The Fine Hammered Steel of Herman Melville

The
Fine
Hammered
Steel
of
Herman Melville
by
Milton
R.
Stern

University of Illinois Press, Urbana, Chicago, and London, 1968

Originally published in a clothbound edition, 1957.
© *1957 by the Board of Trustees of the University of Illinois*
Library of Congress Catalog Card No. 57-6959

252 78408 1

To the

memory

of

my sister

Ruth

Found a family, build a state,
The pledged event is still the same:
Matter in end will never abate
His ancient brutal claim.

—Melville, "Fragment of A Lost Gnostic
Poem of the 12th Century"

The Truest of all men was the Man of
Sorrows, and the truest of all books
is Solomon's, and Ecclesiastes is the
fine hammered steel of woe.

—Moby-Dick

Foreword

Professor John Gerber of the University of Iowa, to whom I am indebted for an astute reading of this manuscript, pointed out an omission whose explanation I had mistakenly taken for granted, and which is the reader's proper due.

I feel much like Jay Leyda, who, anticipating reaction to his *The Portable Melville*, said in prefatory defense, "A Melville anthology without *Moby-Dick*!" For there is no *Moby-Dick* chapter in this study. This may seem especially strange since I indicate several times that *Moby-Dick* is the grandest single illustration of Melville's theme and perception.

I was faced with two approaches soon after I undertook this study. One was to illuminate *Moby-Dick*, and, by extension, the corpus of Melville's prose. The other was to illuminate the corpus, and, by extension, *Moby-Dick*. I chose the latter, secondly, because readings of *Moby-Dick*, in various forms, greatly outweigh all others. But first and more important, I wanted to attempt an approach to Melville's theme and perception through a study of their development rather than through the single book in which their culmination is found. Insofar as a critical study is only as good as the quantity of material it explains, I felt that a view of a totality is most forcefully validated by the tracing of consistent patterns through a variety of instances. The instances which best demonstrate the development of Melville's theme are *Typee, Mardi, Pierre,* and *Billy Budd.* To include *Moby-Dick* would be to make a separate repetition of the incremental argument of this study. In trying to get at the guiding perception which makes an organic, thematic whole of Melville's books, I hope I have implied a reading of *Moby-Dick* as I went along.

The term "naturalism" has been left purposely as a "loose fish" here. By assigning a naturalistic theme to Melville, I do not try to make him a "Naturalist" according to our present understanding of the word as much as to assert for him a prototype of naturalistic perception. Our generally accepted—or at least unchallenged—distinction between literary and philosophical naturalism is, I believe, a spurious one. "Literary naturalism" means "techniques," especially when combined with pessimism and determinism. Usually the techniques mean something that we call "photographic" realism. But we can find the photography in the details of stage-setting in a Walter Scott romance as well as in the bum-in-the-gutter details of, say, James T. Farrell.

Categorizing techniques provided no answer to the definition of naturalism—at least none that satisfied me for the goals of this study. (The definition itself belongs to another book. This book is, in one sense, a set of notes toward such a definition.) It is the purpose to which techniques are dedicated—theme, or "philosophy"—that holds the answers. If a body of romantic symbology, such as Melville uses, is bent to the purposes of an antiromantic theme, then the user of that symbology cannot fruitfully be called a romantic. Romantic symbology generally, and transcendental symbology especially, is aimed by cosmic idealism. It recognizes flux and multiplicity in order to make a unific rather than a relativistic statement. Romanticism demands cosmic symbolism in order to create absolutes.

Conversely, a sociological theme demands the "photographic realism" of Naturalism. But this is to make literature all one thing or the other. What if a man arrives at an antiromantic theme not from sociology but from an antiromantic view of the cosmos? What if experience demands that multiplicity remain multiplicity? What if, because romantic cosmic patterns don't hold for him, he then turns to an evaluation of experience, or history? Obviously, such a perception is going to need for its expression cosmic symbols, whose antiromantic meanings will be tested by experience. Idealism and naturalism in literature begin to divide into broad polar areas according to perception—or, to say it more specifically, according to the use of techniques rather than according to the presence of them. It is the materials by which an author tests his theme that classifies his writing. And Melville is both cosmic and anti-idealistic in a combination which I call naturalistic. Naturalism is a perfect term for Melville's perception. Capital-letter Naturalism, however, does not take account of the fluidity of literature, and it must be redefined.

However, this foreword is not a place for pursuit of the problem. I will be well content if this book indicates what the problem is.

II

It is the custom, when citing primary sources, to make one's references to the standard editions. This poses a problem in Melville scholarship. The standard Melville edition is *The Works of Herman Melville* (Constable, London, 1922-24), 16 volumes. However, a new collected works (Hendricks House, New York), 14 volumes, is to replace the old edition. But the new collection is still incomplete. Moreover, the Constable edition is now a collector's item, and some of the Hendricks House volumes have also become scarce. Modern publishing methods, though, have made many of the volumes easily and inexpensively obtainable. Therefore, for the convenience of the reader, I have used references to editions which can be found on almost any bookshelf, and which offer reliable texts. The *Typee* quotations are from the Modern Library *Selected Writings of Herman Melville* (New York, 1952). This text is most complete, containing the "Sequel of Toby" of the American second edition and the "Appendix" of the British first edition. The *Mardi* quotations are from the less satisfactory but easily obtainable L. C. Page volume (Boston, 1950). For *Pierre*, however, I have had to go to the Hendricks House (New York, 1949), which is superior to the Constable. *Moby-Dick* quotations are from the Rinehart paperback edition (New York, 1954). The *Billy Budd* quotations are, like *Typee*, from the Modern Library Giant. Wherever possible, I have used the same "principle of availability" for other authors as well.

The growth of this book inevitably was aided by the community of scholars who have made accessible the materials which make exploration possible. For permission to study their collections I wish to thank the directors and curators of the Harvard University Houghton Library, the Massachusetts Historical Society, and the New York Public Library. As a student of Melville unknown to them, I owe a debt of gratitude to Jay Leyda for the *Melville Log* and to Eleanor Melville Metcalf for *Herman Melville, Cycle and Epicycle*, for both works have simplified greatly the studies of countless researchers.

To Gordon N. Ray and the University of Illinois I am indebted for encouragement and for grants-in-aid which have eased the burdens of building a book. And I remember with gratitude the invaluable clerical assistance of Mrs. Elizabeth W. Schultz.

To David Mead, Claud Newlin, Herbert Weisinger, Arnold Williams, and especially to Russell B. Nye, of Michigan State University, I am indebted for the kind of patience and guidance and encouragement that acknowledgments, in their formality, never adequately repay.

I owe a very special debt to my friend and colleague, Sherman Paul. A redoubtable transcendentalist, he has offered insights, agreements, and disagreements which have been an education in themselves. To the stimulation and intellectual excitement he has provided must be credited much of whatever value this book may offer. And, finally, I find it impossible to express my debt to my wife, the only secret sharer who (like Huck Finn) can be so "rotten glad" that the "trouble it was to make a book" is over.

Milton R. Stern
Urbana, Illinois, July, 1956

Contents

chapter 1

The Absolute and the Natural

Let fools count on Faith's parting Knell;
Time, God, are inexhaustible.

—Clarel

"I hardly thought that I should find time or even *table* to write you this long while. But it is Sunday at last, and after a day spent chiefly *Jacquesizing* in the woods, I sit down to do what with me is an almost unexampled thing—inditing a letter at night. It has been a most glowing & Byzantine day—the heavens reflecting the tints of the October apples in the orchard—nay, the heavens themselves looking so ripe and ruddy, that it must be harvest-home with the angels, & Charles' Wain be heaped high as Saddle-Back with Autumn's sheaves. —You should see the maples—you should see the young perennial pines—the red blazings of the one contrasting with the painted green of the others, and the wide flushings of the autumn are harmonizing both. I tell you that sunrises & sunsets grow side by side in these woods & momentarily moult in the falling leaves." [1] Come to my Pittsfield woods, Evert Duyckinck, and observe the view, and accept the tranquillity of my new home, Arrowhead.

But two months later, Duyckinck received another letter from Herman Melville, indited from a brain off which a book was being taken, a job "akin to the ticklish & dangerous business of taking an old painting off a panel—you have to scrape off the whole brain in order to get at it with due safety—& even then, the painting may not be worth the trouble." [2] The "wide flushing" landscape remains the

---

[1] Herman Melville to Evert Duyckinck, Pittsfield (October, 1850). Quoted by Eleanor Melville Metcalf in *Herman Melville, Cycle and Epicycle* (Cambridge, Mass., 1953), p. 95.
[2] Melville to E. Duyckinck, Pittsfield (December, 1850). Metcalf, p. 97.

same, with snowbanks and skidding horses. Except for one thing. Extending from the scraped brain to the farthest verge of the horizon lies a world-huge whale, unburied in the back garden plot. It is invisible, but it is there, and its phantom, hooded hump blends with all the cold whiteness of Saddleback and the universe.

Herman Melville never buried the whale. Instead, his own broad, seaman's shoulders became the saddleback on which perched the Old-Man-of-the-Sea burden of knowledge that drove Pip mad. Yet despite the "altered" landscape of the world, Melville did not go mad. Like any other artist worth his dash of salt spray, Melville retained (sometimes precariously) the superior position of playing God to the characters he created. As an individual he was probably never more insane than anybody else. The funks and blue devils and damp drizzly Novembers of the soul were usually checked by the robust spirits and animal vigor of the man who could not only create gloomy philosophers but could also advise that if you can get nothing else from the world, at least make it yield a good dinner. And like almost everybody else, Melville could bear the realization that despite the "escape" trips round the Horn with brother Tom, or the trips to England or the Holy Land, he could not help packing with him the portmanteau of his mind. For periodically the burden of the whale carried deep-diving Melville down into the soundless dark of his own ideas: "Dear Duyckinck: If you have met Allan lately he has perhaps informed you that in a few days I go with my brother Tom a voyage round Cape Horn. It was only determined upon a short time since; and I am at present busy, as you may imagine in getting ready for a somewhat long absence, and likewise in preparing for type certain M.S.S." This on the twenty-first of May, 1860, ten years after the whale had breached, and no one knows how many years after he first had been sighted. The quotation is an epitome of the life of Melville the artist— the immersion in the destructive element, and the flight following the creative response.

Since the beginning of the Melville revival in the 1920's, destructive brooding, creation, and flight have fascinated scholars into hailing the author of *Moby-Dick* as the Dark Man of American letters. It is only fairly recently that more complete, corrective studies have been written.[3] Present students of Melville have begun to see that what is

---

[3] Besides Metcalf's *Melville* and Jay Leyda's monumental *The Melville Log* (New York, 1951), both of which are information pools rather than interpretative studies as such, among some of the most informative recent studies are Newton Arvin, *Herman Melville* (New York, 1950), which, though it compounds much of the Freudian and Jungian psychobiography, does an admirable job of pulling together most of the important scholarship; W. H. Auden, *The Enchafed Flood* (New York, 1950); William Gilman, *Melville's Early Life and Redburn* (New York, 1951); Leon Howard, *Herman Melville* (Berkeley, Cal., 1951), a biography based upon Leyda's *Log;* and Edward Rosenberry, *Melville and the Comic Spirit* (Cambridge, Mass., 1955).

true of Melville the artist is true of Anyone the artist, and that Melville the man is another, if inseparable, problem. Consequently, attention has shifted from the fact of the damned whale-burden to the nature of it. Granting that every author totes his own whale or albatross, why, as Hawthorne noted, did Melville seem to be isolated, "wandering to-and-fro over [metaphysical] deserts," when all the efforts of transcendentalism had already prepared for his own symbolic imagination? [4] Why did Melville feel isolated in his beliefs during an age of tremendous exploratory energy? What was it that led the acute Hawthorne to write that Melville was a devout man, a man who "has a very high and noble nature," but who was not and could not be a religious man? [5]

The "madness" that prompted Melville's isolated perceptual differentness was best objectified in the mad and different Pip, and if that poor little orphan can not provide a total answer, he can point out an important direction. As a metaphor of man in the universe, Pip is placed alone in the disinterested emptiness of the ocean.

The sea had jeeringly kept his finite body up, but drowned the infinite of his soul. Not drowned entirely, though. Rather carried down alive to wondrous depths, where strange shapes of the unwarped primal world glided to and fro before his passive eyes; and the miser-merman, Wisdom, revealed his hoarded heaps; and among the joyous, heartless, ever-juvenile eternities, Pip saw the multitudinous, God-omnipresent, coral insects that out of the firmament of waters heaved the colossal orbs. He saw God's foot upon the treadle of the loom, and spoke it; and therefore his shipmates called him mad.[6]

This is not a picture of an anthropocentric universe, and there is no conscious benevolence here. The white whale is as colorless, blank, ubiquitous, eternal, and blind as the Pacific in which Pip is momentarily abandoned. And the whale is not only the deeps of blank eternity, but he is also a creature of the deeps. One of the heartless, ever juvenile eternities of the unwarped world, he is the symbol of them all. Wisdom teaches Pip that man cannot exist in the God-realm. In one perspective, there is the view of the whale as God, an eternal, disinterested emptiness. In another there is the view of the whale as God's works, heartless, joyous things whose very existence may be a horror to man. From this point of view, Truth cannot justify God or God's ways to man, nor can Wisdom correlate them with man's physical, emotional, and psychic needs. Consequently the metaphysics of cosmic idealism may be noble folly or pietistic humbuggery and rationalization, but not truth. "Try to get a living by the Truth," said Melville "—and go to the Soup Societies. Heavens! Let any clergyman

[4] Nathaniel Hawthorne in his journal (Nov. 20, 1856). Metcalf, p. 161.
[5] Metcalf, p. 161.
[6] *Moby-Dick* (Rinehart, New York, 1954), p. 411.

try to preach the Truth from its very stronghold, the pulpit, and they would ride him out of his church on his own pulpit bannister." [7]

The significance of a naturalistic universe is a greater burden of possible truth than the human mind can bear (even Ahab, in "The Candles" chapter, refuses to accept the possibility), and Pip is driven insane. As "The Doubloon" chapter indicates, identification of experience depends not upon absolute meaning but upon one's own perception.

"Also, we use defects and deformities to a sacred purpose," said Emerson, "so expressing our sense that the evils of the world are such only to the evil eye."

"What does the man mean?" Melville exclaimed. "If Mr. Emerson travelling in Egypt should find the plague-spot come out on him—would he consider that an evil sight or not? And if evil, would his eye be evil because it seemed evil to his eye, or rather to his sense using the eye for instrument?" [8]

Man's perception of the "*visible* truth" becomes his measure for morality, and he will see differently in different situations. And as *Moby-Dick* and *Pierre* suggest, man's soul is more frighteningly vacant and vast than the physical universe because it is within one's own perception that ideal, or God, is born. If an idealistic perception of experience was false for Melville, then indeed he must have felt isolated in a literary age which was concerned with absolutes. The very symbolism of the transcendentalists and of his friend Hawthorne was an instrument forged for a suprarational extension of meaning to absolute definition. Consequently, an approach to the nature of Melville's leviathan burden is given direction by the possibility that his own imagination and perception operated historically as well as—or rather than—idealistically.

At first this appears to be the last characterization of a man whose quality of mind demanded constant and strenuous struggles with teleological problems. In his presentation of the difference between world and ideal, he utilized the ready-made romantic symbology of his age. Yet he stressed a theme that argues for a combination of empiricism and classical rigor whereby the order of art must be applied to the conduct of life. His age, with few exceptions, insisted that one's life must inform one's art.

In short, Melville's romanticism existed in his transcendent use of symbol, but not in his theme. Thematically, Melville was out of keeping with much of the mainstream of thought of his own times, which popularly and philosophically for the most part emphasized an untrammeled individualism, free from the restrictions of the past. The ideologies of political individualism receive little attention here

---

[7] Metcalf, p. 168.
[8] Leyda, II, 648.

simply because they are so important that they are legitimately the subject of another book. Nineteenth-century oratory, for example, furnishes just one demonstration of the sprawling, vaguely edged political concepts of individualism. The past is seen as something to which all debts have been paid, and the present is the birthday of the free individual whose millenium of self is just around tomorrow's corner.[9] Perhaps the subject may be bitten off with the axiom that American political individualism has its roots in Jeffersonian ideas of Adamic individualism rather than in John Adams' ideas of precedent and order, as the opposing sets of ideas were expressed in the cross-currents of that eighteenth-century middle-class upheaval, the American Revolution. And as early as *Mardi* (1849)—there are even glimmerings of it in the earlier *Omoo* [10]— Melville began to align himself with concepts of order without, however, the class-hierarchy specifics that often make this an elitist position.

To recall nineteenth-century economic individualism, one need only remember that Melville's life span was coincident with most of the important change in America's bittersweet technological history. He saw the amassing of great fortunes which were justified by social-evolutionary thought adapted to a commercialism that was aligned with the ideologies, apparent and real, of America's frontier experience. From the 1820's on, America began its real spree of commercial materialism, later to be typified in Twain's *Gilded Age* and the entire tradition of protest literature championed by the advocates of realism and naturalism. And Melville, together with the transcendentalists, incessantly hammered at the inhuman disparities of economic reward and artificial social distinctions that characterized the age's growing pains.

To recall transcendental individualism, we have the tailor-made symbol of Thoreau's castle in the air, which is a perfect emblem of the method of romantic deduction. The Idea is the first logos or basis of primary importance. And this is the castle. Then the Idea is to be domesticated and applied to social use. This is the foundation. For, Thoreau advised, "In proportion as [you] . . . simplify . . . [your] life, the laws of the universe will appear less complex, and solitude will not be solitude, nor poverty poverty, nor weakness weakness. If you have built castles in the air, your work need not be lost; that is where they should be. Now put the foundations under them." [11] In the social domestication of ideas or the putting of foundations, Melvillean thought and transcendental thought are in accord.

It is in methodology, however, that "Melvilleanism" and romantic

---

[9] R. W. B. Lewis, *The American Adam* (Chicago, 1955), is a wonderfully suggestive treatment of the problem.

[10] Sherman Paul's introduction to the forthcoming J. M. Dent "Everyman's Library" edition of *Omoo* calls attention to this aspect of the book.

[11] *Walden*, "Conclusion" (Rinehart, New York, 1950), p. 270.

idealism polarize into the two major opposites of naturalism and supranaturalism. For where Emerson and Thoreau are ultimately social, Melville is primarily social, and he is empirical and environmental where the transcendentalists are idealistic. For Melville, the immediate facts of the historical community are the first logos. Upon this basis of primary importance, the truth of ideas becomes relative, and is judged by effectiveness. History first determines the applicability of the ideas which inform action. So, despite the huge agreement upon sociality and activity, transcendentalism tends to maximize individualism, Melvillean thought tends to minimize it. With Melville the foundation is not built from the top down, from individually perceived oversoul to historical action, but from the bottom up, from worldly experience to historical goal. For the man who cried, "O Time, Strength, Cash and Patience!" solitude is indeed solitude, poverty is poverty, and weakness weakness. Emerson remarked that, "The drover, the sailor, buffets it [the storm] all day, and his health renews itself as vigorous a pulse under the sleet, as under the sun of June." Keeping his eye on the bitter relativities of physical reality and on the external reality of the materials of experience, Melville responded with, "To one who has weathered Cape Horn as a common sailor what stuff all this is!" [12]

The transcendentalist insisted that the first job is to know self. By knowing self he attains Idea from communion with Ideal. Although in the material world an excursion to Walden may be individualistic isolation, in the spiritual world the excursion is not only cosmic but communal. It becomes apparent to the transcendentalist that he must give spiritual being, pure idea, primary importance over the material world; thus, for instance, Thoreau's discernible motif of Eternity and purity in preference to time and earth, or material history. That is the essence of what Melville sees as idealism, and an arbitrary and rigidly channeled definition of idealism and naturalism will serve here as a key to the difference between Melville and the romantic thought of his contemporaries. For idealism there need be little concern with the idealist's view of commodity, or physical unity. Emerson was careful to point out that recognition of the organic in matter is the lowest level of transcendental perception and, indeed, often required only a sharpening of the understanding. The nitrogen-cycle structure of matter, form as a picture of function, had its highest meaning as a symbolic function of spirit. The symbol served to connect phenomena with the essence of God lifted above institutional or programmatic definitions. The ideal becomes *the pattern of the spiritually organic unity of all existence, a pattern absolute and anterior to men, and which exists whether men recognize it or not.* For all the Emersonian

---

[12] Leyda, II, 648.

insistence upon the primacy of mind, such primacy is secondary to the really primal assumption of the Oversoul's existence. In a sense, the symbolic referent is independent of the symbol itself. With Cartesian distinction between ideal and experience gone, the vocation of the idealist then becomes (1) to seek the ideal, and (2) by explaining the ideal and making it available to man, to allow man to fit his own existence to it, and thereby create the proper body of experience. The transcendental idea by which man does so is dependable because the ideal, as the informing essence of all creation, is perfection and purity. Man must have the self-reliance to trust the initial act of ideation attained from contemplation of ideal, and must vault himself into a unity with God, an equality with all creation. It is this that is the motivation for transcendental insistence upon subjectivity and that creates a link between people like Edwards and Emerson in the course of American idealism. Finally, historical experience becomes a result, and idealism is absolutist. For instance, Emerson, in "Nature," implies that his views embrace a total explanation for experience: ". . . to a sound judgment, the most abstract truth is the most practical. Whenever a true theory appears, it will be its own evidence. Its test is that it will explain all phenomena." Philosophically, Melville abhors this position. There is no China Wall for possible unknowns in life, he says in *Pierre*. Championing wide, first-hand experience, he speaks from a more relativistic position which rejects The Truth. For, whatever The Truth may be, it has to wrench experience to fit theory. The overriding abstraction demands that history be seen all one way.

Naturalism, however, does not have at its disposal idealism's basic symbolic equation. "Language, sleep, madness, dreams, beasts, sex" are perceived according to relationships rather than according to what is absolutely equatable. Naturalism assumes that whatever the ideal informing of existence is thought to be, it can offer no guidance for and have no effect upon man's history beyond the limiting, physical facts of birth and death. For the idealist, the pattern of human history and action must be applied from and merged with the ways of a God who is discovered by intuition and exalted contemplation, a God who is independent of the activities of any given society. For the Melvillean naturalist there is no such God. When "God" exists, he is the product of, not the producer of the body of experience provided by society's activity. God is historical existence. As the definition is refined, man is man's God, and the historical actualities man creates are the laws by which he is ruled. The powers of heaven, hell, and earth become one. Melville says it best himself.

By visible truth [he wrote Hawthorne], we mean the apprehension of the absolute condition of present things as they strike the eye of the man who fears them not, though they do their worst to him,—the man who, like

Russia or the British Empire, declares himself a sovereign nature (in himself) amid the powers of heaven, hell, and earth. He may perish; but so
long as he exists he insists upon treating with all Powers upon an equal
basis. If any of those other Powers choose to withhold certain secrets, let
them; that does not impair my sovereignty in myself; that does not make
me tributary. And perhaps, after all, there is *no* secret. We incline to think
that the Problem of the Universe is like the Freemason's mighty secret, so
terrible to all children. It turns out, at last, to consist in a triangle, a mallet,
and an apron,—nothing more! We incline to think that God cannot explain
His own secrets, and that He would like a little information upon certain
points Himself. We mortals astonish Him as much as He us. But it is this
Being of the matter; there lies the knot with which we choke ourselves. As
soon as you say *Me,* a *God,* a *Nature,* so soon you jump off from your stool
and hang from the beam. Yes, that word is the hangman. Take God out
of the dictionary, and you would have Him in the street.[13]

Here is an insistence upon an empirical, disenchanted perceiver.
"Absolute" does not depend upon an eternal and changeless supernatural being, but upon the "visible," the "present." The historical is
"absolutely" real within its own relative context. The particular shark
in the sea, for instance, may not be an absolute entity, and as natural
beings, man and shark ultimately may be one. But, Melville cautions,
if you guide your swimmer's life on that basis, you and shark will
become one in quite a disagreeable manner. You may be proving
the organic unity of existence, but you will wish that you had acted
as though the shark's independent identity were an absolute reality
within the context of your own brief experience.

The "sovereign nature" in Melville's note to Hawthorne seems to
smack of the idealism of Ahab. Yet, what Melville really is saying here
is that man must act as though his momentary truths are absolute.
When man says, "Me, God, Nature," he assumes an absolute truth
that strangles his evaluation of contradictory experiences—an evaluation, fractured as it may be, that is effective in a time and a place.

The pattern of human history and action necessarily is created by
man, and the application is inherent and inevitable in the kind of
creation made. Primacy is given to the materials of human history
rather than to a metaphysical ideal. Instead of being the lowest level
of organic or symbolic function, commodity becomes just about the
only level. Thus, the symbolic power of naturalistic literature depends
not upon a preliminary symbolic system (a religion, a metaphysic,
a political doctrine), but upon the mind's relativistic, independent,
and interior use of relative, independent, exterior fact. Matter is not
controlled by any cause or secret that intentionally creates moral
values purposeful to man's existence. Historical experience becomes
causal. If the idealist believes that what man can creatively perceive
may be absolute, the naturalist believes that it may be universal but

---

[13] Metcalf, p. 105.

not absolute—it can only be relative. Man can only act as though it were absolute for the moment.

Subsequently idealism is ultimately fideistic and subjective; naturalism is rationalistic and attempts to find bases for objectivity. "In reading some of Goethe's sayings [wrote Melville to Hawthorne], I came across this, 'Live in the all.' That is to say, your separate identity is but a wretched one, —good; but get out of yourself, spread and expand yourself, and bring to your self the tinglings of life that are felt in the flowers and the woods, that are felt in the planets Saturn and Venus, and the Fixed Stars. What nonsense! Here is a fellow with a raging toothache. 'My dear boy,' Goethe says to him, 'you are sorely afflicted with that tooth; but you must live in the all, and then you will be happy!' . . . That 'all' feeling, though, there is some truth in. You must have often felt it, lying on the grass on a warm summer's day. Your legs seem to send out shoots into the earth. Your hair feels like leaves upon your head. This is the all feeling. But what plays the mischief with the truth is that men will insist upon a universal application of a temporary feeling or opinion." [14] These suggestions of rationalism, empiricism, objectivity and relativism are the fundament of Melville's naturalism. He takes his place at the head of a tradition that extends (with basic modifications) through Twain, Dreiser, Hemingway, and Faulkner, in distinction to the transcendental continuum.

It is axiomatic that transcendental thought is essentially ethical. The same is true of the transcendental symbol. Its purpose is moral because its basic assumption is the Ideal, and it attempts to connect history with the absolute moral order of cosmic idealism. Given the task he had set for himself, the truly romantic transcendentalist had to make symbolism his literary vehicle. The naturalist's job is more difficult, for the symbol's basic assumption is lost. Instead of being able to deduce a moral order from the Ideal, the naturalist has to create one. Paradoxically, with absolute morality gone, man's relative moralities become even more important, for there is no controlling moral symbol for the cosmos. The naturalist's task does not become one of creating new symbolic functions but rather one of creating new symbolic relationships for every chapter of man's history. This is the basic difference between Ahab's demonism and Melville's. Ahab sought the symbol because, like Lucifer, he sought to challenge the absolute. Melville, also rebelling (not against God, but against a false concept of God), sought the symbol which would allow him to replace a vacuum with relative, human demands. The entire thematic center shifts, for unlike Ahab, Melville immediately becomes earth-oriented rather than heaven-oriented; thus his "unchristian" demonism consists

---

[14] Pittsfield (Spring, 1851). Metcalf, p. 110.

in his seeing the idealistic Ahab as diabolic. "Shall I send you a fin of the 'Whale' by way of a specimen mouthful?" he asked Hawthorne. "The tail is not yet cooked, though the hell-fire in which the whole book is broiled might not unreasonably have cooked it ere this. This is the book's motto (the secret one), *Ego non baptiso te in nomine*— but make out the rest yourself." [15] [Ego non baptiso te in nomine Patris sed in nomine diaboli—Ahab's blood-baptism of the harpoon he reserved for Moby Dick.] The Melville-devil rebels against the assumptions of idealistic symbolization. He too dives to the pre-Cambrian depths of the past, and returns—but with a different message of creation. Because he was the first major American author to turn the symbology already created by the transcendentalists to the relativistic purposes of naturalism, Melville becomes the historical and artistic focal point for one of the two main branches of American literary thought.

Ahab typifies idealistic symbolic thought. It is true that to Ahab the ideal was an evil enemy of man rather than a benevolent perfection. But what is central is that he was an idealist. It is not pertinent that he would conquer the ideal rather than yieldingly merge with it. Indeed, Ahab found the most freezing terror in the thought that there might be no ideal to fight. Though he worshipped satanically like Fedallah rather than conventionally like Starbuck or hopefully like Emerson and Thoreau, he too feverishly sought God and sought to believe in God. It makes no difference how man defines what he considers to be absolute; the error is that he thinks he perceives it at all beyond the infinity of a natural existence which in itself does not have constant (by human standards) moral qualities.

But it cannot be argued that in selecting the demonized Ahab, who believing in an ideal that frustrated and limited man, Melville was stacking the deck against the idealist. For there is always Pierre, who takes action armed with a belief in the ideal as perfect Virtue, perfect Truth. There is always the Confidence Man, who tries and tries to sell his idealistic stock of faith in a benevolent and curative ideal to others. He also tries to secure faith impregnably for himself before opponents armed with experience in the countless adverse indications of history. There is always Clarel, who tries to reconcile the disparities between his own history and the assumptions which a pilgrimage to the Holy Land requires.

All these seekers and their defeats illuminate Melville's view of the quest for the Holy Grail. Melville takes as a central character the individual who makes a philosophical voyage, which is symbolized by a physical journey. The spiritual voyage is a search for the primitivist's paradisiac world, as presented in *Typee* and only incidentally

---

[15] Pittsfield (June 29, 1851). Metcalf, p. 111.

in the picaresque *Omoo*. Or it is a search for the ideal's absolute perfection, as presented in *Mardi*. Sometimes it is a search for an ideal past and an absolute identity, as presented in *Redburn* and *White-Jacket*. Characteristically it is a search for ultimate truth and being, a final triumph for man's cosmic status, as presented in *Moby-Dick*. Occasionally it is a search for the possibility of behavior according to the ideal responses of the human heart, as presented in *Pierre*. And it is also a search for idealistic faith and faith's confidence as presented in *The Confidence Man* and *Clarel*. Despite arbitrary divisions, the books all share each other's problems. The richest books embrace all the problems. The totality of the books presents man's search for an informing ideal that is more than physical causation. Idealists all, the characters search for a causality that is more than something merely external to man's moral sphere.

And Melville always presents the quest as futile.

Unlike the scientists and Chillingworths of the idealist, Hawthorne, Melville's visionary villains are not materialists. Ahab's famous curse upon science indicates the idealist who projects self upon universe and replaces the facts of the material world with his own ideal, which thereby becomes the unarmed vision of monomania. "As if you can kill time without killing Eternity," says Thoreau in *Walden*. "As if you can fashion a harpoon that will kill a zero," answers Melville in all his books. He devotes the totality of his books to piling up disparities between Eternal self and Vision on the one hand and time's history of man (or should it be man's history of time) on the other. Finally the seeker, like Pierre, realizes—when he is allowed to realize—that absolute Vice and Virtue are two shadows cast by the same nothing, and that the seeker of the absolute becomes the fool of the absolute. Be they heroic or pathetic, noble or ludicrous, Melville's idealists are all finally fools. It is the fool quality that is at bottom of the circular, grim jest referred to in Melville's "metaphysical" novels—the deadly-funny joke that man makes the universe play upon himself.

Yet the idealist, or would-be idealist, is not always portrayed unsympathetically, for Melville has no quarrel with visions and visionaries as such. In *Billy Budd* he champions the need for an informing vision by which man can dominate his history. Melville's quarrel is with the vision achieved from idealism rather than from the lessons of temporal necessity. When the transcendentalist posits an ideal, he believes that it is a reality to which action can correspond. Melville insists that this reality is an erroneous assumption. Indeed, Emerson and Thoreau were empirical in that their ideal was achieved from experience. But Melville's empiricism is so much stronger that it is qualitatively different. It would be as ticklish a job as scraping a painting from a panel to separate transcendental empiricism from idealism, for though ideal derived from experience (which is one of Melville's major arguments), ideal in turn informed the epistemology and ontology through which experience was perceived. Finally it becomes a chicken-and-egg problem because ideal and experience were organically merged.

Significantly, it is in Melville's wider historical experience, as it is in Twain's, that his empiricism differs from the transcendentalist's. Melville subordinated ideal to the facts of material history; in the primacy of community-observed lies the perceptual and thematic significance of Ishmael's oft-quoted statement that "a whale-ship was my Yale College and my Harvard." And once he is divorced from the point-present actualities of human existence, then in fact is Melville's idealist tricked by a stacked deck of circumstances. For Melville the divorce and idealism go hand in hand. He completely utilizes the plight of the very pronounced individuals in his books to achieve a constant formula: idealistic vision results in personal vision; personal vision results in separation of self and community; separation results in monomania; monomania results in a sterilizing and frantic quest for the attainment of vision according to the dictates of self; the quest results in obliteration of self and in murder.

For Melville, true identity lies not in Emerson's suprahistorical self-reliance, but, paradoxically, in a highly individuated identification of self with history. Emerson said of the dictates of self, "My friend suggested, — 'But these impulses may be from below, not from above.' I replied, 'They do not seem to *me* to be such;-but if I am the devil's child, I will live then from the devil.' " [16] That is, if man lives according to ideal, he can only do what is ultimately good and right. "This is precisely Mr. Emerson's crack 'right across the brow'," [17] Melville seemed to say as he penciled in the margin of his copy of Emerson— opposite a statement on the malleability and goodness of man—"God help the poor fellow who squares his life according to this." [18] And when Melville created his Tajis and Ahabs and Pierres in the images of fire and hell, he implicitly insisted that the searcher who ignores the history wherefrom society takes its forms is indeed from the devil and must live on the brimstone of his own smoldering heart. Ironically, Melville added a larger diabolic inversion. His sense of isolation stemmed from the discrepancies between his empirical views and the idealities of a Christian society. In his books he reverses the relation-

---

[16] Emerson, *Selected Prose and Poetry*, "Self Reliance" (Rinehart, New York, 1954), p. 168.

[17] In a letter to Evert Duyckinck, dated "Mount Vernon Street [Boston], Saturday, [March] 3, 1849," Melville wrote, "I could readily see in Emerson, notwithstanding his merit, a gaping flaw. It was, the insinuation, that had he lived in those days when the world was made, he might have offered some valuable suggestions. These men are all cracked right across the brow." Metcalf, p. 59.

[18] Leyda, II, 648.

ship, and it is the idealist who is isolated by actualities. His hero-fools present the kind of belief which, in varying degrees of appearance and reality, represents a nation one of whose mottoes is, "In God we trust." By challenging the basis of this sanction, Melville was questing for the destruction of a sanctity that, to the naturalistic mind, is a false identification. "I have written a wicked book," he wrote to Hawthorne upon completion of *Moby-Dick*, "and feel spotless as the lamb."

Noting the isolation of Melville's protagonists, students of Melville have generally called the central searcher the "isolato"—a term conveniently supplied by Melville himself. Yet the term is too inclusive. It characterizes men like *Pierre's* Plinlimmon and *Billy Budd's* Claggart, who have long since withdrawn from a search. (For instance, Plinlimmon's first name is Plotinus, whose main desire was to be alone with the Alone.) "Isolato" must be pinned more specifically to the Melvillean character who, for any number of reasons, has withdrawn from the world and who no longer has any desire to communicate with humanity. The isolation applies to a searcher like Pierre, departed from Saddle Meadows and withdrawn into his symbolic womb-with-a-view in New York. But it does not apply to Pierre the artist. To differentiate the central searcher from the rest of Melville's isolatoes, we can substitute the term "quester." All questers are isolatoes, but not all isolatoes are questers.

The quester may seem to have Promethean characteristics: he defies gods and submits himself to agonies for the advancement of the race. But he is always selfish. His submission to the inner dictates of the "queenly personality" becomes a rejection of all outward circumstance. His search becomes a satisfaction of his own selfwill and idealism, which predispose him toward the search even before circumstances goad him. Either at the opening of his story or sometime later, certain revelations imply that the predisposition had always existed. The quester's characteristics are formed before the book begins, and these characteristics become the fact upon which Melville creates the disparities between world and ideal. The quester must feed upon himself. He is his own vulture to his own Prometheus. He cannot regenerate himself. He can only drive himself with increasing fury as the disparities become more apparent. Once monomania removes him from the human community, he can no longer hope for sustenance from earth. The quest becomes sterilizing and is increasingly portrayed by imagery of fever, parched whiteness, and loss of virility. Because the quester can never bring his plans to fruition, the psychological qualities of tragedy, the pity and terror, are created by irony: even the other-world toward which the quester drives will not offer attainment, sustenance, or refuge because it is a world which does not exist beyond the physical facts of mortality—which the quester rejects.

Consequently, the quester embarks upon a hopeless voyage. For him human life has been one history of crime and error, which he acts to correct. He refuses to accept the human limitations and vulnerabilities—summed up in mortality—which conditions place upon man. Either his antagonistic attitude removes him from the human community, or else he removes himself. With all sustenance gone, the quester's only means of removal from history is death. Paradoxically perpetuating the very history he tried to escape or rectify, he refuses to admit the impossibility of his quest and gives up the final lance with a malediction. Or, still searching, he sails beyond the reef that separates life from death, world from other-world. Or else, admitting the foolish futility of his position, he takes poison from the very person who transformed his predisposition into active quest. In all cases, following ideal moralities in disregard of world and time eventuates in suicide.

Yet more. The separation of self from world demands deceit. The quester invariably is a liar who masks his own conceit and purposes from a disapproving world. In the cases of Taji and Pierre the quester even lies transparently to himself. At the outset, the quester's very need for expediency defeats the ideal he pursues, and belies idealistic belief. The actions of the quester illuminate Melville's almost instrumentalist view of history. Intentions are irrelevant. It is only the act and the consequences of the act that are important, and act and consequence cannot be divorced. It is inevitable consequence that stalks through the pages of Melville's books as the inexorable figure of Fixed Fate.

Again paradox. Man's will can be free to secure the social vision only if will is controlled, only if will is social rather than individual, only if it consciously tries to choose the fate which is fixed in its own act. For Melville, will itself, or at least the choice open to it, has been formed and dictated by the acts and consequences of previous history —again, there is no absolute equation between specific act and specific consequence. This is the blind wall of Melville's impasse. Because Melville's questers are selfish and his populaces are metaphors for blindness, there is no choice for there is no planning. In short, there is no hero in communal form, which is the logical element demanded by Melville's own works for a resolution of their tensions. Yet Melville's estimate of man's general nature made this one possible answer merely facile and unacceptable. His books become an intensified echo of the sound and the fury, a tale told by a woe-smitten man looking at history created by idiots.

Finally, of course, the quester must be a murderer. The consequences of his acts are out of his hands. The humanity he has deceived and coerced is party to the consequence, and the sin of one man is the sin of all. The ship of humanity is sunk by the unattainable object of the impossible quest, and goes down with all hands but one. Or if the effect does not seem to be so far reaching (but it always is), at least the quester is responsible for the death of his goal, as is Taji, and is responsible for the murder of the history of his house, as is Pierre.

The quest motif certainly is not unique to Melville. As a motif which opens infinite problems about all human history, it is as old as human thought, part and parcel of all the myth and ritual of the world. However, Melville's use of the motif, while again not unique, is particularly modern. The quest does not result in purgation of world and time via heaven and eternity. It does not result in rebirth or a clean slate. It simply "ends" in a never ending continuum of human history, with the quester necessarily defeated, with no lessons learned, with even the one real hero, Captain Vere, murdered by the very forces which continue man's blindness. If Melville attained the psychology, he did not attain the reconciliations of tragedy.[19] His works differ from classical tragedy and from myth and ritual in that there is no pause, no moment of communal wisdom, no clean point of perspective from which man takes a clear breath, blinks, and rests before plunging down to begin the cycle all over again armed with new purpose and knowledge. Melville's view of the jagged continuum of history is basic to his position as a political classicist who yet finds an inescapable need to embrace cultural democracy and relativism. His works attest to the need for imposition of order by the complete men who know how to read history, while at the same time the books back away from Nietzscheism by binding the actions and potentialities of the leader to the masses' historical level of social vision. All men of every social, economic, or ethnic condition become truly equal brothers because they are all subject to the limitations of their common mortality and must all bear the burden of the history they create.

Given the quester's predisposition, it is necessary to survey the cause for which he takes action. The being which stimulates the quester may be called the lure. The lure does not exist in all the books, and only by implication in some. In *Typee* the lure is release from duty-ridden and sterile bondage to the brutal and misdirected

---

[19] This may by no means be a condemnation of Melville as a contemporary writer. Theodore Spencer summed up one of the central considerations suggested by many scholars when he said that tragedy demands a communally accepted background of absolutes against which violation of order and resolution of tensions have channeled meanings which extend from the individual to the society. Perhaps modernity and America for this reason cannot create tragedy as a proper genre; and if this guess aims in the right direction, Melville's inability to create tragedy is more significant than would have been his creation of tragedy. At any rate, the queston remains in the framework supplied by Eric Bentley: "Have we not come to a stage when the non-tragic . . . may better represent us than tragedy? Our outlook is not tragic, and perhaps there is no adequate reason why it should be." "Jean-Paul Sartre, Dramatist," *KR*, VII (1946), 75.

order of a technological western world. In *Redburn* the lure is more concretely symbolized in Wellingborough's father's "prosy old guide book." In *Mardi* there is Yillah; in *Moby-Dick* there is the whale; in *Pierre* there is Isabel. The lure is a representative of ideal corporealized in this world. It is the symbol or embodiment of the ideal absolute for which the quester strives, as the whale is to Ahab or as Yillah is to Taji. Or it is a direction to the attainment of ideal, as Isabel is to Pierre. The lure always points toward God's ideal realm of other-world. The lure is not a false front, because it truly has a hunger for other-world, or it has the characteristics of other-world. Rather, it is a false direction, for it is always germane that Melville's perception derives from experience which denies the existence of another world. It is always the idealist, the quester-villain only, who responds absolutely to the lure. In brief, the lure is an external objectification of the quester's own predisposition. When Melville does create his symbolic Christs, he does so to demonstrate that this embodiment of other-world is murderously inoperative in the man-of-war world of actualities. Could Fedallah, who rose again on the third day, have merged living with the force that the whale represented to him, he would have found only an infinite and eternal blind forehead of dumb, white blankness. Melville defines this blank God not as ideal intelligence, perfection, or spirit, but as a zero thing that, blank and nothing itself, yet makes available to man the material existence with which he can fashion stink or perfume, light or darkness, heaven or hell, on earth —and on earth only. In short, Melville's God is time—the physical, infinite reality of eternity—nothing more and nothing less. He agrees that the universe offers physical pattern and material cycle. But as far as man is concerned, it is ethically blind, perceptually dumb, whitely indifferent, intellectually blank, morally patternless. Limited living man must exchange blindness for planning and impose his own patterns of morality upon history by controlling his own fate, for beyond the physical facts of creation, empty time will not do this for him.

The lure thus feeds the reader directly into the mill which works on the tough kernels of seeming contradiction in Melville's attitude toward science. On the one hand, Melville's quester spurns science; he would replace material circumstance with his own metaphysics. On the other hand, man is limited to physical existence, and, as "The Bell Tower" and "The Lightning Rod Man" indicate, man either misuses his technology or else it is not sufficient to protect him from the vulnerabilities of his own limited position in the grinding eternity of cosmic physicality.

That Melville never solved this problem is a statement about the nature of man's present technological state. It is also at the core of the inability of the major American naturalists to make a positive affirmation out of the problems they raise. For affirmation, Melville would need as a subject not whaling but cybernetics. Or he could have found an ersatz resolution of problems in something like our contemporary phenomenon of American satire, science fiction, wherein all things are possible. Yet the conclusion of Melville's theme champions the necessity for an inductive and empirical evaluation of experience. Alway his choice of sides evolves from the choice between primacy of ideal and idea or primacy of history and idea. "The Mast-Head" chapter in *Moby-Dick* is as well-known an indication as any.

Beware of enlisting in your vigilant fisheries any lad with lean brow and hollow eye; given to unseasonable meditativeness; and who offers to ship with the Phaedon instead of Bowditch in his head. Beware of such an one, I say: your.whales must be seen before they can be killed; and this sunken-eyed young Platonist will tow you ten wakes round the world, and never make you one pint of sperm the richer . . . those young Platonists have a notion that their vision is imperfect; they are short-sighted; what use then to strain the visual nerve? They have left their opera glasses at home . . . lulled into such an opium-like listlessness of vacant, unconscious reverie is this absent-minded youth by the blending cadence of waves with thoughts, that at last he loses his identity; takes the mystic ocean at his feet for the visible image of that deep, blue, bottomless soul, pervading mankind and nature; and every strange, half seen, gliding, beautiful thing that eludes him; every dimly-discovered uprising fin of some undiscernible form, seems to him the embodiment of those elusive thoughts that only people the soul by continually flitting through it. In this enchanted mood, thy spirit ebbs away to whence it came; becomes diffused through time and space; like Cranmer's pantheistic ashes, forming at last a part of every shore the round globe over. There is no life in thee, now, except that rocking life imparted by a gently rolling ship; by her, borrowed from the sea; by the sea from the inscrutable tides of God. But while this sleep, this dream is on ye, move your foot or hand an inch; slip your hold at all; and your identity comes back in horror. Over Descartian vortices you hover. And perhaps, at mid-day, in the fairest weather, with one half throttled shriek you drop through the transparent air into the summer sea, no more to rise forever. Heed it well, ye pantheists!

Despite Melville's confusion of transcendentalism and pantheism, his objection to cosmic idealism remains. He rejects any reading of the universe which implies moral or spiritual equation. As pitiful as man's resources are, as limited his identity, as weak his visual nerve, they are all he has. By reordering his history with an earthly orientation, he must make them work for him.

Once more, Melville's disagreement with the transcendentalists is not based upon an informing moral vision for physical existence, but upon the methods by which the vision is extracted. Just as Melville is not anti-vision as such, he also is not anti-quest as such. In later naturalists, like Norris and Crane, it seems apparent that the natural world is no longer a neutral thing without moral pattern. The concept of neutral, albeit possibly horrible, indifference almost changes to Ahab's view of the universe as an agent of evil pattern and conscious hostility. When this is true, it is really idealism, but traveling ninety knots in reverse. Unlike Ahab, Melville sees the world as a blithely unconscious thing of heaps and tasks ("joyous, heartless, and eternal"), and most of the facts of his universe are adverse to man's triumph. In this sense, "the mystic ocean" becomes the realm of natural and human mystery, the realm into which man must continually push the bowsprit of his pioneering exploration. The ocean is the "dark side of life, and two thirds of the world are water."

Melville does not lose sight of his moral metaphor. The sea is not only the mystery of natural existence, but also the "mystery of iniquity." Significantly, as *Billy Budd* states, the one area of mystery out of which historical experience seems to provide no direction is human nature, not the nature of God or the cosmos. Unlike the inverted transcendentalists, Ahab and Crane, Melville demands in his naturalism a seer who feels the compulsion to widen or define the boundaries of action through historical knowledge rather than through the speculations of cosmic idealism; the selfless sailor who escapes the dry rot of the unenlightened lee shore to seek an ethos in the enigmas of world rather than in the enigmas of other-world. The sea of human exploration and control calls forth the Bulkington and Vere; the sea of cosmic ideal and the absolute calls forth the Ahab and the Taji. Always the problem remains the same: when Emerson and Thoreau speak of "higher moralities" they are trying to humanize nature in order to naturalize man up to those moralities. Melville tries to naturalize nature in order to humanize man away from the "higher moralities" of nonexistent ideal.

That is, the cosmic idealist emphasizes the equality, the oneness, of man and nature. Melville also seeks sanity in an organic plan for human life (what man takes from the whale is what man makes of his existence). But he approaches the problem by emphasizing the differing identities of man and nature and of all natural forms. If cosmic idealism glosses the differences into a unity, and the unity is made The Truth, the differences may kill man—as they do the young sailor on the Mast-Head.

The separation Melville makes between the "me" and the "not-me" is not a separation of two consciously contending forces as it seems to be with later naturalists. By its very nature the universe can be neither supranatural nor conscious, benevolent nor malevolent, as Ahab tries so desperately to believe it is. For man alone can be a conscious or spiritual contender. The universe emerges as something not for man's emulation, but for his instruction and understanding through his conquest. Man sometimes has to act according to his own, not "cosmic" truths, and thus sometimes he ought not be assimilated into nature. Moreover, man does not have enough facts to know cosmic absolutes, and thus perhaps he never can be completely assimilated into nature except in death. He may take the facts of a time and a place to be absolute truth. But in that case, cosmic idealism disappears ridiculously into the actualities of human necessity. God, for all purposes, never is. With this particular moral truth operating upon him, and if he would not deny the pathetic, heroic aspirations of his heart, man cannot simply relate himself to human and physical nature. He must struggle with them. For the transcendentalist, man is of utmost importance because of his creative perception of oversoul; for the Melvillean naturalist, man is of utmost importance because his is the only soul there is. One merges with God; the other replaces God.

The thematic differences involved in the problem of perception are highlighted in Melville's comments upon Emerson's dictum that "The good, compared to the evil which [man] sees, is as his own good to his own evil." Responded Melville, "A perfectly good being, therefore, would see no evil.—But what did Christ see?—He saw what made him weep.—However, too, the 'Philanthropist' must have been a very bad man—he saw, in jails, so much evil. To annihilate all this nonsense read the Sermon on the Mount, and consider what it implies." [20] The problem is not one of admitting that there is an order, or orders, of existence beyond the human. The problem is one of identifying the existence beyond man's ken at any given time. Both transcendentalist and naturalist agree that for man existence is not meaningful until it is brushed by human perception. But the transcendentalist makes all existence interior, dependent on the mind. The naturalist, however, insists upon the exterior independence of the world around man. To him, the subjectivity of the cosmic idealist becomes an "atheistic" and blasphemous denial of the life that actually is, regardless of how pleasant or monstrous it may seem to be. Melville's comment upon Bayle's idea that atheism does not shelter us from fear of externally imposed suffering was, "If we assume that the existence of God makes external suffering possible, *then* it may be said that atheism furnishes no defense against the fear of it." [21] Only if the lure's ideal identification is correct, only if there is a supranatural existence which is an absolute morality aimed at man, only then does the religionist's view of "atheism" have meaning.

The lure points toward God as the ultimate basis for human behavior. The lure suggests that God is the answer to all the enigmatic, dark, rushing forms of the ocean. Driven by predisposition and urged by lure, the quester believes. He tries to become a forceful "transparent eyeball," tries to strike through the mask of phenomena to the ultimate. He never realizes that when he abandons the historical world for God's, he abandons the very God and answer he seeks. The

---

[20] Leyda, II, 648.
[21] Leyda, II, 651.

lure, when human, also never understands what Melville considers to be the true nature of the "other-world." And as a representative of other-world, the lure is either a dumb, ubiquitous brute, or is a human significantly inexperienced in this world, unable to communicate with this world, steeped in ancestral memory of an other-world which, ironically always turns out to be a creation of *human* history. The lure, by its very function, cannot be completely human. It is ubiquitous in time, at least in the human disposition for absolute being, if not in fact. Consequently Melville's books are filled with exquisitely mystical light and dark ladies for whom the quester has what is to him an inexplicable and immediate and savage affinity. And, of course, the non-mammalian and nonhuman fish (Ishmael insists that the whale is a fish) becomes Melville's best symbol. The great white whale literally lives in an eternal element in which men cannot and do not exist, but which furnishes, in any moment of time, every possibility that men can wrest from it.

Following the naturalistic insistence upon world and time, we find two more basic characters to be added to the list. They are the western world and the primitive world, which is usually represented by South Seas peoples. As *Typee* concludes, man cannot change worlds. The nineteenth-century search for primitivism becomes a delusion. The fact of western man is his western world, and the two worlds are contrasted not as ethnic groupings (all men are brothers, and Quee-queg is more Christian that Bildad), but as levels of development in man's history.[22]

The primitive world is the world of the body and the heart. The heart is Melville's synonym for sympathetic, unalloyed, and spontaneous humanity. The primitive world's inhabitants are childlike and trusting. They have the confidence for which the western idealist searches, and their experience is significantly like that of the infant. Because body dominates heart in primitive life, the primitive cannot have an aspiring heart. Without knowing it, he can only represent, *to western man,* the beautiful simplicities of human aspiration for perfection. It is the mind that is necessary for an aspiring heart. But the primitives are physical and mindless: they are characterized by beauti-

---

[22] Since the writing of this study, James Baird's *Ishmael* (Baltimore, 1956) has appeared. Mr. Baird places Melville as a primitivist. In Mr. Baird's terms, the true primitivist is the artist who, faced with the failure of authority in the regnant religious symbols of his culture, rejects the systems of belief incorporated in those exhausted symbols, and replaces them with a new symbolic system taken from the Orient, which is made to include the South Seas. While I agree with Mr. Baird's impressive and stimulating discussion of primitivism, symbolism, and cultural failure, I am convinced that primitivism is not Melville's alternative system of allegiance. *Ishmael,* for instance, ignores Melville's rejection of primitive perception in *Typee.* Rather, Melville prefigures the naturalistic alternative, for it was Ahab, not Melville, who symbolized according to the rules laid down by Mr. Baird.

ful bodies and "the quantity of sleep they can endure." The primitive world is the elemental, unartificial world of the child, and is the only world which can embrace what for Melville is the childlike ideal of Christ. Thus Melville sees the missionary as a paradox, for not only does the missionary not represent Christ and not suffer the little children to come unto him, but he tries to destroy those very childlike qualities which are the beauty of the barbarian. There is no question that as a true western idealist, Ahab is infinitely higher and profoundly lower on a moral level than the missionaries of *Typee, Omoo,* and *White-Jacket.* At least, thunders Melville, if you are going to be idealist, know your area and do not be a hypocrite. Contemporary actualities do not apply to Eden. And, heartbreakingly, the converse is also true.

The clock cannot be turned back on the west's adulthood, and primitivism becomes part of the bitter retrogression of idealism. Given man's present condition, which for Melville is symbolized by the concept of the Fall from Grace—fortunate or unfortunate—then the meaning of the Fall is the actuality of a naturalistic universe. Melville uses Original Sin as a metaphor for the nature of reality, not as a theological or orthodox expression. Indeed, history indicates the eternity of a naturalistic universe rather than any initial state of Grace. The primitive is simply inapplicable to the "fallen," complex, present, man-of-war world of the west. Once more, in the issue he takes with the romantic primitivist's call for a return to nature, and thus to God, Melville's disagreement with the assumptions of transcendental methodology becomes central.

The western world is the world of historical knowledge. This knowledge mated with idealistic assumptions turns man into a deracinated being who tries to find his own identity (soul), and his lost God the Father. It is a world of erroneous political, economic, social, and military goals. But it can never retreat into primitivism, for such an escape is a chronological, social, and spatial impossibility. As long as the western world remains blind to the naturalistic meanings of its historical actuality, it remains unconscious and the visual nerve remains atrophied. Although unconsciousness preserves the primitive, it makes the life of western man a hell of unplanned circumstance. Because of the mystery of human nature, even planned and discerning action often results in unanticipated consequences. But abandoning historical foresight for groundless cheer or monomania or spontaniety is blindness, and results in sheer chaos. It is this rejection of baseless optimism combined with the view that hope lies only in communal historical awareness that so attracted Melville to the Hebrew prophets. He sees the western world as the world of mind and technology. Unconsciousness makes it, with all its precious machinery, prey to every mindful idealist: witness the *Pequod.* Technics by itself provides no answer. And unconsciousness perpetuates the western world in a wrong and artificial status quo, as in *Pierre's* Saddle Meadows.

The western world is the area of necessary combat with nature, and herein Melville accepts the romantic view of flux and development as central to man's search for an improved status. But Melville insists that the method by which flux is to be measured is a classical order and control of the community, by the community, and for the community rather than the mystical response of the individual or the mindless spontaneity and simplicity of the primitive. "I stand for the heart," wrote Melville. "To the dogs with the head! I had rather be a fool with a heart, than Jupiter Olympus with his head. The reason the mass of men fear God and at *bottom dislike* Him, is because they rather distrust His heart, and fancy Him all brain like a watch. (You perceive I employ a capital initial in the pronoun referring to the Deity; don't you think there is a slight dash of flunkeyism in that usage.)" [23] Melville demanded control by mind for the western world, and this statement cannot be taken as a rejection of mind. First of all, this is a sudden, emotional outburst directed to Hawthorne, whose "Unpardonable Sin" ["Ethan Brand"] Melville had just read, whose abhorrence of intellectual pride was implicit in everything he wrote, and whose friendship, admiration and agreement Melville warmly desired. Secondly, this same excerpt begins, "It is a frightful poetical creed that the cultivation of the brain eats out the heart. But it's my *prose* opinion that in most cases, in those men who have fine brains and work them well, the heart extends down to hams. And though you smoke them with the fire of tribulation, yet, like veritable hams, the head only gives the richer and the better flavor." What is rejected is the quality of mind which does not recognize the reality of the feelings that experience may impose upon the human heart. It is this rejection that is underscored by his evaluation of Emerson, which, despite Melville's conditional admiration, stated that "[Emerson's] gross and astonishing errors & illusions spring from a self-conceit so intensely intellectual and calm that at first one hesitates to call it by it's right name. Another species of Mr. Emerson's errors, or rather, blindness, proceeds from a defect in the region of the heart." [24]

But whether Melville presents the world of body, or the world of mind, he finds that two elements are common to both worlds. What is held in common is the irreducible that becomes Melville's view of the nature of general man. One is the desires of man's heart. The second is the blindness of man. Concerning the blindness, it is illuminating that general man emerges as what might be called political man, for the final evaluation of even the apolitical Ahab depends not

[23] Metcalf, p. 109.
[24] Leyda, II, p. 649.

so much upon what he does to the whale (the novel's metaphysics) as upon what he does to himself and the human community (the novel's "politics"). Both worlds are belligerent because both worlds are blind to their own mortality and to the nature of God and history. Although in the western world man must struggle to use nature by conquest, and in the primitive world man can use nature by submission to it and integration with it, in both worlds man's body of experience is blind and man's nature is therefore anarchic. It is the final view of chaotic anarchy that underlies the political classicism of *Billy Budd*.

But unlike the antiromanticism of some speculators, Melville does not see man's potentialities as limited. In the idea that man makes his own history is an implication of limitlessness. Rather, Melville sees man's vision as self-limited, for the visual nerve has been strained in false directions. Melville's symbolic emphasis on restraint does not belong to the classicism of our contemporary politically conservative symbolists because it does not positively merge with theology. It is not, finally, dependent upon God. It depends on "political" man, and man is doubly blind. First he is blind to his burden of common mortality in the physical reality and ultimate democracy of history and death. "So," says Melville, "when you see or hear of my ruthless democracy on all sides, you may possibly feel a touch of a shrink, or something of that sort." [25] Second, man is blind to his need for subordination of goal for self to goal for group, since it is the group that creates a kind of immortality in all the possibilities of the sheer physical fact of the group's continuity. Thus man's own negation of his real democracy makes him reprehensible. His blind anarchy creates a situation wherein it is not always wise to translate the democracy of life, which man's actions deny, into political democracy, which man's conceit, selfishness, individualism—and aspirations—demand. "It seems an inconsistency," Melville adds, "to assert unconditional democracy in all things, and yet confess a dislike to all mankind—in the mass. But not so. —But it's an endless sermon, no more of it." [26]

In death the individualized distortions are forgotten as absurdities, and the visual nerve's angle of perception can see grim Dante sitting cheek by jowl with fat Rabelais. But on earth, as long as this common view does not exist, Melville's man cannot advance. Simply, man does not advance gregariously because he is anarchic, and, atomized, is prey to himself and the universe. Melville's world cannot break the vicious cycle until all leaders and most men learn the circumstantial lessons taught by naturalistic perception. When that happens man will not have to break the cycle because it will *be* broken. It is the failure of Melville's experience that his world shows no direction to the

[25] Metcalf, p. 107.
[26] Metcalf, p. 108.

attainment of that goal. Here too Melville is a most significant figure in the tradition of naturalistic American fiction. Such fiction, if it unites in any protest, protests against the conditions of social experience while maintaining that this historical body of experience is of first importance. The very unprogrammatic quality of Melville's works, a quality that usually saves books from being blatant propaganda, is paradoxically what prevents Melville from creating a thematic resolution of problems. Of course, buried within the tremendous artistry with which Melville creates his hopeless cycle, there are countless rich and positive prescriptions for human behavior. The fact that Melville creates characters whose vision has been enlightened by history is the real affirmative optimism in the two-thirds that is dark. For the naturalistic world is indeed a place of terror unless a kind of cosmic faith is transferred from the destroyed God to a belief in man's potentialities. Unlike the eighteenth century, the nineteenth offered no list of perfectibilitarian "facts" that could be taken from either history or the universe. Nineteenth-century optimism (excluding both the more prevalent imperialistic and fadist varieties) was metaphysical rather than reportorial.

Consequently it was only the transcendentalists who could legitimately emphasize joy and benevolence. Because there was no precedent which allowed the nonidealistic nineteenth-century writer to make the transfer of faith rationally, this inability helped dictate Melville's inevitable choice of the symbolic vehicle, and made him the reluctant naturalist who had a part of Ahab as well as much of Vere within him. He could not accept transcendentalist perception, and though he might have yearned for transcendentalist conclusions he could not, therefore, accept them either. He was not made happy by the conclusions which nineteenth-century knowledge offered to naturalistic perception. But he remained loyal to his fact that his own choice of sides was the only honest and disenchanted one. The loss of God and the nature of the universe are secondary to man's ability to replace the loss and to handle the universe. Ultimately, the need for faith in man, which he could not find, was Melville's unburied whale-burden of woe. For man's hope, Melville could find only the depressingly duped and nobly indestructible aspirations of the heart.

But if "there is a wisdom that is woe . . . there is a woe that is madness." It was Melville's tremendous awareness of hard reality that allowed him to retain a sense of life more strongly than a sense of loss. He was able to enlarge his woe beyond private vision, which Ahab could not do. It was Melville's loyalty to life that kept him from the madness of the disenchanted man who finally discovers that his disenchantment is merely personal-political or metaphysical schizophrenia. It is simply inescapable that in evaluating a writer faced with Melville's problem, the reader must recognize the difference between the artist and the moral essayist or tractarian system-builder—and it is to Melville's everlasting credit that in creating an image of his own society, he struggled to join the two.

Beginning with *Typee*, Melville explored the conduct of wrongly informed vision. *Typee* almost certainly is not the same consciously symbolic construct that the later books are, but in this very first book there is an order sheet for the materials Melville is to use characteristically. There are the quester, the lure, the two worlds. Larger considerations of ideal and man's relationship to it do not really enter yet, but the general patterns of imagery with which such relationships will be created are introduced. Use of color, the primitive and the western, description of the human body, height, depth, land, sea, as symbolic imagery, are all here. Moreover, *Typee* sets a constant for the relationships between the four basic characters. Throughout the other books the specific patterns of imagery which present the relationships may change, but the relationships themselves do not.

In *Typee*, Tommo, the embryo quester, is exposed to the horror of primitive mindlessness, and he learns his lesson of cultural relativism. But the devil-quester that remains in Melville is yet to be exorcised. For we come to *Mardi*. *Mardi* is the central book in a study of Melville's thematic development, and it is the least unified of all the works. Still exploiting the South Seas setting (the popular success of *Typee* and *Omoo* simply amazed and delighted Melville), *Mardi* places a western story in costume. The central characters are not mindless primitives but western men, as the geographical allegory alone makes plain. Picking up character-relationships and patterns of imagery where *Typee* left off, *Mardi* is Melville's first determined attempt to tell the story of quest as a symbolic history of civilization.

Moby-Dick is the same story given artistic form and completion. Though it is the best book Melville wrote, it is not included in this study because it demonstrates the focus rather than the development of Melville's theme. But it was expanded in new directions in *Pierre*, a less satisfactory book. In *Pierre* Melville anatomized the would-be redeemer-quester who brings the primitive characteristics of pure, childlike heart to bear upon the western world into which he emerges. It is for good reason that Saddle Meadows, the estate wherein Pierre grows to young manhood, is presented as a bit of primitive Typee set in the west. It is for good reason that Pierre so often is referred to as a sleep-filled child of magnificent physique and paltry experience. The "common sense" instrumentalist cast of light that plays on this book becomes evident in the reflection that Pierre's tactical defeat is one with his metaphysical defeat. And this redeemer-quester goes through all the steps of withdrawal, deceit, a sterile relationship, murder, and suicide. The redeemer-quester, spurned by the world, becomes the hater-quester, the destroyer. *Pierre* demonstrates how

Christ turns into Satan. Actually, Pierre is a more comprehensive protagonist than Ahab. Pierre goes from love to hate. We see Ahab only after he has spit on the altar, only after Christ and Satan have merged. Finding no other-world, Pierre becomes neutral, a zero like the thing he has pursued. Now Melville can allow the quester to state the thematic conclusion—ideals in any form are shadows cast by a nothing, and the champion of the ideal becomes the fool of the ideal. Pierre is carried to a realization of his untenable position once world and time are rejected. Ahab is never educated, and despite his moments of softening and doubt, he never changes. But with Pierre's death, the story of the quester is complete. What remained now for Melville was to create a hero.

What would happen if there were a man who did manage to understand the proper relationship between heart and mind, a man who was not blind to history, a man who had a political or social position—say a ship's captaincy—which would allow him to translate his realizations into action? What if this man were exposed to a choice between pure ideal and "fallen" human history, with its present actuality of a crime-filled man-of-war world? Wanted: a hero.

Captain Vere is the man created to fill this position.

Billy Budd, like the early Pierre, is pictured as the childlike barbarian, the pure creature whose only experience really is just the experience of his own inner purity and ideality. His spontaneous responses preclude control by mind. This Christ figure also deceives by silence, albeit unwittingly, and finally becomes a murderer and a causer of his own death. Billy himself is the lure which Vere painfully rejects with all the insight created by an understanding of human history. Vere is educated, with the reader, to see Claggart as Satan and Baby Budd as Christ. But Vere's one overriding fact is the fact of the temporal world, the reality of his human community to which he owes his primary allegiance. He cannot choose the ideal which, by itself, is beautiful. And Claggart becomes the other facet of Budd. Budd is the ideal, Claggart is the consequence. He is the completely mad and satanized quester who has withdrawn from quest. He is Ahab, retired in his New Bedford home, staring silently and crazily out at the sea. He is Ahab who has given up the chase, but who still watches. . . . This demonized isolato seeks out and hates and yearns to believe in ideal Billy in exactly the same monomaniacal relationship which Ahab has to the white whale. Just as the reader sees that for Ahab the whale is only what Ahab thinks he is, and the whale, in a sense, becomes Ahab, so for Melville, Christ and Satan are ultimately one entity with a dual face. Like all Melvillean dualities, absolute identities are man-made products which unite in the flow of historical consequence in the Great God Time. The bright and the dark are the *same.*

Vere rejects both lure and quester. His heartbroken rejection of Budd as a beautiful impossibility in favor of an ugly reality, his decision to force his position of command to operate according to what his head dictates and his heart detests, is his acceptance of this world as the only possible one. It is not, as many critics have attempted to demonstrate, an acceptance of God and a submission to Fate. It is quite the opposite. It is Melville's reluctant, modified, but final acceptance of historical necessity in a naturalistic universe. It is a consequent call for man to control his fate by controlling his actions in the historical world—and it is also Melville's statement of inability to find the way to do so. Vere decides to remain unwithdrawn, to accept the responsibility of the human community by accepting the responsibility of command. His decision to maintain order because of man's blindness is his sacrifice of self to the necessities of moral responsibility historically defined. Moreover, it is in his sacrifice of individual self to his social self that Vere finds his greatest identity, in the book as well as in the reader's mind. Vere is the polar opposite and instinctive antagonist to the quester. He offers the alternative behavior which had to be created once the quester's behavior was anatomized and rejected.

In *Billy Budd* the cast of characters changes. The quester as such drops out and the hero takes his place. And here the limitations (or perhaps the accuracy) of Melville's nineteenth-century naturalism become most apparent. For even the hero does not create a purged world. The lesson of Vere's sacrifice is lost. The lesson of Billy Budd's final realization is lost. The world gains not social insight but myth, and the cycle continues. Various studies have tried to identify Melville with his questers. But if he is to be identified with any of his characters, it must be with Captain Vere rather than with anyone else except Ishmael. (The two combined offer a very fair approximation of Melville's political, social, and metaphysical perceptions.) He is the man who turns to history for direction, yet who, when faced with the mystery of *human* nature, calls "Billy Budd! Billy Budd!" He calls for the perfection-aspiring human heart, and not in accents of remorse.

If any writer can be said to be prescriptive, Melville was. Necessarily so, because he was trying to tell America what the correct and incorrect courses of behavior and belief are. If it can be said that two thousand years of western idealistic systems ever began to break down at all, the beginnings became most apparent in the nineteenth century under the impact of a new science, a new politic, a new sociology. Feverishly writing during and after the idealistic height of the American Renaissance, Melville became the greatest spokesman of the breakdown. It is no wonder that he so admired Shakespeare and suspected that he and the man from Stratford were in analogous positions. He even wished that Shakespeare were a contemporary so that he would have the political freedom to write the diabolisms he had only been able to hint at! But, like Shakespeare, before Melville could create a new world in art form, he had to wrestle with the meanings of the breakdown of the old. The surface, or at least most conscious products of the main bout, are his books. ("But I don't know but a book in a man's brain is better off than a book bound in calf—at any rate it is safer from criticism," he wrote to Duyckinck.) [27] Magnificently he could create a usable past. But under the limitations which the knowledge of the dawning "new world" placed upon naturalistic thought, he could point to, but not create, a future. His very attempt becomes, for American culture, a most significant symbol in itself.

Melville's warning buoys were placed among the Encantada rocks of much that was and is dear to an entire society. Yet a fairly unified tradition of American literary thought follows the crucial age which Melville saw as a head-on crash between the juggernauts of the dialectics of materialism and the dialectics of idealism. The mysterious stranger in Esseldorf; that black-white Christman, Joe Christmas; and Jake Barnes' last martini in Spain are various reactions to the crash whose impact, of course, was felt under different conditions. But that the reactions occurred within the general perception that Melville indicated is in itself a statement of debt to the bearded voyager, who still gives sustenance to those who believe that he has indeed found one way to place man's hands "among the unspeakable foundations, ribs, and very pelvis of the world."

And now, as then, this is always a "fearful thing."

------

[27] Metcalf, p. 97.

chapter 2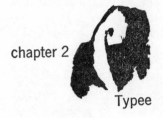

Typee

And man rebounds whole aeons back

in nature.

—Melville, "The House-Top"

Typee does not seem to belong in the same class with the consciously symbolic "metaphysical" novels like *Mardi, Pierre,* and *Billy Budd.* And, in many ways, of course, it does not. But, like a Melvillean character, its face is deceptively bland. Seeing only the face, when a trenscendentalist reviewer wished to tell his readers about a new book called, *Typee, the Narrative of a Four Month's Residence among the Natives of a Valley of the Marquesas Islands: or a Peep at Polynesian Life,* he wrote of the Marquesas which Melville had visited as "these gems of the ocean, in which Nature . . . has hinted the extent of her possibilities . . . perfections which she shall possess in infinite and universal variety when, through the combined industry and wealth and power of a united Race, she shall have become but the image and expression of the Kingdom of God abiding in the souls and societies of Man. . . ." [1] The reviewer went on to explain that the secret of the good social state is abundance; that, contrary to Victor Cousin's beliefs, man must have more than good precepts; that industrialized America, with a more equitable social order of production and distribution, can have a stronger peace and more profound good will than have the Typees. When the writer touched upon the issue raised by Melville's treatment of the missionaries, he said that

It is proper to say in behalf of the author that he does not impeach the . . . Christian character of the missionaries in general. He merely avers that their designs have often been injudicious and that other influences than

---

[1] Unsigned review of *Typee, The Harbinger,* II (April 4, 1846), 263. The author is probably C. A. Dana.

that of the New Testament have operated on the natives, which are undoubtedly the facts. . . . We do not presume to condemn [the missionaries]
individually, but in God's name we condemn a social order which is founded
on such contradictions of the Divine laws, and which devotes to a hopeless
and miserable existence so large a majority of human creatures.[2]

In some ways this pronouncement is typical of the nineteenth-century
reaction to Melville. It interprets the book according to its own pre-
determined findings, and uses the "charming travelogue" as a point of
departure into its own advocations. Yet the *Harbinger* notice does
discuss some of the book's basic themes, at least those of universal
human brotherhood, the aspects of western civilization which are
inhuman, and the obvious discrepancies between the preachments or
intentions and the actions of militant Christianity.[3]

But when it does touch upon the book's themes, it does so either in
a doctrinaire fashion, or accidentally, or indirectly. Consequently,
even the friendly *Harbinger* review, like most of the other contemporary critiques, did not come to grips with *Typee's* symbolic
implications. Melville's reviewers were not accustomed to find in
popular literature the methods and meanings which Melville was to
put into travelogue. In this sense, it is fair to say that as early as the
publication of his first book, after which he was, for a while, a very
successful and popular young author, Melville was "misunderstood." [4]
Indeed, almost without exception, the amusingly literal-minded critics
considered his book in terms of whether or not it was authentic (some
even going so far as to wonder if there were any such person as
Herman Melville), or in terms of enchanting escapism, or in terms
of whether he was to be praised, tolerated, or jailed for his treatment
of the missionaries.[5] But more recent scholarship has made it increasingly clear that however authentic his works may or may not be,

---

[2] *Harbinger,* 266.

[3] There is no need to reopen the arguments about the nineteenth-century missionaries in Polynesia. After reading many of the attacks and defenses, I am inclined to believe that Melville's "sailor's grudge," as Duyckinck called it, was at
least justifiable and not necessarily limited to personal animus. One interesting
item, a letter from one H. R. Hawkins, dated Honolulu, December 10, 1849, to
his father Captain Esek Hawkins, Jr., of Lansingburgh, New York, sheds some
light, but it is only one item among many divergent conclusions. The letter says
in part, "All that Melville ever told about the missionaries in this part of the
world, you may take for gospel." Quoted by William Gilman, "A Note on Herman
Melville in Honolulu," *AL* XIX (1947), 169.

[4] For a discussion of the favorable public acceptance of *Typee,* see two articles
by Charles Anderson, "Contemporary American Opinions of *Typee* and *Omoo,*"
AL, IX (1937), 1-25; and "Melville's English Debut," *AL,* XI (1939), 23-38. An
earlier attempt at the same kind of evaluation is O. W. Riegel's "The Anatomy
of Melville's Fame," *AL,* III (1931), 195-203. See also the unpublished dissertation (Michigan, 1933) by Hugh Hetherington, "The Reputation of Herman Melville in America."

[5] For examples, see Anderson, "Melville's English Debut"; an unsigned review
of *Typee, Douglas Jerrold's Shilling Magazine,* III (April, 1846), 380-83; and
Daniel Aaron, "Melville and The Missionaries," *NEQ,* VIII (1935), 404-8.

it is less and less possible to deny the actuality of symbolic experience in Melville's early books.[6]

There is no way to prove that Melville consciously set out to create a symbolic work in his first book. But the themes arising from *Typee's* symbolic construction do become a point of embarkation for Melville's philosophical voyage into the sea of relationships between the western world, the primitive world, the quester, and the lure. The apparent vehicle for those relationships is the occasional treatment of the contact between Christianity and the Marquesans. The more important and less apparent vehicle is an opposition of mind and body, mind and heart, communication and lack of communication. And again and again, as Melville dives into the depths of his later books, he is to hook these thematic leviathans by the nose, subject them to the try-works of his mind, and boil every last drop of suggestion out of them.

As little as we know about Melville's (or any man's) own feelings and stated intentions, there is some historical evidence that he was not as interested in the factual reporting of his experience as he was in what he could accomplish thematically using those experiences. For instance, when source books like C. S. Stewart's *A Visit to the South Seas* are examined,[7] it becomes clear that the "significance of the discovery of this source material lies in the fact that it constitutes another step in solving the problem of the relationship between Melville's technique of composition and the use of his source materials. . . . At times he borrowed extensively without alteration; at other times he made significant alterations for the purpose of producing a dominant mood or impression . . . again, he seems to be deliberately planning to throw us off the trail." [8] Indeed, in *Typee* the crew of the *Dolly* is painted in heavily uncomplimentary colors. Tommo voices extreme dissatisfaction with his lot aboard ship and with the crew—a gang of debauched immoralists, roughnecks, and ignorant, craven sneaks and bullies. Yet, in a letter to Lemuel Shaw, in which Gansevoort Melville relays news from Herman during the factual period of Melville's "*Dolly*" trip to the Marquesas aboard the whaler *Acushnet,* Gansevoort says: "I am in receipt of a letter from my brother Herman dated August 1841 at Santa Martha, coast of Peru— He was then in perfect health, and not dissatisfied with his lot—the fact of his being one of a crew so much superior in morals and early advantages to the ordinary run of whaling crews affords him constant gratification. By the paper I see that his ship—the Acushnet—Pease [the captain]—was spoken in Dec last—at sea—all well. . . ." [9] There

[6] William Gilman, *Melville's Early Life and Redburn* (New York, 1951) is an excellent demonstration and proof.

[7] (New York, 1831), 2 vols.

[8] Thomas Russell, "Yarn for Melville's *Typee,*" PQ, XV (1936), 27.

[9] New York, July 22, 1842. (Lemuel Shaw Collection, Massachusetts Historical Society.)

is no reason to doubt that even at this early date, Melville was consciously prepared to utilize experience in a sacrifice of fact for thematic purpose. As the London *Athenaeum* put it, "*si non e vero e ben trovato*. . . . We vouch for the verisimilitude, but not the verity." [10] It is not only Melville's desire to spin a good yarn for commercial success that keeps *Typee*, in its heightened color and drama, from being a "true" story. The verity was also manipulated by symbolic creation of theme. Nor is this impossible for a brand-new, twenty-six-year-old author. "Until I was twenty-five, I had no development at all," he wrote to Hawthorne. "From my twenty-fifth year I date my life. Three weeks have scarcely passed, at any time between then and now [June 1, 1851], that I have not unfolded within myself. But I feel that I am now come to the inmost leaf of the bulb, and that shortly the flower must fall to the mould. It seems to me now that Solomon was the truest man who ever spoke, and yet that he a little *managed* the truth with a view to popular conservatism. . . ." [11]

And back "then," in 1846 (or 1845, when Melville was composing the book), the author makes a statement about the author in the "Preface" to *Typee*. "In his account of the singular and interesting people among whom he was thrown, it will be observed that he chiefly treats of their more obvious peculiarities; and, in describing their customs, refrains in most cases from entering into explanations concerning their origin and purposes. As writers of travels among barbarous communities are generally very diffuse on these subjects, he deems it right to advert to what may be considered a culpable omissions." [12] Melville is twitting and protecting himself. Whatever literary sins he may have had, he was hardly ever guilty of sparseness or humility in his books. More important, he did not spend as much time among the Typees as he pretended: he never had time to learn the "explanations" from which he "refrains." [13] This defensiveness is not

---

[10] No. 988 (Oct. 3, 1846), 419.

[11] Pittsfield (Spring, 1851). Quoted by Eleanor Metcalf, *Herman Melville, Cycle and Epicycle*, p. 110.

[12] *Typee*, in *Selected Writings of Herman Melville* (New York, 1952), p. 457. The "Sequel" which this edition adds may be the text of the American third rather than second edition: see Bernard DeVoto, "Editions of *Typee*," SRL, V (1928), 406.

[13] The best study of the authenticity of Melville's books in reporting his stay in the Pacific is Charles Anderson's *Melville in The South Seas* (New York, 1939). Also, Robert S. Forsythe demonstrated that Melville was in the T'aipi valley for four weeks rather than four months. After a painstaking tracing of the true chronology of events, Mr. Forsythe concludes that "Melville confidently believed [that criticism] would seriously impair the success of *Typee* as a genuine narrative. The maintenance of the credit of the volume as a true account of its author's experiences seems to be the object of Melville's solicitude. . . . He rather innocently extended the term of his stay among the Typees in order to make his account more effective . . . . And I do not suppose . . . that the literary seaman, Herman Melville, was deterred by any scruples concerning the veracity of a sailor's yarn from making his narrative more appealing or more dramatic through taking liberties with the time involved in it." "Herman Melville in the Marquesas," *PQ*, XV (1936), 1-15.

a mildly humorous deference to the audience as much as it is a thinly
veiled excuse for thematic organization rather than entertaining
journalism. As Melville complains, whenever the aspiring writer looking for markets wrote the familiar and fashionable travel book, he
crammed his account with as much detail as possible.[14] Yet in his own
utilization of event, Melville rejected the limitation of factual and
chronological exactness of detail, even though his contemporaries considered him to be an anthropologist of sorts and an expert on the
Marquesas.[15] Melville was not ultimately concerned with the reception
of his South Seas books as works of ethnological value, for after he
was fully aware of the favorable reception of his two South Seas books
(*Typee* and *Omoo*), he proceeded to write *Mardi*, a "South Seas"
book which sacrificed for theme any accuracy of ethnological detail
whatever. Melville's commercial and artistic interests were by no
means similar. Prodded by fears and doubts and insecurities, he was
always trying to talk his publishers into the most advantageous terms.
While he remained sober with the American publishers, Wiley and
Putnam, Harper and Brothers, he kept assuring his English publishers,
John Murray and Richard Bentley, that his projected books were
factual, or historical, or "very much more more calculated for popularity than anything . . . yet published of mine." [16] But in intimate
letters, he wrote to his friends that, "I shall write such things as the
Great Publisher of Mankind ordained ages before he published 'The
World'—this planet, I mean—not the Literary Globe." [17] And, "So
far as I am individually concerned, & independent of my pocket, it is
my earnest desire to write those sort of books which are said to

[14] There is no doubt that Melville was received by his contemporaries as just
such an author. One review of *Omoo*, correctly groping for the secret of Melville's
selection of detail, and incorrectly reckoning the extent and purpose of his art,
summed up an attitude thus: "Doubtless we shall hear more of the author's adventures:—for, though the *vraisemblance* of history is well preserved, there are
in the style and about the narrative indications of romance that suggest a power
of prolonging these adventures to any extent for which a public shall demand
them." *The Athenaeum*, No. 1015 (London, April 10, 1847), 384. Recognizing
Melville's different treatment of fact, a friendly magazine, in a notice of *Omoo*,
said, "Treating as they do on familiar topics . . . that we thought had been exhausted by other authors, we are agreeably delighted to find so much of what
is positively new in *Omoo*. There is a freshness and novelty in the graphic
sketches of society as it now exists in these islands, that we look for in vain in
the writings of other travellers. Mr. Melville contrives to throw around his personal adventures all the interest and charm of fictitious narrative. *Omoo* and *Typee*
are actually delightful romances of real life, embellished with powers of description, and a graphic skill of hitting off characters little inferior to the highest
order of novelist and romance writers." In *Albion*, n.s., VI (New York, May 8,
1847), 228. See also the unpublished dissertation (Stanford, 1953), by Howard
C. Key, "The Influence of Travel Literature upon Melville's Fictional Technique."

[15] Arthur Stedman, in an obituarial review of Melville, said, "A reference to
Typee as 'Melville's Marquesan Islands' under which title the book first appeared in England [actually this was the title of the second, expurgated edition],
was given in the *Popular Science Monthly* as recently as two weeks before the
author's death, and shows the ethnological value of the work." "Melville of Marquesas," *Review of Reviews*, IV (1891), 429.

[16] To Richard Bentley (April 16, 1852). Metcalf, p. 135.

[17] To Evert Duyckinck, London (Dec. 14, 1849). Metcalf, p. 71.

'fail.'"[18] And, "Dollars damn me; and the malicious Devil is forever grinning in on me, holding the door ajar. . . . What I feel most moved to write, that is banned, —it will not pay. Yet altogether write the *other* way I cannot. So the product is a final hash, and all my books are botches."[19]

Moreover, if, as the "Preface" says, much detail has been deleted, the questions of what has been retained, and why, remain. In the case of the missionaries, for instance, the "Preface" continues, "The conclusions deduced from these facts [about the missionaries] are unavoidable, and in stating them the author has been influenced by no feeling of animosity, either to the individuals themselves or to that glorious cause which has not always been served by the proceedings of some of its advocates." But Melville had just said that it was *easy* to avoid certain other facts and details. Yet not only in *Typee,* but in *Omoo, Mardi* and *White-Jacket* as well, there is charge after charge against the inhumanities of "that glorious cause" of militant or coercive religion, with some animus reserved for the glory of the cause itself. One suspects the "Preface" of being a good liar. Like any craftsman, Melville did select which of the "unavoidable" facts he would avoid. Further, Melville says, "The great interest with which the important events lately occurring at the Sandwich, Marquesas, and Society Islands, have been regarded in America and England, and indeed throughout the world, will, he trusts, justify a few otherwise unwarrantable digressions." Those "unwarrantable digressions" prove themselves to be an integral part of the book's theme of human behavior in contrasting civilizations.

Whether we approach the book according to what has been deleted or according to what has been reinforced (as is the case here), the conclusion remains the same: *Typee* is a symbolically created thematic construct rather than a haphazard piece of reporting or a tale which is merely picaresque adventure.

II

Immediately after extended statements about the barrenness of sea-life, *Typee* begins with yearning for the lush and exotic land. "The Marquesas! What strange visions of outlandish things does the very name spirit up! Naked houris—cannibal banquets—groves of cocoanut—coral reefs—tattooed chiefs—and bamboo temples; sunny valleys planted with bread-fruit trees—carved canoes dancing on the flashing blue waters—savage woodlands guarded by horrible idols—*heathenish rites and human sacrifices.*" Two features of Polynesia oppose the sterility of life at sea, with which the book opens. One is the physicality

---

[18] To Lemuel Shaw, New York (Oct. 6, 1849). Metcalf, p. 67.
[19] To Nathaniel Hawthorne, Pittsfield (Spring, 1851). Metcalf, p. 108.

and fertility of Marquesan life, and the other is the primitive simplicity, which is barbaric enough to serve as an image of the most basic, pristine human life. The Marquesas are the very beginnings and first curve in the human life cycle, and have not kept pace with western history. "The group for which we were now steering (although among the earliest of European discoveries in the South Seas, having first been visited in the year 1595) still continues to be tenanted by beings as strange and barbarous as ever." The Typee valley itself is further set off from even this primitive group of peoples. Melville's insistence upon the vale's seclusion and isolation increases the dramatic interest; it also makes Typee the constant and unspoiled laboratory test case from which is universalized a general statement about man's primitive life in nature.

The west, with its seamen, missionaries, and French and English conquerors, also represents a single level of value. But it is a level of conquest which clashes with the blissful animal existence of the islanders. The opposition of the two civilizations furnishes the tension in *Typee*, both in the theme and the rising action of conflict. So clear are the tensions in this relatively straightforward story, that the reader can quickly extract a list of opposing characteristics even before he is aware of what Melville is doing in his redefinition of Eden.

WESTERN CIVILIZATION (Mind)	MARQUESAN CIVILIZATION (Body)
1. Heartlessness	1. Heartfulness
2. Conquest	2. Submission, ultimate doom
3. Quest, mobility	3. Seclusion, immobility
4. Consciousness	4. Unconsciousness
5. Sea	5. Land
6. Communication with other worlds	6. Inability to communicate with other worlds
7. Inability to communicate with Typee	7. Spontaneous, childlike, meaningless chatter among selves
8. Sparse food, little sleep, technology	8. Physical gratification, somnolence, unaided nature
9. Planning, scheming, technological and military foresight	9. Spontaneity of animal spirits, innocence
10. Attempt to conquer natural environment	10. Integration with natural environment
11. Artificiality, complexity	11. Naturalness, simplicity

The simplicity of *Typee's* action and characterization can be gauged by the starkness of the list. However, it is in the evaluation of opposing forces that Melville creates the book's complexity of relationships. To do this, once the oppositions were settled, Melville had to give the literal level of action a kinetic thematic energy; he had to hitch "adventure" to the potential symbolism of the motifs. He did this in

Typee as he did in all his first-person narratives—through the plight and observations of the protagonist.

At the very first, Melville indicated the evaluative relationship of the narrator to both sea and land. To Tommo, the sea is a monotone of time and work, and everything about it is repugnant. In his anxiety to leave the whaler, he plans to jump ship. He thinks of the sunny valleys planted with breadfruit groves and of the heathenish rites, and he muses that "Such were the strangely jumbled anticipations that haunted me during our passage from the cruising ground. I felt an irresistable curiosity to see those islands which the olden voyagers had so glowingly described." He is in a fever very similar to that of Ishmael, who, before he set foot on the *Pequod*, was haunted by the image of a humped and hooded phantom like a snow-hill in the air. Compulsively, Tommo is drawn to the objects of tension before the particulars of that tension are introduced either to him or the reader.

Searching for a rationalization which will justify his actions, Tommo offers a legalistic argument for abandoning ship. Although the actions of the captain and the conditions aboard ship form part of the thread of deceit which weaves through the book, Tommo's legalities are really irrelevant. Imaginatively, he is incorrect, for his legal sensitivity has nothing to do with the realities of his desire or the consequences of his actions. While he makes up his own morality as he goes along, Tommo's argument only touches upon its strongest motivation—the simpler and more elemental urge to reintegrate self in the physical and emotional satisfactions of human life. And Tommo has ample emotional inducement. The deceit and brutality of the captain have reduced Tommo's life to a business of elementary survival. Each man thinks that his own comfort is contingent upon his toadying to the captain's despotism. The crew, or populace, has neither realization of, nor courage for, united action, and the sailors blindly accept the consequences of their each-man-for-himself attitudes. Though much degraded, this is the crew of Captain Vere's *Indomitable*. But unlike the enlightened and purposeful rule of the *Indomitable*, the government of the *Dolly* is reduced to all the possible blind egoism and viciousness of western life—the Typee savages are never so debased. Simple savagery in civilized man only results in brutishness. On the *Dolly*, the artificialities of rule do not check and balance each other. The captain's government is not the "law and equity" whereby western society maintains itself. "[The captain's] prompt reply to all complaints and remonstrances was—the butt end of a handspike, so convincingly administered as effectually to silence the aggrieved party.

"To whom could we apply for redress? We had left both law and equity on the other side of the Cape; and unfortunately, with a very few exceptions, our crew was composed of a parcel of dastardly and mean-spirited wretches, divided among themselves, and only united

in enduring without resistance the unmitigated tyranny of the captain." The laws of the west do not apply to Marquesan waters. And
when we first meet Tommo, he has already dissociated himself from
the crew and from the ship.[20] He is enraged by the thought that he
is merely another anonymous member of the *Dolly's* doll-like and sick
society. Giving up the sniveling and anarchic crew as a hopeless job,
he no longer even toys with ideas of union or social betterment. Unlike Vere, he certainly will not risk sacrifice of self for the good of the
community. His solution is evasion, withdrawal from the actualities
of his world as he knows it. Consequently he loses his only possible
individual identity: he becomes like all the other crew members by
dedicating himself to the proposition that as long as life is such an
elemental thing, he might as well make himself as comfortable as
possible. At this point Tommo has no more realization, and no more
ability to change or control fate, than any of the Ancient Mariner's
crew. He rejects and escapes from the inhumanity of quest (the
sea, whaling) and the inhumanity of western man (the dominance of
the captain). He tries to find both comfort and individual identity
by submerging himself in a reintroduction to humanity in the unconsciousness of its very beginnings (Nukuheva's hinterlands). By the
end of the book he discovers that a man does not capture his identity
by such means, because individual identity is contingent upon the
individual's place in the human community of his own history. To
Typee, as a social concept, Tommo is another pig for slaughter.

But supposing, as Tommo does, that the captain might be endured;
what are the added conditions of sea life that make the Marquesas
so attractive in the first place? As if in answer, the very first chapter
introduces a note of hideously parched living. There is no food for
the freshness and completeness of life. The chapter subheadings
begin, "The Sea—Longings for Shore—A Land-Sick Ship. . . ." And the
introductory paragraph continues the lament: "Six months at sea! . . .
six months out of sight of land . . . the sky above, the sea around, and
nothing else! Weeks and weeks ago our fresh provisions were all
exhausted. There is not a sweet potato left; not a single yam. Those
glorious bunches of banannas which once decorated our stern and
quarter-deck have, alas, disappeared! and the delicious oranges which
hung suspended from our tops and stays—they, too, are gone! Yes,
they are all departed, and there is nothing left us but salt-horse and
sea-bisquit." The very food of life offered at sea serves merely to
continue the departure from land and world. Tommo describes the

[20] For an excellent discussion of isolation, see R. E. Watters, "Melville's 'Isolatoes'," *PMLA,* LX (1945), 1138-48. In periodical publication, Mr. Watters'
articles are as keen as any and more so than most. See also "Melville's 'Sociality',"
AL, XVII (1945), 33-49; and "Melville's Metaphysics of Evil," *Univ. of Toronto
Q.,* IX (1940), 170-80.

prodigious preparations for sailing, during which quantities of stale bread, poor meat and roachy water are stored in the hold; and as long as the stores last, the ship remains at sea. "But not to speak of the quality of these articles of sailors' fare, the abundance in which they are put on board a whaling vessel is almost incredible. Oftentimes, when we had occasion to break out in the hold, and I beheld the successive tiers of casks and barrels, whose contents were all destined to be consumed in due course by the ship's company, my heart has sunk within me." Adding to Tommo's heartsickness is the story about the good ship *Perseverance,* whose skipper simply touched port for food and then headed back to whaling grounds. The ship becomes a veritable Flying Dutchman, always seeking, never returning to world and time. Fearing a similar fate, Tommo notes that the meals of salt pork and sea-bisquit are scanty so that the stores will last even longer. At the outset Tommo renounces sea and search and sterility. "Is there nothing fresh around us? Is there no green thing to be seen? Yes, the inside of our bulwarks is painted green; but what a vile and sickly hue it is, as if nothing bearing even the semblence of verdure could flourish this weary way from land."

What the sea says is that like the world of land and body, this life of quest and mind, when limited to a monotone existence, is a cannibal life. It fattens off its opposite member. In its exploitation and scorn of the more elementary levels of natural, animal living, it kills and devours, sucking life and sustenance from land. Western spoilation and cannibalism are presented directly after Tommo bewails the lack of green things. "Even the bark that once clung to the wood we use for fuel has been gnawed off and devoured by the captain's pig; and so long ago, too, that the pig himself has in turn been devoured." Tommo and Toby, when they fight and conquer nature in their struggle to reach the isolated valley, must also live, like the pig, on the bark they can chew off twigs: in the inversion caused by change of worlds, the provisions and foresights of the western man are all lost on Typeean existence. The natives also rape nature, but nature willingly allows the defloration at her own pleasure. Her Typeean seducers never attempt to conquer her. The *Dolly,* however, like the *Perseverance,* will continue to sail until the last reminder of land and animal life, Pedro the rooster, is devoured—and then the ship will touch land again, taking from it the provisions for life which it never replaces in the South Pacific's eternal cycles of growth.

This kind of single-level existence is unmistakably associated with western civilization. All the men who come to the Marquesas from the sea are alien. They are always whalers, traders, conquerors; they are always Americans, Englishmen, Frenchmen; and they come to exploit either the resources of the waters, or the peoples, or the lands. They display behavior values which become represented by a restless striving for conquest, a quest summed up on the personal and philosophical level by Taji and Ahab, and on the political and military level by the missionaries and by Admiral Du Petit Thouars. Totally, this striving is an attempt to extend human power, for all the wrong reasons, over all creation. The argument, however, is not with an extension of human power. Melville does not imply that there should be no ship's captains or French military men as much as he does imply that captain or soldier must make a realistic and humanitarian extension governed by social insight into what he is doing. Realistic because it proceeds from a tactical understanding of the instruments demanded by time and place, rather than proceeding from an external and superimposed set of values. Humanitarian because its goal is what Vere sees as the "lasting peace and welfare of mankind" rather than privilege or power per se. The western, or present-day world—Melville's "world of mind"—is really two worlds in relation to the primitive. It is the philosophical world of mind, and it is the shrewd or technological world of mind. Melville's philosophical characters may set out with social goals, but their cosmic view and their tactics are wrong. His shrewd characters have no cosmic view at all, or if they do it is hypocritical and conventional. Like the "town" characters in *Huckleberry Finn*, their morality does not arise from a firsthand evaluation of experience. They do not care about possible relationships between their own selfishness and the social good. They have technological minds, or political minds, or military minds, but they have no historical and social vision. They are the "practical" men of the world, whose practicality, because visionless and therefore isolated, is ultimately unrealistic and absurd. When Melville devotes his artistic concentration to the world of mind as such, this latter, shrewd quality becomes an element of mindlessness. But in contrast to the primitive, it is the shrewd world of mind, largely, that operates in *Typee*, presenting the semi-picaresque surface which can so easily be mistaken for the totality.

In *Typee*, mind often is objectified in the physical object of the human head, just as mindlessness is objectified in the human body. The sailors know the technics of whaling and the politics of shipboard life. But they eat sparsely of stale food. The Typees, on the other hand, have no technology, and are always feasting. Their food is a profusion of fresh fruits and vegetables, or newly killed and freshly roasted pork. They offer nothing to the world of mind. When the alien western sailors approach the vicinity of the Marquesas, mental activity, toil, and sea-consciousness also become alien, and virtually disappear. Animal existence and somnolence become the only possibility, as though the sailors were approaching a realm of lotus-eaters.

We abandoned the fore-peak altogether, and spreading an awning over the forecastle, slept, ate, and lounged under it the live-long day. Every one seemed to be under the influence of some narcotic. Even the officers aft, whose duty required them never to be seated while keeping a deck watch, vainly endeavored to keep on their pins; and were obliged invariably to compromise the matter by leaning up against the bulwarks, and gazing abstractedly over the side. Reading was out of the question; take a book in your hand, and you were asleep in an instant [p. 473].

And if the "insular green Tahiti" offers no mental refreshment, it reinvigorates and replenishes all the physical and emotional stores robbed by search and consciousness. For instance, Tommo dives from the parching heat of the sea-sun into Polynesia's verdure, which allows oblivion and relief from the perspiration of toil and conflict with nature.

I had come from Nukuheva by water in the ship's boat, and when we entered the bay of Tior it was high noon. The heat had been intense . . . the sun's rays had expended all their fury upon us; and to add to our discomfort, we had omitted to supply ourselves with water previous to starting. What with heat and thirst together, I became . . . impatient to get ashore . . . I rushed forward across *the open ground in the vicinity of the sea*, and plunged, diver fashion, into the recesses of the first grove that offered.

What a delightful sensation did I experience! I felt *as if floating in some new element* while all sorts of gurgling, trickling, liquid sounds fell upon my ear. People may say what they will about the refreshing influences of a cold-water bath, but commend me when in a persperation to the shade baths of Tior, beneath the cocoa-nut tree, and amidst the cool, delightful atmosphere which surrounds them [pp. 497-98, italics mine].

The Marquesas pile mountainous reaches of verdure into a monumental, beckoning emblem of Eden, which stands green and fresh in the sweaty, barren contemporary wasteland of a world, as a cool reminder of the lost Golden Age when life was not touched by time and had not yet become history. The Typee natives, who never leave their homes, are the children of nature, the noble savages of primitivism. They have nothing to do with the deep-sea ships except to bring innocence and physical and emotional gratification. That Typeeans are as much at home in the water as on land is an indication of fertility and integration with physical nature rather than an indication of toil and contemporary quest. Their water is lake or inland stream: it is not sea. The Typees prefer sea fish and sea salt and seaweed as the three delicacies they prize above all else, yet Tommo is surprised that these sea-girt people make only rare excursions to the ocean for those abundant delicacies. Women, who more in *Typee* than in any other Melville book, are representatives of land and land values (particularly body and safety), are not permitted by native taboo to even enter a canoe. It is Tommo, the western alien, who effects the beginning dissolution of native order by effecting the change which allows his mistress Fayaway to break the taboo.

The very first picture of even those Marquesans who are not so isolated as the Typees is an introduction of mindless physicality and simple innocence. The male natives swim up to the *Dolly* surrounded by rings of floating coconuts, which they bring as gifts. At first the *heads* of the natives are indistinguishable from *coconuts*, and when Tommo exhausts this poor pun, he notices that the natives "use their heads" only as a means to push the coconuts through the water. The native females are at first indistinguishable from so many shoals of fish, and when they climb out of the water, they are described as frolicking, cavorting animals.

We were still some distance from the beach, and under slow headway, when we sailed right into the midst of these swimming nymphs, and they boarded us at every quarter; many seizing hold of the chain-plates and springing into the chains, others, at the peril of being run over by the vessel in her course, catching at the bob-stays, and wreathing their slender forms about the ropes, hung suspended in the air. All of them at length succeeded in getting up the ship's side, where they hung dripping with the brine and glowing from the bath, their jet-black tresses streaming over their shoulders, and half enveloping their otherwise naked forms. There they hung, sparkling with savage vivacity, laughing gaily at one another, and chattering away with infinite glee. Nor were they idle the while, for each one performed the simple office of the toilette for the other. Their luxuriant locks, wound up and twisted into the smallest possible compass, were freed from the briny element; the whole person carefully dried, and from a little round shell that passed from hand to hand, anointed with a fragrant oil: their adornments were completed by passing a few loose folds of white tappa, in a modest cincture, around the waist. Thus arrayed they no longer hesitated, but flung themselves lightly over the bulwarks, and were quickly frolicking about the decks. Many of them went forward, perching upon the head-rails or running out upon the bowsprit, while others seated themselves upon the taffrail, or reclined at full length upon the boats. What a sight for us bachelor sailors! how avoid so dire a temptation? For who could think of tumbling these artless creatures overboard, when they had swam miles to welcome us?

Their appearance perfectly amazed me; their extreme youth, the light clear brown of their complexions, their delicate features, and inexpressibly graceful figures, their softly moulded limbs, and free unstudied action, seemed as strange as beautiful.

The "Dolly" was fairly captured; and never I will say was vessel carried before by such a dashing and irresistible party of boarders! The ship taken, we could not do otherwise than yield ourselves prisoners, and for the whole period that she remained in the bay, the "Dolly," as well as her crew, were completely in the hands of the mermaids.

In the evening after we had come to anchor the deck was illuminated with lanterns, and this picturesque band of sylphs, tricked out with flowers, and dressed in robes of variegated tappa, got up a ball in great style. These females were passionately fond of dancing, and the wild grace and spirit of their style excel everything that I have ever seen. The varied dances of the Marquesan girls are beautiful in the extreme, but there is an abandoned voluptuousness in their character which I dare not attempt to describe.

Our ship was now wholly given up to every species of riot and debauchery. Not the feeblest barrier was interposed between the unholy passions of the crew and their unlimited gratification. The grossest licentiousness and the most shameful inebriety prevailed, with occasional and but short-lived interruptions, through the whole period of her stay. Alas for the poor savages when exposed to the influence of these polluting examples! Unsophisticated and confiding, they are easily led into every vice, and humanity weeps over the ruin thus remorselessly inflicted upon them by their European civilizers. Thrice happy are they who, inhabiting some yet undiscovered island in the midst of the ocean, have never been brought into contaminating contact with the white man [pp. 480-81].

This passage would seem to serve as another statement of demarcation between the qualities of primitive and contemporary man. So far there is a stark division between the regenerative Adamic life and the destructive sea life of present western history. But as the distinctions between mind and body lead one to suspect, this passage is more than a statement of opposites, for although the "good" natives are distinct from the "bad" crewmen (Melville discreetly avoids the fact that it takes two to make a bargain), and although they are magnificent animals, they are somehow less than human. Now the relationships between worlds are introduced, and the black-and-whiteness of "good" and "bad" begins to disappear as the worlds are evaluated further. Here is the first hint that the applicability, or correctness, of the elements of man's mysterious nature change as the elements of man's historical condition change. The crew surrenders to the savage which is in all men, and the savage in the civilized character is not purity or artless innocence as it is in the natives. The bestiality of the sailors indicates that what Typee represents is not peculiar to the Marquesas alone; it becomes a universal for the animal in all mankind. Thus Typee is isolated not because it is simply different, but because it serves as an unvitiated example of the animal in pure and innocent state. The Marquesans are the epitome of unsophisticated confidence, and they are doomed in their pure isolation. As Tommo discovers, a man's most important facts are the facts of historical realities. He cannot change his world by jumping back into the past. The present world demands its claim to present life, and the process of adjusting life to contemporaneous reality is historically inevitable. As with individuals, if societies do not recognize this, they forfeit all possible control of their own destinies. If the pitiable and victimized natives share any responsibility for their debased condition, it is only because their level of development and their passive relationship with nature have not allowed them anything but a passive relationship with the impinging world of the present. With a sigh, Tommo notes that it is only a matter of time until the French have their gunboats and troops on the lovely bay and valley, and what has been presented in the extended quote above will occur all over again. Thus *Typee* presents the germ of *Billy Budd's* major argument: the purity of innocence may be beauty, but in the complete inversion that naturalism makes of idealistic tenets, innocence, not knowledge, is a murderous impossibility that becomes original sin.

Eden is deceptive because it is indefensible as a state of being. It is open to all the incursions of history once life has become subject to time. Indeed, Eden is not Eden, but, as historical land, has already been corrupted by the western world of the present. In *Typee* the first visible signs of land, almost immediately contrasted with luxurious and inviting somnolence, are the portentous seafowl led by "That piratical-looking fellow, appropriately named the man-of-war's hawk, with his blood-red bill and raven plumage. . . ." Perhaps Eden was never Eden. Further suspicions are cast upon the state of primitive, pure, and natural life by hints about the quality of its still unspoiled state. Melville is to find that any isolated state of being—mind, body, or heart—which does not review all states of being is untenable. Land in itself is not to be equated with safety or infallible human happiness. The Melville of a story like "The Lightning Rod Man," for instance, envisions the inevitability of fate as something equally embracing whether one is in a howling onshore gale or in the comfort of his easy chair. And particularly in terms of Typee existence, the single luxury of mindless body is bloody murder, a process of rot, a practice of cannibalism; *Typee's* scattered bits of reminders about cannibalism do more than merely sharpen anticipation and suspense. Says Tommo, before he ever lands in Nukuheva,

I had heard too of an English vessel that many years ago, after a weary cruize, sought to enter the bay of Nukuheva, and arriving within two or three miles of the land, was met by a large canoe filled with natives, who offered to lead the way to their place of destination. The captain, unacquainted with the localities of the island, joyfully accepted to the proposition—the canoe paddled on and the ship followed. Soon she was conducted to a beautiful inlet, and dropped her anchor in its waters beneath the shadows of the lofty shore. That same night the perfidious Typees, who had thus inveigled her into their fatal bay, flocked aboard the doomed vessel by hundreds, and at a given signal murdered every soul on board [pp. 493-94].

If untainted natural man in constant communion with nature is Adamic, then this Eden is vastly changed in concept. Rather it is only a different kind of the sharkishness of *Redburn's* land, or the deceptive safety of *Moby-Dick's* Aunt Charity and "The Lee Shore." The initial picture of salvation and pure regeneration associated with Edenic primitivism becomes suspect as only partly true, as factually inaccurate.

Simplicity, innocence, seclusion, isolation, passivity, and avoidance of historical knowledge are not the virtues that either the Christian tradition or transcendentalism thought they were. Melville strengthens this suspicion by adding another detail to the consequences of conflict between the two worlds. The first human who comes aboard ship from the Marquesan land is a tottering, almost comatose, and aged native. He is a drunken old vagabond who "was utterly unable to stand erect or to navigate his body across the deck." And—he is the official pilot for the bay of Nukuheva! He is the man appointed to navigate the microcosm of one entire world into communication with another. The activities of one world simply cannot be bundled into the activities of another without the dehumanization which results from the loss of function and identity. The murder works both ways. Not only is the representative of Eden a ruin to the west, but the west also ruins the representative of Eden. This will not be the only time that Melville is to suggest that the oppressor becomes more debased than the oppressed he debases. As long as the western, contemporary world of mind is the visionless world of "practicality" and selfish conquest, and as long as the values of the primitive world of heart and body remain isolated from contemporary experience, the two can never be joined correctly. The final product is an inability to navigate life, for neither Typee alone nor the *Dolly* alone provide the necessary fullness for complete, correct human behavior. These early hints prepare for the demonstration of Eden's failure, which is the purpose of the rest of the book.

In the purity of Typee terms, the main tasks of body seem to be an innocent partaking of nature's munificence and an avoidance of conflict. For Ahab, in his departure from nature, the area of conflict is imaged in the depths of the ocean. For Pierre, in his departure from nature, the area of conflict is epitomized in the scaling of the Mount of Titans. The Typees avoid both ocean and mountain. Conflict is in ocean, whence come intruders and invaders, and is in mountain, where there is none of the nature that gives sustenance, and where there is the chance to meet battle and death from hostile tribesmen. The Typee existence is so diametrically opposed to toil and conflict, quest and consciousness, that its limitations preclude any hope for human aspiration in western terms, any hope for a widening of man's horizons.

The mountainous tracts which separated their respective territories remain altogether uninhabited; the natives invariably dwelling in the depths of the valleys, with a view of securing themselves from the predatory incursions of their enemies, who often lurk along their borders . . . I several times met with very aged men, who from this cause had never passed the confines of their native vale, some of them having never even ascended midway up the mountains in the whole course of their lives, and who, accordingly, had little idea of the appearance of any other part of the island, the whole of which is not perhaps more than sixty miles in circuit. The little space in which some of these clans pass away their days would seem almost incredible [pp. 496-97].

Isolation and seclusion become not only some of the perfecting charms of the sequestered vale, but also some of its major limitations and defects. *Typee* becomes a natural starting point for themes which will illuminate men who would see all the known world and the infinities beyond it. But always the striking through to infinities is validly meaningful (even if the meaning is negative) only when it is motivated by broad experience in life.

Tommo is impressed by the wholeness, wholesomeness, and perfect magnificence of the islanders' bodies. At the same time, the conscious and injured isolato describes the mindlessness of the Typees. They cannot communicate with or understand the rest of humanity from which they are isolated. They can hear news from outlying valleys only through the agency of itinerant and taboo "communicados" like Marnoo and Jimmy. When the Typees talk—as they always do chatter chatter chatter—the talk is always spontaneous, unplanned, childlike and inconsequential. The Typee's only communication system but serves to continue isolation; the human telegraph system of natives shouting from tree to tree, from the beach to the inmost glen of the valley, announces invasion from either mountain or sea. The very animals of the glen, the physically brilliant lizards and birds, can make no sound. Always, except in its own primitive terms, which are not the terms of Tommo's life, childlike Typee can neither see, talk, nor hear; like Baby Budd, it is beautiful, mindless and blind.[21]

When Tommo does escape to the sea, his greatest opposition comes from a warrior chief, Mow-Mow, who is characterized by a gigantic and wonderfully powerful body, and by the fact that he has only one eye. On the other hand, the leader of the faction which would allow Tommo to leave unharmed is the old man, Marheyo, who (with his daughter Fayaway) is among the few Typees to understand Tommo's plight to the point of compassion. It is true that others (Mehevi the chief and Kory-Kory the valet) also are fond of Tommo, but when the values of Typee conflict with Tommo's values, these others refuse Tommo's wishes, with few exceptions. When they do grant his wishes, they do so believing that his injured body will make him ineffectual in the attainment of his goals—that he will be unable to effect his own destiny. Fayaway has love and sympathy for Tommo because she is his mistress. But it is Marheyo who has the compassion of understanding, and he is the only native aware that there may be in non-Typeean worlds values which also have claim upon human behavior. When Tommo tries to escape, Marheyo consequently is in the van of those who see Tommo as a human being—they have been able to make that much of an extension beyond their own world into history. Those who wish to head Tommo off see him from the

---

[21] Perhaps even when he was a pretentious nineteen-year-old author, Melville was concerned with the idea of apparent beauty marred by dehumanizing defects. The embarrassingly bad second installment of "Fragments from a Writing Desk" by "L.A.V." (*Democratic Press and Lansingburgh* [N. Y.] *Advertiser,* May 18, 1839), offers as a punch line the fact that the delicious "Inamorata" is dumb and deaf.

ahuman perspective of a single and isolated world. They wish only to maintain patterns of belief and behavior which have remained secluded from the history Tommo represents, and if they were to have their way, his identity and destiny would alike be consigned to the sacred "pork" dishes of a Feast of Calabashes. To them Tommo is not a human being as much as he is a sacrificial subject for cannibal rites. Tommo is pursued by the blind, magnificent animal and by the religion of the hidden valley, by Mow-Mow and the priests. As they rush onto the beach in furious chase, they shout "Roo-ne! Roo-ne!" which, judging by its effect upon Tommo, is a reference to the cannibalistic death which he must not be allowed to escape. "In the midst of this tumult old Marheyo came to my side," says Tommo, "and I shall never forget the benevolent expression of his countenance. He placed his arm upon my shoulder, and emphatically pronounced the only two English words I had taught him—'Home' and 'Mother.' I at once understood what he meant, and eagerly expressed my thanks to him." Whether Melville so intended it or not, this is more than a sop to nineteenth-century sentimentality. For suddenly, with no warning Marheyo is the only Typeean who can communicate in the tongue of another history, and the time of departure from Typee is the only moment in the entire book in which he does speak the words he knows. The Typeean Marheyo of the Typeean social group could not have been at all sentimental or lugubrious in his evocation of home and mother, for an entire chapter was devoted to pointing out that family relationships among the Typees were extremely loose and flexible, and that homes are only houses, open to all. Significantly, in the frozen instant of Marheyo's communication, he states a realization of the need common to all mortality, the need for identification with one's world. He is capitulating to worlds which can offer Tommo his identity, something that Marheyo's beloved Typee can never do. This capitulation is crucial not only to an understanding of Tommo's salvation, but also to Melville's naturalism. If isms split on the rock of the problem of man's identity, then it is central to recognize that in Melville's books human identity is attained by its relationship to its historical and social world, and not to any set of ideals which exist outside time.

Marheyo's sorrow when he takes leave of Tommo represents many things. His loss of Tommo on the literal level is the loss of a friend and a son. His loss of Tommo is also a yielding to the claims of consciousness, and is the first drumbeat of Eden's doom. The world moves on beyond Typee, and here is the first intimation for Marheyo that there may be greater areas of being which impinge upon Typee. The loss of Tommo becomes a portent of a loss of Typee's ability to control its own future. As in the climax of all Melville novels, characters and incidents take on added significance in the suddenly quickened tumble of events which bring the action to a close; and here Marheyo, a harmlessly puttering old savage who cannot even build a tiny hut, almost becomes a figure of transition in time. Marheyo and Fayaway tearfully aid Tommo's escape only because they realize that their desires are not consonant with the larger, predatory world outside.

Tommo recognizes the human and emotional meaning of their action, and he would reward their love. He gives to them and to Kory-Kory the cloth and musket which were used as ransom by his deliverers. But just as Marheyo buys his realizations with sacrifice, so Tommo too cannot buy his own deliverance with the fortuitous gun and calico, which are a bogus reprieve because they are external to his own commitments. He had had to translate commitment into action in order to be free of the *Dolly*. He must yet prove in action his own rejection of the level of Typee existence which shouts "Roo-ne!" rather than "Home" and "Mother." The complete deliverance, the consequence, is dependent upon his own manipulation of events, and his personal sorrow over a loss of idealized, innocent, Edenic sexuality and love must not be permitted to bar his choice of histories. In order to capsize the rowboat which carries Tommo out to sea, Mow-Mow swims after his fleeing victim. "After a few breathless moments I discerned Mow-Mow. The athletic islander, with his tomahawk between his teeth, was dashing the water before him till it foamed again. He was the nearest to us, and in another instant he would have seized one of the oars. Even at the moment I felt horror at the act I was about to commit; but it was no time for pity or compunction, and with true aim, and exerting all my strength, I dashed the boat-hook at him. It struck him just below the throat, and forced him downwards." Melville could not have chosen a better representative of Typee to be the last real obstacle between Tommo and his freedom. Tommo's action here is an acutely conscious thing rather than mere physical reflex. In the pitch of the fray he weighs worlds and actions, compassion or force. He is aware of his horror—his action is not spontaneous on every level as is that of the islanders. Also, by this time Tommo's bad leg has almost crippled him, in contrast to the "athletic islander" who opposed him. But the excitement of conscious will, of self-preservation, overcomes his disabilities. With identity itself staked upon the outcome, the world of mind physically utilizes sheer will in order to defeat the physical world of external circumstance. "The strong excitement which had thus far kept me up, now left me, and I fell back fainting into the arms of Karakoee." Finally then, Tommo rejects isolation and his own former escapist role. His horror, like his sorrow, is on a personal level of human pity. He must override this in order to remove Mow-Mow the symbol, although he is pained at the thought of hurting Mow-Mow the man. Yet because his choice is so central to man's historical destiny, he must take the same action which looks forward, over the haze of years, to the actions of Captain the Honourable Edward Fairfax Vere. What makes Melville's meaning especially clear is the clinching detail of Tommo's salvation. He is rescued not by a Typeean, not even Marheyo or Fayaway, but by Karakoee, a tabooed *communicado*, a native who has rejected isolation and primitive existence, a man who can communicate with both worlds. His native Marquesan physical and linguistic abilities are brought to the present world of whalers, which is the world in which he chooses to live. Man cannot run from the present to the past without murder and loss of identity. Tommo will swear to this. Man cannot be abruptly flashed from one history to another without dehumanization. The pilot of the bay of Nukuheva will attest to this. Motion is one-directional. Man can only educate himself from the past to the present in order to find his fullest self. Melville, Tommo, Karakoee, *and* the transcendentalist will honor this.

Communication and isolation, as shaped by the literal characteristics of Marquesan geography, are concentrated in the story of Tommo's and Toby's attempt to reach an inland valley of Nukuheva. The secondary character in these chapters (VI-IX) is physical nature, which battles the intruders every inch of the way. Moreover, the captain of the *Dolly* had offered rewards to the natives for the capture of the two renegade sailors. Tommo and Toby are doubly isolated. As individuals who attempt to transfer into different worlds of space and time, they are met with rebuffs on every hand. As isolatoes, their individualism can never be as overwhelming as the pride and identity of either world. The world to which they flee will not have them (and when it does, there must be unconditional surrender), and the world from which they flee will not let them go.[22]

Tommo and Toby have brought some slight provisions with them, but those provisions turn out to be almost useless in the new environment. Escape into the alien environment only hurts Tommo's body. Tommo's identity at once becomes a residual rather than a complete quality, an emblem of consciousness in a purely physical world, and the body is the only weapon of that world. Once transferred in time, Tommo's consciousness is not only of no help, but it is a danger. Whenever Tommo begins to feel a sharp awareness of his isolation in Typee, and particularly whenever he meditates on the possible meanings of that isolation, at that precise moment Melville always reintroduces the injured leg; and also at that precise moment the leg becomes more acutely inflamed and painful. The failure of Tommo's body is symbolic of his entire plight. The man who evaluates his

---

[22] In every novel except *The Confidence Man* the Melvillean quester either slinks away from his world, or is torn from his world, or is barred from normal society.

actions individualistically rather than historically is ground to a pulp in the warfare between historical conditions. This germinal suggestion is fulfilled in *Pierre,* and is one of the keys to an understanding of that book. The world is not integrated. As Pierre discovers, the world's segments become "banded" only in the act of turning against the man who would withdraw from his historical identity. Tommo's plight sounds the first note in Melville's thematic call to integration and completion. Body needs consciousness (Tommo can strike a Lucifer match, but Kory-Kory must struggle to produce a flame), and consciousness needs body (Kory-Kory must carry the injured Tommo) lest man become an invalid in the undeniable world of physical nature or a childlike animal in the undeniable world of the human mind. Segmentation makes suicide a dual thing: it is visited upon society by the individual who tries to remake the world in the image of his own individual disintegration (Ahab), and it is visited upon the individual by the disintegrated world which tries to deny border-crossing (Pierre). Each segment is more aware of its own absolutist concepts than of the relativistic view demanding integration, and Melville uses this folly to satirize religious dogma, hypocritical social mores, and thoughtless nationalism. Thus there is the need for the complete man, the Vere-hero, whose reinforming vision is historical and communal, and who can effect a border-crossing eclecticism according to what is pertinent to his time and civilization rather than according to a preconceived ideality. It is this crying human need which is the polemical stimulus for Melville's themes of universal brotherhood, cultural relativism, and social democracy, even in the experimental spawn of *Typee.*[23]

Certainly Melville's position was not completed, or perhaps even formed, by 1845-46. For the remaining forty-six years of his life, Melville was to wrestle with his "ontological heroics." But the relativistic mind is observable in *Typee* if only in the embryonic qualities of the hints and possibilities which are to grow to full stature in the later books. In *Typee* the relativism, or early and simple Melvillean "duality," is best realized in the scene wherein Admiral Du Petit Thouars, western conqueror of the Marquesans, meets the chief of the natives of Tior, who have just capitulated to the French.

It so happened that the very day I was in Tior the French admiral, attended by all the boats of his squadron, came down in state from Nukuheva to take formal possession of the place. He remained in the valley about two hours, during which time he had a ceremonious interview with the king. The patriarch-sovereign of Tior was a man very far advanced in years;

---

[23] I emphasize social because Melville had many reservations about political democracy. These reservations are implicit in almost everything he wrote, and are explicit in the Vivenza section of *Mardi* and in *Billy Budd.* Even in *Omoo* and *White-Jacket* there is an implied differentiation between order as a concept and the wrongul imposition of order.

but though age had bowed his form and rendered him almost decrepit, his gigantic frame retained all his original magnitude and grandeur of appearance. He advanced slowly and with evident pain, assisting his tottering steps with the heavy war-spear he held in his hand, and attended by a group of grey-bearded chiefs, on one of whom he occasionally leaned for support. The admiral came forward with head uncovered and extended hand, while the old king saluted him by a stately flourish of his weapon. The next moment they stood side by side, these two extremes of the social scale,—the polished, splendid Frenchman, and the poor, tattooed savage. They were both tall and noble-looking men; but in other respects how strikingly contrasted! Du Petit Thouars exhibited upon his person all the paraphernalia of his naval rank. He wore a richly decorated admiral's frock-coat, a laced chapeau bras, and upon his breast were a variety of ribbons and orders; while the simple islander, with the exception of a slight cincture about his loins, appeared in all the nakedness of nature.

At what an immeasurable distance, thought I, are these two beings removed from each other. In the one is shown the result of long centuries of progressive civilization and refinement, which have gradually converted the mere creature into the semblance of all that is elevated and grand; while the other, after the lapse of the same period, has not advanced one step in the career of improvement. "Yet, after all," quoth I to myself, "insensible as he is to a thousand wants, and removed from harassing cares, may not the savage be the happier man of the two?" Such were the thoughts that arose in my mind as I gazed upon the novel spectacle before me. In truth it was an impressive one, and little likely to be effaced. I can recall even now with vivid distinctness every feature of the scene. The umbrageous shades where the interview took place—the glorious tropical vegetation around—the picturesque grouping of the mingled throng of soldiery and natives—and even the golden-hued bunch of banannas that I held in my hand at the time, and of which I occasionally partook while making the aforesaid philosophical reflections [pp. 498-99].

The cliché, the flip "philosophy" about the undressed-savage-as-happier-man-than-beribboned-admiral is relatively unimportant. It is glib and traditional, and as it appears here, cheap and shoddy. It cannot be believed completely in the context of Tommo's total relations with the savages, nor even in the context of the tone of this particular passage—and tone is always one of Melville's most obvious clues. Tommo lounges and chews bananas while he "philosophises"; he is not greatly bowed under the weight of his thought. What is important is that the "social" differences between the two men are differences in time and levels of development. Although this passage devotes itself to appearance—the apparent evil of civilization's artificiality and the apparent good of primitivism's honesty—what does emerge is the total force of the contrast, the snapshot of the two disjoined segments of the world under analysis at the moment. By calling attention to the Frenchman's lack of nakedness and the native's lack of surface artificiality, the point of view creates expectations for a symbolism of clothing, as it were. It prepares for a statement of modifications, for more than the external relationships between the civilized and uncivilized world.

For instance, there is a modification created by a contrast (which is somewhat extrinsic, appearing in the Appendix) between the westerner, the Englishman Paulet, and the westerner, the Frenchman Thouars. Paulet, also a uniformed man, introduces civilization to primitivism in terms of the primitive world which is to be affected. He attempts to understand, to wisely control, rather than merely to rule this aspect of human existence. Thouars and the missionaries, on the other hand, prove that rule without understanding is not a guiding control, but chaos. It is consequently a denial of the very consciousness which present history represents and which makes control possible. It is only an imposing of the technology and mores of the western world on a world which cannot cope with them, and it becomes a mirror of civilization's sins. Once again the elements of the book return us to Melville's controlling point of view: the government of human affairs must deny mere conquest and utilize consciousness for social goals. The primitive must be evaluated by a cumulative racial experience rather than by that one aspect of it which is called respectability. As a segment of that experience, the natives in a most basic sense are not divorced from western man, and a view of cultural differences which is not motivated by an attempt to guide the civilization from which the differences are seen, simply continues a wrongful and artificial segmentation. As "ethnologist" Melville insists that anthropology must be descriptive only so that it may be properly prescriptive, for "prescriptions" will be forthcoming in any case.

The universality of Typee is suggested not only by its debased manifestation in the primitive savagery of the western ship's crews, but also in Melville's description of the natives on their home grounds. The young men lounge around trying to look important and trying to avoid work. They are interested in weapons, athletics, and girls. The girls are interested in cosmetics and flirtations. The men at the bachelor quarters are interested in eating, drinking, smoking, discussing current events and making casual small talk of male affairs. The description of Tinor is the description of any good middle-class Lansingburgh or Albany or New York or Berkshire housewife—although in conformity to the life symbolized by Typee, Tommo takes care to point out that old Tinor is the only conscientious worker in the entire valley. Melville describes characteristics in these instances as typical not of Typees particularly, but as typical of one's youth, sex, marital status, or office. Except on the literal, narrative level, the Typeean is not unconnected with the you's and me's of Melville's and Tommo's current world. Symbolically he is that ultimately murderous part of all men which is unconscious, spontaneous, and comfortable. Like the sea self, the Typee self is also a robber, and both selves are cannibalistic because in their incompleteness they set man to devouring man. The Typee simply takes. He never plants or plans, never enters into conflict with nature in order to grasp the control that the quest figure constantly seeks. There are times when the breadfruit trees do not bear food, and only the haphazardly stored fruits of past crops sustain the natives, or else they go hungry. For unlike the whaleman, the savage does not store food with any plan, sufficiency, or foresight. This unconsciousness is simple and childlike and beautiful, but it is a luxury which can be afforded only in the limited area of existence wherein man can allow himself to be submissively integrated with nature. And that is the limited quality of Eden. Like Tommo's legal arguments at the beginning of the book, the unconsciousness is inapplicable to the realities of history. It is a fortuitous thing, like the Typeean attributes of Mrs. Glendinning's riches in *Pierre*. The blithe unconsciousness is necessary for the honest and inescapably animal functions of body, and consequently Melville uses it in his exposure of western respectability. It is a necessary part of man's relationship with external physical nature, and cannot be omitted if such a relationship is to be successful. But this primitivism must be recognized as only a part of the necessary human completion, and not as something to be mistakenly adored as the purity which cures the sweat and toil of the life of conscious relationship with both nature and man.

In his praise of the islanders and their happiness, and to the extent that he insists upon a human integration with physical nature, Melville agrees with the Rousseauism that appeared in so many modified and contradictory forms during the era of the transcendentalists. But by no means is his agreement a back-to-nature movement, transcendental or otherwise. For the transcendental back-to-nature doctrine was predicated upon idealistic rather than physical growth. Melville felt that the idealists used the wrong means for given goals. Indeed, Thoreau went to the woods to rid himself of his "scurvy, empirical self." Melville rejects sheer physicality as well as doctrines for human behavior that minimize the physical and the empirical. He never departs from his historical evaluation of primitivism, for his area of concern is that of social integration. Given that integration, man uses time and is not used by it. Given that, the cosmic will follow—at least for man. "We must first succeed alone, that we may enjoy our success together," said Thoreau.[24] Melville inverts the dogma. In presenting his happy Typee community, he says that true individual happiness can never exist unless and until it is conditioned by and given a frame of reference by social happiness. A man alone in a world of woe can find truth but not happiness. The truth must be applied to the world in which the truth is born, or else mere truth becomes a silent and selfish accomplice of murder, as it does with *Pierre's* Plin-

---

[24] "Paradise to Be (Regained)," *The Writings of Henry David Thoreau* (Houghton Mifflin, Boston and New York, 1906), IV, 299.

limmon and *Billy Budd's* Dansker. This approach to morality and identity in *Typee* is at once a foreshadowing of Melville's naturalism and a reinforcement of Tommo's final desire to regain his own self's true place. The rejection of Typee, despite all of Typee's own kind of happiness, is the flight from the unmodified natural level of man's existence. Man must step above the unselfconsciousness of elemental living, yet must not reject the physical world as reality. The fore-shadowing suggests the distinctive qualities of Melville's naturalism: William Faulkner, for instance, is naturalistic in his acceptance of the physical world as reality, yet is in tactical disagreement with the view that man must rise above an unselfconscious assimilation into elemental life.[25] The very answer that is needed by Faulkner's haunted heroes is the answer Tommo learns to distrust. For Faulkner, nature is something that man must emulate, something that is man's positive tutor and moral surrogate. For Melville, nature is something that man must reshape and modify according to his own needs, i.e. the needs of his own society.

Consciousness of self has characterized Tommo from the beginning. He is an exponent of conscious will. He reviews alternatives and makes choices concerning his own destiny. Then he withdraws from the *Dolly*. He forces himself to an act he cannot physically sustain when he uses his body to crush the barriers of physical nature as he and Toby labor through the reed tangles on the slopes. It is Tommo who conceives the plan for use of body in the first place. Even when compared to Toby, who is himself a representative of western civilization, it is always Tommo who prevails in council. It is he who decides where they shall camp, which path they shall follow, into which valley they shall descend. Toby prevails in action, in spontaneous physical en-deavor, and he does not communicate to Tommo except in those terms. Whereas Tommo discusses alternatives with Toby, Toby simply moves when the next move is up to him: he falls off the cliff into the palm tree in the last descent into the Typee valley, leaving the startled Tommo gasping behind him. It is Tommo who first communi-cates to Toby his own plans for desertion, whereas Toby had been harboring similar thoughts in silence, telling no one.

There are, of course, ample instances of Toby's conscious will. After all, he too is alien to pure Typee existence, and it would be surprising indeed to find symbolic subtleties of characterization fulfilled in this first novel. But the relationship between Tommo and Toby (Tommo is always the more enterprising, even in the first, comic introduction to Polynesian food: "By my soul, it is baked baby!" exclaims Toby, while Tommo sets to with epicurean gusto) makes it clear that it is

---

[25]As is Ernest Hemingway. Unlike Melville, Hemingway insists that man must discipline himself to be himself, but must not indulge himself to see himself, for that way lies either madness or sloppy, posed behavior.

the more spontaneous Toby who is best fitted for existence in Typee. His body is unimpaired by Typee. His conversion would not demonstrate the meaning of Typee ethics as much as would Tommo's conversion; Melville permits the natives to be willing to part with Toby—but they will not allow Tommo so much as a glimpse of the sea. These considerations lead one to expect to find not the Tommo and Toby that *Typee* actually presents, but an Ahab and a Flask, a Faust and a happy-go-lucky companion. And it remains true that until Tommo longs to return to his own world, his quality of mind remains "practical," and shrewd, and uninformed by philosophy. But once his attitudes do change, and they do, the implication is that he does begin to think deeply. His "philosophy" must be extrapolated by the reader, because Melville suggests the underlying meaning of Tommo's rejection of Typee only in terms of action. Had Melville been fully conscious of what he actually was doing, he certainly would have given Tommo opportunity for Ahabian soliloquy or dialogue. One can only conclude the obvious: thematically and artistically, Melville was as yet unprepared to express his controlling perception on many levels.

Still, the barrier to the sea presented by *Typee* prepares for the difference between the quester and the lee shore. As demonstrated by Tommo and Typee, the difference is intensified in Tommo's and Kory-Kory's variant reactions to the effigy of the warrior chief in the canoe of death.

In one of the most secluded portions of the valley . . . was the mausoleum of a deceased warrior chief. Like all the other edifices of any note, it was raised upon a small pi-pi of stones, which, being of unusual height, was a conspicuous object from a distance. . . . The sanctity of the spot appeared never to have been violated. The stillness of the grave was there, and the calm solitude around was beautiful and touching. The soft shadows of those lofty palm-trees!—I can see them now—hanging over the little temple, as if to keep out the intrusive sun.

On all sides as you approached this silent spot you caught sight of the dead chief's effigy, seated in the stern of a canoe, which was raised on a light frame a few inches above the level of the pi-pi. The canoe was about seven feet in length; of a rich, dark colored wood, handsomely carved, and adorned in many places with variegated bindings of stained sinnate, into which were wrought a number of sparkling seashells, and a belt of the same shells ran all around it. The body of the figure—of whatever material it might have been made—was effectually concealed in a heavy robe of brown tappa, revealing only the hands and head; the latter skillfully carved in wood, and surmounted by a superb arch of plumes. These plumes, in the subdued and gentle gales which found access to this sequestered spot, were never for one moment at rest, but kept nodding and waving over the chief's brow. The long leaves of the palmetto dropped over the eaves, and through them you saw the warrior holding his paddle with both hands in the act of rowing, leaning forward and inclining his head, as if eager to hurry on his voyage. Glaring at him forever, and face to face, was a polished human skull, which crowned the prow of the canoe. The spectral figurehead, reversed in its position, glancing backwards, seemed to mock the impatient attitude of the warrior [pp. 678-80].

Here is a touch which could be right out of the later Melville. The muffled figure is immediately recognizable as the model of all Melville's questers, and the antithesis of Typee life. His body is hidden; his head demands notice. He is voyaging. He is impatient. He is mounted on an aspiring structure. He is water-bound, sea-traveling, surrounded by and ornamented with emblems of another life than the land's. He is Taji in his canoe, with the backward-mocking specter in the prow grinning out the message that time is more absolute than ideal. He is Ahab furiously staring into the ever gaping mask of the white whale. He is Pierre struggling to complete the rebellious journey of Enceladus. He sees no Heaven, no God, no Answer—as long as he quests, ever trying to streak past the symbol of impossibility, he sees nothing but the face of time: mortality, transiency, death. At this point Tommo becomes momentarily separated from the narrator. The narrator notes that the skull "seemed to mock the impatient attitude. . . ." But how does Tommo react?

Whenever in the course of my rambles through the valley I happened to be near the chief's mausoleum, I always turned aside to visit it. The place has a peculiar charm for me; I hardly know why; but so it was. As I leaned over the railing and gazed upon the strange effigy and watched the play of the feathery head-dress, stirred by the same breeze which in low tones breathed amidst the lofty palm-trees, I loved to yield myself up to the fanciful superstition of the islanders, and could almost believe that the grim warrior was bound heavenward. In this mood when I turned to depart, I bade him, "God speed, and a pleasant voyage." Aye, paddle away, brave chieftain, to the land of the spirits! To the material eye thou makest but little progress; but with the eye of faith, I see thy canoe cleaving the bright waves, which die away on the dimly looming shores of Paradise [p. 681].

It is the material eye which sees the skull. It is the idealistic eye which sees the dimly looming shores of Paradise. Not only is this at the core of the pessimism which often characterizes naturalism (yet which is not necessarily one of naturalism's identities), but it is a significant insight into Melville's perception. For it is at the moment that the idealistic eye and the material eye are differentiated that the figures of Tommo and the narrator barely perceptibly slide apart, like two identical, photographed figures whose outlines momentarily fail to merge on the screen. If the warrior is a symbol of general human aspiration, then there need be no blurring of identities—the naturalist may have his own Faith and Belief. But here the figure represents to Tommo a kind of idealistic faith, for his reaction to the effigy is couched in obvious suggestions of Christian theology. And Tommo sympathizes; he understands the everlasting trip to another world; he himself is a changeling. But the quester as such is not yet. Tommo does not wish to plunge beyond the human world, and wishes only to return to his own true home.

Melville proceeds to use the reactions of Tommo and Kory-Kory to further divide the perceptions of the material and idealistic eye. The innocent animality of the islanders had at first been presented as apparently enviable. Then the relationship of Tommo to Typee presented the same quality as murderous. Now, when the physicality of the native is presented in its hardheaded, simple and materialistic aspects, the tone of the book becomes jocularly sympathetic. If Tommo, who empathizes with the warrior chief, has strong reservations about leaving the human world, Kory-Kory is completely empirical about the whole business, and his vision of the warrior and voyage is projected completely in the matter-of-fact terms of body.

When I first visited this singular place with Kory-Kory, he told me— or at least so I understood him—that the chief was paddling his way to the realm of bliss, and bread-fruit—the Polynesian heaven—where every moment the bread-fruit trees dropped their ripened spheres to the ground, and where there was no end to the cocoa-nuts and banannas: there they reposed through the live-long eternity upon mats much finer than those of Typee; and every day bathed their glowing limbs in rivers of cocoa-nut oil. In that happy land there were plenty of plumes and feathers, and boars'-tusks and sperm-whale teeth, far preferable to all the shining trinkets and gay tappa of the white man; and, best of all, women far lovelier than the daughters of earth were there in abundance. "A very pleasant place," Kory-Kory said it was; "but after all, not much pleasanter," he thought, "than Typee." "Did he not then," I asked him, "wish to accompany the warrior?" "Oh, no: he was very happy where he was; but supposed that some time or other he would go in his own canoe."

Thus far, I think, I clearly comprehended Kory-Kory. But there was a singular expression he made use of at the time, enforced by as singular a gesture, the meaning of which I would have given much to penetrate. I am inclined to believe it must have been a proverb he uttered; for I afterwards heard him repeat the same words several times, and in what appeared to me to be a somewhat similar sense. Indeed, Kory-Kory had a great variety of short, smart-sounding sentences, with which he frequently enlivened his discourse; and he introduced them with an air which plainly intimated, that, in his opinion, they settled the matter in question, whatever it might be.

Could it have been then, that when I asked him whether he desired to go to this heaven of bread-fruit, cocoa-nuts, and young ladies, which he had been describing, he answered by saying something equivalent to our old adage—"A bird in the hand is worth two in the bush?"—if he did, Kory-Kory was a discreet and sensible fellow, and I cannot sufficiently admire his shrewdness [pp. 680-81].

When the ideal is subjected to the empirical view, the blurring between the narrator and Tommo disappears. The incipient naturalism is manifest in the sympathy the Tommo-narrator has with Kory-Kory's implicit suspicion that this life is reality and when it is surrendered, all is surrendered. Melville does here what he is to do in all the books to follow: he suggests the discrepancy between the idealistic belief (especially when institutionalized) and the empirical evidence which makes even the pious man afraid to die. The way is prepared for *Mardi's* bitter "Marmora" passages on the hypocrisy, blindness (the idealistic eye of Pani is literally closed to the naturalist's basic truth), and idiocy of institutionalized religion. Melville as naturalist does have a Truth and a Belief, but it is born of the material eye: he is religious, but cannot be pious. The material eye of Melville's perception explains the idealist's, Hawthorne's, statement that "If he [Melville] were a religious [in context, a pious] man, he would be one of the most truly religious and reverential;" [26] and also explains the "Rabelaisian" quality that all readers notice in Melville. This commonsensical, physical *joie de vivre* stems from the assumption underlying Kory-Kory's doubts, that is, that the purpose of life is not a dying into another life, but the living of the present life. In an impish passage in which Tommo, through satiric tone, again identifies himself with an impious, common-sense attitude, Kory-Kory further displays the primacy he places upon the physical realities of this world. The Typee far exceeds the American in accentuating earthliness and in confining all areas of being to the realm of body.

On the whole, I am inclined to believe, that the islanders in the Pacific have no fixed and definite ideas whatever on the subject of religion . . . In truth, the Typees, so far as their actions evince, submitted to no laws human or divine—always excepting the thrice mysterious taboo. The "independent electors" of the valley were not to be brow-beaten by chiefs, priests, idols, or devils. As for the luckless idols, they received more hard knocks than supplications. . . .

. . . Walking with Kory-Kory through the deepest recesses of the groves, I perceived a curious looking image, about six feet in height, which originally had been placed upright against a low pi-pi, surmounted by a ruinous bamboo temple, but having become fatigued and weak in the knees, was now carelessly leaning against it. The idol was partly concealed by the foliage of a tree which stood near, and whose leafy boughs drooped over the pile of stones, as if to protect the rude fane from the decay to which it was rapidly hastening. The image itself was nothing more than a grotesquely shaped log, carved in the likeness of a portly naked man with the arms clasped over the head, the jaws thrown wide apart, and its thick shapeless legs bowed in to an arch. It was much decayed. The lower part was overgrown with a bright silky moss. Thin spears of grass sprouted from the distended mouth and fringed the outline of the head and arms. His godship had literally attained a green old age. All its prominent points were bruised and battered, or entirely rotted away. The nose had taken its departure, and from the general appearance of the head it might have been supposed that the wooden divinity, in despair at the neglect of its worshippers, had been trying to beat its own brains out against the surrounding trees.

I drew near to inspect more closely this strange object of idolatry;

---

[26] Metcalf, p. 161.

but halted reverently at the distance of two or three paces, out of regard to the religion of my valet. As soon, however, as Kory-Kory perceived that I was in one of my inquiring, scientific moods, to my astonishment, he sprang to the side of the idol, and pushing it away from the stones against which it rested, endeavored to make it stand upon its legs. But the divinity had lost the use of them altogether; and while Kory-Kory was trying to prop it up, by placing a stick between it and the pi-pi, the monster fell clumsily to the ground, and would infallibly have broken its neck had not Kory-Kory providentially broken its fall by receiving its whole weight on his own half-crushed back. I never saw the honest fellow in such a rage before. He leaped furiously to his feet, and seizing the stick, began beating the poor image: every moment or two pausing and talking to it in the most violent manner, as if upbraiding it for the accident. When his indignation had subsided a little he whirled the idol about most profanely, so as to give me an opportunity of examining it on all sides. I am quite sure I never should have presumed to have taken such liberties with the god myself, and I was not a little shocked at Kory-Kory's impiety [pp. 687-89].

Kory-Kory is a simple, earthbound, unphilosophical Ahab who furiously seeks vengeance against any god who would crush him. The Typee, of course, does not function on a metaphysical level, and for just that reason underscores the irony of Ahab's mistake: God is a dumb block of wood whose hurts to man really have nothing to do with any intentional relationship between heaven and earth. It is man who "providentially" keeps the "infallible" god from falling and breaking his neck. Typee's incompleteness, on the other hand, is manifested in Kory-Kory's complete lack of recognition of the god as a concept, as an emblem of human aspiration. Typee is death to informing vision, and thus Tommo has a certain amount of nostalgic sympathy for the dead warrior-chief. Once again, Typee is universalized, for the savage's "practicality" and mindless materialism result in the same limitation as does the shrewd "practicality" of the west, even though it is not the same qualitatively. And every time the universal limitations of Typee are suggested, there is also a focus of Tommo's change. The contemporary world he has abandoned, with all its savage denials and perversions of its own possibilities, is the world of man's largest potentialities. This is Tommo's driving force for an identity which explains action that "Home" and "Mother" on the merely sentimental level cannot justify at all. Significantly, it is Kory-Kory who, as a representative Typee and Tommo's friendly valet and warden, is the man assigned by the islanders to keep the American from breaking taboos or from fleeing toward the sea.

When Karky the tattooer wishes to practice his craft on Tommo, the injured man refuses in horror. At first his refusal is based upon a relatively superficial fear that once he has been decorated, he will no longer have the "face" for western society. But Karky will not be satisfied with a commission to work on Tommo's arm—he wishes to attack the face. The Typee tattoos of the face all include a line which runs across the eyes (either horizontally or vertically, like *prison bars* [Melville's image], or diagonally as part of the two inclines of an equilateral triangle with the base line running across the *mouth*). The Typee designs for tattoo of the head all include a hiding of the agents of communication and understanding. The designs for the body are—as would be expected—animals or vegetable growth. When all the natives, even Kory-Kory and the high chief Mehevi evidence their strong desire to have Tommo's face tattooed, and when all the priests join vehemently in agreement, Tommo realizes that the basis of their desire is conversion. None of the Typees understands why Tommo refuses the tattoo. They are all amazed that the values, symbols, and commitments of luxurious Typee can be refused by anyone. So there is a more basic meaning to Tommo's fear that his face will thereafter be unfit for western society. It is the book's fundamental suspense, the tension between mind and mindlessness. At this moment Tommo's desire to escape mounts to panic. And again the point is made that Tommo is inoperative in Typee; the pain in his useless leg becomes unbearable; his body cannot compete. His will and mind are useless because they cannot communicate the truth of Tommo's position. The truth enrages and insults the Typees. When will and mind do communicate at all, they only betray the wish to escape, and the guard is further alerted. If Tommo remains in Eden, either his will and mind will be altered by the overlay of Typee values, or else they will be consigned to death by the cannibal festivals. To retain physical existence, he must consent to the extinguishing of his mind, the loss of his own identity. The plight of Tommo in the death trap of alien values is summed up in a bit of dialogue with Marnoo. When Tommo pleads with Marnoo to try to get him out of the valley—thus endangering Marnoo's life as well as his own—Marnoo cuts him short. " 'Kannaka [natives] no let you go no where,' he said; 'you taboo. Why you no like stay? Plenty moee-moee (sleep)—plenty ki-ki (eat) —plenty whihenee (young girls)—Oh, very good place Typee! Suppose you no like this bay, why you come? You no hear about Typee? All white men afraid Typee, so no white men come.' " Marnoo's statement works in both major directions. First there is the Faulknerian hint about the universal savage which civilized man is afraid to admit is a truth about himself; secondly, the gravity of Tommo's sin is intensified. He cannot reply, in response to Marnoo's question, "Well, I guess I made a mistake." By the very legalities he claimed when he renounced his own world, he cannot claim the mistake and disclaim the consequence. Indeed Marnoo's conversation immediately heightens the suspense by revealing the symbolic meaning, or reality, beneath the appearance of Tommo's captivity: "Me no hear you talk any more; by by Kannaka get mad, kill you and me too. No you see he no want you to speak to me at all?—you see—ah! by by you no mind—you get well, he kill you, eat you, hang you head up there like Happar [enemy tribe] Kannaka! . . ."

Jealousy for the possession of Tommo, as indicated in the avidly proffered conversion, is a concentration of the conflict and isolation of the two worlds; Tommo has plunged back down into the primitive beginnings of human order only to find that man of the conscious, technological world has traveled too far beyond that Eden to find operation, completion, or even existence possible on that primary, mindless level. In short, man's history teaches that Eden and Adam must be redefined for every period of man's development; that if Eden is to be defined as a positive virtue for human aspiration, it lies not in the primitive past but somewhere in the completely conscious future, and is a goal, not a beginning. Marnoo, who is operative, and who, with his own broken communication, might connect the present with the past, is neither physically limited or debilitated like Tommo, nor isolated like the Typees. His tattooing sets him apart from the Typees: his head and face are clear of any tattoo. His body tattoo is not a collection of isolated items, like those of the Typees. His is one complete and integrated picture, and Tommo points this out quite emphatically. His level of existence is a transition, a hovering below the western world and above the Polynesian. Like Karakoee, he too has broken out of seclusion in time and space and has contacted the west and the sea. In a chronological sense but, significantly, not in the sense of political possibility, Marnoo comes close to the integration of polar values that will characterize the complete man. The real distances are distances of time.

There have been attempts to interpret Tommo's and Toby's literal descent and final fall into the valley as a parallel to the Fall from grace. Actually the parallel exists as a condensation of Tommo's entire voyage, the plunge from the world and time of civilization to the world and time of unconsciousness. It is a plunge that can no longer be accepted in terms of the Christian concept of the Fall from grace. Indeed the very fall in *Typee* is a fall from the barren uplands, which demand toil, into the cushioning verdure of the palm tree, down into greenness and plenty. The barriers of waters, mountains, and ravines are startlingly similar to the traditional barriers between worlds in the literature of Christian mythology.[27] And in inverse parallel to Christian mythology with its fabulous questing heroes, innocent purity and ignorance of worldly ways become a seeming thing. With the refructified lands and running waters, they bring death, for the appearance of innocence and the reality of its consequences are different things. And since the only time is world-time, the death is final, with

---

[27] See Howard Rollin Patch, *The Other World* (Cambridge, Mass., 1950), *passim.*

no dying into anything but time's mocking, backward-glancing skull. This is the naturalist's view of the deadly paradox of limitations hidden beneath the smiling surfaces of Typee-Eden. Indeed it is Melville's consistent view of the deadly-funny grim jest, the lie, which hides beneath the occasionally smiling surfaces of an apparently benevolent universe.

Typee's very use of the luxuriant land reinforces this ironic note. The constant reference to verdure looks forward to the symbolic function of green in *Pierre*, where the color there too merges with the theme of time. In *Typee* green is related to decay in time. The first close view that Tommo and the crew have of land is the bay of Nukuheva, which is described in language vitally cognizant of the time motif: "Nothing can exceed the imposing scenery of this bay. Viewed from our ship as she lay at anchor in the middle of the harbour, it presented the appearance of a vast natural amphitheatre in decay, and overgrown with vines, the deep glens that furrowed its sides appearing like enormous fissures caused by the ravages of time." Closer to home in its application to humanity is the following use of green under the subheading (Chapter XII) "Timeworn Savages":

As we advanced further along the building, we were struck with the aspect of four or five hideous old wretches, on whose decripit forms time and tattooing seemed to have obliterated every trace of humanity. Owing to the continued operation of this latter process, which only terminates among the warriors of the island after all the figures stretched upon their limbs in youth have been blended together—an effect, however, produced only in cases of extreme longevity—the bodies of these men were of a uniform dull green color—the hue which the tattooing gradually assumes as the individual advances in age. Their skin had a frightful scaly appearance, which, united with its singular color, made their limbs not a little resemble dusty specimens of verde-antique [pp. 579-80].

The application of greenness and time has been made to man and nature; all that remains is to find the same applied to the divine. In the description of the idol beaten by Kory-Kory, the use of green-rot is made in just such a way, showing that the gods men worship are themselves decayed by time. That picture recalls the image of the verde-antique natives at the Ti, who always sit motionlessly, Tommo says, like so many idols. And later, at the Feast of the Calabashes, Tommo discovers that they are priests. Everything, including religion and man's conceptions of God, are subject to time. This theme is developed more completely and startlingly in *Pierre*, and is a basis for an understanding of Melville's view of history, religion, and Christ. It is for this reason, for instance, that Melville can dismiss Christian priests, ministers, and missionaries with the same amusement, the same devastatingly ironic tone, the same emphasis on futile and foolishly misdirected effort, that he employs for his treatment of pagan religion. Looked upon as timeless and permanent by its adherents, each religion, like each segment of the world, becomes an isolated caricature of each other religion and each other segment. One of the best examples again is found in the passage on Kory-Kory's beating of the idol:

When one of the inferior order of natives could show such contempt for a venerable and decrepit God of the Groves, what the state of religion must be among the people in general is easily to be imagined. In truth I regard the Typees as a backslidden generation. They are sunk in religious sloth, and require a spiritual revival. A long prosperity of bread-fruit and cocoa-nuts has rendered them remiss in the performance of their higher obligations. The wood-rot malady is spreading among the idols—the fruit upon their altars is becoming offensive—the temples themselves need re-thatching—the tattooed clergy are altogether too light-hearted and lazy—and their flocks are going astray [p. 689].

Tommo, tongue in cheek, is assuming the attitude of the Christian missionary, and, of course, thus seems to blast those very aspects of Typee which have been found good. When the Tommo-narrator's sympathy for certain elements of Typeean materialism and empiricism is remembered, certainly we cannot believe aversion to Typee on *these* grounds. The puckish humor changes the "long prosperity" and the "blackslidden generation" into an obvious and satirical reference to the western-Christian—particularly American—world of Melville's day. Here again, Melville uses Typee not as a separate or ethnic grouping, but as a control for a general Type. Typee alone is not open to charges of decay. Time has affected all. It has reduced the once conscious, aspiring civilization which erected the monumental stone piles of the Typee valley into a memory confused by superstitions. That past civilization is one with all the great conquerors of nature whose works are now misunderstood and degraded to a level of support for a later, unconscious race which has not earned that support. *Mardi* is to state explicitly the implications of this idea; *Pierre* is to use the identical image of crumbling stones and past civilizations to recreate the idea; and *Billy Budd* is to center upon the historical monument perverted into superstitious myth, which becomes man's historical blindness and cannibalism. The idealistic presuppositions of religion repeatedly are seen as folly, not as man's truly highest aspirations. Consider the following savage indictment:

Mehevi and the chieftains of the Ti have just risen from their noontide slumbers. There are no affairs of state to dispose of; and having eaten two or three breakfasts in the course of the morning, the magnates of the val-ley feel no appetite as yet for dinner. How are their leisure moments to be occupied? They smoke, they chat, and at least one of their number makes a proposition to the rest, who joyfully acquiescing, he darts out of the house, leaps from the pi-pi, and disappears in the grove. Soon you see him returning with Kolory [a high priest], who bears the god Moa Artua in his arms, and carries in one hand a small trough, hollowed out in the like-ness of a canoe. The priest comes along dandling his charge as if it were a lachrymose infant he was endeavoring to put into a good humor. Presently, entering the Ti, he seats himself on the mats as composedly as a juggler about to perform his sleight-of-hand tricks; and with the chiefs disposed in a circle about him, commences his ceremony.

In the first place he gives Moa Artua an affectionate hug, then caressingly lays him to his breast, and, finally, whispers something in his ear; the rest of the company listening eagerly for a reply. But the baby-god is deaf or dumb,—perhaps both, for never a word does he utter. At last Kolory speaks a little louder, and soon growing angry, comes boldly out with what he has to say and bawls to him. He put me in mind of a choleric fellow, who, after trying in vain to communicate a secret to a deaf man, all at once flies into a passion and screams it out so that every one may hear. Still Moa Artua remains as quiet as ever; and Kolory, seemingly loosing his temper, fetches him a box over the head, strips him of his tappa and red cloth, and laying him in a state of nudity in the little trough, covers him from sight. At this proceeding all present loudly applaud and signify their approval by uttering the adjective "mortarkee" with violent emphasis. Kolory, however, is so desirous his conduct should meet with unqualified approbation, that he inquires of each individual separately whether, under existing circumstances, he has not done perfectly right in shutting up Moa Artua. The invariable response is "Aa, Aa" (yes, yes), repeated over and over again in a manner which ought to quiet the scruples of the most conscientious. After a few moments Kolory brings forth his doll again, and while arraying it very carefully in the tappa and red cloth, alternately fondles and chides it. The toilet being completed, he once more speaks to it aloud. The whole company hereupon show the greatest interest; while the priest holding Moa Artua to his ear interprets to them what he pretends the god is confidentially communicating to him. Some items of intelligence appear to tickle all present amazingly; for one claps his hands in a rapture; another shouts with merriment; and a third leaps to his feet and capers about like a madman.

What under the sun Moa Artua on these occasions had to say to Kolory I never could find out; but I could not help thinking that the former showed a sad want of spirit in being disciplined into making disclosures, which at first he seemed bent on withholding. Whether the priest honestly interpreted what he believed the divinity said to him, or whether he was not all the while guilty of a vile humbug, I shall not presume to decide. At any rate, whatever as coming from the god was imparted to those present seemed to be generally of a complimentary nature: a fact which illustrates the sagacity of Kolory, or else the time-serving disposition of this hardly-used deity.

Moa Artua having nothing more to say, his bearer goes to nursing him again, in which occupation, however, he is soon interrupted by a question put by one of the warriors to the god. Kolory hereupon snatches it up to his ear again, and after listening attentively, once more officiates as the organ of communication. A multitude of questions and answers having passed between the parties, much to the satisfaction of those who propose them, the god is put tenderly to bed in the trough, and the whole company unites in a long chaunt, led off by Kolory. This ended, the ceremony is over; the chiefs rise to their feet in high good humour, and my Lord Archbishop, after chatting awhile, and regaling himself with a whiff or two from a pipe of tobacco, tucks the canoe under his arm and marches off with it.

The whole of these proceedings were like those of a parcel of children playing with dolls and baby houses [pp. 683-85].

Markedly, this is not the reportage of an "ethnologist." There is not any desire or attempt to understand the religious basis of the ceremony (Moa Artua is a High God, not an underling, Tommo explains); rather the religious ceremony is used as a foil for the narrator's observations of it. All the elements of unconsciousness unite in this incident. Except for the simple deceit which Kolory practices upon his parishioners—the same simple and transparent deceit which the natives practice upon Tommo—there is no disguise. Except for the "chaunt," all action is pictured as spontaneous, not ritualized. There is no attempt to pierce through appearances, no intellection. When Moa Artua is denuded in punishment, he is revealed as nothing more or less than what we are led to believe he is—a piece of wood. As Melville asks repeatedly in his later books, how can men get an answer from a stone, a voice from a silence, a guide from a zero? There is no directive connection between the absolute and the human, and no moral communication. There is only the fact of wood and the credulity, spontaneity, and unconsciousness of childish primitivism. The doll-playing members of Typee are no different than the doll-like crew of the *Dolly*. Religion becomes Melville's emblem of unquestioned values, unexamined behavior, and as a human institution it either demands submission (the missionaries and the natives) or unconsciousness (Kolory and Moa Artua).

The basic lack of communication, and the consequent need for it, returns Melville's thematic material directly to the cause of human brotherhood. Mere imposition of values is neither brotherhood nor integration. It denies communication. It may result in incongruity and farce: the visiting native queen of Mowanna, king of Nukuheva, getting into the spirit of the splendor and pomp of a military review, hoists her skirts to reciprocally display the splendor of her own brilliantly tattooed hindquarters. The French are scandalized and the incident is funny, like the joint-stock nature of the world presented in Queequeg's boarding the ferry to Nantucket, and his voyage to that island. But sometimes denial of real communication results in disease and death, as brought on by the ravages of venereal disease introduced by the western aliens. Often loss of brotherhood brings debasement, poverty, and death as introduced by the missionaries with their shifting, inapplicable laws and mores. Or incompleteness brings a denial of man's potentialities, and it is death as introduced by Typee with its cannibalism.

The treatment of isolation brings Melville's eclecticism to the fore. Tommo needs Kory-Kory: Ahab should have some of Queequeg's characteristics. Kory-Kory needs Tommo: Queequeg should have some of Ahab's. Thus, cultural relativism and democracy. The isolation also becomes part of Typee's social and historical orientation. Man must not tire of his world only to scorn it Byronically from an isolated mountain peak or to hide from it in the depths of an isolated valley. Before Tommo jumps ship he delightedly envisages the former and after he jumps ship he lives the latter. And once he learns the lesson of isolation he rejects both as single possibilities for behavior.

The element of heart has been mentioned, but only casually because it does not occupy much place in *Typee*. It is one of the foreshadowings in which the book so richly abounds. Heart, in Melville's books, is generally related to the Typee world rather than to the western, to the female rather than to the male, to the healthy body rather than to the self-consumed and driven man. As Taji, Ahab, and Pierre become more and more driven in their quests, and as their bodies waste away, their hearts harden. The complete-man hero will emphasize neither heart nor mind, but will subordinate either to the necessities and realities of his world. *Mardi's* Media will slacken his use of shrewdness and advantage, and will intensify and enlarge his heart. Captain Vere will submit to a necessary action of mind which breaks his heart. But like *Typee* itself, these heart-mind fractures can be only a preparation.

Not only because it is chronologically his first book, but also because it looks ahead to so much, *Typee* is the beginning of Melville's voyage. It is a book whose rich display of Melville's craft has been almost overlooked. Tommo's is indeed the central story, enriched by the roles of the characters who become enmeshed in his discoveries. There is never any real doubt about point of view, as there is in *Mardi*, or *Pierre*, or even *Moby-Dick*. *Typee* is not travelogue; its *raison d'être* is not "A Peep at Polynesian Life." Polynesia could have been the Arctic Circle or the Belgian Congo. *Typee* is the story of a man's discovery of his relationship to the world. The narrator enters different worlds, always retaining the consciousness of his original orientation, which is that of contemporary civilization. Focused through this constant consciousness, the forming views of Melville are expressed in Tommo's implied awareness. Perhaps it is the constant consciousness that does it; perhaps it is the external quality of that consciousness; *Typee* yet remains more cleanly readable than many contemporary literary productions which fashionably, and therefore contrivedly, also wrestle with the favorite theme which Melville called "the shock of recognition," the sudden mirror which forces a change of perception and an initiation of sensibility into reality.

Consciousness itself has not been explored by Melville. It has been glimpsed only in relation to the primitivism which is the center of *Typee* and which has been rejected as a way of life. From this beginning in time and ethical values, Melville points Tommo and reader toward the open sea again, wherein he will make the deepest explorations of his great, gliding theme.

chapter 3

Mardi

. . . The tempest bursting from the waste
of Time
On the world's fairest hope linked with man's
foulest crime.

—*"Misgivings"*

Melville presented his friend, Evert Duyckinck, with the three-volume British first edition of *Mardi*. Accompanying the gift was a letter which read in part, "tho' somewhat unusual for a donor, I must beg to apologize for making you the accompanying present of 'Mardi.' But no one who knows your library can doubt, that such a choice conservatory of exotics & other rare things in literature, after being long enjoyed by yourself, must, to a late posterity, be preserved intact by your descendants. How natural then—tho' vain—in your friend to desire a place in it for a plant, which tho' now unblown (emblematically, the leaves, you perceive, are uncut) may possibly—by some miracle, that is—flower like the aloe, a hundred years hence—or not flower at all, which is more likely by far, for some aloes never flower.

"Again: (as the divines say) political republics should be the asylum for the persecuted of all nations; so, if Mardi be admitted to your shelves, your bibliographical Republic of Letters may find some contentment in the thought, that it has afforded refuge to a work, which almost everywhere else has been driven forth like a wild, mystic Mormon into shelterless exile.

"The leaves, I repeat, are uncut—let them remain so—and let me supplementaryly hint, that a bit of old parchment (from some old Arabic M.S.S. on Astrology) tied round each volume, & sealed on the back with a Sphynx, & never to be broken till the aloe flowers— would not be an unsuitable device for the bookbinders of 'Mardi.' " [1]

---

[1] Eleanor Melville Metcalf, *Herman Melville, Cycle and Epicycle*, p. 75.

In this letter of February 2, 1850, the pain of failure had begun to blur, and Melville was merely wistfully defensive about his book. Ten months earlier, in another letter to Duyckinck, he had been able to manage a closer look at the book in what obviously was still a painful awareness of its existence. "I am glad you like that affair of mine [*Mardi*]. But it seems so long now since I wrote it [1848], & my mood has so changed, that I dread to look into it, & have purposely abstained from so doing since I thanked God it was off my hands." [2] And when he reconsidered *Mardi* from the perspective of approximately fifteen years, he was able to condemn Jean Paul Richter's *Titan, A Romance* by stating, "The worst thing I can say about it is that it is a little better than 'Mardi.' " [3]

As Melville came to a closer accord with the critical reaction to his book, he accepted the fact that this particularly bitter aloe never would flower. What his wife had called "the 'fogs' of 'Mardi' " [4] were never swirled away by the sunlight of popularity or pierced by the light of understanding. The reaction to *Mardi* was justifiable. The book is very bad for the same reasons that it is very important. In *Mardi* Melville created the first consciously symbolic statement of his guiding perception, and without the "ballast" which ties *Moby-Dick's* narrative interest to symbol, *Mardi* fell apart at almost every seam. Supposedly, it was to be another book of South Seas marvels. But in the "Author's Preface" Melville offers the mask for his own little lie:

Not long ago, having published two narratives of voyages in the Pacific, which, in many quarters, were received with incredulity, the thought occurred to me, of indeed writing a romance of Polynesian adventure, and publishing it as such; to see whether, the fiction might not, possibly, be received for a verity: in some degree the reverse of my previous experience. This thought was the germ of others, which have resulted in Mardi.

As usual, Melville's prefatory remarks about verities are ironic and deceptive. In its departure from fact, *Typee* is a "romance" much more than it is a "narrative of voyage." As a book which subordinates fact to theme, *Mardi* is as much a "verity" as *Typee*, and more so than *Omoo*, which is largely adventure for its own sake. The groping toward theme, the germ, was as virulent in the man who wrote *Typee* as in the man who wrote *Mardi*. *Mardi* was simply the first book in which the body of Melville's materials succumbed completely to the onslaught of the germ; the book was his first self-indulgence in the writing of his cosmic vision. The book is a self-indulgence because *Typee* and *Omoo* had not yet taught him how to make the closely and consciously sought symbol arise from the suspenseful surface of

---

[2] Metcalf, pp. 60-61.
[3] Metcalf, p. 203.
[4] Metcalf, p. 61.

a well-written story. By 1847-48, Melville could experiment consciously with symbol, or he could write adventure, but he was obviously not yet ready to combine the two on the highest levels; and *Mardi* became the kind of hash and botch that his earlier and later books are not.[5] Surely Melville must have learned more from *Mardi* than from any other book he ever wrote except, possibly, his first. *Moby-Dick* would have been impossible without *Mardi*. "Had I not written & published 'Mardi,'" he said, "in all likelihood, I would not be as wise as I am now, or may be."[6]

This book enters the shadowy realms of consciousness, and *Mardi's* "world of mind" is neither as simple nor as unified a narrative as *Typee's* world of body. Seizing theme in *Mardi* is like catching the phantom great white squid; the hunter is twisted by the pull and suction of many tentacles, and just when it seems to him that this hold or that will result in grasping the Damned Thing's central core, the whole mass sinks out of sight in a sea of botched construction, hashed action, and artificially shifting islands of narration. Structurally *Mardi* is not a single being, but rather a combination of three parallel tales whose occasional unity is accidental. These three tales are (1) the introductory "factual" stories that take place in the "real" worlds of the *Arcturion,* the *Chamois,* and the *Parki;* (2) Taji's story, the Taji-Hautia-Yillah quest which takes place in the symbolic world of Mardi; and (3) Babbalanja's and Media's story, which is symbolic and allegorical, and which takes place everywhere and nowhere.

It is the structural disorganization which makes *Mardi* a difficult book, and there is still much room for a definition of *Mardi's* disorganization.[7] Generally the charge has been that the allegory and symbolism are obscure, that the allegory itself is wild, that *Mardi* becomes a "whaling story gone wrong," a possibly good story deadened and made artificial by clouded symbols.[8] However, the symbolism itself is consistent, the allegory is clear, and the narrative level of story

---

[5] Melville had his own reservations about the artistic completeness of his book. In a letter to Hawthorne, dated Pittsfield, June, 1851, Melville wrote, "Dollars damn me; and the malicious devil is forever grinning in upon me, holding the door ajar. . . . What I feel most moved to write, that is banned,—it will not pay. Yet, altogether, write the *other* way I cannot, so the product is a final hash, and all my books are botches." Willard Thorp, *Herman Melville* (New York, 1938), p. 390.

[6] Metcalf, p. 71.

[7] One argument states that Melville wrote sermons rather than novels, and that he "made only the loosest efforts to tie his sermons into his novels; he was quite content if he could see that his novels illustrated his sermons and was reasonably content if they did not." R. P. Blackmur, "The Craft of Herman Melville," *VQR,* XIV (1938), 281. See also, Newton Arvin, "Melville's Mardi," *AQ,* II (1950), 71-81.

[8] Matthiessen believes that it is the symbolism which kills the allegory, and he certainly is not alone in this view. See also Arvin's "Melville's Mardi"; Stephen A. Larrabee, "Melville against the World," *SAQ,* XXXIV (1935), 410-18; "Melville's Journey," *TLS* (Jan. 12, 1946), 18.

interest, with which the book opens, is perfectly good as long as it exists. The trouble is that Melville was unable to unite all the elements because he did not understand them. Consequently sometimes the book has a symbolic center, sometimes an allegorical center and sometimes a narrative center. The disintegration of structure at times makes it impossible to know just who is narrating the story, whose words are to be taken as a value standard, and whose words are revelation of character. The book opens in the first person, and the narrator is an adventure hero, Taji-not-yet-named-Taji. By implication, this narrator is definitely within the world of the reader's present. He is safe. He is looking back upon his past adventures after the book is finished.

Good old Arcturion! Maternal craft, that rocked me so often in thy heart of oak, I grieve to tell how I deserted thee on the broad deep. . . .
Old ship! where sails thy lone ghost now? For of stout Arcturion no word was ever heard, from the dark hour we pushed from her fated planks. . . .
By quitting the Arcturion when we did, Jarl and I unconsciously eluded a sailor's grave. . . . And for myself I am almost tempted to hang my head, that I escaped the fate of my shipmates . . . [pp. 21-22].

It is logical enough to assume this retrospective point of view, for the hero does survive the "real" world of the book's "factual" beginning. But at the end of the book, the narrator can not possibly be in any position to remember things past because he does not survive the unreal world of Mardi. Yet, well beyond the "factual" beginning, and deep in the Mardian world, the narrator again adopts the retrospective point of view: "As in dreams I behold thee again, Willamilla! as in dreams, once again I stroll through the cool, shady groves, oh fairest of the valleys of Mardi! the thought of that mad merry feasting steals over my soul till I faint!" The first person narrator is suited to the adventure story element of the book, but he is an impossible choice for the allegorical and symbolic sections—and Melville is stuck with him. The fractured structure, unsuited to theme, makes *Mardi* as unreasonable as *Moby-Dick* would have been had the first person narrator been Ahab.

There are certain other disturbing features about the narrator. He slips in and out of control of the point of view as either narrative progression or symbol and theme demand. Although the narration generally is in the first person (usually plural), there are scattered passages wherein Taji is relegated to a third person, and no indication of the new narrator's identity is given—as if Melville is sporadically aware of Taji's eventual doom, which the theme will demand. "Seeing all these indications of hard roystering; like a cautious young bridegroom at his own marriage merry-making Taji stood on his guard. And when Borabolla urged him to empty a gourd or two, by way of making room in him for the incidental repast about to be served, Taji civilly declined; not wishing to cumber the floor, before the cloth was laid." And then again, sometimes Taji is referred to in the editorial third person, with clear indication that the narrator is Taji talking about himself.

"This recital filled Taji with horror.

"Who could these avengers be, but the sons of him I had slain. I had thought them far hence, and myself forgotten. . . ."

The very end of the book spotlights the inextricable dilemma into which the book's disunity has forced Melville and his narrator. During the last bit of action, when Taji abandons the world and murders himself by plunging into eternity, the narration is still first person.

" 'Now I am my own soul's emperor; and my first act is abdication! Hail! realm of shades!'—and turning my prow into the racing tide, which seized me like a hand omnipotent, I darted through.

"Churned in foam, that outer ocean lashed the clouds; and straight in my white wake, headlong dashed a shallop, three fixed specters leaning o'er its prow: three arrows poising." At this crucial point, the first person narrator withdraws—as he would have to if there is to be anyone to write finish to the tale—and some other narrator, who has been dodging in and out of the story as convenience, forgetfulness and necessity dictate, again takes over in order to wave a *mal voyage* to Taji and his specters:

> And thus, pursuers and pursued
> fled on, over an endless sea.

THE END

It is also the end of the reader's bewildered attempt to determine just who is telling the story.

Noting the book's disintegration, readers have attempted to demonstrate a break between the real world of the beginning and the unreal world of Mardi.[9] But such a break is highly debatable, and is not a central explanation of the book's fragmentation. As will be seen, there are strong parallels between the "factual" beginning and the rest of the book.[10] Thematically there is no break. Moreover there are

---

[9] For some of the approaches to the "break" in the story, see Charles Anderson, *Melville in the South Seas* (New York, 1939) pp. 343-44, where Luther S. Mansfield's explanation of change in story is presented from his unpublished dissertation (Univ. of Chicago, 1936), "Herman Melville, Author and New Yorker, 1844-1851." This explanation is largely the same as that presented by Leon Howard in his excellent study, *Herman Melville* (Berkeley, Cal., 1951), pp. 112-32; and by William Gilman in *Melville's Early Life and Redburn* (New York, 1951), pp. 164-67; and by Merrell Davis in *Melville's Mardi: A Chartless Voyage* (New Haven, 1952), p. 66: "In brief, during those first months of 1848, Melville was experimenting with a whole range of new voices which the opening world of books helped to provide." Davis, whose book is the only published full-length study of *Mardi*. divides *Mardi* into the following sections: (1) The Narrative Beginning, (2) The Romantic Interlude (Taji's brief stay with Yillah), and (3) The Travelogue Satire (all the rest of the book).

[10] Leon Howard's and Merrell Davis' studies of Melville's reworkings show that before he got very far into the plans for *Mardi*, he knew that he would commit himself to the allegory. Had he not wanted the narrative beginning, he could have deleted it if he felt that it bore little relation to the rest of the book.

statements in the beginning that indicate a consciousness of what is
to come. For instance, among many other examples of preview, the
end of Chapter XXVII ("In Which The Past History of The Parki
Is Concluded") says, "And such, in substance, was the first, second,
third and fourth acts of the Parki drama. The fifth and last, including
several scenes, now follows." Three chapters later, as the "several
scenes" continue, Taji-not-yet-named-Taji says, "At times, I mounted
aloft, and lounging in the slings of the topsail yard—one of the many
snug nooks in a ship's rigging—I gazed broad off upon that blue
boundless sea, and wondered what they were doing in that unknown
land, toward which we were fated to be borne."

Not only do the several hints of looking ahead prepare the expectations later satisfied, but also the language itself ties the "factual"
beginning to the Mardian consequences. The fight with Aleema and
his sons (at this point the "real" world ends and the unreal begins)
is in no way different from the appearance of the "factual" adventure
which clothed the desertion from the *Arcturion*. The language itself
does not indicate any change from adventure to allegory. Here is the
desertion scene:

"Man overboard!" was now shouted from stem to stern. And directly we
heard the confused tramping and shouting of the sailors, as they rushed
from their dreams into the almost inscrutable darkness.

"Man overboard! Man overboard!" My heart smote me as the human cry
of horror came out of the black vaulted night.

". . . Heave the ship to, and hold fast everything," cried the captain,
apparently just springing to the deck. "One boat's enough. Steward! show a
light there from the mizzen-top. Boat ahoy!—have you got that man?"

No reply. The voice came out of a cloud; the ship dimly showing like a
ghost. We had desisted from rowing, and hand over hand were now haul-
ing in upon the rope attached to the breaker, which we soon lifted into the
boat, instantly resuming our oars.

"Pull! pull, men! and save him!" again shouted the captain.

"Ay, ay, sir," answered Jarl instinctively, "pulling as hard as ever we can,
sir."

And pull we did, till nothing could be heard from the ship but a confused

---

Or he could have condensed it. Davis, however, does not draw the same conclusion: "The apparent inconsistency in addition to the perfunctoriness of Jarl's
dismissal from the book would seem to indicate that the author as well as the
Narrator did not know what was to happen to his travellers when they reached
the paradisiacal islands to the west." *Melville's Mardi*, p. 109. However, Davis
does not reconcile this opinion with his own recognition of the fact of Jarl's
symbolic value: "As Evert Duyckinck was to suggest in his review of *Mardi*, 'the
unphilosophic friend Jarl' of the first volume was apparently not wanted in the
learned company with whom the Narrator toured the islands of Mardi" (p. 109).
Also, Davis recognizes the unity of the narrative beginning with the allegory:
"Aside from the obvious device of chronology, the most significant structural device is the reiteration in almost every chapter of the theme of present and future
danger" (p. 110). Seeing that the narrative level is not fitted to the symbolism, he
points out that many visits to particular islands are unnecessary (pp. 196-97).
For a study which does find symbolic meanings in all the islands, see Nathalia
Wright, "The Head and Heart in Melville's *Mardi*," *PMLA*, LXVI (1951), 351-62.

tumult; and, ever and anon, the hoarse shout of the captain, too distant to be understood.

We now set our sail to a light air; and right into the darkness, and dead to leeward, we rowed and sailed till morning dawned [p. 25].

And here is the saving of the *Parki*, wherein more characters are added to the "factual" beginning.

The boat still gaining on the brigantine, the muskets were again reloaded. And as the next shot sped, there was a pause; when, like lightning, the headmost Cholo bounded upwards from his seat, and oar in hand, fell into the sea. A fierce yell; and one of the natives springing into the water caught the sinking body by its long hair; and the dead and living were dragged into the boat. Taking heart from this fatal shot, Samoa fired yet again. . . .

Enough: darting past the ill-fated boat, they swam rapidly for land followed by the rest; who plunged overboard, leaving in the boat the surviving Cholo—who it seems could not swim—the wounded savage, and the dead man. . . .

At length both Cholo and savage fell dead upon their comrade, canting the boat over sideways, till well nigh awash; in which manner she drifted off [p. 63].

The meeting with Aleema is the first scene in the unreal, symbolic world, yet there is no difference in tone or atmosphere. Even the murder of Aleema is not attended by any change of language.

The knife before dangling in Samoa's ear was now in his hand. Jarl cried out for us to regain the boat, several of the Islanders making a rush for it. No time to think. All passed quicker than it can be said. They closed in upon us, to push us from the canoe. Rudely the old priest flung me from his side, menacing me with his dagger, the sharp spine of a fish. A thrust and a threat. Ere I knew it, my cutlass made a quick lunge. A curse from the priest's mouth; red blood from his side; he tottered, stared about him, and fell over like a brown hemlock into the sea. A yell of maledictions rose on the air. A wild cry was heard from the tent. Making a dead breach among the crowd, we now dashed side by side for the boat. Springing into it, we found Jarl battling with two Islanders; while the rest were still howling upon the dais. Rage and grief had almost disabled them [p. 118].

There is a slight difference in the sentence structure, which has been made more brisk and direct in order to accord with the faster action. But the language itself is as realistic as anything in the "factual" beginning. From this point on, however, the language does begin to change. We have only to turn to the end of the book, where the style has just about ridden itself—and the reader—out, to see the difference:

And now, their torches held aloft, into the water the maidens softly glided; and each a lotus floated; while, from far above, into the air Hautia flung her flambeau; then bounding after,—in the lake, two meteors were quenched.

Where she dived, the flambeaux clustered; and up among them, Hautia rose, hands full of pearls.

"Lo! Taji; all these may be had for the diving; and Beauty, Health, Wealth, Long Life, and the Last Lost Hope of man. But through me alone, may these be had. Dive thou and bring up one pearl if thou canst."

Down, down! down, down, in the clear, sparkling water, till I seemed crystallized in the flashing heart of a diamond; but from those bottomless depths, I uprose empty handed [pp. 576-77].

In the passage on the death of Aleema, the priest is a brown hemlock, an image united to both the literal and symbolic levels. He is a dark Islander, and he is also something that poisons the flow of Taji's life with guilt and pursuit and finally death. The metaphor of Hautia the meteor is also unified to both levels. She is hotly and flashily attractive, and she burns out into nothing when Taji tries to seize the promises of her appearances. There is more contrast between the introduction of the unreal world and the end of the unreal world than between the "factual" real world and the unreal world of Mardi.[11] The language does not change because of a higher charge of symbolic content. It changes because it embraces all the highly stylized artificialities of what Melville thought was allegory. In short, there is no break in the sense that Melville abandoned one story and began another. He changed techniques; he abandoned realistic narrative progression for allegory, but he did not change theme. In the Aleema passage a torch would be a torch, not a flambeau. In the Aleema episode the stage is set by the actions necessitated by the incident itself, not by the emblematic hocus-pocus of maidens floating lotuses in the water. In the Aleema episode the energy of the language arises from narrative action; it does not die into the fixed diction of traditional stylization. And in the Aleema episode, rage and grief, as meaningful as they will prove to be, are rage and grief, not Rage and Grief. Yet, as bad as the stilted qualities of the language become, Melville adds the artificialities skillfully, taking the reader slowly from "another South Seas book" into the world of Mardi. At no point can the reader put his finger on the page and say, "The change is here." It is not until after the disappearance of the "factual" beginning that the gradual change of technique occasions a change of worlds somewhere along the line. Although it is true, it is not apparent that the introduction of Aleema is the introduction of the change, which is a transfer from the point of view of the historical Taji-not-yet-named-Taji in tale one to the point of view of the symbolic Taji in tale two.

The narrative beginning functions as a symbolic preparation for,

---

[11] One critic finds that the significance of the name of the whaling ship, *Arcturion*, dispells the "break" by uniting the "factual" beginning to the satiric design of the whole book. "None of the myths in which Arcturus figures . . . seems applicable to the situations in the book. But there is an association to be made with the name, and one with which we may be sure Melville was familiar, which also provides a clue as to what he intended." From 1840-42, the Duyckincks published a magazine called *Arcturus*. The prologue to the first issue reads in part, "Neither by assuming this designation do we vouch for the literary character of the inhabitants of Arcturus as patrons of the present undertaking; it is sufficient that Arcturus is a star that shines high and brightly, and looks down with a keen glance on the errors, follies, and malpractices of men." Gordon Mills, "The Significance of 'Arcturus' in *Mardi*," *AL*, XIV (1942), 159-61.

and almost a pastiche of, the quest story. But on the narrative level the "factual" beginning does not continue in the quest story. On the narrative level the introductory material only needed the purpose and length it was assigned in *Typee*, that of evaluating the major character and getting him off the whale ship and on the islands. Yet it is expanded far beyond its function. The question is not, "Why does Melville suddenly change stories in the middle of the book?" but rather, "Why has he taken so much time leading up to the unreal *Mardi* toward which he knew he was steering?" The most reasonable —and probable—answers are not completely complimentary to Melville. His publishers expected a continuation of South Seas adventure that would have the popular interest of *Typee* and *Omoo*. Indeed, they were primarily interested in factual adventure. Melville himself was interested, understandably, in the financial success of popular literature. Along with the contempt for popular trash that his letters make manifest were a need and longing for financial success. In the same breath with which he dedicates himself to writing profound books, he yearns for Cash, as well as Time, Strength and Patience. The famous *Redburn* letter says, "I am glad of [*Redburn*]—for it puts money into an empty purse. But I hope I shall never write such a book again—tho when a poor devil writes with duns all around him, & looking over the back of his chair—and perching on his pen & diving in his inkstand—like the devils about St. Anthony—what can you expect of that devil?—what but a beggarly 'Redburn!' And when he attempts anything higher—God help him & save him! for it is not with a hollow purse as with a hollow balloon—for a hollow purse makes a poet *sink*—witness 'Mardi.'" [12] Moreover, Melville was very conscious of patronage. He wrote because he was "bestirring himself to procure his yams" as well as dedicating himself to high truths. There is evidence that in some books he would delete, change, or prettify the truth as he saw it in order to sell books. As annoyed as he was with the missionaries, and as much as he wanted to expose them, he himself suggested to his English publisher, John Murray, that a milder version of *Typee* would sell better in Britain. "Yet *Omoo* was more severe on the missionaries than *Typee* had been, for, as Evert Duyckinck wrote his brother George, Melville owed them a 'sailor's grudge,' which he paid off in his accounts of Tahiti. He was not willing to pay it off, however, at any considerable expense to himself . . . he decided to drop three of the earlier chapters entirely. . . ." [13] In the same spirit he probably extended the "factual" beginning of *Mardi* as a come-on. Indeed, he wrote to John Murray, "Only forbear to prejudge it.—*It opens like a true narrative*—like *Omoo* for example, on shipboard—& the romance and poetry of the

[12] Metcalf, p. 71.
[13] Howard, p. 102.

thing thence grow continually, till it becomes a story wild enough I assure you & with a meaning too." [14] He must have tolerated the beginning of the book as long as he could until either (1) he convinced himself that his current popularity allowed him to thumb his nose at shallow reader interest; (2) he no longer had fun with Taji, Jarl, Samoa, and Annattoo (the manuscript *Mardi* chapters that Duyckinck read, about which he said that here Melville "exhausts the South Seas marvels" were chapters from the "factual" beginning); and (3) the devil-artist in the depths could no longer be restrained. Probably no one reason is truth by itself, and probably all are a truth taken together. For inside the popularity seeker was the man with vision, the artist, who lurked in Melville as Azzageddi lurked in Babbalanja—and who probably caused as much pain. [15] That devil was too honest and deep-diving and all-consuming to conform to the popular Mardi-world. The view of Lombardo writing the Koztanza was Melville's heroic self-portrait of the artist. Paradoxically, the unleashing of the creative devil before he was full-grown put an end to *Mardi's* good beginning.

The premature devil completed the book's breakdown, and went on to write the second tale, which is Taji's. Yet this supposedly central tale exists in only about thirty-six chapters, or, roughly, only 20 per cent of the total book. [16] This second tale is in turn fragmented into three sections. The first is a group of twenty chapters clustered between Chapters XXXIX and LXIV, and this fragment comprises the introduction to the Taji-Yillah tale. [17] The second fragment is a group of seven chapters interspersed throughout the book. In these chapters, pursuit by Aleema's sons and allurement by Hautia's maidens are interjected in a series of mechanical reminders that there is supposed to be an underlying purpose for the voyage. But there is no special pattern in which these reminders occur. It seems as if in the grinding act of composition, preoccupied with the necessity for his characters' ceaseless talk, Melville simply waited what he thought were decent intervals, and reinserted the trappings of Taji's particular quest approximately once every fifteen chapters. As a result, the reintroductions of the three avengers and of Hautia's three heralds are highly

---

[14] Davis, p. 75. Bluff heartiness, or gratitude, or politeness, betrayed (by attempting to mask) Melville's uneasiness in such matters. For examples, see Metcalf, pp. 40-41.

[15] Later, when Herman was experiencing the torment of his own frustrations over his manner of earning a living and over his artistic vision in poetry, he was explaining in postscripts to letters, "I *ain't* crazy." And when his wife, Elizabeth, wrote to her brother Lemuel Shaw, Jr. (New York, June 19, 1877) she said, explaining vacation plans, "I have just written . . . about rooms and *hope* we shall be able to compass a six weeks absence from New York—the only doubt of which is the being able to leave Herman alone so long, in his state of mental health, with a free conscience. . . ." Metcalf, p. 250.

[16] Those chapters are XXXIX-LV, LVIII, LXI, LXII, LXIV, LXXXVIII, C, CI, CXVIII, CXLI, CXLIX, CLXXIII, CLXXXIX-CXCV.

[17] Those chapters are XXIX, XL, XLI-LIV, LVIII, LXI, LXII, LXIV.

fortuitous. Every reminder is monotonously similar to every other. The occupants of Media's canoe are startled by a patter of three arrows intended for Taji. They look up in time to see the avengers' canoe rush away in the distance. Immediately, Hautia's three heralds appear, displaying flowers to Taji. Yoomy interprets the meaning of the flowers (generally: your hope, Taji, is dead; come fly to Hautia's joys). Taji makes a grim avowal of eternal quest for Yillah and scorn for Hautia. And away they all sail into a sea of essay statement, uninterrupted by the symbolic novel for another fifteen chapters or so. The third fragment of this second tale is composed of the last nine chapters of *Mardi*. This fragment sees the quester doomed to failure as he plunges out of the world in pursuit of his phantom. Accidentally, the only thing that tends to save the narrative level of the Taji-Yillah-Hautia tale is the very fragmentation which intermixes it with the Media-Babbalanja tale and thereby lends the two a minimal appearance of unity.

The third tale of *Mardi* is what the second should have been. Babbalanja's and Media's story is the major portion of the book, in bulk as well as in resolution of the thematic problems raised. The first thirty-eight chapters have been exempted for the "factual" beginning. Thirty-six chapters more are allotted to the second tale. That leaves more than half of the total one hundred and ninety-five chapters for the third tale. Ostensibly, *Mardi* is about Taji's quest. In resolution, however, it concerns itself with the development and education of the king and the philosopher. Because Taji rejects the concerns of this world in the first place, the education deriving from the visits to the isles of the archipelago does not by right belong to him. It is not until they reach Hautia's isle (which chapters do belong to the Taji tale) that Taji takes any place in the book again. As they voyage, all the inhabitants of the canoe seek Yillah, but each one defines her differently. Babbalanja learns to reject Yillah ("Odonphi," "Astrazzi," or any of the jargon terms satirically intended to represent metaphysical absolutes) for an earthly value. Media takes a journey, almost imperceptibly, from isolation to membership in the human community. Media and Babbalanja find the same basic answer to the problems of human behavior, and characteristically each one applies the answer according to his personality and his traditional function as contemplative or active man. They become the only truly rounded, developing characters in the book, surrounded by a stableful of puppets. Because each character seeks a meaning in the search for Yillah the symbol, and because Yillah the person is meaningless to everyone (including the reader) except Taji, the parallel between the Taji story and the Media-Babbalanja story exists on the symbolic level more coherently and fully than it does on the narrative level. As would be expected, the total definition of Yillah is given in the parallel. That definition is the sum total of everything the voyagers seek. The voyage throughout the archipelago explains where Yillah will not be found, and each land visited provides implications about what kind of behavior will not yield her. The moment that Taji admits that Yillah is really gone and that he will have to hunt through the world for her, the general purpose of the voyage becomes evident. "But hereafter," says Taji, "*in words* little more of the maiden, till perchance her fate be learned."

The voyage serves two specific functions. First, it makes a negative comment on Taji's quest, and provides background which, together with the "factual" beginning, gives some direction to the meaning of the quest's symbolism. Second, it allows Melville to get down on paper all the satiric statements he had wanted to make about the universal follies of human society and the more specific crimes of his own western civilization. Because of the book's failures, the voyage becomes a mechanical and artificial device which allows Melville to make controlling statements for meanings that he was not able to control symbolically.

In commenting upon the various behaviors observed during the voyage, Babbalanja and Media carry the burden of the book's development. The thematic center drifts away from Taji and into the hands of Media and Babbalanja. Had Taji been Babbalanja, and had he rejected the Serenian vision, still wishing to enter the ultimate heaven by escalade, then *Mardi* would have been a far more unified book. But this great portion of *Mardi's* pages have nothing to do with Taji, on the narrative level, except by the almost gratuitous circumstance which places him in the same canoe with the major commentators of the voyage. Matthiessen pointed out that *Mardi's* symbolism is artificial.[18] But Matthiessen is not wholly correct in attributing the artificiality to an indiscriminate borrowing from many authors, including the rose-oil-and-violets stylizers, the ladies'-magazine third raters. Primarily it is artificial because it is imposed from without; it does not grow from the literal level. The symbolism becomes obscure because it leads back (as it should) to the Taji story, which is the symbolic center of *Mardi*, but which certainly is not the narrative center.[19]

---

[18] F. O. Matthiessen, *The American Renaissance* (New York, 1941), pp. 384-86. See also Gilman, p. 246.

[19] Matthiessen is correct when he says that Melville "was not in control . . . and was often whirled about by his abstractions." But he is not wholly accurate when he adds that "you can hardly construct a coherent view of man and society from the many counterstatements that are made . . ." (p. 381). Matthiessen, in what is one of the most suggestive studies of Melville ever made, makes the mistake of equating now Taji, now Azzageddi, now Babbalanja with Melville. In such a tacit equation there certainly is neither coherence nor symbolic unity. Davis is one of the few critics to indicate a difference between Melville and the Narrator. See *Melville's Mardi*, p. 103, p. 94, n.3, p. 107, and p. 107, n.1. In noting that Melville's perception becomes obvious despite structural difficulties, Matthiessen adds, "but you can follow the urgent drives of [Melville's] mind in the direction in which they were aiming."

Melville was aware of *Mardi's* narrative disintegration, but he was not aware of how fatal it really was, for during the discussion of Lombardo's Koztanza, fragmentation is championed by the sympathetic character, Babbalanja, and condemned by the heartless and thoughtless king Abrazza.

ABRAZZA.—. . . But, Babbalanja, the Koztanza lacks cohesion; it is wild, unconnected, all episode.

BABBALANJA.—And so is Mardi itself:—nothing but episodes; valleys and hills; rivers, digressing from plains; vines, roving all over; boulders and diamonds; flowers and thistles; forests and thickets; and, here and there, fens and moors. And so, the world in the Koztanza.

ABRAZZA.—Ay, plenty of dead-desert chapters there; horrible sands to wade through.[20]

Melville seems to have found in Shakespeare a concept he himself embraced, the concept that art should follow nature.[21] But Melville was not completely aware of the difference between sixteenth- and nineteenth-century nature. He extended the concept into a belief in an unconscious following of the creative impulse, and in this he was close to a persistent romantic idea of the artist as inspired and unconscious medium, or instrument. "Call it what you will, Yoomy, it was a sort of sleepwalking of the mind. Lombardo never threw down his pen: it dropped from him; and then, he sat disenchanted: rubbing his eyes; staring; and feeling faint—sometimes, almost unto death." However, *Mardi's* total pronouncement on the artist cannot be said to defend critical unconsciousness completely. In fact, recognition of the need for a conscious approach to creative composition accounts for Melville's realization that the uncritical upwelling of creative vitality brings to the surface froth as well as deep sea creatures: "My lords," says Babbalanja, "[geniuses] abound in [trash]! more than any other men in Mardi. Genius is full of trash. But genius essays its best to keep it to itself; and giving away its ore, retains the earth; whence, the too frequent wisdom of its works, and folly of its life." Moreover, Lombardo and Babbalanja are highly cognizant of critical necessities. Babbalanja, speaking for Lombardo, says, "For I am critic and creator; and as critic, in cruelty surpass all critics merely, as a tiger, jackals." For himself, Babbalanja adds, "Lombardo never presumed to criticize true critics; who are more rare than true poets. A great critic is a sultan among satraps; but pretenders are thick as ants, striving to scale a palm, after its aerial sweetness." And Lombardo is quoted as saying, "Who will read me? Say one thousand pages—

---

[20] Pp. 526-27. That the discussion of the Koztanza reflects directly upon Melville's own creation was obvious at least to Melville's family. Augusta, who finished the "fair copy" of *Mardi*, wrote to Elizabeth, "Mardi's a book . . . ! Ah, my own Koztanza! child of many prayers! Oro's blessings on thee." (New York, Jan. 27, 1849.) Quoted by Davis, p. 96.

[21] Matthiessen, pp. 386-87.

twenty-five lines each—every line ten words—every word ten letters. That's two million five hundred thousand *a*'s, and *i*'s, and *o*'s to read! How many are superfluous?" [22]

These passages are at once a revelation of, and a rationalization for, a creative method, a bit of forearming against criticism which Melville was sure would be forthcoming.[23] He tried to emphasize the meaning of *Mardi* rather than the vehicle, not seeing that a believable theme cannot be divorced from a successful vehicle—a mistake to which he was prone. Once his fears were realized, he justified the contents of *Mardi* with a defensiveness in which recognition of the book's confusing and obscure qualities is implicit. To Lemuel Shaw he wrote, "I see that Mardi has been cut into by the London Athenaeum, and also burnt by the common hangman in the Boston Post. However, the London Examiner & Literary Gazette; & other papers this side of the water have done differently. These attacks are matters of course, and are essential to the building of any permanent reputation—if such should ever prove to be mine. —'There's nothing in it!' cried the dunce, when he threw down the 47th problem of the 1st Book of Euclid—Thus with the posed critics—But Time, which is the solver of all riddles, will solve 'Mardi.' " [24] And to Richard Bentley he wrote,

The critics on your side of the water seemed to have fired quite a broadside into "Mardi"; but it was not altogether unexpected. In fact the book is of a nature to attract compliments of that sort from some quarters; and as you may be aware yourself, it is judged only as a work meant to entertain. And I cannot but think that its having been brought out in England in the ordinary novel form must have led to the disappointment of many readers, who would have been better pleased with it, perhaps, had they taken it up in the first place for what it really is—Besides, the peculiar thoughts & fancies of a Yankee upon politics & other matters could hardly be presumed to delight that class of gentlemen who conduct your leading journals; while the metaphysical ingredients (for want of a better term) of the book, must of course repel some of those who read simply for amusement.—However, it will reach those for whom it is intended; and I have already received assurances that "Mardi," in its larger purposes, has not been written in vain.[25]

What is important is that Melville recognized the book's fragmentation, yet tried to justify it rather than correct it. For this reason, too, *Mardi* is Melville's greatest literary self-indulgence. Finally, confusing life and art in defense of *Mardi's* haphazard qualities would hardly

---

[22] *Mardi*, p. 530. The *a*, *i*, and *o* signify the petty detail more than once. These same letters describe the girls of Pimminee (Chapter CXXIX, "A, I, and O").

[23] "Melville was . . . anticipating the critical disapproval he was already beginning to expect. He did not mean to give the impression that writing was simply an uncritical outpouring of any author's mind: 'Oh! could Mardi but see how we work,' he exclaimed, . . ." Howard, p. 128.

[24] Metcalf, p. 62.

[25] Metcalf, pp. 62-63.

be a fruitful gambit for the man who had scoffed at seekers of verity and verisimilitude. Least of all is such a confusion a defense for a man who writes symbolism which, like *Mardi's*, is unconcerned with photographic reality.

Melville's confusion of realistic, allegorical, and abstractly symbolic techniques causes other structural breakdowns which are probably less important than those cited, but which also help to destroy the book. For instance, the voyagers travel in a realistic geography in the South Seas. But in Chapter CXLV ("Chiefly of King Bello"), they enter an allegorical geography which is not in the South Seas. Taji-not-yet-named-Taji of the "factual beginning" was painstaking in out-lining his plan to drift eventually to the Kingsmill group of islands. The first few pages of *Mardi* are spotted with details of location. In the Taji tale, the reader may willingly suspend disbelief and accept the Mardian archipelago as a symbolic realm with no possible geo-graphic location. But in the Media-Babbalanja tale, the reader must forcibly suspend disbelief in order to accept, allegorically, an area near the Kingsmills as the whole earth, with the added confusion of specific suggestions of north, south, east, and west. For suddenly, still in the symbolic Mardi, the reader voyages allegorically and literally to England (Dominora), and must accept this bit of the northeastern Atlantic as something which exists in a corner of the southwestern Pacific. Melville further jars the reader's acceptance by precisely associating his allegorical creatures with the geographical earth. For example, when explaining King Bello's (the King of England's) mar-riage to the sea in the world of the Pacific Mardi, the narrator cites similar ceremonies by Jason, Castor and Pollux of Greece, Aeneas of Troy, Mark Antony and Cleopatra of Egypt, Torf-Egill of Denmark, Doge Dandolo of Venice, Kumbo Sama of Japan, and Kannakoko of New Zealand. Allegory, at this point, makes reality an imposition, and the reader has only a confused sense of which world he is in. It would be silly to demand a consistent geography for an imaginary land used for the purposes of political satire, but political satire is only part of the book's intentions. The allegorical portion of the Media-Babbalanja locale cannot so conveniently be divorced geographically from the other, abstract, symbolic Mardi, or from the other concrete, realistic Mardi, simply because the author wills it so. He must make it so, and he does not.

The confusion of allegorical and geographical earth is extended. There is a northeastward voyage around Dominora, between Scotland (Kaleedoni) and Ireland (Verdanna); southeastward to continental Europe (Porpheero), along the coast of France (Franko), where Media is frightened by the potentially regicidal explosions of 1848. Skittering off, the royal canoe then travels westward across the At-lantic-Pacific to the United States (Vivenza), where the travelers visit awhile and travel southward, overland, to the Gulf of Mexico; then out the Gulf, down the east coast of South America (Kolumbo of the South), westward around Cape Horn (the Cape of Capes), and northward to the west coast of North America, where the voyagers observe the gold rush. Then the trip continues across the Pacific (the Pacific-Pacific this time!), past lush isles where Mardi is supposed to be in the first place, southward and westward along the coasts of Asia (Orienda), to Africa (Hamora). Then they skirt the coast of Africa, travel westward around the Cape of Good Hope, and northward to the Straits of Gibraltar, through which they sail eastward, with Europe's Christendom on their left and North Africa's Islam on their right. They paddle to the farthest eastern portion of the Mediterranean, after which they turn around and canoe back out to the wide Atlantic. At this venture, Melville simply asks the reader to disregard the specific geographical and political regions just caricatured, and to believe himself once more in the Mardi of the South Pacific.[26] "As, after wandering round and round some purple dell, deep in a boundless prairie's heart, the baffled hunter plunges in; then, despairing, turns once more to gain the open plain; even so we seekers now curved round our keels; and from that inland sea emerged. The universe again before us; our quest as wide." [27] That universe is the same familiar Atlantic already sailed over on the journey to Vivenza. But— the next chapter opens blithely in Mardi: "Morning dawned upon that same mild, blue Lagoon as erst; and all the lands that we had passed . . . were faded from the sight." Either the "factual" intro-

---

[26] For historical background for the events seen during the voyage, see Davis, pp. 79-94. Davis suggests (p. 94, n.3) that after the visit to the geographically identifiable islands is concluded, "the beginning of the voyage to the fictitious 'world of mind' " is commenced. However, this is debatable. The islands which come after the geographically identifiable islands are no different in quality than the islands which come before. Doxodox's island, for instance, or Abrazza's island, both of which come after the geographically identifiable group, are no more or less symbolic of "mind" and no more or less allegorical or symbolic in any way, than the islands of Mondoldo or Valapee, which come before the geographical group. The geographical islands are inserted in the midst of the allegorical islands as vehicles for specific political and social satire, and in many ways have no less a philosophical overtone than the obviously symbolic and allegorical islands. The entire book, having as it does its symbolic center in Taji's story, is a total exploration of will and mind. The geographical islands were inserted after the completion of the first general construction of the book. Melville added them for thematic as well as self-indulgent reasons, because by this time he must have been seeing ideas for Mardi in every leaf and rock and event. The geographical islands became for him perfect cases in point, taken from the recognizable world, and which satirically illustrated the man-of-war world's behavior patterns which precluded Yillah. The very repetition with which Melville says that Yillah is not here . . . or here . . . or here is the method by which Melville ties the geographical islands to the symbolic quest. Davis recognizes this: "Thus the satirical representation of many of the islands and their inhabitants exposes obvious reasons for Yillah's not being discovered among them" (p. 197). For the composition of Mardi, particularly the later inclusion of the geographical islands, see Davis, pp. 81-94, and Howard, pp. 112-13 and 122-29. For the range of satire in the geographical islands, see Davis, pp. 151-59.

[27] Mardi, p. 486.

duction should have used the safer, traditional device of an unknown sea rather than the real Pacific, or the map of Mardi should not have been such a detailed and transparent duplicate of the real earth. As far as narrative structure is concerned, when the narrator exclaims, "Oh, reader, list! I've chartless voyaged," he makes a truer statement than he knows.

The chartlessness of narrative is noticeable in one other large area of *Mardi*, and that is the incident itself. One of the worst accusations that can be leveled against the quality of the book is that the incident is almost totally haphazard. There is no steady incremental development in the incident, no plan of arrangement. There is no reason, for instance, why the visit to Valapee should precede the visit to Juam. Except for its last paragraph, there is no function for the chapter on "The Sea on Fire." With many other sections developing the qualities of the sea, there is no reason why reiterative chapters like those which tell "More about Being in An Open Boat" are necessary. Nor is there any reason for chapters like CXXI ("They Regale Themselves with Their Pipes") to be included at all.[28]

Sometimes the action that is needed to motivate the major characters is made unnecessarily obtrusive (like the visits of Hautia's heralds) by being injected mechanically and obviously. These bits of action become triggers which launch buckshot projectiles of discourse. For example, Vee-Vee falls and breaks his arm like the obliging little chap he is, only so that Babbalanja may deliver a lengthy sermon on necessitarianism. While the story of Donjalolo's emissaries to the outside world has a meaning reflexive to *Mardi's* theme, it is presented only so that Babbalanja may make a summary statement about the relativity of truth. The ceaseless talk, the mechanical incident are indications of Melville's loss of control over his symbols; he cannot let the incident speak for itself. With the book fragmented as it is,

[28] Davis gallantly suggests that such chapters are not extraneous. After citing sources for some of the extraneous incident, he says, "All of these incidents, though often introduced as digressions ('But all this is an episode made up of digressions'), are appropriate embellishments for the westward voyage of the Parki" (p. 121). However, just how and why these "embellishments" are "appropriate" is not explained—probably they cannot be justified either in themselves or in their sources. As Davis says of Melville's discussion of phosphorescence, "This discussion, of its main outline and in many of its verbal phrases, follows Bennett's essay in his *Whaling Voyage* on 'Marine Phosphorescence and Its Dependence on Animal Matter.' The narrator's account, however, is not a dull recital of facts, but a lively and informal conversation about the phosphorescence of the sea, with the information of the source adjusted to the dramatic and humorous purposes of the narrator. The whole chapter affords an appropriate conclusion, whether or not it was so intended, to the first part of the voyage to the western isles . . ." (pp. 123-24). But again, more must be attributed to Davis' generosity than to Melville's selectivity. Liveliness and informality per se are hardly a very serious justification for inclusion of material, especially in a book so well-nigh unreadable as *Mardi*. Just what the "source adjusted to the dramatic and humorous purposes of the Narrator" means, or how the source is so "adjusted," or what the "dramatic and humorous purposes" are, are left unexplained, as is the judgment that the entire chapter is an "appropriate conclusion" to the narrative beginning.

any one incident is generally unrelated to any other incident, and is related only to editorial statement. Melville limits the possibilities with which incident creates further levels of meaning out of itself and he constantly stretches a topping of statement over a potentially creative drum of incident—and the resulting sound is hollow. One example will serve to illustrate what too high a percentage of *Mardi's* incident is like. As the royal canoe travels to Serenia, one of the oarsmen falls into the sea.

But a sudden splash, and a shrill, gurgling sound, like that of a fountain subsiding, now broke upon the air. Then all was still, save the rush of waves by our keel.

"Save him! Put back!"

From his elevated seat, the merry bowsman, too gleefully reaching forward, had fallen into the lagoon.

With all haste, our speeding canoes were reversed; but not till we had darted in upon another darkness than that in which the bowsman fell.

As, blindly, we groped back, deep Night dived deeper down in the sea.

"Drop paddles all, and list."

Holding their breath, over the six gunwhales all now leaned; but the only moans were the wind's.

Long time we lay thus; then slowly crossed and recrossed our track, almost hopeless; but yet loth to leave him who, with a song in his mouth, died and was buried in a breath.

"Let us away," said Media—"why seek more? He is gone."

"Ay, gone," said Babbalanja, "and whither? But a moment since, he was among us; now, the fixed stars are not more remote than he. So far off, can he live? Oh, Oro [God]! this death thou ordainest unmans the manliest. Say not nay, my lord. Let us not speak behind Death's back. Hard and horrible is it to die; blindfolded to leap from life's verge! But thus, in clouds of dust, and with a trampling as of hoofs, the generations disappear; death driving them all into his treacherous fold, as wild Indians the bison herds. Nay, nay, Death is Life's last despair. Hard and horrible is it to die. Oro himself, in Alma, died not without a groan. Yet why, why live? Life is wearisome to all: the same dull round. Day and night, summer and winter, round about us revolving for aye. One moment lived, is a life. No new stars appear in the sky; no new lights in the soul. Yet, of changes there are many. For though, with rapt sight, in childhood, we behold many strange things beneath the moon, and all Mardi looks a tented fair—how soon everything fades. All of us, in our very bodies, outlive our own selves. I think of green youth as of a merry playmate departed; and to shake hands, and be pleasant with my old age, seems in prospect even harder, than to draw a cold stranger to my bosom. But old age is not for me. I am not of the stuff that grows old. This Mardi is not our home. Up and down we wander, like exiles transported to a planet afar:—'tis not the world *we* were born in; not the world once so lightsome and gay; not the world where we once merrily danced, dined, and supped; and wooed and wedded our long buried wives. Then let us depart. But whither? We push ourselves forward—then, start back in affright. Essay it again, and flee. Hard to live; hard to die; intolerable suspense! But the grim despot at last interposes; and with a viper in our windingsheets, we are dropped in the sea."

"To me," said Mohi, his gray locks damp with night dews, "death's dark defile at times seems at hand, with no voice to cheer. That all have died makes it not easier for me to depart. And that many have been quenched in infancy seems a mercy to the slow perishing of my old age, limb by limb and sense by sense. I have long been the tomb of my youth. And more has died out of me, already, than remains for the last death to finish. Babbalanja says truth. In childhood, death stirred me not; in middle age, it pursued me like a prowling bandit on the road; now, grown an old man, it boldly leads the way; and ushers me on; and turns round upon me its skeleton gaze: poisoning the last solaces of life. Maramma [institutionalized religion] but adds to my gloom."

"Death! Death!" cried Yoomy, "must I be not, and millions be? Must I go, and the flowers still bloom? Oh, I have marked what it is to be dead; —how shouting boys on holidays, hide-and-seek among the tombs, which must hide all seekers at last."

"Clouds on clouds!" cried Media, "but away with them all! Why not leap your graves while ye may? Time to die, when death comes, without dying by inches. 'Tis no death, to die; the only death is the fear of it. I, a demi-god, fear death not" [pp. 547-49; the discussion of Death and God continues for another entire page].

Because Melville has to transfer symbolic growth from the devices of action to the devices of conversation, *Mardi* is a ceaselessly talky book. The oarsmen are mentioned only a few times in the course of the entire book. This particular oarsman, the bowsman, is mentioned here for the first and only time. His sudden introduction is not the only hint of unincorporated action. The dialogue itself, after the first three sentences of Babbalanja's soliloquy, makes no mention of the oarsman. The dialogue centers either upon generalizations about death (which is the real purpose: Melville wants to talk about death, so someone dies), or upon revelations of the speaker's character. Even this latter intention is not realized, because the incident is too mechanical to bestow upon the bowsman the stature of a being. It is obvious, in Media's case, that Melville wished to reveal the King's hardhearted unawareness of human sorrow and limitation, his false image of his own infallible self. But the bowsman merely fulfills the convenient function of dying. He is a cipher about whom neither the narrator, the major characters, nor the reader can have any feeling. Even the supposedly sympathetic characters are not concerned with the oarsman, but with a self-shaken consideration of death as an abstraction. Consequently the sympathetic characters react not only wrongly, but sentimentally out of proportion, and Media, who is supposed to be censured by his own words, makes the only sensible statement. The wooden oarsman might just as well never have been dumped to the fishes. The entire discussion could have been introduced by Media's calling for talk, as he so often does, or by Babbalanja's unstimulated volunteering of talk, which so often occurs. The incident itself remains not only unincorporated into the discussion of the speakers, but it can have nothing whatsoever to do with any action that led up to it, for there was none, or any action which proceeds from it, for there is none.

Indeed, within any single incident the very dialogue itself becomes fragmented. Expanded sections of talk often include segments unrelated to anything but Melville's desire to be heard. For instance, after one of Babbalanja's lectures upon the need for equal balance and cooperation between mind and body, and upon the evolutionary nature of all corporeal beings—including Kings—the conversation shifts unaccountably:

"Babbalanja," said Mohi, "you must be the last of the kangaroos."
"I am, Mohi."
"But the old fashioned pouch or purse of your grandams?" hinted Media.
"My lord, I take it, that must have been transferred; nowadays our sex carries the purse.
"Ha, ha!"
"My lord, why this mirth? [The reader also wonders.] Let us be serious. Although man is no longer a kangaroo, he may be said to be an inferior species of plant. Plants proper are perhaps insensible of the circulation of their sap: we mortals are physically unconscious of the circulation of the blood: and for many ages we were not even aware of the fact. Plants know nothing of their interiors:—three score years and ten we trundle about ours, and never get a peep at them; plants stand on their stalks;—we stalk on our legs; no plant flourishes over its dead root:—dead in the grave, man lives no longer above ground; plants die without food;—so we. And now for the difference. Plants elegantly inhale nourishment, without looking it up: like lords they stand still and are served; and though green, never suffer from the colic:—whereas, we mortals must forage all round for our food: we cram our insides; and are loaded down with odious sacks and intestines. Plants make love and multiply; but excell us all in amorous enticements, wooing and winning by soft pollens and essences. Plants abide in one place, and live: we must travel or die. Plants flourish without us: we must perish without them [p. 444].

As curiously expendable as this passage is, after the words, "And now for the difference," the dialogue becomes totally irrelevant and unilluminating even if considered as a section of an essay. The basic fractures of the book are duplicated in smaller and smaller sections. The topmost stone of idea is built upon a thousand particles of uncemented sand.

Yet the importance of *Mardi* lies in its failure, for its very artificiality makes it a most convenient beginning for an examination of the relationship between Melville's theme and his techniques. All the major characters in the book are usually symbolic characters. Their meanings are dependent upon their relationships to each other and to action, so that they are multi-valued, like Ahab and Starbuck. They redefine their own contexts just as, and at the same time that, their contexts define them. Even the relatively few-faceted characters like Mohi and Yoomy (or Flask and Stubb) are not assigned a total, exterior, one-to-one relationship with a stable and representative quality. When a person, place, thing, action or speech is symbolic, it may be given a one-to-one relationship with a quality. But that quality demands constant redefinition and consequently attaches to itself a multiplicity of meanings and relationships (the relationships and meanings become the same) which, in turn, it lends to the person, place, thing, action, or speech with which it is associated. The allegorical quality, however, is faithful and constant. The symbolic quality molds and is molded by its context. The allegorical quality is independent of it. In symbolism the meaning arises from the relationships of parts, from the context. In allegory the meaning is imposed upon the context. The unreal and artificial faces of *Mardi's* characters (exclusive of the real world in the "factual" beginning) *seem* allegorical. They lead the reader to expect constant meanings which aren't there. On the other hand, the chapters devoted to satire of nations and follies *are* allegorical. Pimminee, for instance, is The Emptiness and Idiocy of The Social Snob. Doxodox is the Emptiness and Idiocy of Orthodox Pretensions. Such chapters are given an equal weighting with the symbolic chapters, such as those devoted to Donjalolo or Hautia, and are treated as though they were the same. The symbolic action of the quest for Yillah is plunged into an indiscriminate mixture of allegorical and symbolic incidents. Consequently sometimes the characters are allegorical (Media is Mr. Worldly Man, Mr. Proud Man) and sometimes they are symbolic (Media is the multiple definition of the governor). The three completely symbolic characters, Taji, Hautia and Yillah, remain aloof from most of the voyage, remain faithful to their symbolic natures, and do not partake of the incidents in the allegorical sections—immediately breaking the unity of symbol and allegory. Indeed, throughout most of the book one tends to forget their existence except for the mechanical reminders. Yet these three symbolic characters are the least human, least flexible, most artificial and apparently allegorical characters in the book. Because of the bastardization of techniques, the reader very quickly becomes unsure of which meanings are yet to be disclosed and which meanings are established and constant—but which he has missed. Consequently, much of the narrative functionally is poorly related to the symbolism, and symbol, story, and allegory get in each other's way. What happens is inevitable. The book falls apart. With the narrative level neglected (except for the mechanical necessities for making characters speak and act) the symbolism is literally disembodied. Point of view is confused. The real world, where narrative level is still important, is divorced from the Mardian world. The Mardian world is in turn split by a division of the major characters who, at any given time, happen to be in control of the bulk of the dialogue and action. Thus there is the "factual" symbolic beginning; the symbolic, unreal Taji-Yillah-Hautia tale; and the allegorical-symbolic Media-Babbalanja tale. Indeed, because the symbolism grows out of the narrative level in the "factual" beginning, that section of the book, which many readers pronounced expendable (and except for its symbolism most of it is expendable), is the most successful part of the book. The rest of the book's symbolism suffers not only from allegory but also from the artificiality that is a consequence of its separation from the narrative level.

A further conclusion is that the fragmentation of the book and the resulting artificiality of symbol and of pseudo-allegorical diction are a consequence of Melville's loss of control over *Mardi's* ideas. He thought he was creating allegorical figures by means of which he could impose idea, begin from idea. But symbolism is a technique of exploration, not imposition. Melville's motivating perception of values determined the symbols, but he discovered that he was suggesting modifications and new meanings at every turn, and he did not have those ideas well enough in hand to control them with true symbolic craftsmanship. So he sank the narration and put what he had into a leaky boat of dialogue to let his characters talk out the mass of meanings accruing from the quest, from the symbolic center of Taji's career. He discovered that a writer must be craftsman enough to understand the power of the symbol, or it would control him and he would not control it. So he kept his meanings channeled by pure statement, and in this manner he managed to salvage a consistently formed theme from malformed structure. He could save his theme only by destroying his novel, and he did. As a result, *Mardi* is a huge, disorganized essay whose statement is buttressed and interrupted by the occasional, disjointed, and recurrent passages of a submerged symbolic novel.

In one important sense, then, the structural failure of *Mardi* is a reflection of Melville's naturalistic perception. He was unsuccessful in attempting to create symbolism which proceeded from the idealistic fount of pure idea or absolute concept, symbolism which Emerson and Thoreau could create. Emerson buttressed ideas with other ideas and wrote essays. Thoreau buttressed ideas with natural experience and almost wrote novels. When Melville used natural experience as a buttress instead of a fount, his books broke down into illustrated essays, but when experience, the narrative "fact," was the fount, he succeeded beyond his wildest expectations. There is as rich an amount of symbolic "business" in *Mardi* as in *Moby-Dick*. But in *Moby-Dick* the conditionings of historical experience are one with the narrative level from which symbol derives meaning. The gams in *Moby-Dick* and the voyage in *Mardi* are the same trick, serve the same purpose. In *Moby-Dick* the gams are introduced with almost the same regularity with which the visited isles are introduced in *Mardi*. But the gams are defined by Ahab's quest at the same time that they redefine Ahab's quest. No particular gam makes an allegorical definition of any particular character who has his own story divorced from Ahab's and Ishmael's; no particular gam can be lifted out of the general symbolism or general narrative of the total book and be assigned to any subdivision. The "ballast" in *Moby-Dick* becomes the narrative, or factual, or historical conditioning which channels meaning without pure essay. It grows symbolic meaning and becomes indispensable symbolic matter that gives the book unity by welding idea to narration, perception to form, form to technique, so that finally perception, narration, form, technique and meaning are all one entity, the total book.

The idealistic perception presupposes an absolute but not necessarily specific relationship between meaning and matter. Allegory is a matter of equation; symbolism is a matter of association. And idealistic perception is, at first, a perception of equation. The equation is one between matter and spiritual meaning, a view of matter as the expositer of God's mind *which provides directive meaning for human behavior.* For instance, when idealist sees "tree," regardless of context, tree is God, or absolute meaning. Tree is not determined by context, but by the imposition of idea: the idealist's presupposition creates a perception that is basically allegorical. Certainly, this is not to say that idealism is allegorical and naturalism is symbolic. The "naturalism" of the 1930's and 1940's is closer to social history realistically fictionalized than to symbolism. And Emerson, the idealist, rejected Swedenborg because Swedenborg would make allegorical equations between particular aspects of matter and particular aspects of God. Emerson insisted that nature is a symbol of God, not an allegory. But his basic presupposition (nature equals absolute meaning that provides direction for human behavior) is fully as allegorical, as much an equation, as Swedenborg's—on that basic equation both agree. Indeed, in the 1840's, when Emerson began to redefine the equation according to experience, he almost became, in a sense, naturalistic. Thoreau lost his highest "reality," became unsure of the basic equation. He wrote *Walden* in an attempt to prove again for himself what he had been sure of emotionally in the past. And, in a sense, he too became almost naturalistic. But his scientific use of nature was used to regain faith (with the loss of which he struggled—the bay horse, the hound, the dove) in the basic presupposition which he did not reject. He struggled heroically to rediscover the lost joy which comes with belief in the idealistic equation, and this struggle was the vocation which he intended in his life in the woods. Rejecting specific equations, the idealist may create symbols upon his fundamental presupposition, just as Thoreau adds the ice on the pond or the chimney of his house to his basic view of general nature. The transcendentalist was not really interested in redefining God as much as he was interested in redefining self, in finding the Godself-creation made possible by his perception. But though his emphasis was on man, on the creativity of man's mind, the emphasis proceeded from the idealistic equation. He may reject institutional religion, may lose faith, may have to redefine his belief, but he never loses the concept of his idealistic presupposition. Consequently he can transcend history itself, matter itself, can find nowhere in the universe anything that is not part of an absolute meaning which provides direction for human behavior.

And it was precisely this equation that Melville rejected. The non-idealistic, or naturalistic perception sees "tree" as a zero, a blank. The blank is not filled in with symbolic meaning that arises from allegorical presupposition, for there is no presupposition. The blank is filled with meaning that arises from the natural context which can only be defined in the history that holds tree and viewer. Melville has Babbalanja report that heaven has no roof, that the very concepts which result in the idea of beatitude, of spiritual union with the All, are erroneous. Melville has Pip fall into the sea, and at the moment that he has Pip see that there are elements in the universe which make it impossible for man to make equations between nature and absolute, directive, spiritual meaning, at that moment he has Pip see—God. When Melville writes these things, he says that there are mysteries in existence which make it impossible to transcend man's own historical context because in his perception experience teaches that once man leaves that context, there is no absolute meaning to which humanity can transcend. He asserts that precisely by the transcendental argument in which man creates his own meanings, that meaning comes from below, from earth, is relative, is historical, and is not a transcendent absolute which allows nature to be seen as an exponent of directive meaning that pervades existence as an ideal and ultimate reality. If a man does not have a science or a politic with which to replace the idealistic equation, a man often will be bitter. As was Melville. He will have a sense of irony and paradox, a sense that man has been robbed of and by what he idealistically considers to be his greatest identity. As did Melville. Significantly, in all Melville's works, the joys—often Rabelaisian—are the joys of earth, material, personal, historical. As Rosenberry pointed out, when Melville's comic spirit is light and buoyant it centers upon the material joys of food, drink, and sex, the personal joys of the joke, of reading, of intellectual development, the historical joy of occasional social justice.[29] Fortunately, it was this sense of life, which his naturalism offered, that furnished the balance which kept Melville from being swept into the complete darkness of a sense of loss, which his naturalism impended. Melville's world, like his Encantada tortoise, is both black and bright. Inversely, with this natural world the only world there is, Melville's rage at social injustice is black and furious. Sometimes the universe furnishes positive meaning for man, but such meaning is disclosed not by idealism, but by the infant science, the technology which Melville rejected as a puny instrument for his own

---

[29] Edward H. Rosenberry, *Melville and the Cosmic Spirit* (Cambridge, Mass., 1955), *passim*.

time. Sometimes the universe presents negative meaning; it presents sharks and men who are loathsome. But sometimes the universe presents a meaning which is meaninglessness; it presents Moby-Dick, and the meaning of his blank whiteness is blank whiteness. For man, this is neither joyous nor loathsome; it is the central, freezing terror and awe of existence. The whole point is that the mistaken idealist, Ahab, once he leaves his historical context, is killed by the meaninglessness which cannot exist according to the idealist's equation—but which kills him. If the universe is a product of the All, it is not an expositor of the mind of the All because it does not provide absolute spiritual meaning which can direct man. If the universe is an expositor of the mind of the All, then God himself, all creation, is positively meaningful, negatively meaningful, meaningless and relative; and it is up to man to choose his expositions according to his relative, historical needs. In any case, experience of the natural world—and not the idealistic equation through which such experience may be viewed —is the basis of perception. When Vere stares at the blank sea he sees blankness. Occasioned by relative historical needs (which in turn have been occasioned by all the consequences of the fact of the blankness), Vere's pain and anger is Melville's. The pain and anger of *Billy Budd* is first seen in *Mardi*, whose rejection of the idealistic presupposition is Melville's first conscious attempt to express his perception, his first explanation of everything that is to follow. It is only in this light that the incomplete *Billy Budd* really can be understood.

Not only are the meanings of the universe relative for Melville, but so also are the social meanings of man's true context, the historical. Melville, deprived of a basic equation, digs with his own nonidealistic insight into the beginningless symbolism of historical experience. There is no beginning point in Melville's perception. There is a beginning point in either of the two sides of an equation; there is a beginning point in allegory. And there is no beginning point in the development of symbolic meaning. Symbol one may have meaning A; symbol two may have meanings B and D; symbol three may have meaning C, and so on. But after symbols two and three are seen, because of the relationships of A, B, C, and D, symbol one no longer has the constant meaning of A. As each symbol is discovered, each symbol changes and grows. And as certain central, more inclusive symbols are discovered, symbol one may no longer even turn out to be symbol one, and may be seen in relation to meanings X, Y, Z and all the infinite possibilities beyond Z. Consequently, every practicing critic agrees that after he has exhausted a successful symbolic work, he knows that anyone else may find something new just as the author knows that he can never be completely conscious of everything he has created. In the practical work of applied criticism there is always a beginning point for analysis whether the technique analyzed is symbolic or allegorical. But this beginning point depends more upon the inexplicable moment in which the critic gains his first important insight than upon the techniques themselves, for hardly any two minds will attack the given job in precisely the same patterns. But the job itself has no beginning and no end, because symbolic relationships (meanings) have no beginning and no end—they only have direction.

The author's perception gives the symbolic relationships a controlled and controlling motion, or energy, and he must translate the control into words with every last bit of craftsmanship at his disposal. By its very nature, symbolism is high powered and unstable, and may break up into charged but chaotic fragments. When one reads successful allegory, meaning is crystallized and hardened with each new discovery. When one reads successful symbolism, meaning shifts, grows, changes with each new discovery. Consequently critics attempt to arrive at an explanation of symbol by emphasizing irony, or paradox, or point of view. In allegory the point of view has to be fairly constant. In symbolism meaning arises not only from relationships between what is viewed, but also from the relationship between what is viewed and the point of view, which itself becomes a shifting thing rather than an absolute from which meaning can be absolutely limited or determined. Point of view becomes, perhaps, the major controlling guide, and in this consideration can be guessed the far-reaching extent of *Mardi's* breakdown. The divorce between technique and perception is central, for Melville's naturalism is relativistic in precisely the same way that symbolism is. In short, *Mardi's* disintegration suggests that certain perceptions (themes) are better suited to certain techniques than to others; that in fact they may be most successful only by uniting with a particular technique. In this sense it is not surprising that although symbolistic technique had widely disparate practitioners, naturalistic perception and symbolistic technique began to flower in American letters roughly at the same time. The Newtonian universe, for instance, is a perfect allegory. And symbolism was not an eighteenth-century technique. The Einsteinian universe is a perfect symbol, and symbolism is a consciously modern technique. Certainly, Melville's age demanded that relativism should precede Einstein just as his age demanded that evolution should precede Darwin. In their symbolism Emerson and Melville were united and antagonistic. They were united in their estimation of the primacy of the human mind. They were antagonistic in defining the relationships between that mind and the exterior universe. Because idealism needed new terms and new perspectives, Emerson's symbolism is a focal point for an understanding of the liberation of thought in nineteenth-century romanticism. Because existence began to need measurements of force and motion rather than absolute definitions, Melville's symbolism is a focal point for an understanding of the change from the supranatural and the ideal and the individual to the material and the natural and the social. Impelled by a fluid universe, Emerson's liberating words solidify into an organic symbolism, which is as firm as the constant moral nature of a unific cosmos for which all definitions become one. Paradoxically impelled by the same new universe, Melville's fluid words remain fluid in a relative symbolism which is as shifting as the inconstant moral nature of a cosmos which has a new definition with each new context.

II

When we turn from the narrative structure to symbol, we discover a more organized, if independent, Mardi. *Mardi* opens exactly as does *Typee*. The protagonist is weary of a stale sea cruise, and his weariness leads him to disclose his characteristics. He is set apart from the ship's community. He differs from his shipmates in desires and sensibilities. "And what to me," he says, "thus pining for some one who could page me a quotation from Burton on Blue Devils; what to me, indeed, were flat repetitions of long-drawn yarns, and the everlasting stanzas of Black-eyed Suzan sung by our full forecastle choir? Staler than stale ale." In the commitments of daily men and daily living he does not find the kind of existence he would like.

The sailors were good fellows all, the half-score of pagans we had shipped at the islands included. Nevertheless, they were not precisely to my mind. There was no soul a magnet to mine; none with whom to mingle sympathies; save in deploring the calms. . . . Under other and livelier auspices the tarry knaves might have developed qualities more attractive. . . . But as it was, there was naught to strike fire from their steel. . . .

Ay, ay, Arcturion! I say it in no malice, but thou wast exceedingly dull. Not only at sailing: hard though it was, that I could have borne; but in every other respect . . . ye lost and leaden hours, I will rail at ye while life lasts [p. 3].

Temper-tossed Taji displays the characteristics of the quest figure early in the book.[30] Life-as-is is a waste of time for him. His view is exalted, and in a curious bit of dialogue indicative of the quester's attitude toward men's lot, the captain and Taji illuminate the motivations for the quester's actions. " 'Captain,' said I, touching my sombrero to him as I stood at the wheel one day, 'It's very hard to carry me off this way to purgatory. I shipped to go elsewhere.'

" 'Yes, and so did I,' was his reply. 'But it can't be helped. . . .' "

Taji will not accept the captain's view of possibilities. The quester has visions of heaven. For him, the very fact of existence points toward more ideal being. If he doesn't like the direction which the world

---

[30] For one possible but not very revealing explanation of Taji's name, see Davis, p. 69.

takes, with its dullness and calms and actualities, then regardless of responsibilities or consequences, he will abandon it. Again, as in *Typee*, the protagonist is introduced as the isolato who wishes to absent himself from either the cruelty or the dusty deadness of society in order to find himself a Golden Age paradise.[31]

Taji-not-yet-named-Taji gazes off into vaults of sky. He drifts loose from the hampering cables of this mother-ship of his own world. The *Arcturion*, the "maternal heart of oak" is the society of the earthly world. And as early as we can see Taji, he carries his visions, "towing argosies by the score," trembling, gasping, and straining in flight to go beyond the shoals (mortal limitations), which are, "like nebulous vapors, shoreing the white reef of the Milky Way, against which the wrecked [historical] worlds are dashed." At first the unnamed Taji's frenzy is not apparent. But as he watches the arching gateways to another world, he evinces his predisposition to leave this world, and then he states his frenzy.

In the distance what visions were spread! The entire western horizon piled high with gold and crimson clouds; airy arches, domes and minarets; as if the yellow Moorish sun were setting behind some vast Alhambra. Vistas seemed leading to worlds beyond. To and fro, and all over the towers of this Nineveh in the sky, flew troops of birds. Watching them long, one crossed my sight, flew through a low arch, and was lost to view. My spirit must have sailed in with it; for directly, as in a trance, came upon me the cadence of mild billows laving a beach of shells, the waving of boughs, and the voices of maidens, and the lulled beatings of my own dissolved heart, all blended together.

Now, all this, to be plain, was but one of the many visions one has up aloft. But coming upon me at this time, it wrought upon me so, that thenceforth my desire to quit the Arcturion became little short of a frenzy [pp. 6-7].

This is really Taji's first view of Yillah. The predisposition to find her is apparent before it can be objectfied in the meeting with her. But predisposition will be activated in the desertion from the *Arcturion* long before Yillah is introduced. In being born, the quester believes, as a human he has signed for heaven and will gain it by escalade if need be, or he will make no voyage at all. Taji knows beforehand that because of his relationship with the historical world, and because of his view of it, he will desert it. Again, as in *Typee*, the legal

---

[31] See the unpublished dissertation (Yale, 1947) by J. R. Baird, "Herman Melville and Primitivism." For primitivism, Baird stresses the Golden Age, without, however, a development of the possibility of classicist thought inherent therein. Although Baird identifies Melville's use of primitives with primitivism, Melville cannot really be considered a primitivist unless the term is extended to include anyone who uses primitive characters. Both *Typee* and *Billy Budd* demonstrate that the primitivist's Golden Age, or Eden, is not a goal for Melville's thought. Since this writing, Mr. Baird has published his book, *Ishmael* (Baltimore, 1956). It must be pointed out that there is a considerable difference between Baird's discussion in his dissertation and in his book.

niceties are the surface appearances that are only a cover for the real motives beneath the desertion and the journey into "worlds beyond." At the moment he thinks of stealing one of the ship's boats in order to desert, Taji waives the legalities in the same breath with which he invokes them. Nor do the legalities and appearances have the same strength they had in *Typee*, where the captain was a brute.[32] "My first thoughts," says Taji, "were of the boat to be obtained, and the right or wrong of abstracting it, under the circumstances. But to split no hairs on this point, let me say now that were I placed in the same situation again, I would repeat the thing I did then. The captain well knew that he was going to detain me unlawfully; against our agreement; and it was he himself who threw out the very hint which I merely adopted, with many thinks to him." In will and predisposition, the Taji who quests through the allegorical archipelago is the same man who abandoned the "real" *Arcturion*. Much later in the book, during the search for Yillah, Taji is shot at and missed by the avengers of Aleema. Taji examines the arrow and says, "Then it missed its aim. But I will not mine. And whatever arrows follow, still will I hunt on. Nor does the ghost, that these pale specters would avenge, at all disquiet me. The priest I slew but to gain her, now lost; and I would slay again to bring her back." Just as Jarl is at first shocked by Taji's revelation of his decision to abandon the *Arcturion*, so Taji's companions are shocked by his revelation of predesigning and murderous will. This same will prevails upon Jarl to help in the act of withdrawal:

> At last he very bluntly declared that the scheme was a crazy one; he had never known of such a thing but thrice before; and in every case the runaways had never afterwards been heard of. He entreated me to renounce my determination, not be a boy, pause and reflect, stick to the ship, and go home in her like a man. . . .
> But to all this I turned a deaf ear; affirming that my mind was made up; and that as he refused to accompany me, and I fancied no one else for a comrade, I would go stark alone, rather than not at all . . . [p. 15].

By the end of Chapter V the character is settled in a mold that never changes throughout the course of the book. As a "man overboard" never afterwards heard of, Taji "dies" to the world of the *Arcturion*. For a while he is a new figure, that of the omoo, or wanderer, aboard the *Chamois*. Then for the first time he becomes captain of the means which can direct his fate when he becomes master of the *Parki*. This life, in turn, "dies" with the sinking of the ship, which, with its Typeean verdant and primitive qualities, was not the vessel for the course of Taji's fate. After the meeting with Yillah, he emerges as

---

[32] Davis points out that the captain of the *Arcturion* is the only captain in the early books who is not a brute. Thus Melville makes Taji's invocation of legalities yet more morally untenable as a justification for the quest.

the christened Taji, a white god from the sun, and this new life, which in its pretentious other-worldly origin is an association with ideality, is the protagonist's major role throughout the rest of the book. However, Taji never undergoes any character change as would be suggested by the immersions in water, the suggested cycle of death and rebirth. He simply changes external identity. *He kills his historical existence in order to pursue his symbolic quest.*

In Taji we have the monomaniac, the quest figure in full stature. He stocks up for pursuit of his private vision by stealing from the world community of the *Arcturion*. He steals as Tommo did and as Ahab did, when Ahab tacitly deceived the shipowners about the purpose for which the *Pequod* was provisioned. The plunder of the means of existence sets up conditions which have been adumbrated in *Typee,* for again in *Mardi* we find that no one willingly allows the quester to transfer worlds. The quester must be a stealthy liar. The world is more concerned with its own status quo and with its own existence than with the quester's attainment of his private vision. The quester, on the other hand, scorns the world's existence because he scorns the conditions of human existence, and he places his individual relationship to the ideal as the highest value in the cosmos. The act of pilfering is symbolic of the spoilation and loss that accompanies the idealistic action which, though negatively motivated by the actualities of the historical world, is not brought to bear upon them. In thematic scope, *Mardi* brings this consideration one step further than did *Typee.* Whereas a change of worlds in *Typee* is chronological, in *Mardi* it is ontological. Tommo's plunge from his western world is a change in time, but Taji's plunge is a change in being. Taji attempts to substitute a non-earthly heaven and ideal for earth and history. The "man-overboard" plunge from the historical world is the first death, the first suicide of self, and the first possible murder of that world. It is accompanied by the remorse and guilt which call for the salve of legal niceties. That these niceties never stop the pursuit of guilt is sometimes stated and often implied, as in Chapter VII ("A Pause"): "And for myself I am almost tempted to hang my head, that I escaped the fate of my shipmates; something like him who blushed to have escaped the fell carnage at Thermopylae.

"Though I cannot repress a shudder when I think of that old ship's end, it is impossible for me so much as to imagine, that our deserting her could have been in any way instrumental in her loss. Nevertheless, I would to Heaven the Arcturion still floated; that it was given me once more to tread her familiar decks."

It is futile to conjecture whether or not two men posted in the right places at the right time would have saved the *Arcturion*. But it is important that Taji's psychological mechanism of repression does not work as well as he says it does, that underlying his absolution of his own sin is the undying shudder of guilt. It is especially important that this early in the book, because Taji acts like a "boy" rather than like a "man" (for all Jarl's sententiousness), quest and guilt, idealism and the death of the historical world, are immediately associated.

Accompanying the stealing, suicide, and murder, there is another deceit. Taji has to make all the plans, for Jarl is too honest and simple for well-executed indirections. Taji confounds his shipmates with a darkly premonitory call of death upon the midnight sea. The "man overboard!" is not only an obituary, but it is also the lie by which Taji manages his escape. He perverts the usage of the means by which life preserves itself, and later that life is extinguished. The deceit that accompanies all of Taji's words, directed as they are toward the monomania of his vision, becomes a blasphemy against the principle of life and not the redemption traditionally associated with ideality.

When Jarl and Taji board the *Parki*, Samoa tells his story in candid detail, thinking that Taji may be a supernatural being. Taji projects his own deceit to Samoa and at first does not believe a single word. He cloaks himself in the mystery that has fortuitously surrounded him, and assumes a superiority which will further as much as possible the desires of his own unyielding will.

My own curiosity satisfied with respect to the brigantine, Samoa himself turned inquisitor. He desired to know who we were; and whence we came in our marvelous boat. But on these heads I thought it best to withhold from him the truth; among other things, fancying that if disclosed, it would lessen his deference for us, as men superior to himself. I therefore spoke vaguely of our adventures, and assumed the decided air of a master; which I perceived was not lost upon the rude Islander. As for Jarl, and what he might reveal, I embraced the first opportunity to impress upon him the importance of never divulging our flight from the Arcturion; nor in any way to commit himself on that head; injunctions which he faithfully promised to observe [p. 77].

Of course Taji has done nothing to prove that he is a better man than the islander upon whose hospitality he intrudes. Yet he gains ascendency over Samoa by means of an implicit lie which is a wordless renunciation of his true historical origins and earthly being. And he uses Jarl's loyalty in a way which makes a dupe out of the honest man, and which finally results in the dupe's death. Melville's first Ahab, Taji is a false and dehumanized Prometheus. When remorse does come to Taji, it is dismissed as quickly as it is by Ahab.

Immediately following his murder of Aleema, Taji feels regret. But at the very instant of realization, he covers his guilt with an inapplicable appeal to appearance (as with the stealing of the boat and provisions) which discloses the selfish will that is the real motivating force.

What iron mace fell upon my soul; what curse rang sharp in my ear! It was I, who was the author of the deed that caused the shrill wails that

I heard. By this hand, the man had died. Remorse smote me hard; and like lightning I asked myself, whether the death-deed I had done was sprung of a virtuous motive, the rescuing a captive from thrall; or whether beneath that pretense, I had engaged in this fatal affray for some other, and selfish purpose; the companionship of a beautiful maid. But throttling the thought, I swore to be gay. Am I not rescuing the maiden? Let them go down who withstand me [pp. 119-20].

Murder, deceit and flight are extended and concretely realized in action when Taji obtains Yillah. The quest itself is attended by murder even before Taji engages in it: the wronged man, Aleema, had himself committed murder in keeping Yillah, and murder had been committed in gaining her. The entire history of the desire for the ideal is steeped in murder, guilt, and revenge. There is no evidence that Melville is saying that an informing vision translated into violence cannot be good. In fact the opposite may be true, for at the end of the book the enlightened Media plunges into possible violence, as conditions dictate, in order to gain a correct social goal. What Melville does say, however, in his development of the quester's career, is that the man who is motivated as Taji is motivated, the man who strives for ideality, is not the man who will bring peace out of violence or order out of chaos. Because of the death of historical world and self in the "factual" introduction, we expect that death will result from Taji's quest. And with every new view of the attempt to gain Yillah, there is an incremental addition of sin to sin.

Devoted to ideality, the quester is isolated from history and more and more feverishly tries to attain what, to him, is the ultimate reality. As *Typee* foresaw, and as the later books confirm, the quester is an insomniac. Aboard the *Parki*, Taji tries to prod his fellows into wakefulness at night in order to keep the ship ploughing on in the direction which his monomania pursues. He complains that the other men allow physical necessities to intervene. "For Samoa, his drowsiness was the drowsiness of one bent on sleep, come dreams or death. He seemed insensible to the perils we ran. Often I sent the sleepy savage below and steered myself till morning. At last I made a point of slumbering much by day, the better to stand watch by night; though I made Samoa and Jarl regularly go through with their allotted four hours each." We know from *Typee* what sleep and wakefulness represent. And Jarl, though not possessed of the death which is the sleep-unconsciousness of the Typee savage, is closer to the values of land-humanity than to the superhuman values of the obsessed and sleepless searoving quester: "Though in all else, the Skyeman proved a most faithful ally, in this one thing he was either perversely obtuse, or infatuated. Or, perhaps, finding himself once more in a double-decked craft, which rocked him as of yore, he was lulled into a deceitful security." Here is the irony of the master deceiver trying to realize his enormous vision. The sleepless awareness of "deceitful security" is the quester's one strong point, the one point at which quester and Melville agree about the tricks that the world and nature can play upon man. Concerned as the quester is with piercing the appearances of existence in order to strike through to an ultimate reality beyond existence, he is more aware than most of human sham and of man's precarious position in the universe. Engaged in his search, his concern with this world is negative; it is the circumventing of events that would deter or wreck his quest. Jarl, however, is quite a different creature.

Jarl is important for two major reasons. First of all, Jarl helps illustrate the shifting patterns of Melville's symbolic imagery. Secondly, it is partly through Jarl that Yillah is defined. "Jarl hailed from the Isle of Skye, one of the constellated Hebrides. Hence, they often called him the Skyeman . . . his long yellow hair waved round his head like a sunset. My life for it, Jarl, thy ancestors were Vikings . . . and are now quaffing mead in the halls of Valhalla, and beating time with their cans to hymns of the Scalds." Jarl is a Skyeman—a proposition seductive to the Melville student. He is fairhaired, like Billy Budd, and the mention of his ancestors relates Jarl at once to sea-quest and a heavenly other-world. He is in alien surroundings, which hints at the isolato. His complexion is dark, like Ahab's, and he is silent. Because of this apparent similarity to a familiar pattern of Melvillean characterization-imagery, Jarl appears to be the isolato—perhaps a quester, perhaps a lure.

No lady-like scruples had he, the old Viking, about marring his complexion, which was already more than bronzed. Over the ordinary tanning of the sailor, he seemed masked by a visor of japanning, dotted all over with freckles, so intensely yellow, and symmetrically circular, that they seemed scorched there by a burning glass [pp. 29-30].

But Jarl, dear, dumb Jarl. . . . Thou didst carry a phiz like an excommunicated deacon's. And no matter what happened, it was ever the same.

I longed for something enlivening; a burst of words; human vivacity of one kind or another. After in vain essaying to get something of this sort out of Jarl, I tried it all by myself . . . till my Viking stared hard; and I myself paused to consider whether I had run crazy or no [pp. 30-31].

Also tempting is a descriptive similarity to Fedallah and Ahab. Jarl, with his streaming yellow hair, is the dark man topped with fairness, like Fedallah with his shroud-white turban. Jarl, with his yellow freckles, is the man burned with light marks, like Ahab with his pale scar. If we wished to find a changeless meaning for Melville's patterns of imagery, we should say that Jarl is another quester. And we would be completely wrong.

Jarl's relation to immortality is no different than that of the great majority of the quester's world mates. Unlike Yillah, who has memories of another life, and unlike Taji, who has visions of worlds beyond, Jarl is conscious only of his terrestrial existence, and this existence is all that fills his memories of his origins. "Now, among the crew was a fine old seaman, one Jarl; how old, no one could ever tell, not even himself. Forecastle chronology is ever vague and defective. 'Man and boy,' said honest Jarl, 'I have lived ever since I can remember.' And truly, who can call to mind when he was not? To ourselves, we all seem coeval with creation. Whence it comes, that it is so hard to die, ere the world itself is departed." The last three sentences of this passage are to become explanations of the *hubris* which prompts Taji's individualism. The agelessness of Jarl is to be representative of the agelessness of general mortality.

As for Jarl's being alone and alien, at the very moment this aspect of his existence is given, it is negated by a passage which makes Jarl one with all men in all time.

Yet Jarl, the descendant of heroes and kings, was a lone, friendless mariner on the main, only true to his origin in the sea-life that he led. But so it has been and forever will be. What yeoman shall swear that he is not descended from Alfred? What dunce, that he is not sprung of old Homer? King Noah, God bless him, fathered us all. Then hold up your hands, oh ye Helots, blood potential flows through your veins. All of us have monarchs and sages for kinsmen; nay, angels and archangels for cousins; since in antediluvian days, the sons of God did verily wed with our mothers, the irresistible daughters of Eve. Thus all generations are blended: and heaven and earth of one kin: the hierarchies of seraphs in the uttermost skies; the thrones and principalities in the Zodiac; the shades that roam through space; the nations and families, flocks and folds of the earth; one and all brothers in essence—oh, be we then brothers indeed! [p. 10].

Here is the quester's cosmic democracy, which—except for the last fervent exclamation—is more concerned with the democracy of essence than with the democracy of fact. Taji's actions and characteristics belie his devotion to democracy of fact (again, it was a bad plan for Melville to merge the quester and the narrator). But it is important that it is from the denial of Jarl's differentness that there arises a statement of the common, human brotherhood of mortality and the belief that the whole world is the patrimony of the whole world.

And what of Jarl's silence? Is his the special Ahab-language which so hypnotizes the crew? Is it the silence or the stutter which is the mark of the lure like the dumb whale, or Isabel or Yillah or Billy Budd? When Jarl does speak, he speaks not the language of quest or ideality, but the language of common and earthbound humanity. "Now, in old Jarl's lingo there was never an idiom. Your aboriginal tar is too much of a cosmopolitan for that. Long companionship with seamen of all tribes: Manilla-men, Anglo-Saxons, Cholos, Lascars, and Danes, wear away in good time all your mother tongue stammerings. You sink your clan; down goes your nation; you speak a world's language, jovially jabbering in the Lingua-Franka of the forecastle." Jarl is no wanderer after other-worlds, nor is he a soarer or a diver into the mysteries of this world's phenomena. Jarl knows nothing of books or geography, cares not at all that a messmate cannot page him a quotation from Burton on Blue Devils, and he cares not that he knows not. His association with the sea is not the association of mind with the metaphysical mysteries of existence, but rather it is the association of the sailor with his work, the care of the earthman that he "act like a man" and perform the labors of his position as well as possible. "True to his calling, the Skyeman was very illiterate." His silence is the silence of the simple man who knows his own business and minds it well. "Ah, Jarl! an honest, earnest wight; so true and simple, that the secret operations of thy soul were more inscrutable than the subtle workings of Spinoza's. Quietly, in thyself, thou didst revolve upon thine own sober axis, like a wheel in a machine which forever goes round, whether you look at it or no. Ay, Jarl! wast thou not forever intent upon minding that which so many neglect—thine own special business. Wast thou not forever at it, too, with no likelihood of ever winding up thy moody affairs, and striking a balance sheet?" His silence has nothing to do with yearnings or philosophical reachings. His moody affairs are metaphysically hollow, which will prove to be his greatest limitation. Jarl's dignity, Taji's foil though he is, is the dignity which, for Melville as well as his romantic contemporaries, gives nobility to the simple and sincere workman, part of the dignity which creates respect for *White-Jacket's* Jack Chase, who is certainly not intellectually empty as is Jarl. "But how account for the Skyeman's gravity? surely it was based on no philosophic taciturnity; he was nothing of an idealist; an aerial architect; a constructor of flying buttresses. It was inconcievable, that his reveries were Manfred-like and exalted, reminiscent of unutterable deeds, too mysterious to be indicated by the remotest of hints. Suppositions all out of the question."

Jarl's most prominent characteristics are honesty, simplicity, and loyalty. It is the outstanding loyalty to friend, even taking precedence over loyalty to work, which accounts for Jarl's friendship with Taji. In an almost parenthetical aside, Taji reveals that his higher and most important interests are not shared by Jarl. "Now, higher sympathies apart, for Jarl I had a wonderful liking; for he loved me; from the first had cleaved to me." The relationship which binds Jarl to Taji has nothing to do with quest generally or with Taji's quest specifically. Rather the relationship is part of the motif of spoilation and pilfering, for Taji "chummies" with Jarl simply because that workhorse will perform for him all the necessary labors of historical existence. True to his own prime characteristics, Taji's reasons for chummying with Jarl are wrapped in self and will—"for he loved *me*; from the first had cleaved to *me*."[33]

---

[33] See *Mardi*, pp. 12-13, for Jarl's and Taji's chummying. For Taji it is almost all take and little give.

So far, Jarl is an emblem of the earnest, common, and sometimes foolishly simple humanity of the workaday world. It is this emblem that is manipulated to obey the will of the quester, and whose death is finally caused by that will. Taji always scrutinizes Jarl with a Machiavellian disinterestedness which underlies the amused affection that the master has for the body servant. Even in jest, the visionary sees the Skyeman, who is entirely the Earthman, as an expendable object and perhaps victim of the quest itself. Says Taji, "In the tragico-comico moods which at times overtook me, I used to look upon the brown Skyeman with humorous complacency. If we fall in with cannibals, thought I, then, ready roasted Norseman that thou art, shall I survive to mourn thee; at least during the period I revolve upon the spit." And of course while Taji is spitted upon his own will, roasted over the hellfire of his own torments, pursued by the cannibalism of a vengeful orthodoxy, that is precisely what happens.

There are other characteristics which allow for a more specific definition of Jarl. It is Jarl, for instance, who is concerned that the water should last. In contrast to his companion of the chartless wandering, it is Jarl who makes a secure hiding place for the compass (which is likened to a human eye), and who is fearful that they might lose the compass and flint. It is Jarl who suggests that they row in case of a calm—a suggestion of homely and necessary work from which Taji shrinks. It is Jarl who keeps track of time by cutting a daily notch in his oar handle. It is Jarl's shoe that serves as a water dipper. It is Jarl, not Taji, who is concerned with the empirical means of life and work, with the maintenance of the boat, with the needs for keeping warmth, time, and direction. Taji, who reclines and philosophizes in the stern, however, keeps control of the voyage's direction at the same time that he is amused by Jarl's concern with historical existence. He cannot understand the worries of the empirical self. He says, "Oh! Jarl, Jarl; to me in the boat's quiet stern, steering and philosophizing at one time and the same, thou and thy [water] breaker were a study." Taji holds himself above the demands of time and circumstance upon the mortal condition; Jarl is always concerned with those demands only.

Jarl is also industrious and thrifty. He stitches and darns and knits. In order to keep his thirst at a minimum and to conserve water, he foregoes his chewing tobacco—tobacco and liquor being his only two indulgences. He is also superstitious. He believes that the pilot fish are a good omen. He believes that the abandoned *Parki* is a ghost ship piloted by specters. Yet true to his thrifty character, he will not be deterred from the main chance. Finding a bag of coins aboard the *Parki*, Jarl rings the gold pieces. "Sounded on the chest lid, the dollars rang clear as convent bells. These were put aside by Jarl; the sight of substantial dollars doing away, for the nonce, with his superstitious misgivings," and the material taking precedence over the supernatural.

Jarl, who was never anxious to withdraw from the world, is most anxious to rejoin it. When they sight the *Parki* in the distance, Taji and Jarl at first think it is a whaler. Jarl wishes to hail it and rejoin humanity. Taji wishes to avoid it in order to pursue no course but his own. "To be sure, we could not be certain what kind of a vessel it was; but whatever it might be, I, for one, had no mind to risk an encounter; for it was quite plain, that if the stranger came within hailing distance, there would be no resource but to link our fortunes with hers; whereas I desired to pursue none but the *Chamois*'. As for the Skyeman, he kept looking wistfully over his shoulder; doubtless, praying Heaven, that we might not escape what I sought to avoid."

The adjectives which emerge from the total presentation of Jarl are clear. He is the honest, simple, loyal, frugal, industrious, superstitious, gregarious, and earnest workingman. Despite his satirized bourgeois qualities, which are sometimes reminiscent of the worst in Ben Franklin, Jarl remains essentially the devoted drone who performs the world's necessary work. It is this man who is first to take the action that gives the *Parki's* occupants time to abandon ship before it founders in a storm. When Taji takes Yillah to a secluded islet off the mainland of Odo, Jarl maintains his loyalty to Taji and his membership in humanity. Not wanted now by Taji, and thus not prompted to desertion, he does not abandon the mainland this time, but builds his wigwam on the shore, facing Taji's island retreat.

Most important, Jarl is the only character in *Mardi* who is not impressed by Yillah. His hardheaded and practical humanity never allows him to become interested in the other-world object of Taji's quest. Contrasting Jarl's behavior toward Yillah with the behavior displayed by everyone else, Taji asks, "But what of my Viking? Why, of good Jarl I grieve to say, that the old-fashioned interest he took in my affairs led him to look upon Yillah as a sort of intruder, *an ammonite siren who might lead me astray*. This would now and then provoke a phillipic; but he would only turn toward my resentment his devotion; and then I was silent" [italics mine]. But Jarl is inoperative in preventing Taji's quest, for he is like the mother hen who can only cluck helplessly at the actions of the duckling she has hatched. Admiring in Taji the brilliance which he himself lacks, Jarl can only allow his simple loyalty to develop into his final character trait, resignation. He bends to Taji's will, turns dumb devotion to Taji's abuses, and at the last even obeys Taji's command that they part company. And even in the parting, in the premonition of the inevitable death to result from the ahumanity of Taji's quest, Jarl's action is one of characteristic, dumb resignation. "Though he spoke not a word, Jarl was long in taking leave. His eyes seemed to say, I will see you no more."

Jarl assumes the outlines of the western world's counterpart of the

Typee savage. He might be representative of the good, staid burgher
who respects authority, or of the obedient medieval serf who cleared
the wildernesses of Europe for purposes he often did not understand,
or of the stereotype of the semi-ridiculous slave who would die for
ol' Massa. In *Typee* there was only one general type of western man.
But *Mardi* displays ambitions for a more complete canvas. Jarl's incompleteness lies in his lack of intellectuality and his inability to
carry his human virtues and practical instincts into physical action
worthy of the man with vision. He can take the action which preserves
the water breaker, but he cannot take the over-all action which would
preclude in the first place the desertion which necessitated stealing
the water breaker. Once committed to a line of action, he is an active
man. But he is unable to form his own commitments. He lacks the
necessary consciousness of historical meaning which could impart the
fullest significance to his own empiricism. Like Samoa, Jarl need not
be limited to geographically representative qualities. In their most
important meanings, both he and Samoa are the limitations of empiricism per se, the practical men whose practicality is finally im-
practical because of its limited scope.

Samoa is Jarl's primitive counterpart. In the incompleteness of his
consciousness and in his commonness he is Jarl's brother. But where
Jarl is active and unconscious virtue, Samoa is active and unconscious
physicality. He too responds to the moment, but without any rational-
izing reserve of virtue. Both men manifest unexamined behavior.
Samoa's physicality will allow itself to be committed to any cause
other than its own destruction. And Jarl, who does have doubts and
questions, can be committed to his own destruction by the very resigned devotion and fidelity which gave rise to the doubts in the first
place. Jarl certainly is not entranced by the idea of the quest for
Yillah, yet his loyalty will not allow him to abandon his friend:

> But fearing anew, lest after our departure, the men of Amma [Aleema's
> sons] might stir up against me the people of the isle, I determined to yield
> to the earnest solicitations of Borabolla, and leave Jarl behind, for a remem-
> brance of Taji; if necessary to vindicate his name. Apprised hereof, my fol-
> lower was loth to acquiesce. His guiltless spirit feared not the strangers:
> less selfish considerations prevailed. He was willing to remain on the island
> for a time, but not without me. Yet setting forth my reasons; and assuring
> him that our tour would not be long in completing, when we would not
> fail to return, previous to sailing for Odo, he at last, but reluctantly, as-
> sented.[34]

Samoa, however, calls quits to the entire business at this point. He is
courageous enough. And he may have talked like a quester. But when

---

[34] *Mardi*, p. 271. Note again that the quester, with self-centered duplicity,
bends the follower's will to suit his own. Taji has no assurance whatever of either
the brevity or success of his search.

he sees his own gratifications, perhaps his own existence, endangered by another man's business, the appearances dissolve:

At Mondoldo, we also parted with Samoa. Whether it was, that he feared the avengers, whom he may have thought would follow on my track; or whether the islanders of Mardi answered not in attractiveness to the picture his fancy had painted; or whether the restraint put upon him by the domineering presence of King Media, who was too irksome withal; or whether, indeed, he relished not those disquisitions with which Babbalanja regaled us: however, it may have been, certain it was, that Samoa was impatient of the voyage. He besought permission to return to Odo, there to await my return; and a canoe of Mondoldo being about to proceed in that direction, permission was granted; and departing for the other side of the island, from thence he embarked. . . .
Yoomy was at a loss to account for the departure of Samoa; who, while ashore, had expressed much desire to roam [pp. 271-72].

Despite their guiltlessness, neither man can escape the consequences of Taji's guilt, for they have been party to his quest. After their departure, both Jarl and Samoa are killed by the avengers of Aleema. Neither the physical being concerned with his own comforts and safety, nor the virtuous man who does not examine his virtues offers the proper course of behavior. The former has no means to foresee the consequences of the action in which he had become ensnared, and the latter has no plan with which to meet the consequences he does foresee, because he does not understand their meaning.

While both represent cultures which have attained different levels of consciousness, both are found wanting in a world where there are more widely and deeply conscious men. One of Melville's social, or political, prescriptions becomes apparent: the Jarls and Samoas are necessary, indeed indispensable. But to preserve their world and their life, they must either attain the consciousness which will allow them to assign goals of action to the quester, or they must refuse to follow the consciousness which leads to a plunge out of and beyond the world. The refusal must be predesigned, for once committed, a man can not refuse early enough to escape the consequences. The attraction of ideality must be nipped in the baby bud. In any case, the western man must join mind to virtuous activity and the primitive man must join mind to physical gratification—or be murdered.

Once the physicality of Samoa and his Annatoo is explored, the "factual" beginning of *Mardi* ends, and the stage is set for an understanding of the symbolic search for Yillah. The story of Samoa does not merely repeat the creation of a Jarl-figure. Samoa's and Annatoo's story is an inverted burlesque of the story of Taji and Yillah, placed on a physical and mundane level which hovers between, and never reaches, either hilarity or pathos.

Just as Taji is directly responsible for the death of three men (Aleema, Samoa, and Jarl), Samoa is also responsible for the death of three men (the two Cholos and the savage). Taji has his moments with his lady before she is snatched away to death. So too does Samoa, and in both cases the lady's corpse remains somewhere in the sea. In his story, when he saves the *Parki* from the Cholos, Samoa becomes the hunting hunted. Throughout his story, Taji is also the hunting hunted. In almost every other respect, Samoa's mundane life with Annatoo is a precise and earthly opposite of the ethereal idyll that is Taji's life with Yillah.

Annatoo is a caricatured parallel of Yillah. She is dark, aggressive, loud, and bawdy. Yillah is fair, shrinking, soft-spoken, and chaste. Annatoo was carried off from a western isle when still a girl, and her kidnapper was soon more than willing to be rid of her: "The woman, Annatoo, was a native of a far-off, anonymous island to the westward: whence, when quite young, she had been carried off by the commander of a ship, touching there on a passage from Macao to Valparaiso. At Valparaiso her protector put her ashore; most probably, as I afterward had reason to think, for a nuisance." If she was taken by the sea captain for any special purpose, that purpose was most earthly and earthy. Yillah, on the other hand, was carried to a western isle when she was a child, and her captors were more than anxious to keep her, and for most unearthly purposes at that. Yillah leads Taji a chartless and eternal chase, leaving him devoid of a sense of time or a sense of his own or Yillah's true humanness, until it is too late. Annatoo leads Samoa a chartless and temporal chase, stealing the compass, destroying the history in the log books, and ruining the *Parki's* chronometer. Annatoo makes constant raids on other people's possessions, laying up great stores of earthly goods and trinkets. Yillah attempts to take something only once, and then she desires something impossible to get, something which is of heaven, not earth.

> She betrayed much surprise at my Viking's appearance. But most of all was she struck by a characteristic device upon the arm of the wonderful mariner—our Saviour on the cross, in blue; with the crown of thorns, and three drops of blood in vermillion, falling one by one from each hand and foot. . . .
> Eventually, through the Upoluan, she made overtures to the Skyeman, concerning the possession of his picture in her own proper right. In her very simplicity, little heeding, that like a landscape in fresco, it could not be removed [pp. 130-31].

Annatoo, however, is attracted to Jarl by his body, and is not so concerned with a thoughtful view of his arm as with a suggestive pinch of his buttocks. Annatoo is what is left after the bloom is gone; Yillah is still the blooming rosebud. Annatoo is flesh and earth; Yillah is flowers and heaven. Samoa becomes vitally enamored of Annatoo. "By chance it came to pass that when Annatoo's first virgin bloom had departed, leaving nothing but a lusty frame and a lustier soul, Samoa, the Navigator, had fallen desperately in love with her." Yet when Annatoo is carried off by the ocean, Samoa shrieks once and thereafter displays no great woe. In fact he seems to ⋅live in huge contentment. He quests no quest for a corpse. Taji also falls desperately in love. But after his Yillah is carried away over the waters, he grieves like a madman. When the subterranean river sweeps her corpse out to sea, Taji can find no contentment, and he leaves the world to pursue her through oceanic eternity.

The narrator gives very little of Annatoo's personal history, but the revelations of action leave little doubt about what she is. The close and constant inverse parallels between Annatoo and Yillah illuminate Annatoo as the earthly, physical female. Mindless in the same way that Jarl and Samoa are, she is the goal of the "quest" made by the representative of earthly, male physicality. She offers happiness for a time, but such happiness is vitiated by the uxorious, petty circumstances of a mundane married life which becomes a subject for satire rather than tragedy. Whereas Annatoo and Samoa have too much time together for the attainment of a very limited earthly goal, Taji and Yillah have not enough time together for the attainment of a heavenly ideal. Annatoo is a comic representative of time's breakdown of behavior based upon sexual attraction, and she too illustrates the limitations of mindless physicality. Purposeless and directionless Annatoo is magnified into another picture of purposeful lust and pride in the creation of Hautia, that other dark lady who, in a much more serious sense, is a counterpart of Yillah. Perhaps one of the most successful integrations of the mythic and the mundane in *Mardi's* methods is the embodiment of the story of man's primal pursuit of ideal in the basic and conventional image of the male's pursuit of the female, so that part of the entire book is an illustrated Grecian Urn. But the male-female motifs are only secondarily concerned with sex, and are devoted to something different from an examination of the libido. As clearly as Annatoo is the satirized (and satyrized) eternal woman, the narrator, tongue in cheek, would make a mystery of her as an emblem of that tired joke, the Riddle of the Female: "Verily, her ways were as the ways of the inscrutable penguins in building their inscrutable nests, which baffle all science, and make a fool of a sage. Marvelous Annatoo! who shall expound thee?" Again the opposite is true of Yillah. The narrator gives a fairly detailed history of Yillah, both "factually" and symbolically. Without ever saying that she is inscrutable, he does, by divorcing her from immediately revelatory action, make her the major mystery of the book.

Annatoo's Samoa himself has a clearly delineated value. He is *Typee's* Mow-Mow reincarnate. Samoa's limitation to physicality encompasses a lack of sensitivity, as opposed to the quester, whose nerves all seem to be on the surface of his skin. Samoa operates on arm or brain with equal indifference. When he has Annatoo swing the axe that will chop off his injured arm, the pain of the amputation is deadened by "the very clumsiness of the operation," the consciousness deadened by the sheer brute weight of the blow. Reminiscent of *Typee's* first presentation of the coconut-bearing Marquesans, *Mardi's* brain operation depicts Samoa stuffing coconut shell into a man's head, with no apparent sense of discrimination between the two, no realization of what the human head signifies. And, of course, the arm operation (body) is successful; but after the brain operation (mind), the patient dies.

The missing member of the body, the incomplete tattoo, the in-complete ability to do a thing, are common Melvillean indications of the man who can not be the hero, the man whose actions can not and will not embrace body, mind, and heart. The incompleteness is the ineffective behavior which leads to harm—Mow-Mow and his one eye, Tommo and his bad leg, Samoa and his one arm and half-completed tattoo, Ahab and his missing leg, Billy Budd and his stutter. Of course, not all the major characters are so marked, but when they are so marked, they become unified in one of the general patterns of imagery which hold constant symbolic meaning in all of Melville's works. With complete equanimity, for instance, Samoa can tell a tale of a remark-able surgeon who succeeded in stuffing a man's head with pig's brains. Samoa sees nothing murderous or funny or perverted in this feat. That the operation was successful and that the patient died is more than just the weary reworking of an old joke. It is a clear statement of Samoa's limited perception, of the butchery which is a consequence of physicality's single level of existence.

The limitation to half a man, to a dead man in terms of conscious-ness, is both symbolized and stated in a passage describing Samoa's superstitions:

But shall the sequel be told? How that, superstitiously averse to burying in the sea the dead limb of a body yet living; since in that case Samoa held, that he must very soon drown and follow it; and how, that equally dread-ing to keep the thing near him, he at last hung it aloft from the top-most stay; where yet it was suspended, bandaged over and over in cerements. The hand that must have locked many others in friendly clasp, or smote a foe, was no food, thought Samoa, for fowls of the air nor fishes of the sea.

Now, which was Samoa? The dead arm swinging high as Haman? or the living trunk below? Was the arm severed from the body, or the body from the arm? The residual part of Samoa was alive, and therefore we say it was he. But which of the writhing sections of a ten times severed worm, is the worm proper?

For myself, I ever regarded Samoa as but a large fragment of a man, not a man complete . . . [p. 67].

Continuing his description of Samoa, Melville uses the tattoo for the same symbolic purpose it served in *Typee:*

In his style of tattooing, for instance, which seemed rather incomplete; his marks embracing but a vertical half of his person, from crown to sole; the other side being free from the slightest stain. Thus clapped together, as it were, he looked like a union of the unmatched moieties of two distinct beings; and your fancy was lost in conjecturing where roamed the absent ones. When he turned round upon you suddenly, you thought you saw someone else, not him whom you had been regarding before [p. 73].

The unmatched moieties display Samoa's own being. Within the shell of sheer physicality is the soul of a man who, like Jarl, has undeniable human value. His superstition is a dumb and groping recognition of values beyond the circumscriptions of his own life. He meets the demands of battle bravely and superbly (perhaps Samoa is fixed yet more certainly when we recall *White-Jacket's* pronouncement that the one overrated virtue that man has in common with the beasts of the field is physical courage). He is a very simple man, and, within his own terms, a constant one. He is different from Jarl only in the different channels into which different cultures pour unexamined activity. The Polynesian and the European are distinct faces of the same being, and Melville hints again and again at this conclusion by re-emphasizing Jarl's and Samoa's distinctly ethnic names and origins.[35] Thus the two hemispheres, the two civilizations, the two levels of historical development, are joined into one Mardi. Socially translated, *Mardi's* theme of unity in diversity becomes the inescapable oneness of human life. For all his appearance and values, Samoa too has the soul of a man:

But there was one feature in Samoa beyond the reach of the innovations of art:—his eye; which in civilized man or savage, ever shines in the head, just as it shone at birth. Truly our eyes are miraculous things. But alas, that in so many instances, these divine organs should be mere lenses inserted into the socket, as glasses in spectacle rims.

But my Islander had a soul in his eye; looking out upon you there, like somebody in him. What an eye, to be sure! At times brilliantly changeful as opal; in anger, glowing like steel at white heat [p. 86].

The loss is that the eye is wasted. But as Melville often demonstrates, he is too much of a cultural relativist to connect good or bad, superiority or inferiority as absolute labels, with savage or civilized man. They are simply different. In certain contexts the behavior dictated by their differences are operative or inoperative, murderous or saving, but they are always given in the philosophical context to which Mel-

---

[35] Jarl is a distinctively Nordic name, and the man is referred to by his place of origin: the Skyeman. Samoa is a distinctly South Pacific name, and the man is referred to by his place of origin: the Upoluan.

"Jarl hailed from the Isle of Skye. . . . Hence, they often called him the Skyeman. . . ." (This passage continues on to relate Jarl to the Nordic. *Mardi*, p. 10.)

"But no more of Samoa; only this! that his name had been given him by a seacaptain; to whom it had been suggested by the native designation of the islands to which he belonged; the Saviian or Samoan group, otherwise known as the Navigator Islands. The island of Upolua, one of that cluster, claiming the special honor of his birth, as Corsica does Napoleon's, we shall occasionally hereafter speak of Samoa as the Upoluan, by which title he most loved to be called" (*Mardi*, p. 86).

ville devotes the greatest portions of his books. So, as mindless humanity, Jarl and Samoa make a whole, Jarl being almost all heart, Samoa being almost all body. When these two die because of the quester, the indispensable, healthy, common, trusting, working humanity part of the world dies. And it is with this portion of humanity that Melville the artist as well as Melville the sailor has his warmest, if not highest, sympathy. When one would speak of Melville's sympathy for the tortured quester who leads mankind to death, he must remember that he speaks of the same Melville whose purpose is to portray the results of that quester's actions, the same Melville who wrote the hotly democratic *Redburn* and *White-Jacket*, the same Melville who had Captain Vere sacrifice a beautiful dream in order to save common and mindless humanity.

Mardi's beautiful dream, Yillah, undergoes a series of transformations just as does her pursuer, Taji. But unlike Taji, Yillah is a dual creature who does change in essence.

The first view of her at once dissociates Yillah from the islanders and from any possibility that as an ideal she may represent the primitivistic paradise anticipated by Tommo before he became aware of the full meaning of the Typee valley. Yillah is out of place—indeed, markedly alien—in this environment. Her language is not that of the islanders, and it rings a note of familiarity only in the ear of Taji. Neither islander or westerner in speech, but an etherealized something that is at once both and neither, she is even more out of this world than the sungod, Taji. She is immediately associated with an inability to communicate.

Melville sets the stage by presenting a cross section of humanity—the man of mind and will, the mindless man of heart, and the mindless man of body. Yillah utters sounds that are vaguely familiar only to the first, and are totally inexplicable to the other two. Also, Yillah represents Taji's greatest joy; yet she is always quiet and sad. Babbalanja, in his Serenian dream of nonexistent and unattainable ideality, is to report that heavenly joy is a white tear, that the essence of the other-world is a sad silence. And Yillah's first characteristics are sadness, silence, and a separateness from humanity which makes her nonexistent and unattainable. When first seen she is hidden in religion's tent. She is physically isolated from the outside world, and is described in mystical religious terms that set her apart from material existence:

Before me crouched a beautiful girl. Her hands were drooping. And like *a saint from a shrine*, she looked out *sadly* from her long fair hair. A low wail issued from her lips, and she trembled like a sound. There were *tears* on her cheeks, and *a rose-colored pearl* on her bosom.

Did I dream?—*a snow-white skin: blue, firmament eyes: Golconda locks.* For an instant *spell-bound* I stood; while, with a slow, apprehensive movement, and still gazing fixedly, the captive gathered more closely about her a gauze-like robe. Taking one step within, and partially dropping the curtain of the tent, I so stood as to have both sight and speech of Samoa, who tarried without; while the maiden, crouching in the farther corner of the retreat, *was wholly screened from all eyes but mine.*

Crossing my hands before me, I now stood without speaking. *For the soul of me,* I could not link this mysterious creature with the tawny strangers. *She seemed of another race.* So powerful was this impression, that unconsciously, I addressed her in my own tongue. She started, and bending over, listened intently, as if to the first faint echo of something dimly remembered. Again I spoke, when throwing back her hair, the maiden looked up with a piercing, bewildered gaze. But her eyes soon fell, and bending over once more, she resumed her former attitude. At length she slowly chanted to herself several musical words, unlike those of the Islanders; but though I knew not what they meant, *they vaguely seemed familiar* [p. 121, italics mine].

Certainly this is the usual nineteenth-century romantic picture of the fair heroine. But even more certainly, it is not just that. Yillah is the inmost message of the Ark, the contents which the chapel is built to bear. To the quester she is the tantalizing and vague stirring of memory which wordlessly recalls the ideality from which he took his origin, trailing clouds of glory which wish only to rejoin the existence-giving nimbus. Not only does this passage establish a relationship between the quester and the lure, but the statement that Yillah also finds something troublingly familiar about Taji prepares for the discovery of the other facet of Yillah's dual being: the ironic fact that their mutual "ideal" origin is mortal and historical. But the "supernatural" Yillah is presented first. In direct contrast to Jarl, Yillah remembers an other-worldly existence before she was reborn.

She declared herself more than mortal, a maiden from Oroolia, the Island of Delights, somewhere in the paradisiacal archipelago of the Polynesians. To this isle, while yet an infant, by some mystical power, she had been spirited from Amma, the place of her nativity. Her name was Yillah. And hardly had the waters of Oroolia washed white her olive skin, and tinged her hair with gold, when one day strolling in the woodlands, she was snared in the tendrils of a vine. Drawing her into its bowers, it gently transformed her into one of its blossoms, leaving her conscious soul folded up in the transparent petals.

Here hung Yillah in a trance, the world without all tinged with the rosy hue of her prison. At length when her spirit was about to burst forth in the opening flower, the blossom was snapped from its stem; and borne by a soft wind to the sea; where it fell into the opening valve of a shell; which in good time was cast upon the Island of Amma.

In a dream, these events were revealed to Aleema the priest; who by a spell unlocking its pearly casket, took forth the bud, which now showed signs of opening in the reviving air, and bore faint shadowy revealings as of the dawn behind crimson clouds. Suddenly expanding, the blossom exhaled away in perfumes; floating a rosy mist in the air. Condensing at last, there emerged from this mist the same radiant young Yillah as before; her locks all moist, and a rose colored pearl on her bosom. Enshrined as a goddess, the wonderful child now tarried in the sacred temple of Apo, buried in a dell; never beheld of mortal eyes save Aleema's [p. 122].

This passage holds the essential definition of Yillah. Although basically of mortal origin, she is transformed by heaven and given back to earth. Oroolia (the supreme God is Oro) as the Island of Delights is an accurate appositive for the heaven of the Polynesian world in which the action exists. In this world, dark complexion is associated with earth and humanity, and whiteness is associated with other-worldliness. Yillah's whiteness is a consequence of God, heaven, ideality. And when Taji is "reborn" as a demigod from the sun, he is accepted as a visitor from another world because he is white. Yillah, in her human infancy on Amma, was dark, and the waters of heaven washed her white. Clearly, the baptism is a removal of humanity, or, more accurately, earthliness.

Yillah is ever after marked by heaven, not only by her complexion, but also by the rose pearl. Yillah is pink and white, not only lily but rose. The hue of the heavenly flower which ensnared the essence of Yillah was rose; the shell which conducted that essence from the shores of heaven was a "pearly casket." And the last token of Yillah is the rose pearl clutched in Hautia's hand. What then, is the essence, human and divine, pink and white, formed by heaven? The narrator states the definition when he describes what it is that is separated from corporeal being and is ensnared in the flower: "Drawing her into its bowers, it gently *transformed her into one of its blossoms,* leaving her *conscious soul* folded up in the transparent petals." It is this essential spirit, conscious soul, that is released from the flower. "At length when her *spirit* was about to burst forth in the opening flower, the blossom was snapped from the stem." Man's conscious soul, the immortal and divine faculty in his animal being, is to be deposited on earth pure and unvitiated in the substantial being of the transformed Yillah. Yillah is a perfect symbol of the idealist's ontological view of man, whose material identity is not as characteristic as his celestial identity. Melville simply gives her a body by means of obstetrical imagery which could attract any good Freudian. Yillah has to be as nonhumanly etherealized as possible. Thoreau's "scurvy, empirical self" is indeed denied in Yillah—in her that self is practically accidental, necessitated only by need for human form. She does not have a body that anyone can believe in. She is a bodiless symbol of man's concept of ideality. If only for the purpose of narrative, let alone Melville's view of "heavenly" tokens on earth, this corporeality, material being, would have to exist. And the rose pearl is the symbol of Yillah's disembodied spiritual state in heaven, the essential existence within the rose-flower womb and the pearly casket womb before rebirth in substantial form.[36] The pearl is Yillah herself, a symbol of

[36] I cannot prove that Melville was familiar with the medieval tradition of pearl as a symbol of spotless, pure being, and as an emblem of the purity of heavenly ideal. However, the same symbol exists in Renaissance literature, which, as Sealts'

ideality. It is inevitable that idealistic Taji, all consciousness and will, should be attracted to Yillah and should wish to claim her "for his soul," should worship her and want her for himself.[37] She is all that he has ever longed for.

Either as the virgin Yillah, untouched by material experience, or extrinsically as an absolute ideal of pagan or Christian belief, conscious soul in pure state has long been the western world's ideal of existence. It is the unvitiated Adamic intellect, fresh from God, blessed with a Golden Age transcendent, innocent, believing perception which makes beatitude possible. It is the one divine faculty which, even in its vitiated form, lifts man above earth and beast in the great chain of being and makes it possible for man to rejoin his ideal origin. It is the purity of the prelapsarian days when Astraea walked the earth. None of these considerations are made specific by any means, but they are overtones of Yillah's definition. For Melville suggests all myths eclectically in order to create his absolute of innocent purity. In all cases, Yillah is the lone bird Taji saw, which "flew through a low arch" of heaven "and was lost to view." She is at once other-worldly, pure, ideal, and absolute. Regardless of specifics, the important irony is Taji's desperate attempt to unite natural and ideal origins. He tries to make Yillah believe that he too is a supernatural being with a heavenly right to keep her, and that she too is a natural being who belongs on earth with him. To Taji, Yillah is the bliss which was man's right before all the dullness and heaps and tasks and blocks of history were thrown at him. The frantic attempt to regain the heavenly bliss of a divine state of being is the attempt to drive back beyond history, beyond natural time, which is the only time there is, as *Typee* and *Pierre* demonstrate. Immediate history becomes secondary—becomes, in fact, an obstacle, like Emerson's "understanding" and Thoreau's "scurvy, empirical self"—and heaven becomes the primary goal. And Taji's love for Yillah illuminates again his own predisposition, which claims ideal origin, with all the transcendent cosmic status attendant thereon, and which rejects historical origins, with all the dullnesses, deaths, duties, and limitations attendant thereon. Until much later, the allegory of conscious soul is the only story of Yillah's

---

lists of "Melville's Reading . . . Owned and Borrowed" and Melville's own letters make apparent, Melville did read. Moreover, the pearl symbol has a long literary and exegetical tradition which existed actively through Melville's own times. Indeed Hawthorne used the symbol consciously in *The Scarlet Letter* and "The Intelligence Office." See Don Cameron Allen, "Symbolic Color in the Literature of the English Renaissance," *PQ*, XV (1936), 81-92; also Allen's "Arthur's Diamond Shield in *The Faerie Queen*," *JEGP*, XXXVI (1937), 234-43; also my "An Approach to 'The Pearl'," *JEGP*, LIV (1955), 684-92.

[37] For an account of Taji as the positive actor and of Yillah as "beauty and mystery and passion," see Stephen A. Larrabee, "Melville against the World," *SAQ*, XXXIV (1935), 410-18. For a view of Yillah as the traditional heroine as chaste innocence and of Melville as the man afraid of experience, particularly sexual experience, see F. I. Carpenter, "Puritans Preferred Blondes," *NEQ*, IX (1936), 253-72.

origins that Taji knows, but Taji cannot reject Yillah as ideality any more than he can reject his own perception. Taji's predisposition is objectified and transferred to love (stimulated by, but not based upon, physical desire alone) for the maiden, and it is the story of Yillah's supernatural associations that gives the transfer consistent and symbolic meaning. Yillah, as lure, becomes an objectification of Taji's own motivating predisposition, and thus she is an integral part of Taji's own self.

For Taji, then, attainment of Yillah is the happiness of attainment of the total ideality beyond history, the attainment of his own ideal identity. But happiness, when used as part of Yillah's definition, must be anchored specifically in the idea of Yillah held by any particular searcher. For Taji, for instance, happiness does not center around the primary, sexual energy that characterized the Samoa-Annatoo episode, nor the wealth and luxury which characterized the desires of the early King Media. Taji's happiness transcends the happiness of the material world, and he, Ahab, and Pierre are basically the same man in quest: none of them know what Babbalanja is to learn about the sad, silent, white, empty endlessness which is all there is beyond historical life and which makes beatitude an empty word. Thus Yillah is more than conscious soul. As an embodiment of ideality, she is all things to all men. She is sought by all the voyagers, all of whom seek different things. Yoomy seeks the truth of transcendent beauty as a proof of heaven.[38] Throughout *Mardi* he sings fragments of one composite song which identifies Yillah as the lone bright fish of the sea, the far departed Astraea, the bright maid.[39] In the quest for truth, Yoomy sees the ideal in its romantic aspect as beauty, the Keatsian and Emersonian Truth-and-Beauty-are-One.[40] It is this which is the lost, bright

[38] One of the best thematic analyses of Melville is Robert Penn Warren's "Melville the Poet," *KR*, VIII (1946), 208-23. Mr. Warren sees the "fundamental ironic dualities of existence," the relationship of one's own truth to more total truth, the irony of unanticipated consequences which, in Hawthornesque manner, make impossible an absolute differentiation of good and bad. In Melville's poetry of the Civil War, Warren finds a key to the divergent views of Mohi, Babbalanja, and Yoomy—the significance of official truth to those enlightened by the bullet or the whale or the demon.

[39] When speaking of Yillah as a quest object for all the voyagers, and when speaking of Hautia, I use terms like "Astraea," and "Duessa." While such terms are not verbally substantiated in *Mardi's* text, they are sometimes almost explicit analogies. Certainly the Astraea and Faerie Queen and Faustus myths are implied in *Mardi*. Melville made increasing discoveries about Renaissance authors, and read them with startling perception—particularly Shakespeare. He found in those writers standards and ideals which were tailor-made for his theme, and he constantly went back to them. For a good discussion of the Astraea theme, which can shed much light on Melville, see Marjorie Hope Nicolson, *The Breaking of the Circle* (Evanston, 1950), *passim*, and Francis Yates, "Queen Elizabeth as Astraea," *Journal of the Warburg and Courtauld Institutes*, X (1947), 27-82. For Spenser material, see Nathalia Wright, "A Note on Melville's Use of Spenser: Hautia and the Bower of Bliss," *AL*, XXIV (1952), 83-85; and Leon Howard, "Melville and Spenser—A Note on Criticism," *MLN*, XLV (1951), 291-92.

[40] For Yillah as "Ultimate Truth," see Tyrus Hillway, "Taji's Quest for Certainty," *AL*, XVIII (1946), 27-34. Also see Davis, pp. 184-90.

Yillah of Yoomy's search. Mohi is constantly fearful of death and cringes from the premonitory aches and twinges of his old age. As the historian who records chronology rather than meaning, he is constantly aware of the statistics of death. He is characterized by officialness, grayness, and age. The few times that Mohi is permitted personal words about his fears and desires, he voices fear of death and desire for long life. It is not until the Serenian conversion and acceptance of human limitation that he can accept Babbalanja's prescription, "Mohi! Age leads thee by the hand. Live out thy life and die, calmbrowed." And it is only after this acceptance that Mohi tries to restrain Taji from further search for Yillah. For Mohi, who of all the voyagers can least be called a searcher after anything, if Yillah is something she is long life.[41]

Media, until he finds his true goal in Serenia, tries to find his own kind of happiness during the quest. It is the happiness of the wealthy and untroubled aristocrat, and he visits his cousin kings and demigods solely for the wealthy, healthy good times they offer. As a follower of the median path of least resistance, he hugs his kingship, which is an authoritative guarantor of his own selfish wealth and health. After his Serenian conversion, he returns to Odo to universalize in the just society the wealth and health which the perversions of his dictatorial artistocracy had wrung from his slaves to be given to him alone. Until he rejects the search for her, if Yillah is to be defined for Media —who had displayed his own let's-have-a-good-time interest in finding her—she is the happiness of wealth and health.

In one sense, Babbalanja and Mohi seek the same thing for totally different reasons. Babbalanja seeks one glimpse of immortality as proof of heaven, cosmic unity, cosmic design, and purpose. Only immortality could invest with meaning and reason the earthly woes of beings who are crammed with life apparently only to suffer and perish. This is the despondent Babbalanja, who, before his Serenian conversion, fears that man's last hope of immortality is lost and gone.[42] For him, Yillah is the last, lost hope of heaven, the last lost hope of reason and purpose, the last lost hope for the glimpse of the ultimate, for beatitude. Hautia, the Duessa, knows what is sought, and falsely says that only she can offer the ideal to all who search. In one speech she uses some capital-letter terms which are names for Yillah, and to make the suggestion stronger, these terms are associated with Yillah's most prominent trademark, the pearl. "Hautia rose; hands full of pearls.

---

[41] Mohi's mind is the least metaphysical of the group, and the historian should not be thought to be more of a searcher than he is. Nor can he be assigned a goal less pedestrian than he has. He is associated with a search for an ideal mostly by virtue of the fact that he happens to be one of the people taken along by Media. But it is interesting that as the man most dispirited by mentions of old age and death, even Mohi speaks of death in images recalling search and voyage. See *Mardi*, pp. 548-49, and Davis, pp. 166-73.

[42] See also Davis, pp. 173-84.

" 'Lo! Taji; all these may be had for the diving; and Beauty, Health, Wealth, Long Life, and the Last Lost Hope of man. But through me alone, may these be had. Dive thou, and bring up one pearl if thou canst.' "

It is meaningless to call Yillah Happiness or Truth, for both those concepts emerge as relative things dependent upon the searcher, and Yillah as absolute is a no-thing—which is all of Yillah that all the searchers find, and which is the point of the book. The relativity of Yillah's definition (and the fact that those definitions add up to the ironic unity of zero) is not only mockery of the goals of human aspiration idealistically defined and pursued, but is also a parallel to the idea that all manifestations of existence, all phenomena, are united parts of a single entity, time.[43] This unification of symbol's meaning is best exemplified in one episode which takes place on that rock of time, the "Isle of Fossils," whereon Babbalanja settles an argument by explaining that a petrified footprint in the rock indicates both three toes and one foot. He tells the foolish disputants, "Unite and both are right; divide and both are wrong. Every unit is made up of parts, as well as every plurality." There is no absolute either in time or in space, in quality or in quantity, yet the very relativity of existence makes it impossible to separate any part from any other. And once existence is placed on the natural level only, the catalog of traditional sins and virtues is reversed. The attempt to shun relativity and history is the attempt to shun time, is the attempt to shun existence, is the blasphemy of lifting elements of existence away from natural life, which is the blasphemy of lifting them into death. It fits concisely that Taji should fail in his quest, ridden as he is by a monomania of will which would sin and sin again in order to regain a presupposed and transcendent purity outside of time, a state of ideal rather than natural existence. It is inevitable that Taji's initial pursuit should begin in sin and be tinged with guilt. And Taji's guilt stems from the sin that in varying degrees characterizes all five seekers: the desire for a personal, timeless infallibility which is based upon ideal and which is lifted away from, and which implicitly or explicitly rejects, history and society. Significantly, when the true Serenian goal is provided, action is aimed at, not away from, this earth and time. That which informs behavior (Alma, Christ) is judged by historical experience (right

---

[43] Davis notes the inclusiveness of Yillah's meaning as well as he does the error of equating Yillah with one particular thing only, as Hillway, Larrabee, Carpenter and others have done. Yet, the total definition of Yillah is composed of specific qualities. In the selection of King, Poet, Historian, and Philosopher, in addition to the wide range of isles visited, and in addition to Jarl and Samoa, Melville presents a group representative of all humanity. The specifics of Yillah's meaning depend upon the perceptions of the specialized members of the book's cast, although the total meaning of Yillah is the goal of unspecialized man. The relativity of meanings further emphasizes the need for informed and eclectic completeness.

reason). Right reason, in context, is a view of the common denominator, mortality, which demands brotherhood and humanitarianism. The Serenians say that it is impossible to choose between Alma and right reason. And despite the idealistic language, Alma, or Universal Soul, or Christ, is seen naturalistically as the human necessity for love which has been projected to, not drawn from, a supernatural absolute. For, the Serenian ambassador continues, if it should ever be possible to choose, Alma, rather than right reason, would be rejected. The ideal no longer takes precedence as something anterior to history—it is quite the opposite. Thus, the true idealist, or antinaturalist, can not be innocently guiltless, for the consequences of his perception are bound to be criminal in the natural world because of the rejection of historical necessities. The Galahad and Parsifal literally are impossibilities, for they are innocent of the world yet regenerate it; whereas as *Pierre* and *Billy Budd* demonstrate, that very innocence is a sin. As Taji and Ahab symbolize and as Plotinus Plinlimmon will state, the idealist can not find justification for his actions in the world, but only by insisting that his own perception is that of pure and absolute reality. And again, as Taji and Ahab and Pierre demonstrate, if idealism, consequently, is to be active at all, it must be characterized by a will that is murderous because it is blind to its consequences in the natural world.

It is not surprising, then, that Jarl should feel foreboding and uneasiness for Taji at Yillah's presence. In one brief and important chapter, the relationship between the natural and the ideal, between "Yillah, Jarl, and Samoa" is sketched. At first the pure conscious soul shrinks from sheer physicality, but after earthly experience, comes to accept its existence as one of the actualities and necessities of natural life. But she remains aloof. "As Beauty from the Beast, so at first shrank the damsel from my one-armed companion. But seeing my confidence in the savage, a reaction soon followed. And in accordance with that curious law, by which, under certain conditions, the ugliest mortals became only amiably hideous, Yillah at length came to look upon Samoa as a sort of harmless and good natured goblin. Whence came he, she cared not; or what was his history; or in what manner his fortunes were united to mine." Yillah can be friendly with the virtuous Jarl. But she can not be interested in the earthly life of the body. At the least, Yillah can only shun physicality as a principle. At the most, the ideal can woo man away from the most barbaric manifestations of physicality and savagery: "Now, as every where women are the tamers of menageries of men; so Yillah in good time tamed down Samoa to the relinquishment of that horrible thing in his ear, and persuaded him to substitute a vacancy for the bauble in his nose. On his part, however, all this was conditional. He stipulated for the privilege of restoring both trinkets upon suitable occasions." Despite his superstitious reverence for Yillah as a being not of this world, Samoa is dedicated to the actions of this world and will not relinquish his own characteristics when the need for preservation demands his own special attributes. "On suitable occasions" recalls the motif of incompleteness by recognizing the interdependence and relativity involved in man's necessities. For instance, when the *Chamois* group comes ashore at Mardi, Yillah's qualities can not cope with the earthly needs demanded by a physical meeting with earthmen in alien lands. Yillah remains cowering in the closed tent aboard the boat. It is Samoa who springs ashore, determining beforehand whether it is safe to land. Melville immediately suggests that ideality in that otherworld outside of Plato's cave is an incompletion on earth and is inoperative in the potentially martial, historical situation. That Samoa acts as he must "on suitable occasions" is also part of *Mardi's* castigation of religion. Melville insisted that all men really believed the same: i.e., disbelieved in the outside of the cave and believed that the cave itself is the eternal and infinite All that there is. For him the test of truth is simple experience of human behavior: when the chips are down, men act according to history rather than according to ideality. Men wish to cling to the natural life of the cave. In religion, however, Melville sees the storehouse from which man takes the delusion and smugness with which he perverts and hypocritically justifies and makes foul and selfish the actions dictated by his real belief. In his letters and his books, Melville has metaphysical contempt for the delusion and political contempt for the sham involved in the religious doctrine that man must die to this world in order to attain salvation in an eternal other-world.

Samoa may or may not recognize Yillah as conscious soul, a meaning reserved for Taji and the reader. He is aware that she is essentially "different," but he is no more aware of *Mardi's* definition of ideality than he is of his own symbolic meaning in *Mardi's* story. Not realizing that her existence will demand his own literal and symbolic death, he acts toward her as he acts toward no one else in the book, not even toward Taji—for Samoa's primitive, mindless, and superstitious awe of the supernatural is stronger than his submission to a demigod with whom he can deal on a physical level.

But if thus gayly the damsel sported with Samoa; how different his emotions toward her? the fate to which she had been destined, and every nameless thing about her, appealed to all his native superstitions, which ascribed to beings of her complexion a more than terrestrial origin. When permitted to approach her, he looked timid and awkwardly strange; suggesting the likeness of some clumsy satyr, drawing in his horns, slowly wagging his tail; crouching abashed before some radiant spirit.

And this reverence of his was most pleasing to me. Bravo; thought I; be a pagan forever. No more than myself; for after a different fashion, Yillah was an idol to both [p. 130].

Not only Samoa, but all mortal men recognize the emblem of what they think is supernatural, and tremble superstitiously before something which ironically is a reading of their own erroneously idealistic projections. The idealism of Taji, the western man, is the misdirection of conscious mind. The idealism of the islanders is the spontaneous superstition of the primitive and unconscious mind. "Until now, enveloped in her robe, and crouching like a fawn, Yillah had been well nigh hidden from view. But presently she withdrew her hood.

"What saw the Islanders, that they so gazed and adored in silence: some retreating, some creeping nearer, and the women all in a flutter? Long they gazed; and following Samoa's example, stretched forth their arms in reverence." The reverence is what creates the warmth as well as the hopelessness of Melville's view of man. Man will always recognize and worship his own highest aspirations and his own highest self —even though they may be destructively wrongly defined and directed.

III

Once Yillah is given a dramatic weighting, a discernible value, she disappears. If her identity is known, the meaning, or evaluation, of her identity remains to be exposed. As is true of the other lures, Isabel, the whale, and Billy Budd, the story is not Yillah's. She continues to exist only as a motive, a cause for activation, and it is in the consequences of the quester's actions and the actions of the characters with whom he has contact that the story is built.

One episode which helps reveal Yillah's nature is the story of her sojourn with Aleema. Aleema at first is identified by his boat. When it is first seen, the craft is mistaken for one of the white birds of the sky. It is confused with heaven, but closer inspection reveals growing discrepancies between that all-colorlessness and Aleema's religion.

It looked like one of many birds; for half intercepting our view, fell showers of plumage: a flight of milk-white noddies flying downward to the sea.

But soon the birds are seen no more. Yet there remains the speck; plainly a sail; but too small for a ship. . . .

As the sail drew nigh, its failing to glisten white led us to doubt whether it was indeed a whale-boat. Presently, it showed yellow; and Samoa declared, that it must be the sail of some island craft.[44]

When the boat sails within description distance, it is presented in images identical with those of *Typee*, especially the fruit-laden altars of primitive religion. "The yard, spreading a yellow sail, was a

---

[44] *Mardi*, p. 112. The bird imagery is almost always associated with the otherworld. It is a bird in the heavens that first stirs Taji's restlessness to a frenzy; Yillah's companion is a snow-white bird that flies away toward the head of the vale, where God (Apo) is; it is one of the snow-white sea birds with which religion's ship is first confused; and when Taji forgets Yillah long enough to touch Hautia, a dead bird drops down from the sky, signifying the unmistakable fact of Yillah's death.

crooked bough, supported obliquely in the crotch of a mast, to which the green bark was still clinging. Here and there were little tufts of moss. The high, beaked prow of that canoe in which the mast was placed, resembled a rude altar; and all round it was suspended a great variety of fruits, including scores of cocoanuts, unhusked. This prow was railed off, forming a sort of chancel within." The marks of land and greenness which identify the craft immediately differentiate it from the whitness of the quester and his concerns.

Aleema, the priest, is characterized by two recurrent sets of images: oldness and timelessness on the one hand, and on the other, the stern qualities of the Aaron, the militant follower of the demanding, harsh, and vengeful Jehovah.

> Meantime, old Aaron, fastening the two silks crosswise over his shoulders, like a brace of Highland plaids, crosslegged sat, and eyed us.
> It was a curious sight. The old priest, like a scroll of old parchment, covered all over with heiroglyphical devices, harder to interpret, I'll warrant, than any old Sanskrit manuscript. And upon his broad brow, deep-graven in wrinkles, were characters still more mysterious, which no Champollion nor gipsy could have deciphered. He looked old as the elderly hills; eyes sunken, though bright; and head white as the summit of Mont Blanc. . . .
> . . . that old sire, Old Aaron; who, no doubt, reposed upon his sons, as an old general upon the trophies of his youth [pp. 115-16].

The sons of Aleema also introduce characteristics of Mardi's religion. It is supported by the physical savage in everyman; as in Maramma, religion is supported by the sword. If Maramma is a denunciation of the religious institution, Aleema represents general religious practice. Both demand conformity. Just as Emerson and Thoreau had to leave general religious practice and the specifics of religious institutions in order to redefine their own aspirations and true, individual reverence, so Taji had to take his ideal away from religion to live with it by himself. And just as Maramma kills the boy who thinks God is more important than the institutionalized forms in which he is worshiped, so Aleema's sons seek to kill the man who would rescue ideality from religious convention. It is, of course, the martial, superstitious, primitive and physical Samoa who first identifies Aleema's boat. It is he who wishes to meet it, he who feels an immediate kinship and uncowed familiarity, he who can fight with Aleema's sons on their own terms. "Seeing that flight was useless, the Islanders again stopped their canoe, and once more we cautiously drew nearer; myself crying out to them not to be fearful; and Samoa, with the odd humor of his race, averring that he had known every soul of them from his infancy."

Aleema is presented as a lost vitality, a being whose present shrunken stature is masked by his sternness and by the mystery of his hieroglyphics. But his fourteen sons who are the "sword" of religion, are presented in images of physicality: food, animality, and martial strength:

The rest were a youthful and comely set; their complexion that of Gold Sherry, and all tattooed after this pattern; two broad cross-stripes on the chest and back, reaching down to the waist like a foot-soldier's harness. Their faces were full of expression; and their mouths were full of fine teeth so that the parting of their lips were as the opening of pearl oysters. Marked, here and there, after the style of Tahiti, with little round figures in blue, dotted in the middle with a spot of vermilion, their brawny brown thighs looked not unlike the gallant hams of Westphalia, spotted with the red dust of Cayenne [p. 115].

And it is upon these "foot-soldiers," these "gallant hams" that the priest depends for the force which backs up his pronouncements. The gallant hams are further defined as a continual process in human history. They are the new generations molded by religion for dedication to the purposes of religion. They are fathered, despite a variety of mothers or families, into one uniform, conforming family of identical beings who literally do support religion. "But what a marvelous resemblance in the features of all," Taji notes. "Were they born at one birth? This resemblance was heightened by their uniform marks. But it was subsequently ascertained, that they were the children of one sire; and that sire, old Aaron; who, no doubt, reposed upon his sons as an old general upon the trophies of his youth. They were the children of as many mothers; and he was training them up for the priesthood."

What is the quality of this religion which was once vital but which now depends upon constraint? The answer to this question is Melville's development of the relationship of religion to man's conscious soul. Aleema preserves Yillah only to sacrifice her. The preservation for sacrifice is an act which finally preserves not the soul but the status of the priest, and mystagogy becomes identical with politics. The priest does not wish all men to share Yillah. He wishes to be her sole, unchallenged custodian. During Yillah's seclusion in the valley of Ardair, a youth seeks out Yillah and finally sees her. Either Aleema himself kills him or he has his sons, the guardians of the valley, kill the youth.

Moreover, religion would deny the natural origin of man's aspiring consciousness by surrounding it with a fantasy about a supernatural origin which does not exist. And when one recalls that Aleema's sons' pursuit of Taji as the man who would attain ideality by his own will (thus negating the jealously guarded role of religion) is a parallel to the murder of the transcendental boy by the priests of Maramma, the total implication emerges. The most persistent and strongest deterrent to man's search for perfection is religion itself. By subordinating man's conscious soul to the "hieroglyphical devices," religion ahumanizes or dehumanizes the very essence which could allow man whatever he can reach of the high status to which he aspires.[45]

---

[45] See Davis, p. 132.

In his own aspiring and intense dedication of self to the pursuit of ideality, the impious, "godless, godlike" quester is never hypocritical, although he may be deluded. Taji is not taken in by the restricting superstitions of religion—Yillah is a different idol to him than she is to Samoa. Taji tries to relate himself, as a human, to his divine heritage by forever seeking that heritage, by trying to capture it by escalade, and by convincing himself and Yillah that that heritage itself is originally a human thing. In one speech, Taji lays bare the vision behind the quest story, and he embraces the beginning and end of that story with images that make this speech the most significant concentrate of his entire quest.

Now re-entering the tent, she again inquired where tarried Aleema. "Think not of him, sweet Yillah," I cried. "Look on me. Am I not white like yourself? Behold, though since quitting Oroolia the sun has died my cheek, am I not even as you? Am I brown like the dusky Aleema? They snatched you away from your isle in the sea, too early for you to remember me there. But you have not been forgotten by me, sweetest Yillah. Ha! Ha! shook we not the palm-trees together, and chased we not the rolling nuts down the glen? Did we not dive into the grotto on the sea-shore, and come up together in the cool cavern on the hill? In my home in Oroolia, dear Yillah, I have a lock of your hair, ere yet it was golden: a little dark tress like a ring. How your cheeks were then changing from olive to white. And when shall I forget the hour, that I came upon you sleeping among the flowers, with roses and lilies for cheeks. Still forgetful? Know you not my voice? Those little spirits in your eyes have seen me before. They mimic me now as they sport in their lakes. All the past a dim blank? Think of the time when we ran up and down in our arbor, where the green vines grew over the great ribs of the stranded whale. Oh Yillah, little Yillah, has it all come to this? Am I ever forgotten? Yet over the wide watery world have I sought thee: from isle to isle, from sea to sea. And now we part not. Aleema is gone. My prow shall keep kissing the waves till it kisses the beach at Oroolia. Yillah, look up" [pp. 126-27].

On the narrative level, Taji is again employing deceit in order to win Yillah. But even though on the surface Taji's speech is part of his campaign of conquest, Taji speaks in images which are an undeniable part of the book's general symbolism. Again there is the emphasis on origins presented in a suggestion of man's prelapsarian state. Yillah, ere she was golden, was Fayaway, or whatever name we choose whereby to designate the Edenic, primitivistic ideal which was smashed by *Typee*. In that happy and faraway time, Taji and Yillah-Fayaway traveled together, alive and human, from the sea grotto to the cavern in the hill, coming inland. At the end of the book, inhuman, in despair, and dead, they travel from the cavern in the hill out to the final seas. The other-world changes the ideal from dark to white, from earthliness to pure being. Conversely, the story of Ozonna and Rea shows that pride of this world, Hautia, corrupts the ideal from white to dark, from purity to perversion. As the ideal is associated with pink and white flowers, lilies, roses, with white birds, and with rose pearls and heaven, so the corruption represented by Hautia is pictured by a false front of birds, flowers, and pearls on earth. Taji's speech here moves from the early view of the pure ideal to the foreshadowing of the destruction of that ideal. Moreover, Taji makes the definite statement that he did hunt for Yillah long before he knew of her or met her incarnation. The passage ends with Taji's determination not to rest until he and Yillah can re-enter heaven together, until the final withdrawal from earth is complete, and the victory of man's escalade is realized. Of course Taji and Yillah do make a final withdrawal from the world, and the irony of the whole affair is clinched by the unfounded conclusion to the passage: "Sunk the ghost of Aleema: Sweet Yillah was mine!" [46]

Aleema has an easier task than Taji. Religion beats the quester hands down. Religion merely has to dehumanize and sacrifice aspects of human existence in order to maintain its own favored and authoritative position. When the priest's status is threatened by men clamoring for the release of Yillah, Aleema spirits her away to destruction in the whirlpool of Tedaidee. Release of religion's grasp on man's ideals is something that the priest cannot allow, and it is by stealth and force that he circumvents the demands of general humanity. He buries the ideal, consciousness, and human aspiration. The god of Aleema, Apo (a possible play on ape: anthropocentrism, anthropoidism, animality, imitation, conformity) is a "grim profile of a human face; whose shadow, every afternoon, crept down the verdant side of the mountain: a silent phantom, stealing all over the bosom of the glen." It is to this idea of God that old Aleema tries to marry man's ideals. "At times, when the phantom drew near, Aleema would take Yillah forth, and waiting its approach, lay her down by the shadow, disposing her arms in a caress, saying, 'Oh, Apo! dost accept thy bride?' And at last, when it crept beyond the place where he stood, and buried the whole valley in gloom; Aleema would say, 'Arise Yillah; Apo hath stretched himself to sleep in Ardair. Go, slumber where thou wilt; for thou wilt slumber in his arms.' " And just as Apo buries the greeness of the valley in gloom and covers man's conscious soul with shadow, so Aleema buries the quester's thoughts in gloom and makes the very waters over which Taji sails a place of shadow and death.

Although the ritualistic aspects of religion ahumanizes Yillah, Taji,

---

[46] For a similar view, see George C. Homans, "The Dark Angel: The Tragedy of Herman Melville," *NEQ*, V (1932), 699-730. This early article is still one of the best, even though it reflects the earlier passion for "the dark man," "tragedy," and Freudian overtones. The article sees some of the major connections that exist between the books, such as that between Hautia and Fedallah, although it does not see Yillah completely. Homans makes the very suggestive statement that "The dualism of *Mardi* and *Moby Dick* becomes . . . a unity with mutually annihilating sides . . ." (723); and that "The moral of the Melville tragedy . . . [is that] Even if the Titans had mastered the power successfully to pass the penultimate, they would have found the Ultimate a silence" (729).

paradoxically, who leads to the greatest ahumanity, tries to humanize Yillah. Religion becomes the false path to God. It becomes a killer of natural aspiration and consciousness, which is the true divinity, and therefore religion becomes the direct opposite of what it professes to be. The conscious quester, on the other hand, is so acutely aware of an ideal birthright that he tries to capture it by storm, ignoring the actualities of a humanity that does not exist in Eden. In the attempt to storm the ramparts of the other world which is not there, the quester is also a killer. Religion is the life that kills aspiration; the quest is the aspiration that kills life. Either way, the attempt to depend behavior from ideality is murder and suicide and genocide; but it must be remembered that in Melville's world although the quester's attempt is wrong, it is based upon what, for Melville's sincere idealist, is the most honest, sham-piercing, and most splendidly gigantic vision of man's cosmic status. Religion demands unqualified submission, a denial of consciousness for belief and obedience. Quest demands unqualified individual independence, a rising to equality with God, or, if need be, revenge upon him. Whereas Aleema merely has to fill Yillah's head with fairly tales and then kill her, Taji must on the one hand identify himself with heaven, and, on the other hand, he has to identify that state of being, Yillah, with earth and humanity. Having differentiated between earth and heaven, he has to claim both. If, for Melville, religion represents the selfish perversions of ideal, then Taji represents the basic self-contradiction and impossibility of the idealistic position. Chapter LI, "The Dream Begins to Fade," sums up Taji's relationship with Yillah and ideality.

Stripped of the strange associations, with which a mind like Yillah's must have invested every incident of her life, the story of her abode in Ardair seemed not incredible.

But so etherealized had she become from the wild conceits she nourished that she verily believed herself a being in the land of dreams. Her fabulous past was her present.

Yet as our intimacy grew closer and closer, these fancies seemed to be losing their hold. And often she questioned me concerning my own reminiscences of her shadowy isle. And cautiously I sought to produce the impression, that whatever I had said of that clime, had been revealed to me in dreams, her own lineaments had smiled upon me; and hence the impulse which had sent me roving after the substance of this spiritual image.

And true it was to say so; and right it was *to swear it, upon her white arms crossed. For oh, Yillah: were you not the earthly semblance of that sweet vision, that haunted my earliest thoughts?*

At first she had wildly believed, that the nameless affinities between us were owing to our having in times gone by dwelt together in the same ethereal region. But thoughts like these were fast dying out. Yet not without many strange scrutinies. More intently than ever she gazed into my eyes; rested her ear against my heart and listened to its beatings. And love, which in the eye of its object ever seeks to invest itself with some rare superiority, love, sometimes induced me to prop my failing divinity; though it was I myself who had undermined it.

But if it was with many regrets, that in sight of Yillah, I perceived myself thus dwarfing down to a mortal; it was with quite contrary emotions,
that I contemplated the extinguishment in her heart of the notion of her
own spirituality. For as such thoughts were chased away, she clung the
more closely to me, as unto one without whom she would be desolate
indeed.

And now, at intervals, she was sad, and often gazed long and fixedly into
the sea. Nor would she say why it was that she did so; until at length she
yielded; and replied that whatever false things Aleema might have instilled
into her mind; of this much she was certain; that the whirlpool on the coast
of Tedaidee prefigured her fate; that in the waters she saw lustrous eyes,
and beckoning phantoms, and strange shapes smoothing her couch among
the mosses.

Her dreams seemed mine. Many visions I had of the green corse of the
priest, outstretching its arms in the water, to receive pale Yillah, as she
sunk in the sea [italics mine].

Symbolically, Taji and Yillah have become inseparable. Every revelation of one is a revelation of the other, until in this chapter—one of
the last wherein Yillah is seen—a final statement is implicit. Yillah,
as pure being, cannot *be* without a conscious, natural state in which
to exist. Ideality becomes the impossiblity of either belief or object
of belief without the material man who makes the believing. Ideal
must be actualized, humanized. And it is the very act of actualization
and humanization that kills her. The ideal needs humanity and experience in which to exist at all, but once it touches humanity and
experience, it undergoes another transformation which is the death
of the pure state, the death of Yillah. By the very fact that Taji must
naturalize himself and Yillah, his idealism and his quest are fore-
defeated. The pure ideal cannot exist pure once it is mixed with mortality and the demands of earthly living, or else it must wrench
mortality away from those demands. The buildup for the resolution
made by Captain Vere's much debated expediency takes on its con-
textual meaning in this light. For, *Mardi* insists, it is in *this* world that
we live. Mortals cannot breathe the air of heaven; mortality is the
only state of existence; and spirit exists only as long as mortality does.
Babbalanja can accept this after he visits Serenia, but Taji is never
able to accept the limitations of time and mortality, the limitations of
the modern world's materialistic view of man.

To this point, *Mardi* has provided innumerable suggestions that the
entire traditional concept of God, heaven, immortality, the other-
world, must be scrapped. Traditionally, natural existence is a state
of becoming and ideal existence is a state of being. But *Mardi* provides for nothing but the total dehumanization of nonexistence beyond natural life. So religion points to the other-world and is murderous. It dehumanizes. The quester points toward the other-world and
is murderous. He is dehumanized. The pure ideal lures to the other-
world and is murdered. It is dehumanized and it dehumanizes. Even

the "gallant hams" become dehumanized when, doubly ensnared by the crossed paths of religion and the quester, they pursue the pursuer of the other-world.

When the sons of Aleema are first seen they are dark and physical. And Aleema's sons undergo the isolation and alienation of quest. Like the quester they literally become denaturalized, losing their human citizenship. They become white. They become the monomaniacal and self-appointed avengers of religion who will sacrifice all to murder the blasphemer, and who will pile sin upon sin to have revenge upon sin. Their hatred and thirst for vengeance is a white hatred that parches and shrivels and bleaches what it touches:

the same double keeled craft, now sorely broken, the fatal dais in wild disarray: the canoe, the canoe of Aleema! And with it came the spearmen three, who, when the Chamois was fleeing from their bow, had poised their javelins. But so wan their aspect now, their faces looked like skulls. In my delirium I rushed upon the skeletons . . . the pale specters foamed out their curses again and again:—"Oh murderer! white curses upon thee! Bleached be thy soul with our hate! Living, our brethren cursed thee; and dying, dry-lipped, they cursed thee again. They died not through famishing for water, but for revenge upon thee! Thy blood, their thirst would have slaked!" [pp. 267-68].

It is neither just nor profitable to force an allegorical equation between the three sons of Aleema and the Trinity or the Furies. Whether they are religion's symbols of ideality or religion's guardians of ideality, they demonstrate the very opposite of the love that religiosity is supposed to practice. From this point on, they are not "comely" any longer, but are referred to as the "pale" strangers, the "wan" specters, or as "ghosts." Whiteness, other-worldliness, and death are again connected, and the obverse side of ideality's coin is revealed: the lure is associated with purity, but pursuit of the lure is associated with annihilation.

In *Mardi*, from the point of view of the primitive and all he symbolizes, there is a good demonstration of the association between otherworldliness and whiteness. In his dream story of Yillah's origin, Aleema pictured her as a bud torn from the flowering plant. Aleema's sons, when reciting the historical account of Yillah's origin, employ the same image, showing that their father's fable was simply the association made between the whiteness of western man and other-worldliness:

"Of Yillah, we know only this:—that many moons ago, a mighty canoe, full of beings, white, like this murderer Taji, touched at our island of Amma. Received with wonder, they were worshipped as gods; were feared all over the land. Their chief was a tower to behold; and with him, was a being, whose cheeks were of the color of the red coral; her eye, tender as the blue of the sky. Every day our people brought her offerings of fruit and flowers; which last she would not retain for herself, but hung them round the neck of her child, Yillah; then only an infant in her mother's arms; a bud, nestling close to a flower, full-blown. All went well between our people and the gods, till at last they slew three of our countrymen, charged with stealing from their great canoe. Our warriors retired to the hills, brooding over revenge. Three days went by; when by night, descending to the plain, in silence they embarked; gained the great vessel, and slaughtered every soul but Yillah. The bud was torn from the flower; and by our father Aleema, was carried to the valley of Ardair; there set apart as a sacred offering for Apo, our deity. Many moons passed; and there arose a tumult, hostile to our sire's longer holding custody of Yillah; when foreseeing that the holy glen would ere long be burst open, he embarked the maiden in yonder canoe, to accelerate her sacrifice at the great shrine of Apo, in Tedaidee.—The rest thou knowest, murderer!" [p. 269].

Just as western consciousness, Tommo, was held as the most prized captive by the Typees, who would eventually kill him, so too Yillah was held captive. In *Typee* irrational ritual and death-dealing, mystical beliefs were objectified in the taboo and the cannibal feast. In *Mardi* they are translated into the whirlpool and Apo. *Typee* prepares for *Mardi*, for Tommo, like Yillah, is jealously guarded in an inland glen for religious purposes, and he is unable to communicate. So too *Mardi* prepares for *Billy Budd*, where Melville again has the bud torn from the flower, the pure, ideal innocent placed in a worldly existence and reborn again in the context of history. In the same context, Aleema, who represents not ideality but an earthly, anthropomorphic perversion of it, is a mid-point between the white Taji and the dark perversion of earthliness, Hautia. First Aleema pursues Taji, then Hautia immediately follows. And both Hautia and Aleema, as pursuers opposed to idealistic aspiration, are darkly united.

In Taji there is the white incompleteness which is the disordered and incorrectly oriented error of idealism. In Hautia there is the dark incompleteness which is the disordered and incorrectly oriented error of earthliness. Before the reader approaches Hautia's isle of Flozella-a-Nina, he is prepared for a definition of Hautia by two general sets of circumstances. One is her opposition to and union with the sons of Aleema. The second is her opposition to and union with Yillah. It is she who kidnaps Yillah; Hautia is introduced in a direct relationship to Taji and Yillah even before one discovers that the person introduced is Hautia.

Upon the third day, however, there was noticed a mysterious figure, like the inscrutable incognitos sometimes encountered crossing the tower-shaded Plaza of Assignations at Lima. It was enveloped in a dark robe of tappa, so drawn and plaited about the limbs, and with one hand, so wimpled about the face, as only to expose a solitary eye. Now it was fixed upon Yillah with a sinister glance, and now upon me, but with a different expression: However great the crowd, however tumultuous, that fathomless eye gazed on; till at last it seemed no eye, but a spirit, forever prying into my soul. Often I strove to approach it, but it would evade me, soon reappearing [p. 164].

The reader does not discover until the end of the book why Hautia
hates Yillah, or that the glance given Taji is a glance of seduction.
Yet Hautia's introductory emblem, the moss rose, immediately relates
her to Yillah. The rose as well as the lily is an emblem of Yillah; the
moss is a reminder of the mosses in the whirlpool which is to be Yillah's death.[47] There is at once a prefiguring of the dual presentation
of the single being, the hint that Hautia is Yillah's death and that
Hautia is somehow a form of Yillah. And one comes closer to a definition of Hautia with the reflection that Yillah is part of Taji's own
self.

The Yillah-Hautia opposition is continued in Yoomy's song of Yillah, as well as in the dark-white contrasts. When Yoomy sings of Yillah
as the wondrous bright, lone light in the gloom and mystery of the
oceanic universe, he instantly opposes Yillah to Hautia. He sings:

> Like the fish of the bright and twittering fin,
>   Bright fish! diving deep as high soars the lark,[48]
> So, far, far, far, doth the maiden swim,
>   Wild song, wild light, in still ocean's dark.
> "What maiden, minstrel?" cried Media.
> "None of these," answered Yoomy, pointing out a
> shallop gliding near.
> "[Hautia's] damsel's three:—Taji, they pursue you
> yet" [p. 234].

The flower language by which Hautia's three heralds communicate
with Taji then tells Taji that to fly to Hautia is to fly to love, that
Hautia has wrought a death, and that Hautia offers Taji all "rosy"
joys and sweets. Yoomy then recites verses that differentiate between
the roses and lilies of Yillah and the roses and lilies of Hautia.

> Oh! royal is the rose,
>   But barbed with many a dart;
> Beware, beware the rose,
>   'Tis cankered at the heart.
>
> Sweet, sweet the sunny down,
> Oh! lily, lily, lily down!
> Sweet, sweet, Verbena's bloom!
> Oh! pleasant, gentle, musky bloom!
>
> Dread, dread the sunny down;
>   Lo! lily-hooded asp;
> Blooms, blooms no more Verbena;
>   White withered in your clasp [p. 235].

---

[47] For the flower symbolism, see Davis, "The Flower Symbolism in *Mardi*,"
MLN, II (1941), 625-38.
[48] The soaring and sinking of Yillah as quest object fits perfectly. In the chapter
on "Dreams," Taji's soul sinks and soars in the torments of quest. Yoomy soars to
seek his ideal, Babbalanja sinks to seek his. There is constant contrapuntal play
upon depths of sea and heights of sky.

Consonant with the repeated rejection of appearances (the very next chapter begins, "Judge not things by their names"), the warning is given that Hautia's flowers are not what they appear to be, but are cankered at the heart. The white withered bloom is Yillah, the death which Hautia wrought. By the third time, then, that the reader meets Hautia or her heralds, her characteristics are given. She is deadly; she hates the ideal; she clothes herself in deadly flower appearances which are the same as those of the ideal; and she would lure the quester, asking him to take her at face value, claiming that she can offer what he seeks.

We must turn to the history of Hautia, again a story of origins, to discover the meaning of her characteristics. This is the story of Hautia's ancestry:

In the beginning, there were other beings in Mardi besides Mardians; winged beings, of purer minds, and cast in gentler molds, who would fain have dwelt forever with mankind. But the hearts of the Mardians were bitter against them, because of their superior goodness. Yet those beings returned love for malice, and long entreated to virtue and charity. But in the end, all Mardi rose up against them, and hunted them from isle to isle; till, at last, they rose from the woodlands like a flight of birds, and disappeared in the skies. Thereafter, abandoned of such sweet influences, the Mardians fell into all manner of sins and sufferings, becoming the erring things their descendants are now. Yet they knew not that their calamities were of their own bringing down. For deemed a victory, the expulsion of the winged beings was celebrated in choruses throughout Mardi. And among other jubilations, so ran the legend, a pean was composed, corresponding in the number of stanzas, to the number of the islands. And a band of youths, gayly appareled, voyaged in gala canoes all around the lagoon, singing upon each isle, one verse of their song. And Flozella being the last isle in their circuit, its queen commemorated the circumstances by renaming her realm [Flozella-a-Nina, "The Last Verse of The Song"].

That queen had first incited Mardi to wage war against the beings with wings. She it was who had been foremost in every assault. And that queen was ancestor of Hautia, now ruling the isle [p. 569].

The parable, the retelling of Genesis, is transparent. It is the moment of loss of the Golden Age, the beginning of history, the loss of ideality, the earthly inversion of the expulsion of Lucifer from heaven, the inverted fall of man. The original beings were all Yillahs. Be they angels, or whatever order we may choose to call them, they were the divine aspects of existence, the ideal which could live with man in the paradise of prehistory. However, the pride of man-as-is made earth untenable for purity—it was Hautia's ancestor who led the revolt, and when we remember that Taji the quester abandons his world because of a rejection of life-as-is, Hautia's meaning begins to take form. Heaven did not kick man away from bliss as a punishment; man kicked bliss away from earth. Melville's retelling of the myth makes man principle and agent, not subject, and places the qualities of existence in man's hands. Hautia is pride born of pride, the continuer of a universal behavior pattern of man's haughty pride in himself, admitting of no change or betterment or possibility of integration with his own highest potentialities. Natural time, not nonexistent ideality, has been identified as the proper orientation for human behavior. Hautia represents the limitations of naturalism when it is perverted by the destruction of aspiration, to which destruction Hautia is committed. Aleema kills aspiration by denying the natural, conscious senses. Hautia too kills aspiration, but by emphasizing only the animality of the natural senses. Always the symbolism comes back to *Mardi's* rejection of segments and of behavioral opposites, back to its search for the completion of the mind with vision joined to feeling heart and joyful body, and dedicated to the highest aspirations of natural existence. Hautia is the human arrogance which cannot tolerate the pure ideal because it represents something above, beyond, and incompatible with that very arrogance. Taji is man's erroneous spiritual pride, and Hautia is man's erroneous animal or materialistic pride. Throughout *Mardi,* Melville implies that the concept of ideality, that idealistic perception itself, stems from the self's unwillingness to admit that the world goes on while it itself is extinguished. Thus Melville makes the self's desire for natural existence the central reality from which transcendent, eternal existence is projected to the self from and by the self. Thus the voyagers' cries about the pain of death; thus too Melville's religionist's use of ideality, which he is supposed to represent, for purposes of, and in hopes of, bettering the self's natural existence. Hautia is the insanely unjustifiable pride that arrogates to the individual, animal self the eternity of natural existence. The tormented Donjalolo and Borabolla, who reeks of mortality, have prepared for Hautia. For her, sensual gratification, natural existence, and immortality are one, and it is this impossible lie that the pig-Circe offers the world, and with which she enchants consciousness into being a pig-servitor. She would deck herself out in the appearance of the ideal and hold herself forth as man's highest attainment. She is an empty lie. To grasp Hautia, as Taji discovers, is to grasp thin air. Hautia's pride not only denies the other-world (which, thematically, is correct), but it bewitches and drugs men into losing awareness of the possibilities of bettering this world (which, thematically, is wrong). Melville's ironies, that is, the right-and-wrong incompletions, the relativity of truth, of mind, of aspiration, of pride, of body, are the ambiguities that continue in all his books. Just as Yillah is seen again as Isabel, and Hautia is seen again as Mrs. Glendinning, so Taji is seen again as Ahab—with the single change that whereas Taji sees the other-world as something good and desirable, Ahab's experience, capped by the destruction of his leg, sees it as something hostile and ugly. Ahab's enmity toward the whale (idealistic pride, or pride of consćiousness) and Mrs. Glendinning's enmity toward Isabel (animal pride, social pride) are prepared in the symbolism of *Mardi*.

In perfect keeping with the cleavage between body and aspiring mind, Hautia's enticements are all the physical pleasures of earth corrupted into a bewitching intensity which can find meaning only in the pride taken in unregenerate humanity rather than in human potentiality. It will admit neither mind nor love, and is actively hostile to both. It is not the physicality of Samoa, who uses body as the occasion demands. It is not the physicality of Jarl, who uses body in devotion to duty. It is the physicality of a madness which takes the greatest and perverse joy in mankind divorced from any aspects of creative behavior. It is destructive and sterile. It offers sex, but not love. The bloom which represents it is withered at the heart. Hautia, as a behavior value, is not limited to Flozella-a-Nina. The feast of Abrazza is a concretion of Hautia's way of life. It is empty and hollow, and leads to the deprivation and oppression of humanity. And the slow death of Donjalolo who, in reaction to limited existence gives way to wild abandon, is a surrender to Hautia's way of life. It offers witchery, frenzy, and extinction. There is no real food for humanity in the tantalizing and sumptuous appearances offered by Hautia. The fruits of her orchards hang "high in air, that only beaks, not hands, might pluck." The irresponsible sumptuousness is again presented in the "good fellowship" of Borabolla, who gorges himself into a gout-ridden caricature of a man. Except for Serenia, all the symbolic isles display a ruining of the natural existence that man has at his disposal, and they all prepare for Flozella-a-Nina, "the last verse of the song." The isle itself is a symbol of Hautia. Beyond the luxuriant orchard which is "the frontlet of the isle," the appearance, is all the rest of the realm, the reality, which is a "lengthening plain" that terminates in a hill which hides the sea caverns that lead to death.[49]

Hautia cannot admit the conscious being whom Aleema's sons would avenge. Neither god, priest, or devil can have any place in her world. This is the basis of her opposition to the three avengers. And Hautia's opposition to Yillah is clear in the story of her ancestry. Taji, in his attempt to leave the world in pursuit of pure being, is doubly opposed. He is enticed and lured by the world's false happiness which kills man's aspirations. And he is pursued by the self-appointed guardians of man's conscious soul, guardians who will kill and devour the man who would attain pure being on his own terms rather than on the terms of a religiosity which would deny that very attainment. Taji's entire plight is solidified in one revealing image. Night falls as Taji, following the three heralds of Hautia and pursued by the three

---

[49] For an interpretation of the topography of the islands, see Nathalia Wright, "The Head and Heart in Melville's *Mardi*," *PMLA*, LXVI (1951), 351-62.

sons of Aleema, steers for Flozella-a-Nina. "When day dawned, three radiant pilot-fish swam in advance: three ravenous sharks astern. And, full before us, rose the isle of Hautia." Chapter XVIII ("My Lord Shark and His Pages") had already shown that the bright and beautiful little pilot fish serve only to steer the shark toward his murders. Hautia's three lovely heralds, who promise safety and joy, would steer Taji toward his own death. Thus the three avengers, the sharks, and the three heralds, the pilot fish, become different parts of the same team. In this way Hautia and the avengers are unified. They are all death lying in wait, like the green corpse of Aleema, in the oceans the quester travels; and that the consequences rather than the motivations are the unifying band that ties the "banded world" which opposes the quester, is a constant ⸿xposure of the pragmatism which informs Melville's naturalism.

What remains to be discovered is the unity of Hautia and Yillah. The unity can be approached through Yillah's duality. She is at once ideal and human, as her histories suggest. And when Yillah is in Ardair, she has a milk-white bird, a symbol of the ideal half of Yillah. Indeed, the bird is named Lil (Lily, Yillah), and is called the "blest soul of the maidens," the unsullied ideal. Yillah looks into the bird's eyes, and seeing her double reflection, makes a statement of her own dual character: "Yillah, looking into its eyes, saw strange faces there; and said to herself as she gazed—'These are two souls, not one.'" Immediately that Yillah states this realization, the bird flies away, leaving Yillah alone, human, and unaided outside of heaven.

"But at last, going forth into the groves with the bird, it suddenly flew from her side, and perched in a bough; and throwing back its white downy throat, there gushed from its bill a clear warbling jet, like a little fountain in air. Now the song ceased; when up and away toward the head of the vale, flew the bird. 'Lil! Lil! come back, leave me not, blest soul of the maidens.' But on flew the bird, far up a defile, winging its way till a speck." [50] Like the disappearing bird for which Taji had yearned, ideality flies away. It may exist in human emotions as yearning, or in the human mind as imagination projected into memory, but it can not exist in actuality. The blest soul of the maidens is gone. The transformed and corrupted maidens of Hautia are all that is left. Human pride kidnaps the ideal, and either transforms it or kills it; in the Taji-Yillah-Hautia story is a retelling of the Faustus myth. Taji's selfish will motivates the attempted attainment of the ideal; natural existence and pride kill it, for Hautia is but the quester's own selfishness, his own perversion of natural being. Taji renounces pride and earth and is left only with his deadly will, which has no human existence left to rule over, and he is a dead man.

---

[50] The head of the vale is the place where the stone profile of God glowers.

Taji dives into the pool in Hautia's cave to find the single pearl which is Yillah. He dives deep and can find nothing but flashing emptiness there. Hautia tells Taji what the pearls are: Health, Wealth, Long Life, and the Last Lost hope of man. Taji too would call the pearls by the same names, but differing as they do in their definition of those names, only Hautia can find the jewels in her realm and Taji must find nothing. Only if Taji abandons Yillah and accepts Hautia's values, becomes the Circefied pig, can he find the pearl. And as the Ozonna-Rea story specifies, the acceptance can only turn out to be a transformation which would be the death of Taji's aspiring self. Taji will not accept. He will not forget Yillah, for she gives his self its motivations and definitions. Taji would search forever for the fulfillment of man's possibilities in ideality and would not rest content with man's natural state, much less with that state when it is degraded.

Down, down! down, down, in the clear, sparkling water, till I seemed crystallized in the flashing heart of a diamond; but from those bottomless depths I uprose empty handed.

"Pearls, pearls! Thy pearls! thou art fresh from the mines. Ah, Taji! for thee, bootless deep diving. Yet to Hautia, one shallow plunge reveals many Golcondas. But come; dive with me:—join hands—let me show thee strange things."

"Show me that which I seek, and I will dive with thee, straight through the world, till we come up in oceans unknown."

"Nay, nay; but join hands, and I will take thee, where thy Past shall be forgotten; where thou wilt soon learn to love the living, not the dead."

"Better to me, oh Hautia! all the bitterness of my buried dead, than all the sweets of life thou canst bestow; even were it eternal" [p. 577].

Better to die in dead ideality than to live only animal existence. Taji would plunge into the other-world (where there is only eternal nothing, although he does not realize this) rather than find satisfaction in the ready and apparent joys of a depraved society whose life and values are shallow. Like Babbalanja and Yoomy, Taji is the deep, deep diver, the high, high soarer.

The fault which keeps Taji from being the true Prometheus is revealed again at the very moment he rejects Hautia. "Show me that which I seek, and I will dive with thee straight through the world, till we come up in oceans unknown." It is the same disability implicit in Taji's desire to voyage alone with Yillah until their prow kisses the beach of Oroolia. Taji will do anything, will sacrifice world to gain ideal, will abandon man's only reality to gain the goal of his monomaniacal vision, which demands the essential selfishness and egomania of idealistic faith. He has already sacrificed the largest and most wholesome part of humanity to his will, and he will continue to obey his queenly personality in order to find a self whose existence is denied by material history. Like Aleema he too hid Yillah from view. If he could attain his ideal for himself, he would be willing, is willing, to relinquish his humanity and dwell in oceans unknown. The true hero must be able to share Taji's grand vision and to know in what terms it is impossible, to cast his eyes to both heaven and history in order to understand how and why he must act to preserve this world. An informing goal coupled with an understanding of the impossibilities of idealism must underlie the expediencies of earthly action in order that the hero may be motivated positively and purposefully for the possibilities of natural life, and not be stimulated by idealism, or degrading selfish gratification, or random behavior.

It is the misplaced pride of Taji's idealism that attracts Hautia. The guilt attached to pride follows Taji in the form of vengeance and sin. Hautia follows vengeance. At the moment Taji learns of the murder of Jarl, occasioned by the guilt Taji leaves behind him, Hautia's message reads, "Still I follow swiftly behind revenge." At one point, and too late, Taji realizes that in the moment he drew Yillah into humanity, for all the wrong reasons, he was her real murderer. The predisposition to find the ideal turns out to be the predisposition to find an absolute self, and thus is inseparable from the pride which prompts the predisposition. Ideal and pride are two faces of man's quest, just as Yillah and Hautia are inextricable parts of Taji. When Taji subjects ideality to monomaniacal pride, he himself murders the ideal. The conflictingly unifying views of self, quest, and Hautia-Yillah sweep through Taji at a single moment. He is undone by the instantaneous recognition that the two females are one, that they are fused, through him, so that the unity of the two are ironically made apparent in the death of Yillah.

But how connected were Hautia and Yillah? Something I hoped; yet more I feared. Dire presentiments, like poisoned arrows swept through me. Had they pierced me before, straight to Flozella would I have voyaged; not waiting for Hautia to have wooed me by that last and victorious temptation [the promise that she can show him what he seeks]. But unchanged remained my feeling of hatred for Hautia; yet vague those feelings as the language of her flowers. Nevertheless, in some mysterious way, seemed Hautia and Yillah connected. But Yillah was all beauty, and innocence; my crown of felicity; my heaven below;—and Hautia, my whole heart abhorred. Yillah I sought; Hautia sought me. One, openly beckoned me here; the other dimly allured me there. Yet now I was wildly dreaming to find them together [p. 569].

But the same, mysterious, evil-boding gaze was there, which long before had haunted me in Odo, ere Yillah fled.—Queen Hautia, the incognito! Then two wild currents met, and dashed me into foam [p. 572].

On the literal level, this is only the shock of recognition, the realization that Hautia was always a threat, the dire presentiment that Hautia has kidnapped and killed Yillah. But in relation to all of Melville's other books, and especially in relation to all the symbolism in *Mardi* that has led up to this climax, the reader's shock of recognition must be wider. It was not until he came to the world (Mardi) with Yillah that Hautia appeared, and then Taji did not recognize her. Now she emerges, and Taji is horror-stricken at what he sees: a soul mirror, a reflection of the guilt and crime of the pride that inevitably attends the objectification of idealistic yearnings and that shadows him, like the phantom reminder of Aleema's green corpse, throughout his voyage.[51] In either case actuality kills pure ideal. If not captured by Taji, Yillah would have been sacrificed to the whirlpool of superstitions. When captured by Taji she is drawn into the whirlpool of pride. Yillah had foreseen the mosses of the whirlpool: they were the one thing of which she was always certain. Now she is drowned in the moss-rose whirlpool of Hautia, who uses the vortex image to describe herself in assuming the dimensions of general pride: "Come, let us sin, and be merry. Ho! wine, wine, wine! and lapfuls of flowers! let all the cane-brakes pipe their flutes. Damsels! dance; reel, swim, around me:—I the vortex that draws all in."

Mohi, the historian, has seen Taji's story repeated throughout the ages and in all the different forms created by man's myth-making abilities. The Ozonna-Rea story is, like Taji's story, but one more chapter in man's ancient pursuit of ideality. Man chases the thing beautiful to his own eye only to find that in the course of the pursuit pride eventually transforms the ideal into something other than what it was and draws it into pride's far-reaching vortex. Mohi knows what Hautia's slave-damsels are. He says to Taji, "Listen; and in his own words will I recount the adventures of the youth Ozonna. It will show thee, Taji, that the maidens of Hautia are all Yillahs, held captive, unknown to themselves; and that Hautia, their enchantress, is the most treacherous of queens." [52] It is significant that although Melville has not allowed Mohi to earn the right to explain Hautia to Taji (if Mohi suddenly emerges as someone not blinded by official statistics, why had he not revealed Taji's mistake at the beginning of the voyage?), still, it is the historian who reveals the consequences of the perception that is idealistic rather than historical. The very predisposition which is the stimulus for Taji's quest is the same thing that is instrumental in the death of his goal. He can no longer find Yillah on earth, and life has even less meaning than it had before he met her. Babbalanja, while still the seeker with no answer, made a statement which sums up Taji's plight, although unlike Babbalanja, Taji is not reluctant to leave this world: " 'tis not the world *we* were born in; not the world once so lightsome and gay; not the world where we once merrily danced, dined, and supped; and wooed and wedded our long buried wives. Then let us depart. But whither? We push ourselves forward—then, start back in affright. Essay it again, and flee.

---

[51] "Is not that, the evil eye that long ago did haunt me? and thou, the Hautia who hast followed me, and wooed, and mocked, and tempted me, through all this long, long voyage?" [p. 572].

[52] See Homans, "The Dark Angel," 727, for Ozonna as Ether and Rea as Rhea.

Hard to live; hard to die; intolerable suspense! But the grim despot at last interposes; and with a viper in our winding-sheets, we are dropped into the sea." But Taji will pursue his object into death if need be, even though all that has gone before shouts that heaven cannot be regained in this way; that just as man banished heaven from this earth, man will gain heaven on this earth or not at all. Once the white bird has flown, man cannot pursue the myth that the bird represents, but must breed new and real and realized ones. Taji, whose vision is bound to be greater than his effectiveness, blinds himself to both truth and consequences, and will not rest content. "I am the hunter that never rests!" he says, "the hunter without a home! She I seek still flies before; and I will follow, though she lead me beyond the reef [which bounds Mardi, the world, natural existence]; through sunless seas; and into night and death. . . ."

The irrevocable decision, once made, completes the dehumanization of the quester, kills his heart, submerges him in the consequences of his greatest blasphemy—the denial of life—and changes his quest from heavenly aspiration to the diabolism of pride: "Then sweet Yillah called me from the sea;—still must I on! but gazing whence that music seemed to come, I thought I saw the green corpse drifting by: and striking 'gainst our prow, as if to hinder. Then, then! my heart grew hard, like flint; and black, like night; and sounded hollow to the hand I clenched. Hyenas filled me with their laughs, death-damps chilled my brow; I prayed not, but blasphemed." Here is the terrible, terrific Ahab prefigured complete. When the despised world would hinder, for good or bad, for right or wrong, then the Titanic self becomes rock-hard and murderous in its frustrated rage and would substitute itself for history and does substitute its dedication for humanity. The irony is now final. Just as Taji becomes the false Prometheus, the murderer rather than the savior, so Yillah, in the other-worldliness of her dual being, becomes the false lure, the beckoning of the bleached skeleton finger which points only to the eternal zero beyond the reef. Literally, the book cannot continue with Taji beyond that reef. Were he to find Yillah and unwrap the cerements that bind that once fair face, he would be greeted only by the hideously blank whiteness, not pearls, that once were eyes. And in that moment that he looks upon ideality, Yillah, God, heaven, he would be only his own non-being, both he and history unmade in the white zero of eternity. The only possible presentation of nothing is nothing, and the blank whiteness of the page beyond the words "The End" makes more words impossible. Hautia knows that she cannot hold Taji, who has recognized her, this side of the reef. In his revulsion for life which can not be had on his own terms, Taji rejects the possibilities that life may offer. The true hero would have to combat Hautia; Taji flees to other realms, and remains merely a bleached specter of idealistic will. So, when Taji rejects

Hautia, offering neither to submit to her or to remain and contest her rule, she makes the only possible answer to him: "Go, go,—and slay thyself: I may not make thee mine;—go, dead to dead!—There is another cavern in the hill." Rejecting the cavern of the shallow joys of animal existence, Taji races to the cavern of the death pride wreaks. He finds Yillah (but only *vaguely* Yillah—he does not know that with him she has undergone the final transformation from ideal to monstrous apparition) dead in the depths of—of course—a whirlpool. The dead ideal is swept out to sea by the eddies, and Taji says his frenzied goodbye to the world. "Ah! Yillah! Yillah!—the currents sweep thee oceanward; nor will I tarry behind.—Mardi, farewell!—Give me the helm. . . .

"And why put back? is a life of dying worth living o'er again?—Let *me*, then, be the unreturning wanderer. The helm! By Oro, I will steer my own fate . . . Mardi, Farewell!"

At this point the statement exceeds the wildest blasphemy. In effect, what Taji says is that having lived a life of dying to this natural world, he will now commit himself to the only identity for self he has left. If this is what I now am, so be it! He will not recognize the world, existence itself, humanity, man's plight, time, or man's limitations in time. He would, by Oro! be God and would transcend time. In a pride far exceeding Hautia's, a pride not of this world but rather the pride which drives him to replace the historical cosmos with himself, he pursues Yillah into suicide. The enormity of the suicide is the atheism of denying man's vision for life by hurling it into death with a loathing for historical existence. It is suicide not only of Taji, but it is murder of man's possibilities. It is this complete denial of life itself, the unforgivable sin, which is intended in Yoomy's last, screaming plea, "Nay, Taji: commit not the last, last crime!" It is the unforgivable sin suggested in Babbalanja's statement that one had "Better slay the body than the soul; and if it be the direst of sins to be the murderers of our own bodies, how much more to be a soul suicide." The murder of man-self implicit in Taji's crimes can only add up to that final butchery of soul-murder and soul-suicide. Taji's soul is now no soul. Its ideal is dead and it denies conditions and humanity to its self. Ideality is demonized, God is Satan, life is death; the ultimate, time, wears both faces facelessly, and Taji's denial of limitations is his final submission to them, his final relinquishment of soul or self. Mohi shouts, "He's seized the helm! Eternity is in his eye! . . ." And Taji replies, "Now I am my own soul's emperor; and my first act is abdication! Hail! realm of shades!" Time, history, God, seize Taji's bark, as the emperor will of man, abandoning its dead subject soul, shoots out of the world. Only man's own doings, the good or the bad, and in Taji's case sin, guilt, crime, error, and revenge, can pursue the quester into the grave as he is seized by the hand of time. "And turning my prow into the racing tide, which seized me like a hand omnipotent, I darted through.

"Churned in foam, that outer ocean lashed the clouds; and straight in my white wake, headlong dashed a shallop, three fixed specters leaning o'er its prow: three arrows poising.

"And thus, pursuers and pursued fled on, over an endless sea." [53] The endless sea is eternal nonexistence in death. The suicide is the destruction of all the possibilities of man's consciousness, and the white waves of time record the passage of all the sins of man's inhumanity to himself. The visionary who denies the needs and realities of natural existence turns his guns inboard and calls down death and destruction upon himself and his society. The nothingness of time, if it allows anything to continue beyond the grave, allows a pursuit by consequences. The only immortality is racial, collective, not individual; the only ghost is not the visiting angel—it is human history.

IV

The involved tale of what man does to his ideal and to his consciousness, and of what consciousness misdirected by idealism does to man, is not Taji's story alone. Taji's demonism is, like Ahab's, the diabolism of frustrated human will. If man cannot meet God, he will turn to the devil—not realizing that he barters with the same nonentity. Babbalanja, who quests with Taji, is subject to the diabolism of the man of insight, who, unable to find the last lost hope of immortality is unable to find the reconciling answers to the conflicts of natural existence. Babbalanja is like Hamlet, the man who tries to find an absolute which will at once dictate, explain, and justify the actions which must be taken to meet events. Unlike his polar opposite, Samoa (who had no stomach for Babbalanja's disquisitions), Babbalanja finds that mere action is meaningless. Next to Taji, Babbalanja is the most distinct idealist in the book. He plunges deep into the mysteries of experience, trying to prune away modifications and repetitions, ripping away phenomena to find the essential reality. The essential reality lies in the definition of God and the other-world, and Babbalanja's despair lies in the freezing suspicion that there is no God but time by which to explain the diversity, energy, and limitations of natural life. In sheer quantity, Babbalanja talks more about immortality and causality than about anything else.

Yoomy, the poet, tries to find the meaning of experience in beauty, but he too is a socially and physically inactive man. He soars high into

---

[53] See Tyrus Hillway, "Taji's Abdication in Herman Melville's *Mardi*," *AL*, XVI (1944), 204-7. "The flight through the reef barrier into the outer ocean [necessitates that] . . . the belief that the search goes on in a world similar in form and substance to Mardi itself must be rejected . . . Taji is willing to sever all his ties with life" (205). "And here 'abdication' is difficult to account for if it refers to something other than suicide" (207).

etherealizations of phenomena, also trying to find an essential reason. Yoomy, soaring into the magnificently awe-inspiring beauty and hopefulness of the universe, is the most optimistic of all the voyagers that Yillah will be found. Babbalanja, diving into the magnificently awe-inspiring deadliness of the universe, tries to find the ultimate reason, and of all the voyagers he is the least optimistic that Yillah will be found. One sees the creativity and brightness of time, the other sees the destructiveness and darkness. (Melville always places hope and joy in the mouths of his youths, like Yoomy; the wisdom of grief-taught experience is always placed in the mouths of his wiser and older characters, like Babbalanja.) At one point, in a sudden feeling of kinship with Yoomy, Babbalanja declares, "Yoomy: poets both, we differ but in seeming; thy airiest conceits are as the shadows of my deepest ponderings; though Yoomy soars, and Babbalanja dives, both meet at last." Babbalanja makes the statement which demands the realizations given him by his Serenian dream, for it is a most accurate definition of natural existence, which, in all its dualities, height and depth, life and death, meets itself in the time source. Like the sperm whale, Babbalanja dives deep and deeper and deeper still, down to the darkness of creation wherein lurk all the heartless, joyous horrors, the eternal monstrosities of being. And wishing to find the all-saving light, Babbalanja sees only the naturalistic universe, which is the wisdom that is woe. He must yet learn to find the brightness, the hope and beauty which are man's consciously intelligent use of the natural life and universe he has. In this black-bright light, Taji's abdication assumes historic proportions, for it is not the mortal story of one man's sins, but the immortal story of mankind's self slaughter with the mammoth engine of delusion, which finally consigns life to darkness only, to "night and death" and the "realm of shades." Babbalanja's statement cuts through the delusion. Whether one soars with the angel or dives with the devil, if he seeks the metaphysical ultimate, he finds the same negative reality. The soarer and diver meet in the reality of ultimate time, symbolically if in realization, literally if in death—which is Melville's ultimate democracy, where all meet and sit cheek by jowl. Realization must demand morality, but it must be aware that morality is a set of qualities which are projected for and by man to the positive reality of natural existence, to history. Appearances only are dual; the reality is an impersonal and unconquerable unity, for natural existence is simultaneous with eternity, is the substance which manifests nonexistence, is man's only positive reality. That *Mardi's* philosophical resolution sounds so similar to transcendentalism, to classical idealism, to theories of compensation, suggests an obvious idea that has often been stated: the real contention between naturalism and idealism does not lie in disputing the existence of infinite eternity, but rather in the definition of that concept.

Babbalanja's Serenian vision of worlds beyond takes him farther
and farther into eternity and infinity, into realms increasingly characterized by white brightness, sadness, and silence. Finally, beyond the
uttermost realm are a brightness and a silence comprehended by none,
and this is the realm of Oro. Babbalanja is lifted out of mortal being
in the dream, and his very spirit cannot reach that last boundless
realm. No one can. Indeed, as long as he has any kind of existence
whatever, even in the dream, Babbalanja can hardly breathe in
the realm but once removed from his own. Babbalanja's heavenly
guide admonishes, "But know that heaven hath no roof. To know
all is to be all. Beatitude there is none. And your only Mardian
happiness is but exemption from great woes—no more." There is no
ultimate state of *being*. There is only a state of becoming. For just
as each angel reaches greater heights, so there are other angels, each
from a realm incredibly higher than that of his lower brothers. Unlike
Taji, Babbalanja accepts a limitation to natural existence. He does not
wish to storm the ultimate which is boundlessly nonexistent and therefore unattainable, but to preserve himself in a manner compatible
with earth. "My voyage now is ended," he says. "Not because what
we sought is found [Yillah is again defined in this implication]; but
that I now possess all which may be had of what I sought in Mardi . . .
Taji! for Yillah thou will hunt in vain; she is a phantom that but mocks
thee; and while for her thou madly huntest, the sin thou didst cries
out, and its avengers still will follow." When Babbalanja despaired of
finding God, he despaired of finding Yillah. Now he lets Yillah go for
totally different reasons. Now that he is convinced that the other-
world is the negative reality of natural infinity and eternity, he is
sure that nothing which leads away from natural existence can be true
or attainable. In his realization that pride-killed Yillah is not a desirable goal but a mocking phantom, Babbalanja asserts that the lure to
the absolute is herself a murderess by the very nature of the zero to
which she lures.

Babbalanja's answer, however, does not embrace all the necessities
for behavior.[54] Babbalanja's final position is one of retreat. It is not
Taji's withdrawal; it is rather an action consonant with Babbalanja's
character, and is a retirement into a life of contemplative serenity.
Babbalanja gently disengages himself from the Mardi of the Samoas
and Pikos and Hellos and embraces the *vita contemplativa*. Taji's
career has demonstrated that withdrawal from the world begins a
chain of disastrous consequences, but Babbalanja's decision to remain
in Serenia, although strictly a first-person-singular solution, harms no

---

[54] I do not intend to imply that Melville's complete man is simply a hodge-podge
of all possible behavior patterns. That Melville rejects unselective and thoughtless
eclecticism is evident in chapters LXVII ("Little King Peepi") and LXVIII
("How Teeth Were Regarded in Valapee").

one because it attempts to lead no one into unlivable spheres. Yet, Bab-balanja's Serenian answer is a disappointment. Granted that his acceptance of limitations is one of the book's major necessities, and granted that his new and serene life is in keeping with his character, there is still a great deal of evasiveness attached to his withdrawal. Although it is true that Serenia emphasizes humanity, Christ's human principles and human reason, and is not other-worldly centered, still it represents a philosophical sweetness and light that is not accepted by the rest of the man-of-war world of Mardi. The islands have proved that if you turn your other cheek, someone knocks your head off. Yet Serenia would maintain that repeated love will conquer the ornery streaks in man. Babbalanja had been caught in all the torture of wrestling out a meaning for existence, of trying to ascertain the best course of human action, and of trying to define his relationship to man, God, and society. All that emerges from his enormous anguish is the anti-climactic picture of the philosopher who dwells by the side of the road (presumably in a rose-covered cottage named "Dunrovin") and is a friend to man. When he was demonized, Babbalanja's sententious and sometimes foolish pronouncements were often tolerable. Now that he has taken the cure and must be listened to seriously, he gives every indication that he may be a crashing bore were it not so close to the end of the book. Babbalanja has all the good insights and realizations, and he talks the good fight, but as one of the possible interpretations of his name suggests ("babbling tongue"), he merely talks it.

Babbalanja's Serenian visit has re-ordered his experience, and therein lies the trap. According to everything the voyage has taught, experience should first evaluate Serenia, and this never happens. Serenia comes into view merely as a very unreal paradise in a generally unreal and demented world. Consequently, although Babbalanja's realizations are results of his Mardian experience, his retirement in peace is a direct contradiction of what the man-of-war world has taught about actualities. We have no more right to believe that the rest of predatory Mardi will leave Serenia unmolested than we have to believe that the priests of Maramma will leave the transcendental boy unmolested. Had Melville meant to use Babbalanja as an incomplete representation of proper behavior, he should not have made him such a sympathetic character throughout so much of the book, should not have made it appear that Babbalanja resolves the problems. If Melville intended to use Babbalanja as a representative of the proper course of action, then such action is sadly out of whack with the political thematic implications built up by the entire voyage. Babbalanja's remaining in Serenia, the insular and green Tahiti of the soul, is a driving of the silver stake through Azzageddi's heart. The demon, which is the unanswered recognition of the horrors, accidents and inequities of existence, will remain dead as long as Babbalanja retains his Serenian answer of love, limitation, and reason. But the sweetness and light is insupportable here because Azzageddi is quieted only by a glib dismissal of the experience which gave Azzageddi life—as if one could say to a demented man, "There, there, now, be happy and quiet," and have the man become happy and quiet. In every way short of withdrawal from existence, Babbalanja's "solution" is a withdrawal from the very life which he has learned is the only one there is.

Although the Serenian episode results in behavior badly out of proportion to the stimulus (one old man talks and all are miraculously convinced), the behavior itself is prepared for as an alternative to the behavior observed in all the other isles. Whatever the old Serenian says about Serenia is what all the voyagers but Taji have long wanted to hear. But Babbalanja's pronouncements become irritating simply because he has not earned the right to offer prescriptions for living to the other characters, and the pronouncements appear—and are—facile and shoddy. Babbalanja should have accompanied Media as chief spear bearer or chief pacifier; and this objection is best made in terms of thematic structure rather than extrinsic morality.

The other major character who must be examined more closely is Media, for he emerges as more than just one more fragmented section of human behavior. He is the only character who unites heart and consciousness with the action that experience dictates. The thematic shortcoming of the Babbalanja story is extended to Media's career: Melville lost his best bet by dismissing Media with secondhand mention, for actually in Media he created the hero which the conditions of Mardi demanded. Perhaps Melville realized this and was too "written out" after his revision, which included the political allegory, and allowed the wrong man, Babbalanja, to make whatever summary statements were needed. Or perhaps he was not yet ready to tell the story of the Media-Vere hero. Perhaps the proper resolution was killed by something as simple as Melville's haste to have his sister, Augusta, get the "fair copy" of the manuscript into the hands of the publishers. At any rate, Media should have been a major protagonist, coequal with Taji. His re-entry into society, armed with power and historical insight, would have been the true major resolution instead of being just one more episode which managed to get itself included into the book's vital action.

Media is first seen as a man who considers himself withdrawn from humanity by being above it. The infallible demigod, he is the center of things. He is surrounded by, and he affects and directs the concentric rings of human classes subject to him. But he is insulated from humanity by his protective aura of divinity. Unlike Taji, Media presumes falsely to superhumanity in blithe unawareness of his self-deceit and social delusion, believing himself to be entitled to godship by his origins. When Taji and Yillah and Media enter the temple to dine, Media calmly removes the idols that look like Taji and himself, and the two seat themselves in the idols' places, blissfully signifying that the sacred objects are but proxies for the real thing. Media's detachment from human limitations is symbolized by Odo's custom whereby the subjects remove stone walls from the path of the king, demonstrating that he need swerve from nothing and that he is immune to everything.

Yet in the midst of this treatment of Odo's religion, reminiscent in style and attitude of *Typee*, Media is exposed as a man after all, one who very much enjoys some of the necessary conditions of humanity.

> Did deities dine? . . . Self-sacrilegious demigod that I was, was I going to gluttonize on the very offerings laid before me in my own sacred fane? . . .
>
> But hereupon, what saw we, but his cool majesty of Odo proceeding to lunch in the temple?
>
> How now? Was Media too a god? Egad, it must be so. Else why his image in the fane, and the original so entirely at his ease, with legs full cosily tucked away under the very altar itself. This put to flight all appalling apprehensions of the necessity of starving to keep up the assumption of my divinity. So without more ado I helped my self right and left. . . .
>
> Our hunger appeased, and Media in token thereof celestially laying his hand upon the appropriate region, we proceeded to quit the inclosure [p. 150].

Always, immediately after the appearance is the insertion of the humanity, the indication that this central dictator is fooling himself, for he is as human and as subject to the conditions of mortality as anyone else. Media is not only politically *in media res*, but also within Media, in dead center of the appearances, is the human being.

The man himself has a mind, and a good one. He has all the acuteness necessary for the conscious hero. At one point he angrily protests that he, a demigod, cannot be conquered by the bottle (the old toper!), rages that Babbalanja should think otherwise, stammers . . . and passes out, dead drunk. But even while inebriated, he is able to confound the subtle Babbalanja, and convincingly, too. "Babbalanja rose to his feet, muttering to himself—'Is this assumed, or real?—Can a demigod be mastered by wine? Yet, the old mythologies make bacchanals of the gods. But he was wondrous keen! He felled me, ere he felled himself.'

" 'Yoomy, my lord Media is in a very merry mood today,' whispered Mohi, 'but his counterfeit was not well done. No, no, a bacchanal is not used to be so logical in his cups.' " At first his intellect seems to be only practical shrewdness. But Media, a sham himself, sees through sham, and his shrewdness is necessary to preserve all the rationalizations which allow him to believe in his own infallibility. He sees through human foibles, and knows how to exploit them; but he prefers to believe himself above the conditions which expose human weakness in the first place. When speaking of power politics, specifically the relationship of England to Ireland, Babbalanja asks. "And may the guardian of an estate also hold custody of the ward, my lord?" Media cuts short Babbalanja's moral insinuations with a statement of stark realism. "Ay, if he can. What *can* be, may be: that's the creed of demigods." This response reveals the limitations of Media's realism. Although what Media says is true, his statement is not cognizant of the fact that this demigod creed is devoid of any direction, devoid of any purpose but an unoriented pursuit of power for its own sake. Very aware of his power position and of the realities of power politics, he is harsh and dictatorial. That his harshness never blinds him to his subjects' falsenesses is made clear in his treatment of the demagogical old men who plead for a common right to trial by jury. But he prefers to be blind to his own humanity, and he is therefore oblivious to suffering and unsympathetic to woe and human feelings. Consequently, he is unaware of his own vulnerability. He is tyrannical in defending the divine right of kings because at all costs he will preserve the power given him by the pretense to divinity. His rule is selfish. As governor he is solipsistic. His isle of Odo, consequently, is no heaven of freedom and peace. Media is at first incomplete because his consciousness of realities is denied the companionship of an understanding heart.

The common sort, including serfs, and Helots, war-captives held in bondage, lived in secret places, hard to find. Whence it came, that, to a stranger, the whole isle looked care-free and beautiful. Deep among the ravines and the rocks, these beings lived in noisome caves, lairs for beasts, not human homes; or built them coops of rotten boughs—living trees were banned them—whose mouldly hearts hatched vermin. Fearing infection of some plague, born of this filth, the chiefs of Odo seldom passed that way; looking round within their green retreats, and pouring out their wine, and plucking from orchards of the best, marvelled how these swine could grovel in their mire, and wear such sallow cheeks. But they offered no sweet homes; from that mire they never sought to drag them out; they open threw no orchard; and intermitted not the mandates that condemned their drudges to a life of deaths. . . .
  Now needs it to be said, that Odo was no land of pleasure unalloyed, and plenty without a pause?—Odo, in whose lurking-places infants turned from breasts, whence flowed no nourishment.—Odo, in whose inmost haunts, dark groves were brooding, passing which you heard most dismal cries, and voices cursing Media. There, men were scourged; their crime, a heresy; the heresy, that Media was no demigod. For this they shrieked. Their fathers shrieked before; their fathers, who, tormented, said, "Happy we to groan, that our children's children may be glad." But their children's children howled. Yet these, too, echoed previous generations, and loudly swore, "The pit that's dug for us may prove another's grave" [p. 169].

  Once more origins are introduced: the characteristics of the present generation, ruler and ruled, oppressor and oppressed, are the legacy of all the past. Because his awareness is heartless, it is incapable of making the social resolutions of history's tensions, and Media's selfishness prepares the destruction of his self's own social identity. In his delusion of invulnerability and superiority to time, Media is the Lear, the Richard II, the Oedipus, who all learn through loss. When Media gains humanity by losing his kingship and demigodship, he goes one step beyond the role of tragic hero. He does not become the indirect redeemer-by-negative-example, whose insights are socialized by external agencies like Albany and Theseus. Rather he attempts to apply his knowledge himself. He abdicates the throne and retains the scepter in direct opposition to Taji, who abdicates his humanity in order to retain his other-worldliness. Media's loss of kingship becomes the gained knowledge of the governor's true role and of human completeness. If there is the possible stuff of tragedy anywhere in *Mardi*, it exists in the Media story. Taji's story is only the rising action of tragedy, the incremental sin that has neither purgation nor resolution at the climax. Media cannot be considered the Theseus to Taji's Oedipus, because Taji's changeless blindness and self-delusion prevent him from being the hero. The ambivalence of Media's divinity-humanity becomes another implication of the name: he is a half-and-half man, not really a god, not yet a complete human.

Moreover, until Serenia, Media is a passive follower of circumstance. He pursues the bland median way and will not become involved in extremes or in any attempt to change the haphazard flow of events which have always been good to him because his origins have exempted him from consequences. He will not disturb the comforts of his royal, divine status by considering the inequities of existence. To be a centralist, to take things as they come, to disturb nothing with demonized views of the status quo, is to behave in a manner that presents another implication of the name Media:

"Why, Babbalanja," said Media, "I almost pity you. You are too warm, too warm. Why fever your soul with these things? To no use you mortals wax earnest. No thanks, but curses will you get for your earnestness. You yourself you harm most. Why not take creeds as they come? It is not so hard to be persuaded; never mind about believing. . . .

"Why think at all? Is it not better for you mortals to clutch error as in a vice, than have your fingers meet in your hand? And to what end your eternal inquisitions? You have nothing to substitute. You say all is a lie; then out with the truth. Philosopher, your devil is but a foolish one, after all. I, a demi-god, never say nay to these things. . . .

"Babbalanja, if you have any belief of your own, keep it; but, in Oro's name, keep it secret" [pp. 373-74].

Media's wisdom is the shrewdness that squares incontrovertibly with the evidence of unregenerate life-as-is. But it denies any aspiration to life-as-may-be. Media's response to the philosopher comes in answer to a speech in which Babbalanja states a rejection of idealistic aspiration and yearns feverishly for an intelligent use of the natural world. Despairing, as he does, that all the evidence seems to deny that man will ever behave intelligently, still he insists that life-as-may-be might be earned if man will turn his attention to the uses of life and stop chasing the vapor trails of angels' wings. "Ah! let us Mardians quit this insanity. Let us be content with the theology in the grass and the flower, in seed-time and harvest. Be it enough for us to know that Oro indubitably is. My lord! my lord! sick with the spectacle of the madness of men, and broken with spontaneous doubts, I sometimes see but two things in all Mardi to believe:—that I myself exist, and that I can most happily, or least miserably exist, by the practice of righteousness."

As the voyage continues, Media is worn down by the torments of humanity, and his heart grows and greatens—just as Taji's hardens and shrinks. His sterile, metallic qualities begin to disappear. After the visit to Vivenza, Media lets slip a remark (he is drunk again) which reveals a sense of moral relationships lurking just beneath the surface of his power-conscious realizations. "Fools, fools!" cried Media, "these tribes hate us kings; yet know not that Peace is War against all kings. We seldom are undone by spears, which are our ministers.—This wine is strong."

In Chapter CLXXII the change in Media becomes more apparent. The wearing away of his delusions liberated the submerged anxieties of his human consciousness, and he dreams that he has returned to Odo only to find that he must earn his right to kingship. The man becomes increasingly more apparent than the demigod. When Media hears that on the isle of Hooloomooloo the corpse of an ape had been confused with the corpse of a king, he maintains a thoughtful silence —no longer does he shout out against anything that detracts from kingship, as he did when he witnessed the revolution in Franko.

During the visit with King Abrazza, it is Media who champions the right of Babbalanja's interior devil, Azzageddi, to speak his view of woe—even though Media's own peer, Abrazza, is outraged by the realities Azzageddi utters. For the first time, Media actually sides with the subject rather than with the ruler's pretense to an immunity to the woes of history. There is yet another indication that there is hope for Media. When the company discusses Lombardo's Koztanza, that Mardian epic is associated with great heart, great truth, great humanity. Abrazza, characteristically, has never read it. But surprising all, Media leaps to his feet and says, "And I have read it through nine times." Babbalanja, starting at this unexpected disclosure, exclaims, "Ah, Lombardo! this must make thy ghost glad!"

Finally, on the Isle of Serenia, Media experiences his full conversion. He renounces his delusion and recognizes the oneness of human existence, subject to time and mortality. "No more demigod," cried Media, "but a subject to our common chief. No more shall dismal cries be heard from Odo's groves. Alma, I am thine." Alma, Christ,

Soul, is presented as a quality of earthly felicity, not as a quality which religion believes was issued from the other-world. As the son of Oro, Alma is the human soul, the all-embracing, collective consciousness and virtue of the total race. As soul, Alma becomes the emblem of the highest possibilities of man's positive reality, natural life. The relationship of Serenia to Taji is apparent when one recalls that when Taji renounces life he is called a "soul-suicide." The old Serenian's anti-absolutism, his rejection of orthodox, dogmatic revelation, is the statement that humanity can gain heaven by its own behavior in this life only. Thus, Melville's use of God is not as inconsistent as it appears to be. When he refers to God in man he means that man must be his own God, and he is making a naturalistic reference to man's most creative possibilities. When he refers to God as a metaphysical concept, he refers to the emptiness of time. Significantly, Media becomes the complete man when he renounces association with metaphysical divinity to align himself with natural divinity. And when we last hear of Media, he is the true governor. He combines heart and mind and body and does not withdraw from history, but attempts to reshape it. He fights against the consequences of the past, whose forces are led, properly enough, by the three vengeful sons of Aleema. He will try to create a re-ordered and humane state out of chaos, or he will die in the attempt.

Arrived at Odo, Media had been met with yells. Sedition was in arms, and to his beard defied him. Vain all concessions then. Foremost stood the three pale sons of him, whom I had slain, to gain the maiden lost. Avengers from the first hour we had parted on the sea, they had drifted on my track; survived starvation; and lived to haunt me round all Mardi's reef; and now at Odo, that last threshold, waited to destroy; or there, missing the revenge they sought, still swore to haunt me round Eternity.

Behind the avengers, raged a stormy mob, invoking Media to renounce his rule. But one hand waving like a penant above the smoke of some sea-fight, straight through that tumult Media sailed serene: the rioters parting before him, as wild waves before a prow inflexible.

A haven gained, he turned to Mohi and the minstrel:—"Oh, friends! after our long companionship, hard to part! But henceforth, for many moons, Odo will prove no home for old age, or youth. In Serenia only, will ye find the peace ye seek; and thither ye must carry Taji, who else must soon be slain, or lost. Go: release him from the thrall of Hautia. Outfly the avengers, and gain Serenia. Reck not of me. The state is tossed in storms; and where I stand, the combing billows must break over. But among all noble souls, in tempest-time, the headmost man last flies the wreck. So here in Odo will I abide, though every plank break up beneath me. And then—great Oro! let the king die clinging to the keel! Farewell!" [p. 579].

The three avengers are recognizable as a type of Furies. And in keeping with *Mardi's* naturalism, there can be no *deus ex machina* from heaven to represent the ultimate justice of existence, no Athena to calm the troubled waters of the state. Man alone must provide for himself. So Media sends poetry and history beyond the tumult, while

he stays immersed in society to fight the Furies, to combat the chaos
and retribution engendered by the sins of the past, sins which he
himself had helped perpetuate. The name Media takes on its final
meaning: the man who remains positively and actively and humanely
in media res; the new center who tries to reorganize about himself a
new social state from the chaos that howls out of the breakdown of
the old. Youth and age, poetry and history are unsafe in the chaos
where past and future are suspended in the uncertainty of the re-
organizing present. The results will determine the retrospect which
will record a new song and new legend—a new and different pean
than that which was celebrated in Flozella-a-Nina. And neither Media,
Odo, nor Mardi can re-emerge from the chaos in the same pattern
in which they entered. If Media is successful, there will be a spiral
toward the Golden Age; or, if he is unsuccessful, there will be a murder
of mankind by the three avengers. Media must provide the means,
the media, which will reinvigorate life. Once more, Melville's healer
of the wasteland is not the idealistic Christian knight, but the informed
and heartful social strategist.[55]

Clearly, in *Mardi* Melville does not relegate history to philosophical
and ethical considerations only. The description of the serfs in Odo,
the starving people in Abrazza's domain, the constant threat of revolution and further revenge, the description of the march on Parliament
by the Chartists, described as hammer-and-sickle-bearing workers who
are betrayed by agents of the ruler, all indicate an awareness of the
social and economic forces working in the ferment of Melville's contemporary history.[56] The allegorical Mardi is by no means divorced
from the world which saw the Paris Commune, the rise of Marxism,
sharpening class conflicts, the beginnings of nineteenth-century im-
perialism, the American pre-Civil War tensions, and the sincere and
hypocritical attempts of the deep divers and shallow skimmers on
every side of ideological problems to find a resolution for tensions in a
planet breaking into Mardian islets and fragments. In terms of the
Mardian world, the day of Mars which Melville used as the backdrop
for his quester, the plan of *Mardi* would have been an inevitable
choice for almost any writer. But in the naturalism of its author's informing perception lies the book's unique modernity.

Like Shakespeare, whom he idolized, Melville was also searching for
the Complete Man, the Perfect Governor. But Melville's search could
not take place against the background of absolutes which the Eliza-
bethan dramatist was able to assume for himself and his audience.
Melville had to take his symbols from the history of his own experience. Whether he saw plunder of planet (*Typee, Moby-Dick*), or

[55] For suggested sources for the names Media and Mardi, see Davis, p. 77, and
p. 77, n.2.
[56] For the political satire, see Davis, pp. 79-99, and 142-59.

colonial exploitation (*Typee, Omoo*), or the murder of freedom and happiness in the hell of nineteenth-century mechanized society (*Redburn, White-Jacket,* "The Tartarus of Maids"), he saw that philosophical protest had to find its form in the materials of social protest. The willingness to conduct his search by means of a perception born of experience in a changing culture is what made Melville the great writer he is. This willingness, as much or more than any rejection of Calvinism, as much or more than any personal, family bitternesses, as much or more than his love of rhetoric (rhetoric which was often in bad taste), is what enabled Melville to reach conclusions so much more universal than anything produced by most of his contemporaries, who began with an attempt at the universal. It is an old, paradoxical mystery of literary greatness. Melville's contemporaries talked about beneficent cosmic tendencies. Or they talked about the individual's first concern with his own soul. Or they talked about individual self-help and moral regeneration, about thrift and industry and success. Whether apologists for a growing industrial capitalism, or defenders of a middle-aged genteel tradition, or the really brilliant expositors of transcendentalism, Melville's contemporaries ideologized their arguments in terms of natural plans or universal designs that either are anthropocentric or absolute, demanding man's emulation. The conscious idealism of the fountain, Plato, and the superstitious idealism of that earlier fountain, man's need for myth in the face of what he does not understand, transmogrified and intensified by the middle and Renaissance ages, continued through the rationalism of the eighteenth century, and did not seem to begin to dwindle (if they ever have) until they reached a century which combined materialism with technology. By now it is a cliché to say that human history seems to speed up, to pack itself more densely with every increment of time. The nineteenth century was the first era in which a Thoreau and a Carnegie, a Whitelaw Reid and a Longfellow could exist within the same fifty-year span and all be representative. And whatever clothing disparate thinkers allowed language to give an ideology, there was an increasing need for an epistemology and an ontology based upon pragmatism and empiricism. Melville did not dismiss the political institutions, whale ships, financial structures, and factories. Like the transcendentalists, he talked not only about the qualities of the cosmos but about man's prime responsibility to his century and his society. But unlike the world of his literary contemporaries, Melville's cosmos had no final end, no absolute beyond the realities of the social conditions which are seen as the forms of human, mortal, material existence in the Mar-di-an journey. His world is like Babbalanja's Serenian dream of heaven. It is bottomless and roofless. Melville had to probe on and on into the nature of man and society in order to find relative goals that make human existence meaningful and good. The relativity of goodness and meaning made his symbolic task endless, but for his final and personal rest. "Would that a man could do something," he said, "& then say—It is finished. —not that one thing only, but all others—that he has reached his uttermost, & can never exceed it. But live & push—tho' we put one leg forward ten miles—it's no reason the other must lag behind—no, *that* must again distance the other—& so we go till we get the cramp & die." [57]

---

[57] Metcalf, pp. 60-61.

chapter 4

Pierre

The running battle of the star
and clod
Shall run forever—if there be
no God.

—Clarel

Reframing the quest in *Moby-Dick*, Melville created his most magnificent book. He united all the implications of his perception in a
central masterwork whose thematic place in the totality of his books
is seen clearly by the light of *Mardi* and *Pierre*. *Mardi*, coming before
Moby-Dick, is the conception of that book, just as *Pierre*, coming just
after it, is *Moby-Dick's* extension. Both Taji and Ahab are the Titans
who storm the battlements of ideality, but in neither case do the books
illustrate the process of disillusionment which led the quester to a
rejection of life-as-is. What had Ahab seen in life to make him spit
on the altar before his predisposition had been activated by and objectified in the white whale? What had Taji seen in life to make him
rail at the *Arcturion's* leaden hours before his predisposition had been
activated by and objectified in Yillah? It is not until *Pierre* that the
answer is dramatized. Pierre is Melville's most detailed portrait of
the quester. Pierre begins life accepting life-as-is as a joyful fulfillment of the human heart's demands. When he recognizes that the
appearances of life-as-is may be lies which deny those demands, he
proceeds to tilt with the cosmos, bearing a pennant whose motto is
"The Heart! The Heart!" And, ironically, like Taji and Ahab before
him, his great heart is fired and hardened to the zero humanity of
stone. It is this development of the quester that Melville had yet to
dramatize. "Lord, when shall we be done growing?" Melville asked

Hawthorne. "As long as we have anything more to do, we have done nothing. So now let us add Moby Dick to our blessing, and step from that. Leviathan is not the biggest fish;—I have heard of Krakens." [1]

Pierre, like *Billy Budd,* comes to closest grips with the problem of idealism by placing it squarely in the actualities of contemporary society. Ahab was the captain, who could rewrite the law each morning and who had command over the direction of his activities. Taji too, as sun god, could not be hindered in his monomania by the rest of the world. But Pierre is not his own social emperor. He must fight his battle as just one more nameless inhabitant of New York City. Also, there is another important difference between Pierre and Taji-Ahab. One wonders what would happen if Taji and Ahab had been able to catch their lures. Melville allows Pierre to attain and keep the lure, Isabel, and then crashes the whole weight of his theme down upon Pierre's head, showing that still beyond, there is nothing. "Even if the Titans had mastered the power successfully to pass the Penultimate, they would have found the Ultimate a silence." [2] And in *Pierre,* largely by means of a beautifully worked pattern of stone imagery, of which the hero's French name is not the least pertinent part, and by means of the imagery of greenness introduced in *Typee,* Melville defines the Ultimate for which the quester strives.

The problem shapes itself in familiar terms. There is the repeated insistence upon the characters' origins. There are the repeated white-dark tensions. There is the repeated problem of communication and isolation. There is the repeated half-and-halfness, or "ambiguity" attributed to many of the major characters. And there is, associated with the origins, the familiar illustration of characters by a display of their relationships to the world they inhabit. Lucy Tartan, whose relationship to Pierre determines much of the book's meaning, offers one of the best approaches to the novel.

As in the case of *Mardi's* Jarl, were one to shadow forth Lucy Tartan by working from apparent symbol to character, he would reach an erroneous conclusion. At first Lucy appears to be the bright lady, like Yillah. She is fair, ethereal, described by words like "angelic" and "heavenly." Her very name, Lucy, suggests light, Lucifer, the bright angel. To extend this to the symbolic value of Lucy the person is to see her as the lure to ideality, or at least as the unearthly nineteenth-century blonde heroine. When one thinks of the warfare between the amaranth (white heavenly flower) and the catnip (green domestic plant) and extends the imagery to Lucy, one would conclude that in the warfare between Lucy and Isabel, Lucy is the amaranth. But one of the "ambiguities" in *Pierre* stems from a half reversal of

[1] Eleanor Melville Metcalf, *Herman Melville: Cycle and Epicycle,* p. 129.
[2] George C. Homans, "The Dark Angel: The Tragedy of Herman Melville," *NEQ,* V (1932), 729.

symbolic imagery. In *Mardi* the dark maiden was earthly—proud and perverting, but earthly. But in *Pierre* the white maiden is earthly—well meaning and pure, but earthly. When we look closely at Lucy's other-worldliness, we see that she is described as angel by the converging perspective of characters whose judgment we cannot accept at all. "Wondrous fair of face, blue-eyed, and golden-haired, the bright blonde, Lucy, was arrayed in colors harmonious with the heavens. Light blue be thy perpetual color, Lucy; light blue becomes thee best—such the repeated azure counsel of Lucy Tartan's mother." But Mrs. Tartan is satirized as a brainless woman who has no real human heart and who cannot see realities at all. She never understands the real strength of which her daughter is capable. When Lucy comes to live with Pierre, Mrs. Tartan furiously storms into that young author's quarters in an attempt to reclaim Lucy. And she might have succeeded had "Mrs. Tartan been a different woman than she was; had she indeed any disinterested agonies of a generous heart, and not mere match-making mortifications, however poignant. . . ." Not only is her heart faulty, but her brain power is weak, "for, like many other superficial observers, forming her previous opinion of Lucy upon the slightness of her person, and the dulcetness of her temper, Mrs. Tartan had always imagined that her daughter was quite incapable of any such daring act." Like the lady-world she represents, Mrs. Tartan lives only by and for appearances, and has no insight into the true meanings or virtues or fitnesses of things. In the early portions of the book, by trying to bring Lucy and Pierre together, she blindly and gaily and preposterously gilds the lily. Conversely, she would also hopelessly mate incompatibles in her matchmaking, as attested to by the rumor of the young men's club formed to warn eligibles away from her clutches. "Preposterous Mrs. Tartan. . . . Exceedingly preposterous Mrs. Tartan!" the omniscient narrator hoots at her. Her equation of Lucy and heaven is not to be taken seriously.

Mrs. Glendinning, proud queen of this world, proud of her appearances, her social status, her body, the prerogatives of her sex, and her sensuality, sees herself as the dark, potent liquid, attractive to men of consequence. She sees Lucy as a pale, ethereal, light liquid fit for boys who have not yet grown to stronger stuff. Lucy is "a very pretty little Pale Sherry pint-decanter of a girl; and I—I'm a quart-decanter of—Port—potent Port! Now sherry for boys and Port for men. . . ." Again, "there was ever a slight degree of affectionate patronizing in the manner of the resplendent, full-blown Mrs. Glendinning toward the delicate and shrinking girlhood of young Lucy." And Mrs. Glendinning is partly correct, for at this point in the satirically lyrical presentation of life at Saddle Meadows, Pierre is a rather sickeningly sweet and unconscious little boy, and Lucy a rather sickeningly sweet and unconscious little girl. But Mrs. Glendinning is not a reliable judge either, for she too cannot see beneath the surface. She would reject the real man who does not submit to her own appearance values, just as she rejects her husband's chair portrait. Mrs. Glendinning's household is run by heartless and cold pride. There is merriment and comfort only as long as appearances are not disturbed, and Pierre himself later realizes that his mother dotes on him only because he is a perfect appearance, a mirror for her own pride and her own values. Were he a cripple, he suspects, his mother would not love him. For Mrs. Glendinning everything is but layer upon layer of appearances to be manipulated into conformity with her will—a will not of aspiration but of Hautia-like social pride. As Ishmael repeats after Solomon, all, ALL is vanity. Pierre's young love for Lucy is, to Mrs. Glendinning, nothing but a happy juxtaposition which is manipulated to meet her demands. While juxtaposition may account for the youthful Pierre's attraction to Lucy, it cannot account for the general passion of which he is capable. "Mrs. Juxtaposition, ah! And in your opinion, Mother, does this fine glorious passion amount only to that?" "Only to that, Pierre. . . ."

That it is *Mrs.* Juxtaposition is a revelation of Mrs. Glendinning's superbly overriding willful maternalism, which bends everything to its own queenly needs. It sees everything in its own image, seeing only what it will tolerate, perpetually lost in the self-deceiving projection of finding only what it wants to find. Mrs. Glendinning, like Mrs. Tartan, demonstrates that the opinions of Lucy are not definitions of that girl; rather they are the comic technique by which Melville has his characters unwittingly reveal themselves. In order to further direct the reader, Melville's typically nineteenth-century narrator steps in to suggest that the apparent and real Lucys are two different beings, regardless of what the other characters think.

Looking beyond the present period, Mrs. Glendinning could not but perceive, that even in Lucy's womanly maturity, Lucy would still be a child to her; because, she, elated, felt, that in a certain intellectual vigor, so to speak, she was the essential opposite of Lucy, whose sympathetic mind and person had both been cast in one mold of wondrous delicacy. But here Mrs. Glendinning was both right and wrong. So far as she here saw a difference between herself and Lucy Tartan, she did not err; but so far—and that was very far—as she thought she saw her innate superiority to her in the absolute scale of being, here she very widely and immeasurably erred. For what may be *artistically* styled angelicalness, this is the *highest essence compatible with created being;* and angelicalness hath no vulgar vigor in it. . . . Therefore, benevolently, and affectionately, and all-sincerely as thy heart, oh, Mrs. Glendinning! *now* standest affected toward the fleecy Lucy; still, lady, thou dost very sadly mistake it, when the proud, double-arches of the bright breast-plate of thy bosom, expand with secret triumph over one, whom thou so sweetly, but still so patronizingly stylest, The Little Lucy.[3]

---

[3] *Pierre*, p. 69. Italics mine.

Mrs. Glendinning, blind like Mrs. Tartan, cannot offer a true picture of Lucy. Isabel does not meet Lucy until the end of the book, so she provides no direct clue to Lucy's identity. Pierre is the only remaining character whose opinion of Lucy can be heard, and through Pierre's eyes we get another view of Lucy as something unearthly. To him she is not even the fragile pearl of maidenhood that she is to Mrs. Glendinning. In Pierre's estimation she is not of this world at all. "I to wed this heavenly fleece? Methinks one husbandly embrace would break her airy zone, and she exhale upward to that heaven whence she hath hither come, condensed to mortal sight. It cannot be; I am of heavy earth, and she of airy light." When Pierre first greets Lucy at the very beginning of the book, he greets her as though she were not involved in mortal circumstances: "Truly, thought the youth, with a still gaze of inexpressible fondness; truly the skies do ope, and this invoking angel looks down.—'I would return thee thy manifold good mornings, Lucy, did that not presume thou hadst lived through the night; and by heaven, thou belong'st to the regions of an infinite day!'" Despite puns upon the airy zone and the fact that no one seriously considers for one moment that Lucy is anything but a mortal, everyone feels, like Pierre, that the seemingly Yillah-like Lucy is not suited to a historical world which might include night and grief. But the Pierre who feels this way about Lucy is the early Pierre, whose eyes have not yet seen truth, whose soul has not yet known grief. He is a magnificent animal, like one of his well-fed and well-bred colts, but he and his horses can see just about equally far into realities. The early Pierre is a satirized creature, revolving like a well-trained satellite about the strong gravitational pull of his mother's dominating pride, a male lady-in-waiting whirling about the Hautia vortex. We cannot believe what the early Pierre believes, not only about Lucy, but about anything.

The narrator, on the other hand, is quite reliable—often obtrusively so. On the one hand the narrator satirizes Lucy, and on the other hand he furnishes direct hints about Lucy's very earthly being and her common mortality and humanity. Says he, "My proper province is with the angelical part of Lucy. But as in some quarters, there prevails a sort of prejudice against angels, who are merely angels and nothing more; therefore I shall martyrize myself, by letting such gentlemen and ladies into some details of Lucy Tartan's history." After all the sugar water and treacle of the too pretty life at Saddle Meadows, the satire is of course obvious in the words "I shall martyrize myself." The moment of "martyrdom" is the excuse to introduce Lucy's origins; the introduction is itself wrapped in another presentation of Lucy's apparent unearthliness.

At this moment, Lucy just upon the point of her departure, was hovering near the door; the setting sun, streaming through the window, bathed her whole form in golden loveliness and light; that wonderful, and most vivid tranparency of her clear Welsh complexion, now fairly glowed like rosy snow. Her flowering, white, blue-ribboned dress, fleecily invested her. Pierre almost thought that she could only depart the house by floating out at the open window, instead of actually stepping from the door. All her aspect to him, was that moment touched with an indescribable gayety, buoyancy, fragility, and an unearthly evanescence [p. 67].

But the reader knows what Pierre does not. A sad silence, not buoyant gaiety, is the characteristic of heaven. Lucy's unearthliness is the fragility of inexperience and of blind and youthful joy. The repeated words "fleece" and "fleecy" and "fleeciness" associated with Lucy indicate that perhaps this sacrificial lamb will indeed be fleeced of her youthful characteristics, for

Youth is no philosopher. Not into young Pierre's heart did there then come the thought, that as the glory of the rose endures but for a day, so the full bloom of girlish airiness and bewitchingness passes from the earth almost as soon; as jealously absorbed by those frugal elements, which again incorporate that translated girlish bloom, into the first expanding flower-bud. Not into young Pierre, did there then steal that thought of utmost sadness; pondering on the inevitable evanescence of all earthly loveliness; which makes the sweetest things of life only food for ever-devouring and omnivorous melancholy [p. 67].

So much for what others think of Lucy—all the opinions are but so much noise and clatter, none of them correct. "Yet how would Lucy Tartan shrink from all this noise and clatter! She is bragged of, but not brags. Thus far she hath floated as stilly through this life as thistle-down floats over meadows. Noiseless, she, except with Pierre; and even with him she lives through many a panting hush. Oh, those love-pauses that they know—how ominous of their future; for pauses precede the earthquake, and every other terrible commotion! But blue their sky awhile, and lightsome all their chat, and frolicsome their humors." Lucy's stilly essence, which none of the characters recognize, is what Sedgwick accurately defined as the land sense.[4] There is little sea-land tension as such in the imagery of *Pierre*, but the exact same opposition of worlds that includes the general Melvillean sea-land tension does exist here. Lucy, for instance, was "born among brick and mortar in a sea-port, [but] she still pined for unbaked earth and inland grass," and "though her home was in the city, her heart was twice a year in the country." Isabel, Lucy's direct opposite and other-worldly counterpart, highlights the tension by her longing for the sea. The ocean swell is but a dim memory for Isabel, buried deep in her Yillah-like, vague remembrance of things past; and when she once more feels the motion of the departing sea waves, her frenzy to travel outward to the infinite beyond becomes so uncontrollable

---

[4] William Ellery Sedgwick, *Herman Melville: The Tragedy of Mind* (Cambridge, Mass., 1944), *passim*.

that Lucy and Pierre have to restrain her forcibly from irrevocable immersion in the other-worldly, destructive element of ocean.

But the land sense which Lucy represents is fairly specific. It is not the cruel land sense of Mrs. Glendinning, or the foolishness of Mrs. Tartan, or the man-of-war conventionality and propriety of Lucy's own brothers. Nor is it the shark-cold brutality of the city, for Lucy wishes to flee from the city in order to return to the area of peace and fertility, the human, "domestic felicity" of the green Tahiti. The land sense of the youthful Lucy is much like that of the childlike and warm-blooded Typees. "So the sweet linnet, though born inside of wires in a lady's chamber on the ocean coast, and ignorant all its life of any other spot; yet, when spring-time comes, it is seized with flutterings and vague impatiences; it cannot eat or drink for these wild longings. Though unlearned by any experience, still the inspired linnet divinely knows that the inland migrating season has come. And just so with Lucy in her first longings for the verdure." Lucy as land sense must be divorced from land as the symbol of smug convention, human cannibalism, and dry rot, the land from which the Bulkingtons, the true seers of reality, flee. Falling on the debit side of the ledger are the Aunt Charities, the Bildads, the man-sharks of *Redburn,* the Mrs. Tartans and Glendinnings, the hypocrisy and selfishness and heartlessness and blindness. On the credit side is the warm safety of human love and sympathy, the Lucy-being which is bright earthliness and perpetuation of life. Lucy is indeed a gossamer thing like Yillah, unexposed to experience; but whereas experience kills the other-worldly Yillah, it brings out the steel in the land sense which is Lucy. She can determinedly face all experience but the denial of life itself, and near the end of the book, the grief-informed Lucy reappears divested of the roseate glow of superficial appearances, whitened and hardened to an intense determination to support and protect Pierre. She would lead back to true humanity at the same time that she rejects false and apparent humanity, as indicated by her rejection of her family. As soon as Lucy appears at the Apostles, other-worldly Isabel feels a strong displacing agency. All the rest of humanity consti- tutes what Isabel calls the "banded world." Lucy literally is related to all the false people, and in all cases is of this world and earth; therefore, like the rest of the banded world, she too is ultimately aligned against Isabel. But Lucy's unrealized opposition to Isabel operates from totally different motives: when she comes to New York to support Pierre, she thinks of herself as supporting true human morality and aspiration. Lucy would lead Pierre to completion. But for one thing.

Lucy's consciousness is incomplete. Although she becomes able to see through the appearances of Saddle Meadows, she is unable to see through her own or Pierre's idealism until it is too late. When she does reappear, purged of softness and blindness, she herself is the new enthusiast, beginning the quest all over again, believing herself to be prompted by God, to be aiming at heaven. She has had a social enlightenment, but no ontological, no true historical enlightenment. In short, she duplicates exactly, in relation to Pierre, the very career that Pierre began in relation to Isabel. Like Pierre's idealism and because of it, the element of humanity that can provide the proper answers becomes misdirected by an erroneous view of its own proper function and its own proper goal. While still the unconscious pink-and-white girl in Saddle Meadows' false bliss, "at bottom she rather cherished a notion that Pierre bore a charmed life, and by no *earthly* possibility could die from *her*, or experience any harm, when she was within a thousand leagues" [italics mine]. The irony is inherent not in Lucy's notion, but in her inability to see that every possibility is an earthly possibility, that her very woe-smitten idealism will defeat the redeeming qualities of her preserving essence—and even when it is too late, Pierre still feels in Lucy's presence a vestige of the force that would return him to humanity. Significantly, at the very moment that Pierre would treat sea-hungering Isabel according to human and earthly needs rather than according to the virtues of ideal absolute— at the moment that he is on the verge of incestuous, bodily relations with her—he appeals to her with a term that would be extremely strange were it not reflexive to the symbolic value of Lucy and to the entire mistake of idealistic quest: "'Hark thee to thy furthest *inland* soul'—thrilled Pierre in a steeled and quivering voice" [italics mine]. Always the irony indicates that the answers to the very questions the idealist pursues are only to be found in the historical actualities of earth's natural existence.

It is not only in her own intentions and in the words of the narrator that Lucy is related to earth: her very actions betray her fear and unwillingness to depart the level plain of earth for the chilly mountain heights of God-seeking. In *Pierre*, as in the other books, sea, mountain, and brooding forest are associated with the mysteries of existence and the quest for absolute values. The Delectable Mountains are really the barren mountains of the Titans, a reminder of the unassailable other-world. The earthbound pine tree which reaches upward higher than any other tree of the forest is the mournful reminder of Isabel's enigmatic face. And to anyone who has read *Moby-Dick*, the sea is a familiar symbol. Just as the narrator reveals Lucy's positive relationship to land when he has her restrain Isabel from suicidal diving, so, in one revealing instance, the narrator exposes Lucy's negative relationship to mountain.

When Pierre and Lucy ride to the mountains for a picnic together, Pierre turns passionately to Lucy, mistakenly seeing in her an Isabel (as he later mistakenly sees a Lucy in Isabel), a being of mystery by whom he has already been attracted. The very traditional language with which Pierre addresses Lucy is imagery which, in his terms, applies to Isabel. "Thou art my heaven, Lucy; and here I lie thy shepherd-king, watching for new eye-stars to rise in thee. Ha! I see Venus' transit now;—lo! a new planet there;—and behind all, an infinite starry nebulousness, as if thy being were backgrounded by some spangled veil of mystery." Lucy is too inexperienced to realize that she has just heard the voice of Pierre's predisposition. Yet the land sense is vaguely troubled by the outburst, as if it intuits the operation of powers inimical to its well-being. The land sense knows that its lover does not make love to it, but to something else for which he mistakes it. His words do not describe Lucy. "Is Lucy deaf to all these ravings of his lyric love? Why looks she down, and vibrates so; and why now from over-charged lids, drop such warm drops as these? No joy now in Lucy's eyes, and seeming tremor on her lips.

"Ah! thou too ardent and impetuous Pierre!"

The saving aspects of common humanity sense that the fierce fires of the quest burn too hot for life, burn along a path that leads away from the only existence there is. The bursting of the hot heart's shell, the lurid and satanic fires of the soul's tryworks will kill earth and humanity and quester in Pierre as they have in the other books, and in the first presentation of Lucy, the narrator provides a direct statement of this: "Thus, with a graceful glow on his limbs, and soft, imaginative flames in his heart, did this Pierre glide toward maturity, thoughtless of that period of remorseless insight, when all these delicate warmths should seem frigid to him, and he should madly demand more ardent fires." The early Pierre does not burn actively for the ideal absolutes simply because he believes that he has them, that they exist all about him in the appearance-world of his youth. It is only when appearances are pierced by remorseless insights that the fires of truth roll their black billows in Pierre's soul and that the flames of his predisposition burn upward fiercely to consume all in the activated desire for ideality, which Pierre designates by the terms absolute Truth, Virtue, and Honor. Lucy, vaguely stirred to uneasiness by the sudden hint of what lies within Pierre, correctly senses the direction of his ardor: "Blue is the sky, oh, bland the air, Pierre;—but—tell me the story of the face [Isabel's],—the dark-eyed, lustrous, imploring, mournful face, that so mystically paled and shrunk at thine. Ah, Pierre, sometimes I have thought—never will I wed with my best Pierre, until the riddle of that face be known. Tell me, tell me, Pierre; —as a fixed *basilisk*, with eyes of steady, *flaming mournfulness*, that face this instant fastens me" [italics mine]. She wishes to know the identity of the power with which she must contend for Pierre's dedication, and again Lucy correctly assesses the nature of her opponent's

attractions when she continues to plead with Pierre that he share
with her every last agitation and troubling thought "that ever shall
sweep into thee from the wide atmosphere of all things that hem
mortality." When she is in the mountains, the home of the amaranth,
Lucy is exposed—via Pierre's outbursts—to the appallingly vast and
vacant atmosphere of all things that hem mortality. Mountain is not
her home. She must return to earth, the dooryard, the domestic habitat
of the catnip. " 'Up, my Pierre; let us up, and fly these hills, whence,
I fear, too wide a prospect meets us. Fly we to the plain . . . lo, these
hills now seem all desolate to me, and the vale all verdure. . . .' Now
they rolled swiftly down the slopes; nor tempted the upper hills; but
sped fast for the plains. Now the cloud hath passed from Lucy's
eyes; no more the lurid slanting light forks upward from her lover's
brow. In the plain they find peace, and love, and joy again."

But Lucy's flight cannot answer the problems that cause her to flee,
for it becomes evident that Melville is retelling his one major story.
Life is both black and bright, both mountain and vale, both ocean and
land, both the mysterious and the known, both the aspiring and the
bodily, both the heartful and the comfortable. One must not, the
complete man cannot, choose one over the other. He must reform
existence by using each half of the duality to condition his approach
to the other half. Again, experience, maturity, becomes primary. One
cannot extend from self to exterior universe, from impulse to experience, but must work quite the other way round. Only as new experience revalues old assumptions, only as man's reconstruction of
history grows, can man's mastery over self grow, can the brightness
grow.

The fact that Lucy is to become vale-rejecting, mountain-climbing
Titan, just as now she is mountain-rejecting, vale-seeking innocent,
exposes the basic error of choosing one side over another. As usual,
the unity of existence, in the character of Lucy, is to be found in her
dual origins. On the one hand, her father was "an *early and most
cherished friend* of Pierre's father." Pierre's father, as a young man,
pursued not the conventional and proud world of Mrs. Glendinning,
but he pursued the ideal. Through association with Pierre's father
when he was young, part of Lucy's heritage is the aspiring and the
heaven questing. Mixed with this secondhand strain of heaven is the
more preponderant element of artificial society. Her brothers are
naval officers, conventional, obtuse, cold, and proud. They are not
the kind of seamen that either Bulkington or Ahab were; rather they
are guardians of the cold society and glittering proprieties which land-
lord this man-of-war world. And Lucy's brainless mother is a known
quantity. There is in Lucy's origins yet one more element which
associates her most deviously and tenuously, but most strongly, with
an anti-idealistic orientation. She is Welsh. In that one moment when

she is pictured as an angel caught in the rays of the setting sun, the narrator curiously calls attention to her clear Welsh complexion. It is also curious that Lucy's aunt, the most minor character in the novel, one who appears but few times, is twice mentioned by name—and that name is unmistakably Welsh: Aunt Llanyllyn. Even were the aunt a major character, the name would be strange did it not serve a special purpose. In sound and in national origin it recalls another Welsh name that plays an important role in the book: Plinlimmon. And the name Plinlimmon is directly associated with a philosophy that warns men to abstain from idealism, to be expedient, to realize that the morality of heaven and the teachings of Christ are inoperative and inapplicable on earth. Yet there is one important distinction between Lucy and Plinlimmon. Plinlimmon is heartless, and does not wish man good. Lucy is motivated by her highest, divine humanity, by her "angelicalness" as Melville defined it. She is benevolent and heartful. Indeed, when Pierre first tells her that he is claimed by another, Lucy clutches her breast and cries "My heart! My heart!" In context, this is more than the trite image of brokenheartedness. In similarity to Tommo and his leg, it is by means of a wounded heart that Lucy's consciousness is awakened to see that the state of her own emotion and the state of the exterior world are quite disparate. It is the quester's first murder—a murder, ironically and inevitably, of the very innocent heartfulness under whose banner he quests and whose ideals he seeks. The early Lucy dies, and unconsciousness is dropped like scales from the eyes. When she reappears after the purging and maturing heart wound, she is Taji-white. This whiteness, purged of social and religious illusion, represents the same rightness and wrongness that dualizes all the questers. The rightness is, of course, the increased consciousness, the loss of deluding, illusive innocence. Lucy is now the human being who is ready to attempt to control the conditions of life rather than to surrender to their appearances. The "Little Lucy" can no longer be pushed here and prodded there by the landlords of the conventional world. It is Lucy who brings up the topic of breadwinning in Pierre's poverty-stricken household. It is Lucy who initiates action by coming to Pierre, Lucy who rejects the comfortable, lifelong, haphazard ride upon the tide of events, Lucy who represents the moral recognition of necessity. The wrongness is the misdirection of Lucy's conscious morality. Lucy cannot be eclectic any more than any of the other questers. She has rejected one half of life which, though evil in its historical forms and circumstances, is necessary. Along with the rejection of the appearances of Saddle Meadows is the familiar rejection of the nourishing fertility and necessary material fulfillment which Saddle Meadows and Typee can offer. Even Lucy's instrument for the attainment of nourishment, her easel, is now stripped of the greenness of her earlier life: the pots of clinging ivy in which the legs of the easel had been planted are gone. The whiteness of Lucy's intense white dedication is now the same sterility that is Pierre's baleful red, fiery light of Satan. Lucifer and Lucy, example and disciple-twin. Prompted by Pierre, in the complete rejection of Saddle Meadows, the preserving, fertile land sense is destroyed as the characteristic of Lucy's being. With her real identity gone, Lucy cannot provide the very support which she sets as her task. She does not, cannot by the very irony of her situation, succeed in breadwinning. Indeed, she denies herself the bread of life, the bread which is food for natural existence, and uses it (as an eraser) in the sketching by which she impossibly hopes to earn bread. Only a taking-away, and growing blank whiteness can result from the rejection of history.

The sterility to which Pierre's example has reduced Lucy is the counterpart of the consciousness he has afforded her; in killing her true identity's ability to function, Pierre murders the regeneration of earth itself. Were there no mountain of evidence concerning the definition of Lucy, one would need no more than the single crucial question asked by Pierre as he prepares for quest. Pierre has to choose between human history, the human community, regenerative natural life on the one hand, and the idealistic predisposition which hungers for superhistorical absolutes (which underlies his championing of Isabel and which makes Isabel merely ancillary) on the other. And the narrator says, "Then, *for all time,* all minor things were whelmed in him; his mother, Isabel, *the whole wide world:* and only one thing remained to him;—*this all-including query*—LUCY OR GOD?" [italics mine].

In order to understand the development of this question in *Pierre,* one has to turn back. One must reorder Pierre's experience, as it is given by the book, in order to understand why the tension of Pierre's choice is the entire book in miniature.

II

Saddle Meadows as paradise is presented in honeyed phrases which are to be taken no more seriously than the "banded world's" evaluations of Lucy. "Instead of showing a sudden and inexplicable loss of taste, or the debilitating influence of cheap, sentimental fiction [Melville] is known to have thought ridiculous, his style reveals a satirical purpose." [5] It is especially important to notice that the gaudy giftbook dialogue in which *Pierre* abounds is fitted largely to a comic revelation of the speaker. Thus, a typical mid-nineteenth-century horror such as this: " 'Curses, wasp-like, cohere on that villain, Ned, and sting him to his death!' cried Pierre, smit by this most piteous

[5] William Braswell, "Melville's Opinon of *Pierre,*" *AL,* XXIII (1951), 285.

tale. 'What can be done for her, sweet Isabel; can Pierre do aught?' "
The flamboyant speech reveals Pierre's conventionally melodramatic
reaction to fornication in which, later in the novel, he himself would
like to indulge—incestuously at that—and which suggests not sin but
the supremacy of the complex intermixture and interindebtedness of
all mortality.

Although any reader can discover frequent stylistic atrocities
throughout the novel (indeed, one can hardly avoid them), most of
the florid language serves satiric and ironic purposes. It is true, though,
that once fairly caught in the cadences of artificial dialogue, Melville
never completely freed himself. However, although the dialogue is
often pompous and stilted, in those scenes in which the narrator
is intensely earnest, truer and more natural diction and speech
rhythms emerge as the more constant standard of that elusive thing
called style. The satiric tone extends beyond the dialogue itself, and
includes the entire lyrical, idyllic quality of life in Saddle Meadows.
We are as much as told that such existence may seem to be pure milk
and honey, but that it is actually a lot of unreal nonsense. In the
narrator's own words, "In a detached and individual way, it seemed
almost to realize here below the sweet dreams of those religious en-
thusiasts, who paint to us a Paradise to come, when etherealized from
all drosses and stains, the holiest passion of man shall unite all kindreds
and climes in one circle of pure and unimpairable delight." After
Mardi we know what to expect of Paradise to come, and when we
balance this passage against the career of Pierre the enthusiast, all
the sweetness and light crumbles under ridicule. The very next
sentence points the satire by injecting a neatly counterpointing touch
of reality, reminiscent of Taji's wonder that deities should dine so
well: "There was one little uncelestial trait . . . [Pierre] always had
an excellent appetite and especially for his breakfast. . . ." As Melville does with the presentation of "divine" Media's postprandially
distended belly, he uses "Mrs. Juxtaposition" to undercut the idealized
appearances by means of natural and common actuality. Moreover,
the essentially antihuman, antinatural qualities of the appearances are
always made manifest: during the breakfasts with his mother, Pierre
eats tongue. And it is during those breakfasts, as at all other times,
that Pierre can communicate with his mother only in terms of appearances; he must indeed eat his tongue and remain mute when he would
talk about realities.

The steady condescension with which the narrator sees the early
Pierre as a very, very young and docile boy intensifies the satire, for
as in Lucy's case, the omniscient narrator's view of Pierre is never in
agreement with the view of the characters who see the boy. It is not
until the last third of Book Two that the tone relents at all. And even
then, until the end of the novel, the tone seldom entirely loses its
edge of distaste and sarcasm. It is true that the tone also indicates

sympathy, perhaps love, for Pierre. But one must reject an identification between Melville and Pierre, for the tone always works hard to enable the narrator to show the reader that Pierre's goal is pathetically hopeless and foolish and murderous. Melville's careful choice of words creates a tone that makes a rejection of Saddle Meadows' values inevitable. The narrator takes great care to destroy the apparent attractiveness of Mrs. Glendinning and the social world that Saddle Meadows represents. She ". . . had never betrayed a single *published* impropriety . . . [she never displayed] one *known* pang of the heart. . . . With Mrs. Glendinning it was one of those spontaneous maxims . . . never to appear in the presence of her son in any dishabile that was not eminently becoming" [italics mine].[6]

Mrs. Glendinning is "a lady who *externally* furnished a singular example of the preservative and beautifying influences of unfluctuating rank, health, and wealth, when joined to a fine mind of medium culture, uncankered by any inconsolable grief, and never worn by sordid cares." Just as the early King Media (like Donjalolo and Abrazza and Borabolla) is a reflection of Hautia, so again we meet him here, with all his wealth and health and unfluctuating rank, in feminine disguise. Mrs. Glendinning's queenly relationship with her son, like Media's relationship with his subjects, allows no room for basic human needs and feelings:

a reverential and devoted son *seemed* lover enough for this widow. . . . This romantic filial love of Pierre *seemed* fully returned by the triumphant maternal pride of the widow, who in the clear-cut lineaments and noble air of the son, saw her own graces strangely translated into the opposite sex. . . . There was a striking personal *resemblance* between them; and as the mother *seemed* to have long stood still in her beauty, *heedless of the passing years;* so Pierre *seemed* to meet her halfway . . . where his pedestaled mother had so long stood; . . . they were wont to call each other brother and sister. Both in public and private this was their *usage;* nor when thrown among strangers, was this mode of address ever *suspected* for a sportful *assumption;* since the amaranthiness of Mrs. Glendinning fully sustained this youthful *pretension* [p. 2, italics mine].

Thus the opening of the novel furnishes a picture of the social Typee queen of the western world. Saddle Meadows, as the western Typee,

---

[6] The coverings-up constitute a major motif symbolic of the quester's deceit of society and himself, and society's deceit of the quester and itself. Everything is covered by something else. The chair-portrait's smile covers what to Pierre at first seems to be mildew and rot. The father's cousin lays the chair-portrait face down so that it cannot be seen, and paints in secret, leaving the picture otherwise covered. Isabel's true history is hidden by a recital of vague memories that she can scarcely communicate. Plinlimmon's writings are written by others. Reverend Falsgrave's snowy white napkin covers the symbol of his own shortcomings. The hall-portrait of the father is a varnishing-over of him. Words are sublimated into the disguising muteness of pictures, which play as constant actors. There are innumerable instances of disguise, which parallel Pierre's own plight. No one can be completely honest, for the world does not live by chronometers. But Pierre attempts (he thinks) complete honesty ("I will write it! I will write it!"), and meets death in his chronometric attempt.

has no more true consciousness than the Marquesan Typee. In one sense it is an exact duplicate of Mehevi's inland valley. The young Pierre and Lucy are physically beautiful and healthy; their environment is lush and verdant; they themselves are unconscious; their actions and feelings are spontaneous and childlike. In another sense, the western Typee goes one step further than its Polynesian counterpart. In the valley behind Nukaheva, although there were ruler and ruled, there was no social maladjustment, no economic inequity involved in government. The Typees were completely equal children of a benevolent nature. Saddle Meadows, however, sees rule consciously and selfishly perpetuated for the advantage of the ruler. Mrs. Glendinning wishes to see everyone about her saddled with docility. Blindness to basic human equality becomes mandatory. Saddle Meadows becomes a social, economic, as well as a physical Typee, and its ruler must insist upon the false appearances and prerogatives which will allow her to rule her subjects as if they were malleable children. Thus the Marquesan Typee, of and by and for itself, while still outside contemporary historical actuality, was, like *Peer Gynt's* troll, enough unto itself. It was not true to man, but it was enough. The western Typee, however, by its very being, is, of and by and for itself, an empty and inadequate lie. It is part of the actualities of western history (Melville takes great pains to demonstrate this), and, like its queen, must be supposed to be impervious to time. It is inevitable that Pierre's rebellion should be one with the exposure of the history of his house, and therefore with the destruction of his house.

Therefore, regardless of what one might like to read into the book as a discovery of what may have been hidden in Melville's libido, the brother-sister routine played by Pierre and his mother serves to spotlight Mrs. Glendinning's blindness to time and mortality and to the common origin and status of all humanity. Pierre puts up with it as long as he too is unconscious, as long as it is only a pleasant little game that pleases mommy. The fact that there is a real, blood relationship beneath the false brother-sister appearances is a preparation for the final murder of sex, generation, and history in Pierre's becoming neuter and in the suicide of his dehumanized being. *Pierre's* constant brother-sister, mother-child, and cousin-cousin relationships are one with the Enceladus-incest motif. Coelus and Terra, heaven and earth are one; all concepts are products of natural history. Melville never presents sex and genesis without tying them in some way to the convenient symbols of Adam and Noah—all mankind is one. All the children of "the sons of Adam" and the "irresistible daughters of Eve" are one. Thus all relationships are incestuous, inward-bearing, and outward-driving at once. Narcissism, incest, and homosexuality are one. Simply, Melville's sexual implications (when they are not used for "Rabelaisian" humor) are not intended for psychological purposes, and "psychiatric" approaches to Melville's books are bound to wrench those writings into an assortment of badly understood Freudian and Jungian freaks. Melville's sexual implications have symbolic overtones which are socio-ontological. Man's sex is an inevitable courting of his own continued existence; the dualities of Melvillean characters are finally unions of man's aspiring and man's animal facets, a joining of the parts of man-self with the parts of man-self, a unifying hetero-sexuality which in itself philosophically includes narcissism, incest, and homosexuality. In social terms, Melville's meaning is that love of one-self (inevitably futile), which attempts to exclude man-self, is the final unsexing, pretentiousness and heartlessness that ultimately deny life. Conversely, love of man-self, the realization of the one-self's common, mortal unity with all men, is the only love that can bring fruition and completeness to the one-self. Always the individual loses individuality and identity in individualism, which is blind to history; always the individual gains individuality by subordinating his one-self to the needs and actualities of the total race. Mrs. Glendinning prefers to be unconscious of mankind's common democracy in the universal capitulation to time. Like the quester, like Bartleby, she "prefers not to" recognize that the one-self cannot be isolated from the man-self—even though the world the blind man-self makes may be rotten. (Ah, Bartleby! Ah, humanity!) Thus Mrs. Glendinning lacks the realization of mankind's interindebtedness and lacks what Media gained through the canker of grief and sordid care—a time-wise and consciously informed heart. Pierre seems to be Mrs. Glen-dinning made male. He is the early King Media, not a female trans-lation. For, like the early Media, Pierre too has a huge and dormant heart.

What is it then, that prevents him from becoming the complete man? The answer to this question is the underlying philosophical materialism, the naturalistic perception, that emerges from the book's theme: whereas Media, when his heart was activated, reimmerses himself in world and time in order to institute the correct social state, Pierre immerses himself in the chronometrics of "purity," of idealism. And in the same relationship which Taji has to Media, Pierre too thus loses the very means to the realizations of his driving aspirations, or predisposition, and he too becomes a suicide and murderer on a vast historical scale. Melville repeatedly comes back to the same point. Because of the discrepancies between history, natural life, on the one hand, and ideal on the other, the idealist by his very nature, and regardless of the altruistic uses he intends for his mammoth engine of delusion, must reject history and natural life by rejecting its evi-dences of the mess man has made. The tactically wrong turn to idealism in the morally right revulsion to hideous history becomes an evasion of reality and of the correction for which history cries.

The idealist confuses the history of material existence with the potentialities of material existence, just as he confuses the blankness that allows every possibility with his own absolutes. Thus, although he becomes acutely aware of experience, he really uses experience to murder experience. Inevitably he can find justification only in his own being and becomes the monomaniac. Ironically, regardless of his Prometheanism, he becomes the being who subordinates man-self to one-self despite his belief in his own protestations to the contrary, thereby annihilating man (murder) and obliterating his own identity (suicide).

Mrs. Glendinning, in the apparently unchangeable bloom of her wealth, health, and beauty (she is called "this widow Bloom"), cannot admit social realities or time realities without admitting a changed view of herself and the world she landlords. Her smashing the world-mirror would be about equivalent to the impossibility of Hautia's committing suicide. In this hauteur inheres Mrs. Glendinning's seeming "amaranthiness," which, when placed in the context of the warfare between the amaranth and the catnip, sums her up as another cold and sterile opponent of the "domestic felicity" that Lucy represents. And, within the everpresent duality of results rather than intentions, Mrs. Glendinning, as earthly pride, is as opposed to the amaranth itself (ideality) as Hautia is to Yillah. It is his mother, Pierre realizes, who would be the last person to admit Isabel into the society she governs. Again, in the effects of her actions, Mrs. Glendinning, like Hautia, denies the true generative and conscious aspects of human life just as much as does their mutual other-worldly opponent.

Thus the apparent similarities of Pierre and Mrs. Glendinning are broken. Highlighting the vast difference which underlies the surface resemblance of the two, the narrator says, "I beg you to consider again that this Pierre was but a youngster as yet. And believe me you will pronounce Pierre a thorough-going Democrat in time; perhaps a little too Radical altogether to your fancy." The antidemocratic and narrow-viewed Mrs. Glendinning is further associated with royal prerogative. Even the land she rules is described in queen-imagery; "the country, like any Queen," says the narrator, "is ever attended by scrupulous lady's maids in the guise of the seasons." [7] And in a parallel that re-emphasizes their antinatural mother-son relationship, Pierre attends Queen Glendinning with the appearance-tokens of ribbons and bows, calling himself "First Lady in waiting to the Dowager Duchess Glendinning." The queen imagery fixes Mrs. Glendinnings origins. The words noble, haughty, aristocratic, tradition, privilege of rank, land-lord, are constantly associated with her so that she becomes delineated

---

[7] For a Freudian view of the queen imagery, see Henry A. Murray's introduction to *Pierre*, xxxiii-xxxix.

as the traditional and historical force which has always perpetuated
the status quo of Saddle Meadows life by hereditary and unchanging
rule. She is descended on both sides from heroes; Mrs. Glendinning
was sired and born by Mrs. Glendinning. She is self-generating, with
differing names and appearances throughout the generations, going
back to the beginning of hauteur, so that pride is not even a matter
of choice for Mrs. Glendinning.[8] The changeless position of Queen
of This World invests her with the insightlessness and grieflessness
which allows her the self-delusion that she is set apart from and above
mankind and time. (Even her servant, whom the young Pierre so
gaily orders about, is the old man, *Dates*.) Her origins and her name
—Mary—place her squarely in position in the list of opposing-
complementing characters.

When talking about Lucy's beauty, the narrator introduces a brief
and heavily satiric section on queens in general (of course relating
Lucy to the beautiful queens of earth), and in this section the anti-
idealism of Queen Mary of Earth is made clear.

A beautiful woman is born Queen of men and women both, as Mary Stuart
was born Queen of Scots, whether men or women. All mankind are her
Scots; her leal clans are numbered by the nations. A true gentleman in
Kentucky would cheerfully die for a beautiful woman in Hindostan though
he never saw her. Yea, count down his heart in death-drops for her; and go
to Pluto, that she might go to Paradise. He would turn Turk before he
would disown an allegiance hereditary to all gentlemen, from the hour
their Grand Master, Adam, first knelt to Eve.

A plain-faced Queen of Spain dwells not in half the glory a beautiful
milliner does. Her soldiers can break heads, but her Highness can not
crack a heart; and the beautiful milliner might string hearts for necklaces.
Undoubtedly, Beauty made the first Queen. If ever again the succession to
the German Empire should be contested, and one poor lame lawyer should
present the claims of the first excellingly beautiful woman he chanced to
see—she would thereupon be unanimously elected Empress of the Holy
Roman German Empire;—that is to say, if all the Germans were true, free-
hearted and magnanimous gentlemen, at all capable of appreciating so
immense an honor.

It is nonsense to talk of France as the seat of all civility. Did not those
French heathen have a Salique Law? Three of the most bewitching creatures,—immortal flowers of the line of Valois—were excluded from the
French throne by that infamous provision. France, indeed; whose Catholic
millions still worship Mary Queen of Heaven, and for ten generations refused cap and knee to many angel Maries, rightful Queens of France. HERE
IS CAUSE FOR UNIVERSAL WAR [p. 27, capitals mine].

---

[8] See the passage including, "Then, high-up and towering, and all-forbidding
before Pierre grew the before unthought-of wonderful edifice of his mother's
immense pride;—her pride of birth, her pride of affluence, her pride of purity,
and all the pride of high-born, refined, and wealthy Life, and all the Semiramian
pride of woman. Then he staggered back upon himself, and only found support
in himself. Then Pierre felt that deep in him lurked a divine unidentifiableness,
that owned no earthly kith or kin. Yet was this feeling entirely lonesome, and
orphan-like" [p. 105].

The tone of the entire passage, as well as the implications of the last paragraph, explode the appearances and idealizations. Men will act according to more basic realities of self-interest or according to the demands of real idealism, be they sons and Pierres or German politicians. Just as the beautiful Isabel is rejected and scorned by a heartless world and is recognized neither as Queen of Earth nor Queen of the Heaven she represents, so the beautiful Mrs. Glendinning and the beautiful Lucy and the beautiful Isabel are killed by Pierre when their lives lie at cross purposes. When the chips are down, the Kentucky gentleman bleeds not one drop, but quietly enjoys his southern comfort. The last paragraph is a satirical recasting of the general question, "LUCY OR GOD?" The primary competitor of Mary Glendinning of Saddle Meadows is Mary of Heaven. Mary Glendinning is "Sister Mary" to Pierre only in terms of the greatest irony, for the "Brother" will reject the Typee offerings of "Sister Mary" in an idealistic attempt to be a "brother" to Isabel. When he owns a "true sister" or a "Mother Mary," that female is the lady of heaven, or ideality.

The association of France with other-world, and pursuit of otherworld, and homage to other-world, exposes Pierre's father in a revelation of Pierre's own origins. Once upon a time, Pierre's father loved and pursued the Mary that was not Glendinning. He was the incipient quester, seeking values not allowed by the queens of this world, and the "chair-portrait" of the father as a young man provides the clue to the symbolic value of the Frenchwoman that was the father's first love. "Once upon a time, there was a lovely young Frenchwoman, Pierre," says the portrait. "Have you carefully, and analytically, and psychologically, and metaphysically, considered her belongings and surroundings, and all her incidentals, Pierre?" In youth, the father was a man of ideal aspiration, a quester, and as such he had to be an isolated deceiver; he masked his true self from the conventional world, even from the unconventional family member who wished to paint his portrait. He masked himself with a smile, "the vehicle of all ambiguities." And, in a parallel that further reveals the differences between the earthly Mrs. Glendinning and the earthly Lucy, Mrs. Glendinning is unable to tolerate the portrait of that smile because she senses that it reveals, at the moment it disguises, a man who was not her subject. She prefers not to accept the portrait as a true picture of her husband, and sensing alien and hostile values in the canvas, she will allow it to hang only in the secrecies of Pierre's closet. For Pierre the portrait has a constant and mystifying attraction which the boy associates somehow with the idealities he thinks his life realizes. Pierre becomes universal in history as the final male member, the inheriter of the paternal origins of the house of his fathers. His own father's history, however, is a repetition of *Mardi's* Rea and Ozonna. The father, as the fathers before him, had to succumb to the rule of Queen Hautia-

Glendinning, and under the impact of time and the impossibility of the early and rebellious love, had to yield to one of the alternatives history offered, the continuing, heartless rule of life-as-is. In the final action which ends the house of Glendinning, Pierre, unlike all his fathers who "returned to earth" in the wrong kind of surrender, plunges from earth in the wrong kind of quest. And precisely as Mrs. Glendinning rejects the masking, revealing chair-portrait, she rejects the son who becomes the inflexible summation of that portrait—as the horologicals always reject the chronometricals.

The chair-portrait tries to explain the surrender at the same time that it apologizes for surrender. It tells Pierre that the glimpse of humanity in rebellion, following the heart, may be the true and essential reality of human greatness, but it must be able, somehow, to realize this greatness in world and time. And world and time offer not only potential, but more to the point, the heartless mess man has made of that potential. Time, it says, allied with convention, allied with what man has made of the possibilities of life (again the pragmatic unity of opposed forces), makes aspiration knuckle under at last. The weakness of humanity is also an essential truth of humanity: "Pierre, believe not the drawing-room painting; that is not thy father; or, at least is not *all* of thy father. . . . In mature life, the world overlays and varnishes us, Pierre; the thousand proprieties and polished finesses and grimaces intervene, Pierre; then, we, as it were, abdicate ourselves, and take unto us another self, Pierre; in youth we *are*, Pierre, but in age we *seem*. Look again. I am thy real father, so much the more the truly, as thou thinkest thou recognizest me not, Pierre." Pierre recognizes the weakness of humanity, while refusing to understand or forgive it. *His* youth has been but a seeming, for his youth has been nothing but a continuation of the father's age. Frenzied, furious, betrayed, Pierre resolves that if the father capitulated and abdicated his true self, then he, Pierre, will reverse youth and age and will abdicate the abdication. He will pursue the quest. He will take up his young father's heart-shaped banner and will not break faith with ideality. His pursuit of ideality will be constantly stimulated, he knows, by an agonized heart which will remind him of all the abdications with which the chair-portrait seems to smilingly mock him. He will revenge himself upon the father and disown the father by the very act of trying to complete the father. The portrait is like the whale or the gold doubloon in *Moby-Dick*, another of Melville's devices which demonstrate the relativity of truth and the dependence of meaning upon perception, while the device itself remains indeed an external reality. Pierre and his mother each see different meanings in the portrait, and the reader, seeing both, sees more. Pierre sees only the lies of history's and life's appearances, and, dedicating himself to the Absolute Truth with which he will replace appearances, he rejects the father along with the abdication—thereby, like Taji, in rejecting human origins, rejecting history and committing the completest abdication.

When Pierre rejects Saddle Meadows, he turns in rage upon the portrait whose living self had been the cause of Pierre's sudden realization that "the time is out of joint;—Oh cursed spite, That ever I was born to set it right!" [9] At the moment he burns the portrait, he commits himself to the consequences of a rejection of history, the father, the broken quest, and of a rejection of the present, the mother, the banded world which breaks the quester. The father is horrified to see Pierre reject human potentialities along with human error. The appeal of the father shines out one last time as Pierre casts the portrait into the flames—as Pierre commits his own human heritage and his only identity to the hell fires of a heart which now hungers for more ardent fires. Pierre does not understand the direction or the kind of aspiration in which man can find his greatest identity in the social reordering of history—for this understanding, too, is conveyed by the ambiguous smile which reveals the knowledge of a dead man. "Steadfastly Pierre watched the first crispings and blackenings of the painted scroll, but started, as suddenly unwinding from the burnt string that had tied it, for one swift instant, seen through the flame and the smoke, the upwrithing portrait tormentedly stared at him in beseeching horror, and then wrapped in one broad sheet of oily fire, disappeared forever." Because of his initial errors, it is too late for the father to do anything but watch the history he has perpetuated being visited in incremental sin upon the son as the son burns humanity itself. At the same frozen moment, from Pierre's side of the tableau, life is rejected and the scene already is viewed "through the flame and smoke"; and once committed to the mania of his predisposition and the consequent burning of history, it is also too late for Pierre. "Yielding to a sudden ungovernable impulse, Pierre darted his hand among the flames, to rescue the imploring face; but as swiftly drew back his scorched and bootless grasp." The scorched and bootless grasp is an objectification of Pierre's entire plight. Once he enters the hell of his own furious heart, he cannot come back out to human identity through the archway over which stands the inscription

> Through me you pass into the city of Woe;
> Through me you pass into eternal pain;
> Through me, among the people lost for aye.
>
> °   °   °   °   °   °
>
> All hope abandon, ye who enter here.[10]

---

[9] The introduction of *Hamlet* is not only a fine stroke of thematic parallelism, but it is also an indication of the sensitivity of Melville's reading of Shakespeare. Like Hamlet, Pierre also turns to a frenzied search for absolute, cosmic justifications for his historical actions.

[10] See G. Giovanni, "Melville and Dante," *PMLA*, LXV (1950), 329; and "Melville's *Pierre* and Dante's *Inferno*," *PMLA*, LXIV (1949), 70-78.

The fact that man can only present a history of crime and woe and error allows the idealist but a one-directional thrust through the mask. For the conventional world allows the quester an either-or choice of rejection or submission. The transformation of the chair-portrait to drawing-room portrait is all Mrs. Glendinning's doing. That portrait was made "during the best and rosiest days of their wedded union; at the particular desire of my mother; and by a celebrated artist of her own election, and costumed after her own taste . . . as he had really appeared to her," Pierre muses. Convention, traditional rule, status quo, will not allow aspiration to be translated into social and historical terms. If the aspiring man is not the social and historical strategist, then he must either succumb to life-as-is or turn to supersocial, super-historical, supernatural absolutes. Since Pierre is not the social strate-gist, his mother is, then, his greatest external enemy. (The absolutes, the zero, can be neither friend nor enemy; they can only not be.) At the moment Pierre challenges appearances with suggestions of reality ("You are too proud to show toward me what you are this moment feeling, my mother"), Mrs. Glendinning says, "Beware of me, Pierre. There lives not that being in the world of whom thou hast more reason to beware, so you continue but a little longer to act thus with me."

Pierre's great-grandfather was also once a rebel and a fighter. He led the western incursions against the aboriginal Typees, who are translated into the American setting of *Pierre* as the Indians. On be-half of his own contemporary history, the great-grandfather made sweeping inroads against those primeval, noble savages. But Pierre's great-grandfather was unhorsed in the struggle, and from the fallen aspiring man in the fallen saddle, Saddle Meadows takes its com-memorative name: "On the meadows which sloped away from the shaded rear of the manorial mansion, far to the winding river, an Indian battle had been fought, in the earlier days of the colony, and in that battle the paternal great-grandfather of Pierre, mortally wounded, had sat unhorsed on his saddle in the grass, with his dying voice, still cheering his men in the fray." But by the time we come to Pierre's grandfather, another rebel and fighter, we discover that the great-grandfather had simply defeated the physical Typee in order to extend the traditions and the rule of western Typee. His taking the land became not an act of liberating human potential, but was an act of expropriation, for the deeds to the land itself, "those deeds, as be-fore hinted, did indeed date back to three kings—Indian kings—only so much the finer for that." In the way of life for which it prepared, that battle loses its possibilities as a struggle for consciousness and becomes reduced to the spoilation of earth (startlingly similar to Faulkner's Ikkemotubbe and Sutpen and de Spain and McCaslin) in a conflict of cultures; the battle is finally just another struggle for rule and the denial of mortality's common existence.

The grandfather in turn rebels against colonization by Britain. The mansion is full of mementos of the grandfather's victory in his revulsion to traditional rule. Yet the granfather too makes no new synthesis of human society, but also succumbs to and turns to his own kind of convention, the rule of the Mrs. Glendinnings. Pierre's "grandfather had for several months defended a rude but all-important, stockaded fort, against the combined assaults of Indians, Tories, and Regulars. From below that fort, the gentlemanly, but murderous half-breed, Brant, had fled, but had survived to dine with General Glendinning, in the amicable times which followed that vindictive war." After the war, the grandfather in his own turn becomes the type of the polite and patriarchal aristocrat:

in a night-scuffle in the wilderness before the Revolutionary War, he had annihilated two Indian savages by making reciprocal bludgeons of their heads. And all this was done by the mildest hearted, and most blue-eyed gentleman in the world, who according to the patriarchal fashion of those days, was a gentle, white-haired worshipper of all the household gods; the gentlest husband, and the gentlest father; the kindest of masters to his slaves; of the most wonderful unruffledness of temper; a serene smoker of his after-dinner pipe; a forgiver of many injuries; a sweet-hearted, charitable Christian; in fine, a pure, cheerful, childlike, blue-eyed, divine old man; in whose meek, majestic soul, the lion and the lamb embraced—fit image of his God [p. 33].

Chapters could be spent on the ironies and double meanings in this passage alone, but it can be left with the reflection that unmarked by any real woe in all his experience, the grandfather also fights an ultimately meaningless fight. The banners and drums and batons captured by the grandfather become pride-ornaments in the household of Mrs. Glendinning, who made the father a colony in his turn, and who attempts to keep her son saddled with prideful convention in her British, colonial rule. So just as the rebels, great-grandfathers, grandfathers, fathers, all become exponents of Typee, they hand down the dual heritage of Titanism and submission to the son.

The unhorsing image helps to relate the fight against time to the fight against convention. The act of rebellion is the same in both instances. Pierre, when considering the consequences of his choice between Lucy and God, invokes the wisdom of the Terror Stone. "If the miseries of the undisclosable things in me shall ever unhorse me from my manhood's seat . . . then do thou, Mute Massiveness, fall on me." [11] Pierre is, of course, unhorsed from his manhood's seat. And at the same time, he snatches the reins from Mrs. Glendinning's hands and ceases to be a trained horse himself. In one highly revealing and premonitory soliloquy, Mrs. Glendenning uncovers her portrait of

---

[11] *Pierre*, pp. 157-58. Ironically, the predisposition and its object are more completely interior than Pierre, in the very act of appealing to the symbol of the object, can realize.

Pierre, in which he is seen as a splendidly trained and magnificent animal, a most beautiful Typee with the overlay of western convention and the consciousness only of "his place."

"A noble boy, and docile"—she murmered—"he has all the frolicsomeness of youth, with little of its giddiness. And he does not grow vain-glorious in sophomorean wisdom. I thank heaven I sent him not to college. A noble boy, and docile. A fine, proud, loving, docile, vigorous boy. Pray God he never becomes otherwise to me. His little wife that is to be, will not estrange him from me; for she too is docile,—beautiful and reverential, and most docile. Seldom yet have I known such blue eyes as hers, that were not docile, and would not follow a bold black one, as two meek, blue-ribboned ewes follow their martial leader. How glad am I that Pierre loves her so, and not some dark-eyed haughtiness, with whom I could never live in peace; but who would ever be setting her young married state before my elderly widowed one, and claiming all the homage of my dear boy—the fine, proud, loving, docile, vigorous boy!—the lofty-minded, well-born, noble boy; and with such sweet docilities! See his hair! He does in truth illustrate that fine saying of his father's, that as the noblest colts, in three points—abundant hair, swelling chest, and sweet docility—should resemble a fine woman, so should a noble youth" [p. 21].

The lack of essential humanity, the desire for her subjects' mindlessness in Mrs. Glendinning's idealized description, almost does characterize the early Pierre who, as a noble, docile colt, has the same relation to the proud name of Glendinning that his own noble colts have to him. When he sees the clothes and trophies and pictures of his sires, his feelings are mingled pride, fealty, and inferiority. He has the haughty hope that some day he too may measure up to the stature of the great Typee masters of the past. Perfectly does the description of the colts parallel Pierre's relationship with his mother and his house. "They well knew that they were but an inferior and subordinate branch of the Glendinning's, bound in perpetual feudal fealty to its headmost representative. Therefore these young cousins never permitted themselves to run from Pierre; they were impatient in their paces, but very patient in the halt."

Lucy and Pierre go riding in the huge old phaeton that is an emblem of the great girth—in every sense—of the grandfather's past. And, "Though the vehicle was a sexagenarian, the animals that drew it were but six year old colts." Pierre is haltered and saddled in Saddle Meadows. He is horse and horsed. He is both the well-trained and docile colt and at the same time the new young "headmost representative" of the Typee world—and will remain horsed as long as he remains horse. Thus the son draws the dual burden of the heritage of the generations. When Pierre puts his colts through their paces, showing off their obedience by crawling beneath their potentially murderous legs, he is rewarded by foam-flake epaulets, himself being made general like the grandfather before him through approbation of the horse-world of Saddle Meadows. He is at once an obedient animal and a Mrs. Glendinning, delighting in the obedience, fealty, and docility of his subjects. He feels that he but follows in other's footsteps, and Pierre's pride wheels to new heights. "How proud felt Pierre: in fancy's eye, he saw the horse-ghosts a-tandem in the van. 'These are but wheelers'—cried Young Pierre—'the leaders are the generations.'" And it is perhaps here that Melville's satirical irony reaches its height in the lyrical early books of *Pierre*. The tableau epitomizes the theme emerging from the insistence upon origins: here is an oblique picturing of man's moral responsibility for man's past, present, and future. On and on goes history in incremental spiral, the generations past preparing a context for generations future, leading them on, harnessed and saddled, head to buttock, drawing the horse-slave-humanmaster queens and colonies of the Saddle Meadows world.

Thus Pierre's was a double descent of subjection. On both sides he sprung from slaves. Also "Pierre's was a double revolutionary descent. On both sides he sprung from heroes." But the young Pierre, as yet untouched by woe, is blind to the real essence of his burden. Drawing the burden of the western Typee is pleasant indeed, as long as that is the only burden and the real burdens remain undisclosed. "Well, life's a burden, they say; why not be burdened cheerily?" asks Pierre. Indeed, history-blind "Pierre little foresaw that this world hath a deeper secret than beauty, and Life some burdens heavier than death." The horse imagery continues as Pierre, "laden with shawls, parasole, reticule, and a small hamper," sees his burden simply in terms of appearance.

"But look ye, Lucy, I am going to enter a formal declaration and protest before matters go further with us. When we are married, I am not to carry any bundles, unless in case of real need; and what is more, when there are any of your young lady acquaintances in sight, I am not to be unnecessarily called upon to back up, and load for their particular edification."

"Now I am really vexed with you, Pierre; that is the first ill-natured innuendo I ever heard from you. Are there any of my young lady acquaintances in sight now, I should like to know?"

"Six of them, right over the way," said Pierre; "but they keep behind their curtains. I never trust your solitary village streets, Lucy. Sharp-shooters behind every clap-board, Lucy" [p. 25].

When Pierre is unhorsed by unmanning himself, he is also unhorsed with the withdrawal of support by the horselike and heartless world of the very appearances in which the early Pierre lives. His flight from Saddle Meadows is made in a horse-drawn stagecoach, and for the first time in the book, Pierre is in acute physical discomfort. When he arrives in the stony city, his first difficulty is with a horse-cabby. The driver is not only insolent (rank, station, wealth, are gone), but balks Pierre's will. Pierre even has difficulty finding a horse-cab with which to make his necessary arrangements. His new life is introduced by the losing of his way; by the coldness, the hostility, the loss of control over circumstance, which the change of worlds first presented in *Typee*; and by stone, which comes to enclose the novel's meaning.

III

Pierre is first seen "issuing from the embowered and high-gabled old home of his fathers." He is "dewily refreshed and spiritualized by sleep," and "half-unconsciously" he wends his way to Lucy. The very countryside is also one "verdant trance" and even "the brindled kine [are] dreamily wandering." He is just emerging from the womb, as it were, and is on the verge of introduction to history; yet before the narrator does much more than portray Pierre's experiential, if not chronological, infancy, he reveals the boy as one who has the beginnings of the quester's predisposition.

"Oh, had my father but had a daughter!" cried Pierre; "some one whom I might love, and protect, and fight for, if need be. It must be a glorious thing to engage in a mortal quarrel on a sweet sister's behalf! Now of all things, would to heaven, I had a sister!"
Thus, ere entranced in the gentler bonds of a lover; thus often would Pierre invoke heaven for a sister; but Pierre did not then know, that if there be any thing a man might well pray against, that thing is the responsive gratification of some of the devotedest prayers of his youth [p. 6].

And again:

But his profound curiosity and interest in the matter [Isabel's identity]— strange as it may seem—did not so much appear to be embodied in the mournful person of the olive girl, as by some radiations from her, embodied in the vague conceits which agitated his own soul. *There*, lurked the subtler secret: *that*, Pierre had striven to tear away. From without, no wonderful effect is wrought within ourselves, unless some interior, responding wonder meets it [p. 59].

But the infant Pierre fully believes that Saddle Meadows, the circumstances of life, history, and the entire external world, are all not only in accord with ideality but also prove ideality by their very existence. For him mankind never really fell from grace, or in more Melvillean terms, man had never played his own actual Satan to his own potential God. His father, for Pierre, is at once a happy combination of God the Father (a smiling, perfect, and benign being), the prelapsarian Adam, and, as continuator of Saddle Meadows goodness and summer mornings, the redemptive Christ—but a Christ who never really had to have anything to do with sin. It is impossible for Pierre to conceive of the heritage of history as one of possible error and sin.

But he discovers that the father was not just his smiling appearance. The God changes. The Adam falls. The father had sired and neglected an illegitimate child begotten on the Mary of France, whose "circumstances" he could never really possess. The product of the entrance into "heaven" is not happy humanity, but humanity denied entrance into any potential Eden that the world might make of itself.

The Christ had indeed known sin and had redeemed nothing. Pierre's view of Isabel, the mournful, eternal, orphaned bastard, knocking at the gates of peace and happiness, is a new view of life and man and history. The final outrage is that the "banded world" represented and landlorded by Mrs. Glendinning will not admit Isabel. That is, Pierre's view of Isabel offers one definition of her: she is the reality of mankind's cosmic position, a reality that deluded and deluding men will not admit to themselves. Then the very cornerstone of the shrine to appearances built in Pierre's innocent heart crumbles, and the white marble edifice topples into the foul dust of an entire cosmos disjointed in world and in time. But Pierre has already established himself as an enthusiast and idealist. When truth sears him, he will not deny the flame—cannot by the very aspiring elements of his human being. He has to cast off everything as a lie. He abandons the very concept of history as a paltry thing because he can trust none of its evidences. Once more, exit the saving eclecticism and naturalism; once more enter the destructive monomania. Pierre will sink the world in order to seek and publish The Truth for mankind. In the very instrument with which he must search, the quester is foredoomed: he can only search with the being that is natural man, and natural man cannot reach ideality with nonideality. The ultimate irony is that existence cannot be anything but natural. When Pierre burns his father's chair-portrait, he says, "so, so—lower, lower, lower; now all is done, and all is ashes! Henceforth, cast-out Pierre hath no paternity, and no past; and since the Future is one blank to all; therefore, twice-disinherited Pierre stands untrammeldly his ever-present self!—free to do his own self-will and present fancy to whatever end!" [12] The double disinheritance, however, is larger than Pierre realizes. Because he is disinherited in time, he is also literally disinherited in space. At this point, were this classical drama in modern dress, there should be a sudden blankness where Pierre stands, a sudden view of chaos, and then the thunderclap as the forms of existence rush in to fill the vacuum so suddenly created. But Melville does not have these means at his disposal, and therefore must continue an impossibility which makes the novel so agonizing and long. The Pierre who, according to the theme and philosophy of the book, can not and does not exist beyond this point, has to be continued in order that he may learn both the fact and the reasons for the fact that he has long since ceased to exist. He is not even a ghost, and we must accept him as a physical being.

As a physical actor, for Pierre the question is never really

---

[12] When one considers the backward-reaching of this language—to Pierre's distaste for humanity when he reads Isabel's letter—and the forward-reaching of the language—to Mrs. Glendinning's disinheritance of Pierre and to Pierre's realization that he is also cast off by the other-world—one has but a single example of the richly reflexive character of Melville's use of words. The same quality is created by the association of "Future" (time) with "blank."

What must I do? . . . such question never presented itself to Pierre; the spontaneous responsiveness of his being left no shadow of dubiousness as to the direct point he must aim at. But if the object was plain, not so the path to it. *How* must I do it? was a problem for which at first there seemed no chance of solution. But without being entirely aware of it himself, Pierre was one of those spirits, which not in a determinate and sordid scrutiny of small pros and cons—but in an impulsive subservience to the god-like dictation of events themselves, find at length the surest solution of perplexities, and the brightest prerogative of command [p. 103].

There is at once the isolation, deceit, scheming, and stealing in preparation for withdrawal from the world—Pierre's taking of his belongings out of the ancestral house from which he was already banished. The lie of independent self-will is revealed. Pierre becomes the most helpless pawn in the river of events which flows not to the brightest prerogative of command but to the ultimate unmanning of the self-deluded "commander." Again man-self and external reality are replaced by one-self. The final conclusions of hero and hero-worship simply were not for Melville, for the flow of time always proves greater than the individual in all the novels—greater even than the heroic individuals who direct aspiration correctly.[13] In comparison with Captain Vere, Pierre's plight explains one of Melville's central ambiguities. The man who bows to time and remains in the world in recognition of external, historical realities is the only man who may attempt to reform the future by carefully weighted action in the present, action which, in turn, is determined by the history of the past. The man who leaps to "command" in an attempt to transcend history and to pierce time, believes himself to be superior to events and allows his heart and mind to be subjectively swept by events. He is unhorsed, unmanned, uncaptained, and unkinged, and has no command.

So Pierre's career becomes familiar. He lies to Mrs. Glendinning about Isabel three times. He lies to Lucy. And he lies to himself and Isabel when he believes that he, a terrestrial, inland being, can enter a relationship that will be governed by nonterrestrial, sealike absolutes. Melville's irony is heightened by his own italics when he restates the very blindness and lack of experience with which the youthful Pierre undertakes a task which is impossible even for the Captain Ahabs: "do not blame me if I here make repetition, and do verbally quote my own words in saying that *it had been the choice fate of Pierre to have been born and bred in the country.*" And in depicting the unforgivable sin that results because Pierre does not know how to behave the first time the abyss opens beneath him, the narrator states one of the central premises of Melville's naturalistic perception: "Thus, in the Enthusiast to Duty, the heaven-begotten Christ is born; and

---

[13] Lawrance Thompson provides a suggestive statement of the divergence of the Carlyle-view and the Melville-view. See *Melville's Quarrel with God* (Princeton, 1952), especially the first few chapters, *et passim.*

will not own a mortal parent, and spurns and rends all mortal bonds." And thus becomes Satan. The association of Pierre and Christ continues the heritage of the generations. Pierre's Father-God is one of duplicity, but only because in terms of what the world believes, he does not exist at all. Pierre himself now becomes at once the Prometheus and the Christ, who, as he writes his novel, would bring the flame of truth to man and thus redeem men from appearances. But again, the human heritage, itself dual, is the only real heritage: Pierre is human, and as he undergoes crucifixion by the world, he changes from lover to hater, from redeemer to murderer. In Pierre's own career is a demonstration of Plinlimmon's thesis: the heavenly Christ is the killer of the race because he espouses an absolute from which men's moralities do not and can not depend. Rebuffed by earth and heaven, he becomes not the optimistic confidence man but the diabolized confidence man, whose confidence in the existence of an attainable ultimate may be merely the last illusion of hatred rather than reverence. It is a working out of the old idea that by his very nature Satan is the devoutest believer in God.

Again within the central character we find the tension that is externalized in the dualities of the major female characters. Just as Pierre in a sense creates and kills and recreates and annihilates Lucy and Isabel and Mrs. Glendinning, so he is universal mankind in whose mind and heart the "universal war" of heaven and earth, aspiration and convention, is fought throughout history. In Pierre's apostrophe to the God which is not there, the madness of the war is hinted.

Guide me, gird me, guard me, this day, ye sovereign powers! Bind me in bonds I cannot break; remove all sinister allurings from me; eternally this day deface in me the detested and distorted images of the convenient lies and duty-subterfuges of the diving and ducking moralities of this earth. Fill me with consuming fire for them; to my life's muzzle cram me with your own intent. Let no world-siren come to sing me this day, and wheedle from me my undauntedness. I cast my eternal die this day, ye powers. On my strong faith in ye invisibles, I stake three whole felicities, and three whole lives this day. If ye forsake me now,—farewell to Faith, farewell to Truth, farewell to God; exiled for aye from God and man, I shall declare myself an equal power with both; free to make war on Night and Day, and all thoughts and things of mind and matter, which the upper and the nether firmaments do clasp! [p. 126].

The imagery here suggests all the dualities which the novel offers, and when Pierre recognizes the ironic unity of his own hatred and his own reverence, and recognizes that the being he once was contained within itself all the alternatives and all the consequences, he realizes that he has thrown away all that he has prayed for. Neutralized out of all existence, the salvation of human love that Lucy offers Pierre is now unobtainable. "Dead embers of departed fires [of both love and quest] lie by thee, thou pale girl; with dead embers thou seekest to relume the flame of all extinguished love." It is the extinguished love of the humanity which he has rejected for the absolute which does not exist; it is extinguished love of God, too. It is extinguished love of all existence. In his final malediction to Lucy and Isabel, he announces his final understanding of the madness of his career: "the fool of Truth, the fool of Virtue, the fool of Fate, now quit ye forever!" When Lucy and Isabel visit him after the murder which is the logical extension of his gamble, he sees himself precisely in the Memnon Stone's point of balanced disinheritance from man and God; he himself is now a Terror Stone. Isabel, who would lure him to the nonexistent values on which he stakes his gamble, becomes the bad angel. Lost to the world that is and the world that isn't, Pierre's only and inevitable alternative is extinction. "Away!—Good Angel and Bad Angel both!—For Pierre is neuter now!" In his total loss he is made a stonelike neuter by the impulses which followed the "French" heritage of the father. (Is it too obvious to suggest again that the French for stone is *pierre*?) In his realization of the diving and ducking moralities of earth is the realization that man jails himself with delusion and hypocrisy. At the moment of insight into the conventional appearances of the world, Pierre cries, "Oh, men are jailers all; jailers of themselves; and in Opinion's world ignorantly hold their noblest part a captive to their vilest. . . . The heart! the heart! 'tis God's annointed; let me pursue the heart!" And just as Pierre proceeds to jail himself with a heartful, idealistic illusion, he is jailed by the world which cannot tolerate his insights. When the new Lucy, reborn a quester, hears Isabel call Pierre "brother," she realizes that her exemplar has been living a lie himself (just as Pierre discovered his father before him). Her own sacrifices become the madness of another fool of virtue, and Lucy dies. Like Pierre, she too sees through the mask of Gorgon and drops dead on the stone floor of the stone prison cell. Insofar as she would have redeemed Pierre, she is the good angel. Because she became another Pierre, she is the bad angel, too. Pierre, stone, kills earth and quester when he kills Lucy. So too, Isabel lures Pierre to stone, and is the bad angel. Yet she activates Pierre's heart and consciousness, and she represents aspiration; she is the good angel, too. Pierre kills human aspiration when Isabel dies because of him. The "Good Angel and Bad Angel both" refers to each of the girls as it refers to both of them together. And when one considers that Pierre is earthman and lure and quester, the embodiment of all external tensions, one sees that Pierre again performs Taji's total murder when he commits suicide. At the moment of the triple-single all-inclusive death, the jailer opens the cell door to admit Charlie Millthorpe, who has come to find Pierre, and Lucy's brother, who has come to find Lucy. The jailer decides to accommodate them both at once, and as he throws open the door, he makes a remark which reaches far from the literal level of his conversation with two peripheral characters. In the heartbreaking irony that it is a jailer who speaks and who is totally blind to the meaning of his words, plot and theme unite in the tableau which is balanced upon the turnkey's seven words of dialogue: " 'Kill 'em both with one stone, then,' wheezed the turnkey gratingly throwing open the door of the cell." The structure of the setting, which is balanced between Saddle Meadows and the stone city, becomes the structure of the plot, which is balanced between Lucy and Isabel, becomes the structure of the theme, which is balanced between the almost endless list of dualities, becomes the structure of the whole book, which is the structure of the Terror Stone. Like the inscribed Terror Stone, the inscribed book is a mute massiveness, for no printed page and no character can be the zero they are to represent.

IV

Pierre is a more hopeless book than *Mardi*. There is no informed, heartful Media left to fight the social and historical fight. Charlie Millthorpe is a good and heartful man, but he is an unconscious child. He has not earned the right to sum up Pierre in a final statement. As Millthorpe bends over Pierre, saying, "Oh, I would have rallied thee, and banteringly warned thee from thy too moody ways, but thou wouldst never heed!" Melville makes up for what could have been a bad mistake. The reintroduction of Millthorpe is much like the knocking at the gate in Macbeth, but this is not the kind of action that should end the book. Although there are no "types" left but Millthorpe and the man-of-war brother—the Saddle Meadows with which the book opened—no one can, as hero, inherit the stage of *Pierre*. So Melville has Isabel repudiate Millthorpe. "All's o'er, and ye know him not!" the dying girl whispers. No indeed. Charlie Millthorpe is not the hero. His mindlessness keeps his sweet and good heart from being able to cope with—or even recognize—the problems raised. The Apostles were asked by Christ, "Know ye not me?" How utterly impossible for the Apostle, Charlie Millthorpe, to recognize the Pierre-Christ or that other leader of Apostles, Plinlimmon.

The disparate Christ-figures all add up to one unified statement about human aspiration. Christ is all the characters except the heartless or mindless people of the "banded world." At one point or another, Lucy, Isabel, Pierre, the father, and Plinlimmon all act or think or are described in terms which recall Christ. His association with the different characters accounts for much of the duality and ambiguity which become the unity of the total Christ character, the archetypal quester. This character may be summed up as one who has the highest moral and ethical perception (the heart, aspiration, the true and natural "divinity" or "God" in man—the good angel) but who assumes that those perceptions have absolute, other-worldly origins rather than the true origins of the history of immortal mortality (and he becomes the Titan, the Satan, the bad angel). Because he chronometrically misdirects his horologically good perceptions, he directs mankind to its murder via the murder of mankind's ability to recognize the nature and direction of its perceptions; or he fails to communicate the realities he sees. His followers consequently can never understand or worship the right things. In either case, because of idealism, the wrong aspects of Christ are what Christ leaves to man. The right aspects could become part of the human heritage only if those aspects themselves fought to make the banded world change its concept of itself and therefore the concept of its Christ—only if the ontological is transferred to the social. In all events, the action must be earthly, not heavenly. In *Pierre* Melville does not make the same mistake he made in *Mardi*. In this later book there is no sudden and mechanical development of a character who will carry the lessons of Pierre's career into social action. In its greater artistic purity, *Pierre* is further than *Mardi* from fitting the demands of tragedy. The integrity and hopelessness of this book remains fairly intact: "from the fingers of Isabel dropped an empty vial—as it had been a run-out sand-glass—and shivered upon the floor; and her whole form sloped sideways, and she fell upon Pierre's heart, and her long hair ran over him, and arbored him in ebon vines." The time-glass has run out and time conquers. Isabel claims Pierre, and there is nothing left to claim. All that remains is the tableau in the stone dungeon, another evidence, like the stones of Palmyra, of mistaken aspiration. Not Isabel—all's o'er and she knows him not—nor anyone who died because of Pierre understood zero. And certainly none of the people left alive can properly decipher the tableau. The darkening day closes over silence and stone.

V

The silence and sadness of heaven characterize the person who lures Pierre to the quester's doom. The pine tree, which is the introductory symbol of Isabel, presents her leading qualities; "while both trees are proverbially trees of sadness, yet the dark hemlock hath no music in its thoughtful boughs; but the gentle pine-tree drops melodious mournfulness." And as Pierre sits at the tree's "half-bared roots of sadness," he says, "How wide, how strong these roots must spread! sure, this pine-tree takes powerful hold of this fair earth: Yon bright flower hath not so deep a root. This tree hath outlived a century of that gay flower's generations, and will outlive a century of them yet to come." The thing which has its roots in earth (Isabel has her human origins) and which echoes the mournful melodies of unearthly sadness (Isabel's songs echo the echoes of her heavenly mother's guitar) is the consciousness of woe, the aspiring Titanism in man which needs but man to shape it and act according to it (Pierre constantly "shapes" and "moulds" and "forms" Isabel). The tree is the only thing in Saddle Meadows which introduces sadness to Pierre. "Yet I have never known thee, Grief . . . but thou, Grief! art still a ghost story to me," says Pierre to the tree. It is stronger than the as yet unconscious existence of that bright flower, Lucy, and woe outlives all the pretendings of appearances. Isabel, Yillah in dark disguise, has a human history and that history is confused in her memory into an otherworldly fantasy. Therefore, like Yillah, this malleable lure wishes to enter the world and find her champion, yet at the same time she believes that the mystical confusions of her real history prefigure her true fate, and she wishes to leave the world.

Her initial attraction to and for Pierre is also familiar. Pierre continues, "the wind,—that is God's breath! Is He so sad? Oh, tree! so mighty thou, so lofty, yet so mournful! . . . Hark! as I look up into thy high secrecies, oh, tree, the face, the face, peeps down on me!—'Art thou Pierre? Come to me'—oh, thou mysterious girl. . . . What, *who*, art thou? Oh! wretched vagueness—too familiar to me, yet inexplicable —unknown, utterly unknown! I seem to founder in this perplexity." Again, here is the tantalizing familiarity in which Taji foundered; again the man recognizing his own predisposition. And Pierre, who is as yet young, and can not fathom the identity of the mysterious allurements, senses the associations of the thing that beckons him. He apostrophizes the tree in words that unmistakably recall the stone and fire imagery of his own doom. "Hark, now I hear the pyramidical and numberless, flame-like complainings of this Eolian pine. . . ." And when Pierre begs God for the meaning of the mysterious Isabel, he sums up the consequences of his idealistically directed predisposition.

Now, never into the soul of Pierre, stole there before, a muffledness like this! If aught really lurks in it, ye sovereign powers that claim all my leal worshippings, I conjure ye to lift the veil; I must see it face to face. Tread I on a mine, warn me; advance I on a precipice, hold me back; but abandon me to an unknown misery, that it shall suddenly seize me and possess me, wholly,—that ye will never do; else Pierre's fond faith in ye—now clean, untouched—may clean depart; and give me up to be a railing atheist . . . deprived of joy, I feel I should find cause for deadly feuds with things invisible [p. 48].

Pierre then makes a temporary and understandable reversion to Typee. As yet the vague stirrings of the things within him are but presentiments, objectified in a pine tree and a girl he does not know. There is no experience which has verified the presentiments which must, at this point, be a "vagueness" and a "muffledness"—no ghost has yet walked the battlements to disclose awful secrets. "Now, then, I'll up with my own joyful will; and with my joy's face scare away all phantoms:—so, they go; and Pierre is Joy's and Life's again. Thou pine-tree! —henceforth I will resist thy too treacherous persuasiveness. Thou't not so often woo me to thy airy tent, to ponder on the gloomy rooted stakes that bind it." But once Isabel's letter is received, Pierre needs no more verification of the letter than Hamlet needs of the ghost's words.

Melville introduces the Hamlet analogy at just the proper time. Just as the ghost, as an external concretion of what lies within Hamlet, is something that must be shaped by Hamlet in his own career, so Pierre, according to each new experience, must constantly recast Isabel. She, lure, ideal, Yillah, ghost, can only find expression as her champion will express her. "Thy hand is the caster's ladle, Pierre, which holds me entirely fluid. Into thy forms and slightest moods of thought, thou pourest me; and I there solidify to that form, and take it on, and thenceforth wear it, till once more thou moldest me anew. If what thou tellest me be thy thought, then how can I help its being mine, my Pierre?" Once shape and activity have been found in the being of the quester, the lure really has no further function. The predisposition exists only to prod into continuation the process that has been begun—like the ghost's "Swear! . . . Swear!" Yillah could disappear—had to disappear by the very essence of her definition. Isabel continues to exist only so that the plot can continue Pierre's isolation. But even this consideration is not really valid, because Pierre can never go home again, whether Isabel lived or died. And in the attainment of Isabel, there is no solace of the ultimate. Pierre does live to see that the hunger for the absolute destroys the fertile "inland" soul of man, destroys the means by which he can grow and harvest the fruits of life. " 'The small white flower, it is our bane!' the imploring tenants cried. 'The aspiring amaranth, every year it climbs and adds new terraces to its sway! The immortal amaranth, it will not die, but last year's flowers survive to this! The terraced pastures grow glittering white, and in warm June still show like banks of snow:—fit token of the sterileness the amaranth begets! Then free us from the amaranth, good lady, or be pleased to abate our rent.' " Isabel is as sterile as the amaranth. Her bosom hides the time-shaped death vial with which she and Pierre find death. " 'Girl! wife or sister, saint or fiend!' [cried Pierre]—seizing Isabel in his grasp—'in thy breasts, life for infants lodgeth not, but death-milk for me and thee!—The drug!' and tearing her bosom loose, he seized the secret vial nestling there."

Isabel longs for sea-sky and an all-encompassing emptiness. Her desire to enter the world "for which the dear Savior died" is satisfied once she claims Pierre. Like Yillah she only knows that now she must return to time and lifelessness, feeling that non-being is the goal toward which her life is tending. She yearns for a re-entrance into the still point of the turning world, the zero from which all existence derives. She is completely non-active, and is not interested in man or earth. "My spirit seeks different food from happiness," says Isabel, "for I think I have a suspicion of what it is. I have suffered wretchedness, but not because of the absence of happiness, and without praying for happiness. I pray for peace—for motionlessness—for the feeling of myself, as of some plant, absorbing life without seeking it, and existing without individual sensation. I feel that there can be no perfect peace in individualness. Therefore, I hope one day to feel myself drank up into the pervading spirit animating all things. I feel I am an exile here. I still go straying." The transcendentalist's oversoul may make fine theory, but in the face of the reality of the "pervading spirit," it is self-deluding murder. She denies not only the individuality of the quester, finally, but also the individuality of the selfless man who gains his identity through his sacrifice of self to social realities. Isabel, in short, never goes "home" until she dies. It is the surrender to vacuum, which man erroneously redefines and re-creates within himself, which Melville sums up as soul, lure, time, heaven, and God, when he says, "Appallingly vacant as vast is the soul of man." When Isabel sees the external emblem of her mistaken time-sense, the sea horizon, she displays no "inland" soul whatsoever. "Bell must go through there!" she cries. "See! See! out there upon the blue! yonder, yonder! far away—out, out!—far, far away, and away, and away, out there! where the two blues meet and are nothing—Bell must go!" The two emptinesses, "which the upper and nether firmaments do clasp," where sinking depth meets soaring height and soul meets time and all dualities merge in the unity of zero, that place, heaven, is—nothing. Indeed, Melville iterates, it is better that a man be pushed beyond the farthest distance of physical space than to once feel himself fairly loose and adrift within his own vast and vacant self. Once again, in his relationship to all the characters external to himself, Pierre becomes the general man who is prey to all the conflicting beliefs and aspirations and necessities which exist within the total realm of human memory and consciousness. When Pierre, Isabel, and Lucy attend the exhibition of pictures in the gallery, Pierre stares at the portraits of the mysterious young man and the young woman who look ambiguously at each other, above the heads of the crowd, from opposite walls. He senses a strange identification with the portraits. And he senses that the pictures demonstrate, externally in strangers, the same suprarational affinity between himself and Isabel's face when it was still an unknown enigma that seemed to stare at him from the pine tree. For the first time he begins to recognize the true horror. Isabel need not be—may not be—his wronged sister. He was not acting selflessly to uphold "honor." His actions really had nothing to do with a saintly championing of Isabel as his sister. These pictures are as much himself and his "sister" as he and Isabel are. He begins to see that what he begins to recognize may be only an externalization of himself.

Isabel journeys, as does Pierre, in her search for the "Father" and the champion-quester. And like Pierre, necessarily, Isabel also is universal in time for her search for her father is her search for her human identity and heritage. As the stone imagery indicates, before each crumbling world was a crumbled world which in turn was built upon a crumbled world. Isabel's first home is a crumbling remnant of a once proud civilization. The only inhabitants of the glory that was Europe—in this case France—are two old people, inhuman, black with age. These remnants of outmoded tradition (the identification and worship of the Queen of Heaven) observe and abhor Isabel. But Isabel herself is a child of Coelus and Terra, of general man and God. She is the Christ, the God-child sin-child who yearns for the divine parents ("earthly mother had I none"). The world's rejection of this child prepares for the contemporary and conventional world's rejection of Pierre. The book constantly goes back to ultimate beginnings in the history of mortality's plight, and finds none; constantly hints forward to the end of mortality's plight, and finds none. In *Pierre's* own image, there is no China Wall (Plinlimmon's pamphlet makes China a synechdocal metaphor for earth and history and natural existence) that man can build in his life and say, "This is the final conquest." For ever the frozen and sterile north, in itself a blank whiteness, sends out teeming hordes as evidence that time will always furnish new, external experience which man must define and with which man must cope. No sooner is the whale boiled down and the ship cleared than the cry goes up again, "Tha-a-ar she blows!" and all weary mankind rushes out once more for another bout with the mysteries of existence. So Isabel's first home is *a* beginning and *an* end. A remnant. Empty, once grand rooms, crumbling marble mantlepieces, boarded up, once-glassed windows, are all she sees. Beyond the house is the immortal and timeless forest, the immortal and timeless mountain. Somewhere beyond, within the forest and the mountain is another outpost of humanity in eternity, an outpost from which interdependent man lugs back his watery wine and his thick, black bread. The creatures of animal existence are no more hospitable to what Isabel represents than are the last remnants of a particular decaying conventional society which is already a thing of the past. The cat, the only other inhabitant of the house, scratches on the floor, claiming a nest in the world, and when Isabel tries to befriend it, it hisses and claws at her. Terrified, she runs back to her own fainting loneliness, rests on a stone, and feels the coldness of stone creep up through her entire being. Neither in the banded world, nor in the pristine animality of existence, nor in the absolute zero of time is there hope or heart for the reality, the time-child, who lurks beneath the conventional appearances of religion's silken sash, beneath the accepted image of the child in the warm manger. Catholic France, the bread and the wine and the ancientness, all represent religious tradition. Certainly the old couple can not accept Isabel, for the reality of her identity threatens the very basis of their own identity. Mankind is hateful because it is blind and selfish. Primitive, animal life, the "unrunugate cat" and the catnip, is hateful because it wars with the amaranth and extinction. And the absolute Isabel represents is stone-cold and hateful only because it can not, does not, care. And when present history acts toward Pierre as the cat and the old couple and the stone acted toward Isabel, then there is another picture of man content to live but one more spatial and temporal lie on the thin veneer of the present which coats the decay of the past. Therein is another picture of the world's never having been redeemed from, or made aware of, the oneness and the immortal continuity of mortality. All is a Palmyra. And the refusal to accept this one basic fact of existence for any given time and place makes ALL vanity.

Isabel's second home, the madhouse, is another view of mortal society. The house is peopled with creatures whose hearts were broken by their inability to attain God. They argue Fate and Hell and Heaven and Free Will, and they clutch their breasts and murmur, "Broken—broken—broken." They are all Pierres who have not been lucky enough to die. They are all Pips, whose introduction to God has given him a wisdom that is madness in men's eyes. And, of course, the conventional world locks them up and once again Opinion makes jailers all of men. Yet Isabel wishes to find the very escape from existence that drove these people mad, since to her the suprahuman and supranatural are a positive God. They are, indeed, her identification with her mother, which necessitated in the first place that she should have to search for her humanity. She is hardly human, and the madmen are completely human. The ocean that drove Pip mad would have been the final peace to Isabel, just as it was the final home for Yillah. Isabel constantly has to remind herself of her humanity. "When I saw a snake . . . I said to myself, That thing is not human, but I am human. When the lightning flashed, and split some beautiful tree, and left it to rot from all its greenness, I said, That lightning is not human, but I am human." Yet despite her life of hard work, Isabel never really gains the human identity which could ever allow her to feel that she is anything but a stranger in and to life. China's time and Greenwich's time simply do not exist on the same terms, and as with Yillah, herein is the reason for the fantastic in Isabel, for the confusion and muteness and malleability. Once more it must be emphasized that the lure has to be divorced from history and from a comprehending reading of experience. The fatal error is not that Ahab and Taji and Pierre were activated by the whale, Yillah, and Isabel, but that they could not see the meaning of the direction which the lure forces them to chart.

So the passive lure finds that it is defined from without. It is but one part of the quester's vast self which the self pursues and uses. Just as Isabel lies within the hollow of Pierre's hand, she lies in the hollow of time-imposed events. Even the succession of houses wherein she lived, in mountain or in plain, were all in hollows, slope surrounded. And the narrator observes about God: "He holdeth all of us in the Hollow of his hand—a Hollow truly." And just as it is "Hollow" that is capitalized and not "his," so it is the truth of time and not what particular men would believe about God that is lasting—and truly nothing is as lastingly hollow as zero.

Counterpointing Isabel's tale of woe, and punctuating the story of her history, are the footsteps of Delly Ulver. Isabel yearns for the nothing beyond the heights which surround her homes; her griefs are the antihuman consequences of birth in the misdirected aspirations of the past. Delly has always been identified with the dell, and her griefs are the antihuman consequences of the animal fact of childbirth in the inescapable present. The introduction of Delly literally merges all woe into a consequence of birth, a corollary of existence. The world that lives by appearances casts out the child of Coelus and Terra (to Isabel, the father is Terra; to Pierre he is Coelus); but the same world also casts out the child and parents who on a natural, terrestrial level do not conform to the antihuman rigors of Opinion and convention. In the affinity of like predicaments (Isabel is the bastard, Delly bears the bastard), Isabel allies herself with Delly, who, in terms of her common humanity, is really Isabel's metaphysical opponent. Again, the more one explores the book's characters, the more one finds that identity is pragmatically judged, in a fine parallel to the total view of the book's anti-idealism. Like Pierre, the only solution that Isabel can offer to Delly is isolation, seclusion, and withdrawal from the world.[14] Effected the same by the banded world of convention, Delly's history is part of Isabel's. Isabel can no more renounce Delly than the up-reaching pine tree can renounce the staked roots that bind it deeply in the earth. No more can Pierre renounce his own history, as much as he deludes himself into thinking that he can. Ironically, it is the same idealistic act of apparent renunciation which leads to the acceptance of Delly—Delly who is Lucy minus potentialities. In a fine rendering of the irony of Pierre's and Isabel's situation, Delly is the humanity that they forsake and yet bring with them as an inescapable burden of their history and their very act of renunciation.

---

[14] Indeed, Isabel's first letter to Pierre asks him to take action which will necessitate his withdrawal from the world. "Art thou an angel, that thou canst overleap all the heartless usages and fashions of a banded world, that will call thee fool! fool! fool! [how neatly this prepares for Plinlimmon] and curse thee, if thou yieldest to that heavenly impulse which alone can lead thee to respond to the long tyrannizing, and now at last unquenchable yearnings of my bursting heart?" *Pierre*, p. 74.

When the three move to the Apostles, it is Delly who is closest to the warmth of life and everyday, common humanity. Her room is in the kitchen, where the warmth-bearing stovepipe originates. Isabel comes between Pierre and humanity. Once the quest process is begun, she cannot, even when she will, return Pierre closer to the roots that he can never deny in the first place. There is no room for compromise in the choice between Lucy and God. At the very beginning, Pierre "became vaguely sensible of a certain still more marvelous power in [Isabel] over himself and his most interior thoughts and notions; —a power so hovering upon the confines of the invisible world, that it seemed more inclined that way than this; —a power which not only seemed irresistibly to draw him toward Isabel, but to draw him away from another quarter—wantonly as it were, and yet quite ignorantly and unintendingly; and besides, without respect apparently to anything ulterior, and yet again, only under cover of drawing him to her." So Isabel's room in the Apostles pushes Pierre to the farthest corner from warmth and common humanity. The stovepipe continues through Isabel's room, and just enters Pierre's quarters before it turns out through the wall; "moreover, it was in the furthest corner from the only place where, with a judicious view to the light, Pierre's desk-barrels and board could advantageously stand." The barrels and board are, as one would expect, the desk at which Pierre will explore and publish the absolute. The publication will be his grand gesture, his great blow struck back against inhuman humanity.

In creating Isabel, Melville made one unavoidable mistake. As the representative of nothing, she, like Yillah, is mutely uncommunicative and must be interpreted only by her relationships with the book's other characters. Yet Yillah, with very few lines of dialogue, was truly mute. The narrator was able to present her words through Taji and was able to present her history second hand, either through Taji's rewording or through the sons of Aleema. But in *Pierre* Melville had to allow Isabel to tell her own story to the reader—had to allow the reader to see Isabel's communications. Thus the person who is supposed to be inarticulate becomes one of the most articulate characters in the novel. She is an impossible concept. True, Melville tried to live up to his intentions by emphasizing Isabel's confusions and lapses of memory and her repeated admonitions to Pierre that he be silent while she collects herself from her mystical mazes in order to arrange her thoughts. But after three or four pages of dramatic and melodramatic articulation, the sudden interjections of, "But let me be silent again. Do not answer me. When I resume, I will not wander so, but make short end," become peremptory and ludicrously unconvincing. The admonitions come at regular and mechanical intervals that do not have any special connection with Isabel's story at the moment, so that even though they have a definite symbolic function, they become as annoyingly artificial as the appearances of Hautia's messengers. Further, Yillah was always kept in seclusion, and had good cause to be steeped in other-worldliness. But Isabel has had a life of work and experience. On the one hand, by the strength of contrast, her earthly experience sharpens the essentially nonexperiential qualities of Isabel. On the other hand it is simply unconvincing. In getting away from either the dumb whale or the cardboard figures of *Mardi*, Melville partly defeated his own purpose. The self-defeat, though, is in itself a revelation of theme and of the unavoidable use of Isabel: how can a human being represent the suprahuman? How can Isabel have so much voice to tell of so much silence? Emily Dickinson, also stricken by a naturalistic glimpse of the universe, and toying with the woe and the ironic laugh engendered of that perception, created the being that Melville needed and used intricately in *Pierre*: not Isabel, but the stone which is as independent as the sun.

VI

The stone to which Isabel lures is mirrored from another angle in the person of Plotinus Plinlimmon. There is a huge difference between the man and the Pamphlet, "IF," which first introduces Plinlimmon's name. The pamphlet espouses a doctrine of comfortable expediency. The absolute and Greenwich time are one, earth and China time are one. The absolute ideals of Greenwich time are practicable only in heaven, where there is no need to strive for ideal in the first place. Therefore, men must live by China time, and must model their actions after whatever behavior will make things most immediately comfortable for themselves as individuals. The individual should benefit others only if it is comfortable at the moment to do so, only if it preserves the individual and does not bring him into the danger of the Greenwich-time action that the rest of China time will not accept or understand. Men must turn their backs upon the other-world and live according to the necessities of earth.

At first glance, this pamphlet, highlighting Pierre's plight as it does, would seem to be the very doctrine that Melville calls for in all his books. Yet, a moment's reflection shows that it is the pamphlet's kind of behavior which exactly characterizes the behavior of the conventional world. It is precisely by the pamphlet's standards that Glen Stanley, the Reverend Mr. Falsgrave, and Mrs. Glendinning gauge their own actions. The pamphlet offers merely a set of short-term expediencies which relate to nothing but individual comfort, as if each individual could be hermetically sealed from grief by an indefinite number of contiguous, momentary selfishnesses. Even the title, "IF," implies a comfortable recognition of heaven: IF there is absolute being, then surely paying lip-service to it while living by one's own very temporal doctrines is only so much added insurance.

The pamphlet offers only insightlessness, both social and metaphysical, which is masked by cheerful comfort, just as its author, Plotinus, is masked. In its emphasis on personal rather than general human security, and in its heartless evasion of men's interdependence, the pamphlet only provides for a continuation of the human woe that ostensibly it seeks to ameliorate. "IF" merely continues the status quo while divesting it even of the religious idealism which, inoperative and misdirected as it is, at least asks that man should consider his potentialities for altruistic aspiration. The central meaning of the pamphlet immediately strikes out the possibility of the hero: it is concerned with a billion one-selves, not with man-self. It makes self-sacrifice impossible and precludes the Media and the Captain Vere. Coming as it does at the moment of Pierre's departure for the quest, it does not explain (as it seems to, and which makes it insidious) the correct behavior which Pierre should follow; it explains the behavior which the banded world, opposing Pierre, will follow. The pamphlet is not a reformation; it is an apologia. Like the quester and the lure, it is both right and wrong. Insofar as it makes God to be the impossibility and the idealistic assumption of Greenwich time, the pamphlet is right. In its reasons for rejecting the absolute, and because it swings to a polar denial of human aspiration or the upward reaching of man-self, it is wrong. Most crucially, the pamphlet allows for a relaxingly vague consideration of the positive existence of the absolute. Its conclusions, while justifying historical evidences of human behavior, are not based upon the historical truth which Pierre must discover from that same evidence. Like its opponent, the idealist, the pamphlet uses experience to murder the proper use of experience. It denies any perception that can see mortality as an entity. In this sense, the pamphlet is all wrong, for it offers no solution to the problems of existence raised by the plight of Pierre at the moment he reads the pamphlet. Finally, "IF" belongs to a world of Hautia-like sophistry; it can only be a statement of, and justification for, the "diving and ducking moralities" which evade the realities of history and existence.

The Reverend Mr. Falsgrave, when cornered in a choice between a humane action and comfortable expediency, cannot find an answer. For he cannot find a solution which is compatible with the realities of humanity and also compatible with the appearance values of his benefactress, the formidable Mrs. Glendinning. He evades by saying that there are no absolutes or ideal moralities that can govern every situation. Coming from this man, such a statement does not provide a true, relativistic basis for behavior, but is merely the cowardice which is unwilling to accept moral responsibility to man and to history. Melville deliberately places arguments which seem to be his, which seem to be correct, in the mouths of heartless characters in order to say that he finds no fault with either the fact or the intentions of Pierre's heartfulness, for it is basic and necessary; rather he finds faults with the direction and tactics. By the simple expedient of creating the inhumane Machiavel, Melville rejects the kind of Machiavellianism to which his philosophical materialism can so easily be applied. Falsgrave demonstrates that the time-serving qualities of the pamphlet are time serving in the most ironic and pragmatic sense. In his time serving, the blind and unchristian "Christian" man of God serves a God whose real identity he rejects. He leads indeed to a false grave, for death does not lead to what his hypocritically used Christian idealism espouses. In the inhumanity of his actions, he can only lead to the real grave of murderous extinction. As always, the actions taken in accordance with accepted appearances ironically turn out to have consequences that accord with the rejected realities—perhaps this is at the heart of the "ambiguities" in Melville's fiction, for none of his characters are "either-or" people. Thus Pierre's rejection of history leads to his forced acceptance of his most common mortality; Falsgrave's social time serving results in teleological time serving and the destruction of the very appearances (the Glendinning family and estate) from which the preacher drew his sustenance and for which he time served. Thus all the characters embrace the false God and the true God, and are united in their murder of human aspiration and human existence although their motivations may be completely different. In the moment that Falsgrave murmurs that there are no moral rules to apply to the case of Delly and Ned, his white, surplice-like napkin drops from his collar, revealing a cameo brooch depicting the union of the dove and the serpent. The allegorical meaning of the brooch is obvious enough in the religious terms of Christianity and in the moral terms of purity and duplicity. In context, the dropping of the napkin has a triple, ironic, symbolic weight which reflects back upon Plinlimmon's pamphlet. First, Falsgrave reveals what he is supposed to believe, and he reveals that he does not live according to that belief; rather he covers it with the appearance values of his "surplice-like" napkin, a token of institution and patronage, of the meal being fed him by Mrs. Glendinning. Second, he reveals that what he believes in seems to be, but is not, the unity of all life. Finally, as a conclusion of the other revelations, he reveals that he, like all the other characters except the very late Pierre, does not understand the unified message of experience, and that he is a one-self actor.

Thus, the objection to Plinlimmon's pamphlet lies in the observation that it makes community disappear into atomistic chaos. The pamphlet does not strike through to truth, but merely to a misunderstanding of the truth that lies beneath hypocritical appearances. The pamphlet offers no shock of recognition by which the brooch beneath the napkin may be understood and by which history may be reordered.

But when we see the man whose name appears on the pamphlet,

we see something else again. Plinlimmon, we are told, did not really write the pamphlet. The printed word is the garbled version constructed (from Plinlimmon's former public lectures) by disciples who are called Apostles. The pamphlet is garbled heartlessness; Plinlimmon is conscious and intentional heartlessness. Plinlimmon does not write, Plinlimmon does not read, Plinlimmon does not communicate, Plinlimmon knows that he does not communicate, and Plinlimmon does not want to communicate. And that is central to his definition. For Plinlimmon is a very different kind of Christ-figure. He is withdrawn both from this world and from other-world. He is totally withdrawn into self. Not only does Plinlimmon not communicate, but he literally lives apart and above, in the highest inhabitable room of the Apostles' tower. "Very early after taking chambers at the Apostles', [Pierre] had been struck by a steady observant blue-eyed countenance at one of the loftiest windows of the old grey tower. . . . Only through two panes of glass—his own and the stranger's—had Pierre hitherto beheld that remarkable face of repose,—repose neither divine nor human, nor anything made up of either or both—but a repose separate and apart— a repose of a face by itself." The non-being of Plinlimmon's repose and the selfishly anti-idealistic orientation of whatever ideas the Apostles had written into "IF" indicate that Plinlimmon has had his insight into the true nature of God as a zero. At one time, the narrator muses, Plinlimmon must have read, written, searched. But Plinlimmon has withdrawn from the search because of what he found; he has also withdrawn from man because of what he does not find. Unlike the quester, he is committed to nothing, and to nothing he withdraws— to the vacant vastness of his one-self, ever sealed off as by two panes of glass (by the bewilderment of those who see him, and by the silence of Plinlimmon himself) from contact with existence. He locks himself away with the truth because his only identity is the repose which is the neutral balance between reality and realization, between preservation and annihilation—the balance of the Memnon Stone, the balance of zero. Plinlimmon becomes, like stone-cold time, the still center of feverish activities and fevered actors. He has reached the state for which Isabel yearns, and he will not abandon his withdrawal and thereby lose his state of equilibrium. This zero, unlike Isabel, does not talk or act. All his doings are reported by others, and he himself is a pasteboard image, changeless and unblinking, of his realizations.

Vain! vain! vain! said [Plinlimmon's] face to [Pierre]. Fool! fool! fool! said the face to him. Quit! quit! quit! said the face to him. But when he mentally interrogated the face as to why it thrice said Vain! Fool! Quit! to him; here there was no response. For that face did not respond to anything. Did I not say before that that face was something separate and apart; a face by itself? Now, any thing which is thus a thing by itself never responds to any other thing. If to affirm be to expend one's isolated self; and if to deny be to contract one's isolated self; then to respond is suspension of all isolation [p. 345].

This is a description of time and stone and God. The "Vain! Fool! Quit!" indicate that Plinlimmon understands the reason why the quest is a foolish and hopeless impossibility. But though Plinlimmon is the definition of God, he is not God. As a man, he gives heartless, empty, ahumanity a social equivalent. He is Melville's view of the quietist, as well as a view of the naturalistic perception of God. He has not been introduced before into the list of Melville's characters—indeed, "One adequate look at that face conveyed to most philosophical observers a notion of something not before included in their scheme of the Universe." Plinlimmon will not risk involvement in the world as does Media, and will not court extinction as do the active world spurners, Ahab and Pierre. Involvement always places the self in risk. And while refusal to become involved is, for God, only an inevitable inability, in man it is the last and ultimate selfishness. So selfish that it is the emptiness which can be forgivable only when it is God's.

Plinlimmon, despite his realizations, cannot be the needed hero. He is not the complete man—he is no longer really man, for he has bartered his humanity for his repose. His selfishness is the superiority of the man who does not risk the possible failure that is always inherent in the activation of human insights. In his complete willingness to let the rest of the world bash its brains out on stone walls against which he will never tilt, Plinlimmon is the essential heartlessness and atomized one-self that ultimately is a nothing-self and that characterizes the conventional world for which his pamphlet becomes an apologia. He is beyond caring in any way, beyond wishing good or ill to anything exterior to himself because he does not see himself in anything exterior. The very assumptions of quietism are self-sufficient imperturbability and inviolability in historical existence.

The whole countenance of this man, the whole air and look of this man, expressed a cheerful content. Cheerful is the adjective, for it was the contrary of gloom; content—perhaps acquiescence—is the substantive, for it was not Happiness or Delight. But while the personal look and air of this man were winning, there was still something latently visible in him which repelled. That something may best be characterized as non-Benevolence. Non-Benevolence seems the best word, for it was neither Malice nor Ill-will; but something passive. To crown all, a certain floating atmosphere seemed to invest and go along with this man. That atmosphere seems only renderable in words by the term Inscrutableness. Though the clothes worn by this man were strictly in accordance with the general style of any unobtrusive gentleman's dress, yet his clothes seemed to disguise this man. One would almost have said, his very face, the apparently natural glance of his very eye, disguised this man [p. 341].

His human appearance is a lie, for he has consciously chosen isolation from any involvement and cannot be associated with any moral considerations; he is not to be judged by the unavoidable familiarity of exterior form. He is the mask, he is the inscrutability which is the consequence of his choice. To describe the zero is to describe himself; to describe himself is to expose himself; to expose himself is to lose his apartness and repose. So he chooses his cheerfulness at the cost of universal woe. Taji, Ahab, and Pierre at least all have positive moral centers. Their morality might have been Satanic or angelic, but even their final amorality stemmed from human aspiration. But Plinlimmon does not care that either man-self or one-self should prove its equality with time. He does not care that he does not care. He has seen Gorgon, and instead of living to instruct man, his humanity has been turned to stone. Taji, Ahab, and Pierre also finally end as stone. But they do not choose or look for such an existence; indeed, by the very nature of their endeavor they cannot exist once their humanity is removed. But Plinlimmon chooses ahumanity as the characteristic of his existence. In so doing, he becomes nonexistent, a moral zero. We begin to see what metaphysical truth and what horrible moral emptiness have been reduced by the Apostles to the pamphlet "IF." Plinlimmon is Melville's most terrifying villain. To the Pierre who pours his heart out trying to instruct humanity in woe, the self-centered quietism of Plinlimmon begins to assume its true horror. In the negative effects of its nonaction, the repose is more than non-benevolence. It is passive and general malignance. "Though this face in the tower was so clear and so mild; though the gay youth Apollo was enshrined in that eye, and paternal old Saturn sat cross-legged on that ivory brow; yet somehow to Pierre the face at last wore a sort of malicious leer to him." In comparison with this new monster —he would be Moby-Dick were he not terrifyingly human—Pierre finally begins to merit some sympathy. While it may be true that Pierre hurries life to death, Plinlimmon knows it—and lets him. In short, the man who knows all and does nothing is the worst murderer.

Plinlimmon's disguise hides his dual aspect. He is Christ, and he is the Father of Lies. Of course, as in one of the meanings of Falsgrave's brooch, the two are finally one, but Plinlimmon does not care what his followers believe or what they believe he believes. He lets them scrub away with their transcendental flesh brushes because otherwise he would have to replace all the peripheral nonsense of their satirized transcendentalism with the zero of his own realizations. And of course he will not share the repose, for, as the narrator explained, the very act of sharing destroys the isolation which is central to Plinlimmon's being. He is a fraud to the whole world because the world thinks he is a something.

Finding Plinlimmon thus unfurnished either with books or pen and paper, and imputing it to something like indigence, a foreign scholar, a rich nobleman, who chanced to meet him once, sent him a fine supply of stationery, with a very fine set of volumes,—Cardan, Epictetus, the Book of Mormon,

Abraham Tucker, Condorcet, and the Zend-Avesta. But this noble foreign scholar calling next day—perhaps in expectation of some compliment for his great kindness—started aghast at his own package deposited just without the door of Plinlimmon, and with all fastenings untouched.

"Missent," said Plotinus Plinlimmon placidly: "if any thing I looked for some choice Curacoa from a nobleman like you. I should be very happy, my dear Count, to accept a few jugs of choice Curacoa."

"I thought that the society of which you are the head excluded all things of that sort"—replied the Count.

"Dear Count, so they do; but Mohammed hath his own dispensation."

"Ah! I see," said the noble scholar archly.

"I am afraid you do not see, dear Count"—said Plinlimmon; and instantly before the eyes of the Count, the inscrutable atmosphere eddied and eddied round about this Plotinus Plinlimmon [pp. 342-43].

There is no need to live by the man-imposed concept of idealistic absolutes which have no basis, Plinlimmon realizes. But in the very choice of gifts is the repeated statement of his refusal to share realizations. He rejects a gift of the means of communication in favor of a gift of personal comfort. In this way, like Hautia, Plinlimmon has no reason for his human existence beyond the misdirected naturalism of selfish animal enjoyment in the brief span of life allotted to the one-self. His becomes the naturalism of a pig, not of a man; and like Hautia he becomes, as a human being, the zero emptiness of thin air.

It becomes less important that Plinlimmon's followers are fools than that they are human. In comparison to Plinlimmon, Charlie Millthorpe, Pierre's boyhood friend, is exposed as a lesser kind of confidence man. He deceives himself with his egotism; he deceives himself into believing that he has insight and brilliance, whereas he is but a good-natured fool. "Our Grand Master, Plotinus Plinlimmon!" says Charlie to Pierre. "By gad, you must know Plotinus thoroughly, as I have long done." Of course this man can never know Plotinus, but he is, in a way, more important than Plinlimmon. Plotinus is but an inoperative mask. Charlie has, beneath the coverings of conceit and well-meant stupidity, a genuinely good heart. He is the kind of man who would champion Delly Ulver as that other "Apostle" of Plinlimmon, Falsgrave, would not. Millthorpe scatters goodness quite as easily and unconsciously as he scatters stupidity; like Jarl, he is the wholesome, necessary mankind which might make regeneration possible. After helping Pierre, Charlie skips gaily out of the apartment, and Pierre stands staring at the closed door. " 'Plus heart, minus head,' muttered Pierre, his eyes fixed on the door. 'Now, by heaven! the god that made Millthorpe was both a better and a greater than the god that made Napoleon or Byron [and certainly a better than the god that made Plinlimmon]. —Plus heart, minus head—Pah! the brains grow maggoty without a heart; but the heart's the preserving salt itself, and can keep sweet without the head.' " The God that made all, however, is the same stone-making God that destroys the heart.

VII

The first stone Pierre casts down is the supposedly eternal marble of the shrine which he builds in his heart to the memory of his family. It is the stone of acceptance of unenlightened idealism, and, consequently, unconscious vanity. One remembers the narrator's purpose in emphasizing the fact that Pierre was born in the country. It is the apparent Eden, and "in Pierre's eyes, all its hills and swales seemed as sanctified through their very long uninterrupted possession by his race. That fond ideality which, in the eyes of affection, hallows the least trinket once familiar to the person of a departed love; with Pierre that talisman touched the whole earthly landscape about him." This is the first stone to crumble, the fond ideality which will disappear and leave the world unhinged. The early Pierre, "the only surnamed male Glendinning extant . . . in the ruddiness, and flushfulness, and vaingloriousness of his youthful soul . . . fondly hoped to have a monopoly of glory in capping the fame-column, whose tall shaft had been erected by his noble sires." The appearances and glory stones created by men are supposedly condoned and insured by the traditionally accepted God: "Thus in Pierre was the complete polished steel of the gentleman, girded with Religion's silken sash; and his great-grandfather's soldierly fate had taught him that the generous sash should, in the last bitter trial, furnish its wearer with Glory's shroud; so that what through life had been worn for Grace's sake, in death might safely hold the man." And then in immediate juxtaposition, the narrator presents the warning that the secret reality of the God of religion gives the lie to appearances, and that the realization of the lie is humanity's burden of a woe that must recast the very frame of woe's reference: "But while thus all alive to the beauty and poesy of his father's faith, Pierre little foresaw that this world hath a secret deeper than beauty, and Life some burdens heavier than death." Now Melville identifies the God that tumbles all appearances into meaninglessness by using the stone imagery to associate the killer-creator God with time. The narrator adds this crucial paragraph directly after the picture of Pierre's marble shrine: "In all this, how unadmonished was our Pierre by that foreboding and prophetic lesson taught, not less by Palmyra's quarries than by Palmyra's ruins. Among these ruins is a crumbling, uncompleted shaft, and some leagues off, ages ago left in the quarry, is the crumbling corresponding capital, also incomplete. These Time seized and spoiled; these Time crushed in the egg; and the proud stone that should have stood among the clouds, Time left abased beneath the soil. Oh, what quenchless feud is this, that Time hath with the sons of Men!" The parallel to the early Pierre as an uncompleted "capital" is no less obvious than the parallel of the later Pierre to Enceladus, the Titan who "should have stood among the clouds," but who was "left abased beneath the soil"—the Titan who tried to storm the ramparts of heaven to regain equality with God.

And Enceladus, who like the quester has an earthly heritage in the incest of his origins, can never conquer zero and is abased because he concerns himself with zero instead of with the immortality of his mortality. There is no doubt about the definition of God. In presenting Pierre's dream of Enceladus, Melville ties in the stones of Palmyra, the origins of Isabel, and the goal of the quester, all united in the identification of Pierre with the Titan. A heap of rocks and stones on the approaches to the mount of the Titans has been cast from the heights so that they form a rough-hewn form of the sky-assaulting Enceladus. Abased like the stones of Palmyra, there was "Enceladus the Titan, the most potent of all the giants, writhing from out the imprisoning earth; —turbaned with upborne moss he writhed; still, though armless, resisting with his whole striving trunk, the Pelion and the Ossa hurled back at him; —turbaned with upborne moss he writhed; still turning his unconquerable front [this becomes all of human history] toward that majestic mount eternally in vain assailed by him, and which, when it had stormed him off, had heaved his undoffable incubus upon him, and deridingly left him there to bay out his ineffectual howl." Moreover, from a distance, this mount of Titans is the "Delectable Mountain," and presents a pure and de-lightful appearance that is termed "heavenly," a "purple promise." Closer inspection reveals a forbidding, ageless, silent barrenness. And also characterizing the approach to the unassailable mountain is the warfare between the catnip and the amaranth.

Soon you would see the modest verdure of the [catnip] itself; and where-soever you saw that sight, old foundation stones and rotting timbers of log-houses long extinct would also meet your eye; their desolation illy hid by the green solicitudes of the unemigrating herb. Most fitly named the cat-nip; since, like the unrunugate cat, though all that's human forsake the place, that plant will long abide, long bask and bloom on the abandoned hearth [like something out of the message of Isabel's history]. Illy hid; for every spring the amaranthine and celestial flower gained on the mortal household herb; for every autumn the catnip died, but never an autumn made the amaranth to wane [p. 405].

Then, in order that there be no doubt left about the time-God identifi-cation, the narrator adds, "The catnip and the amaranth!—man's earthly household peace, and the ever-encroaching appetite for God." And lest even at this point there be any doubt that under the amar-anth-reaching influence of Isabel, which is the idealistic direction of his own predisposition, Pierre is really assaulting time in his God-quest, the narrator makes the last equation between Pierre and the Enceladus-stone. In his dream, Pierre watches as the stone Titan "turned his vast trunk into a battering-ram, and hurled his own arched-out ribs again and yet again against the invulnerable steep.

'Enceladus! it is Enceladus!'—Pierre cried out in his sleep. That moment the phantom faced him; and Pierre saw Enceladus no more; but on the Titan's armless trunk, his own duplicate face and features magnifiedly gleamed upon him with prophetic discomfiture and woe. With trembling frame he started from his chair, and woke from that ideal horror to all his actual grief."

The cyclic life-death continuum—the immortality of mortality—is symbolized by greenness and is incorporated into the stone imagery. Enceladus is "that deathless son" of earth. The green catnip dies each fall in autumnal rot and yet is reborn each spring. The cat is still "unrunugate" after all the centuries have passed since Isabel's first home. The images of stone and green suggest that man's only immortality is his collective and historical mortality—the heritage of each generation handed down to the next in all the awful responsibilities of time.[15] For instance, even though the Mount of the Titans is presented as sterile and hideous upon the close view which belies the distant appearances, "Nevertheless, round and round those still enchanted rocks, hard by their utmost rims, and in among their cunning crevices, the misanthropic hill-scaling goat nibbled his sweetest

---

[15] It might be well to briefly restate here Melville's idea of fate, or predestination. Too often Melville's insistence on Fate has been interpreted in terms of the Calvinism of Melville's family background. Yet, whenever there is an allusion to fate, it is not made in traditional Christian context, but rather in unchristian Solomonic context. If God is removed from all conscious purposes and is resolved into the vacancy of time, how can there be a working of fixed fate and predestination, an apparently conscious force? The answer lies in the motif of origins. Insofar as any man is allowed freedom by the history handed down by his fathers, and insofar as his heart or heartlessness, mind or mindlessness, are operative upon specifics in the present circumscribed by the demands of mortal history, so far the Melvillean character has free will. The heart and memory infuse into the character (if he is the quester) a desire for a status that is not compatible with the experiences offered by his present history, but which have their roots in the total actions of the total past. This is the quester's predisposition. This is part of his fixed fate. Insofar as the sins of the fathers are visited upon the child in the circumstances of human history, there is a real cause and effect. Once the act is made, the consequences are inseparable from the act. Once Pierre accepts and believes Isabel's letter, then the whole course of his life is predestined by the acts of his fathers and by his own predisposition, which in turn is an inheritance from the past. The demon Principle, the three Weird Ones, do not originally dictate acts. They dictate the consequences of acts which in turn dictate future acts. Once the original act is past, then the demon Principle does indeed dictate acts. For the original act, Melville finds his convenient symbol—in an unchristian sense—in Adam. And Adam in turn was predestinated by the fact of his mortality. The problem is not so much one of "where did evil come from?" as it is one of seeing that the earliest human history, in not attempting to be its own God (man's relegation of control to the hands of an apparent God), dictated that all the future would be a consequent history of uncontrolled chaos—mistake, crime, and hence evil. The center of action and consequence is placed in the hands of man, who can change the *kind* of predestination (free will) by changing the inevitable consequences by changing history (fixed fate). Nor is Melville's use of fate an existentialist doctrine, for always Melville sees the reality of existence exterior to and independent of the self. Just as all woe is a corollary of birth, so the pattern of one's life cannot be totally attributed to self-choice, for in some facts, birth, for instance, the reality of externalities which are nature's surprises to the individual are made manifest. Either continuation or reformation, it is man's own creation of history that is fate.

food; for the rocks, so *barren in themselves*, distilled a subtle moisture, *which fed with greenness* all things that grew about their igneous marge." Time is both killer and creator, a barrenness itself which yet provides the conditions for life, provides, as it were, the necessary segments of time in which to exist.

When the narrator equates Pierre's proud marble glory-structure with the stones of Palmyra abased beneath the soil, he makes a transition into the next section, in which he examines human history in relation to time. "Certainly that common saying among us, which declares, that a family, conspicuous as it may, a single half-century shall see it abased; that maxim undoubtedly holds true with the commonalty." In this observation, Melville couples Pierre's present American history with Isabel's ancient, European, French history. In their mortality they are basically the same; there is cycle beyond cycle, ruined home beyond ruined home. Indeed, in this entire section, Melville not only makes European history as transient as American, but in tracing the uncharted aristocracy of old American families, he makes American history as permanent as European. Then he follows through from the generalities by placing the deed to the specific place, Saddle Meadows, in the beginnings of history, in the aboriginal hands of three Indian Kings. The democracy of history always, everywhere, goes back to the symbolic Adam, who is simply the beginning of humanity. Using the debased stone as the point of departure, Melville adds the motif of greenness and explains the common history and heritage of all men. "The monarchical world very generally imagines, that in demagogical America the sacred Past hath no fixed statues erected to it, but all things irreverently seethe and boil in the vulgar cauldron of an everlasting uncrystallized Present."

Once he associates time and history, Melville goes on to explain why the American everlasting and uncrystallized Present is a truer picture of the fact of time than the vainglorious pretensions of the European "eternal" aristocratic families. At once he introduces France, which is representative of crumbling European history as well as of the "other-world" that is only time. And he unites the two with an image of greenness that works both ways, to past and future, to death and life.

In our cities families rise and burst like bubbles in a vat. For indeed the democratic element operates as a subtile acid among us, forever producing new things by corroding the old; as in the south of France verdigris, the primitive material of one kind of green paint, is produced by grape-vinegar poured upon copper plates. Now in general nothing can be more significant of decay than the idea of corrosion; yet on the other hand nothing can more vividly suggest luxuriance of life, than the idea of green as a color; for green is the peculiar signet of all-fertile Nature herself [p. 8].

In short, democratic time, as eternity, by the very nature of its definition and relationship to mortality, supplies the passage of ages which rot one mortal structure only to supply more ages which create new structures out of the fertilizing rot of the past. And so the blank, empty, barren rocks, themselves sterile, distill the liquids which birth the greenest things. Thus the act of time's creation is necessarily the act of time's killing; coupled with the woe which is humanity's realization that no bright roselike Lucy lasts forever—not the physical being nor the individual soul "safely" bound in religion's silken sash —is the strength and aspiration potential in humanity's realization of its own collective and racial immortality. Only the quester, only man, can really murder man with no regenerative results. Time left alone to itself must create by the fact of its killing, and so Terra is as everlasting as Coelus, each being relative to, one with, the other. Melville simply offers another way to give an explanation of the quester's sin in rejecting history. It is the rejection of the very immortality, equality, God, or absolute which the quester, as Enceladus, seeks: "Herein by apt analogy we behold the marked anomalousness of America; whose character abroad, we need not be surprised, is misconceived, when we consider how strangely she contradicts all prior notions of human things and how wonderfully to her, Death itself becomes transmuted into Life. So that political institutions, which in other lands seem above all things intensely artificial, with America seem to possess the divine virtue of a natural law; for the most mighty of Nature's laws is this, that out of Death she brings Life."

Pierre, the enthusiast and country bred, does try to emulate what he considers to be God. At least he tries to follow the chronometric Christ which the Falsgrave, in actuality, denies. When Isabel's letter sends him off on his search for God, Pierre realizes that his appeals to the traditional view of God, all the heavenly and invisible powers he had so freely invoked while formed by Joy instead of Grief, are no longer operative or meaningful. And when he apostrophizes his new realities, the new and unknown God who lurks behind the drawn visor of events, he speaks to the stone-maker. "Thou Black Knight, that with visor down, thus confrontest me, and mockest at me; lo! I strike through thy helm, and will see thy face, be it Gorgon!" And the equilibrium of time poised between killing and creating is further extended in a description of—a stone. This stone, the Memnon, or Terror Stone, is related to earthly existence only by this one tiny point of equilibrium. Otherwise, time is totally out of touch with human cares and needs. Time is the ultimate indifference as well as the ultimate silence.

It was shaped something like a lengthened egg, but flattened more; and, at the ends, pointed more; and yet not pointed, but irregularly wedge-shaped. Somewhere near the middle of its underside, there was a lateral ridge; and an obscure point of this ridge rested on a second lengthwise

sharpened rock, slightly protruding from the ground. Beside that one obscure and minute point of contact, the whole enormous and most ponderous
mass touched not another object in the wide terraqueous world. It was a
breathless thing to see. One broad hunched end hovered within an inch of
the soil, all along the point of teetering contact; but yet touched not the
soil [pp. 154-55].

The other end of the stone hangs above a vacancy large enough to
admit a crawling man. The stone is described as ageless, as belonging
to the history of the whole world, as being an emblem of time itself—
the theory being offered that perhaps the stone was transported by
some members of the wandering tribes of Israel. The time-blind Typee
dwellers do not account the stone any great miracle, for they are
unable to read history, "Because, even, if any of the simple people
should have chanced to have beheld it, they, in their hoodwinked
unappreciativeness, would not have accounted it any very marvelous
sight." The stone is inscribed with initials that "in their antiqueness,
seemed to point to some period before the era of Columbus' discovery
of the hemisphere." The initials are "S. ye W." "But who,—who in
Methuselah's name,—who might have been this 'S. ye W.'?" Once, a
"not-at-all-to-be-hurried white-haired old kinsman," after "reading
certain verses in Ecclesiastes . . . had laid his tremulous hand upon
Pierre's firm young shoulder, and slowly whispered—'Boy; 'tis Solomon
the Wise.'" The young Pierre, when told this curious conceit, had
laughed. But the Pierre who laughs is the young Pierre who builds in
his heart a marble shrine to appearances, "For at that period, the
Solomonic insights [had] not poured their turbid tributaries into
the pure-flowing well of the childish life." The ungriefed and young
Pierre has yet to learn that Methuselan age's curious conceit has a
wider knowledge of experience and thus a closer approach to truth.
Melville is very unambiguous about this point; as long as history remains what it is, man must gauge his actions and beliefs according to
the conclusions that lurk beneath the experience of that history. If the
young Pierre and Billy Budd are beautiful, they are not representative
of proper action, and will not be so until there is made by man
the new history which will be the fact of their beauty. Thus, when the
young Pierre, who writes "pretty" verses and is the idol of the critics,
presents himself to an elderly friend as an accomplished artist, the
friend asks him how he can say this. Pierre replies (on the basis of
a sonnet significantly entitled "The Tropical Summer") that he is an
artist simply because he is the idol of the critics—not recognizing that
the "critics" are the fawning, Falsgrave representatives of the illusive
and deluding status quo. "Ah," is all the elderly friend says, and
dismisses the subject.

Pierre is a unified enough book so that one need not go outside the
book itself to find in Pierre's gradual education the greater insights
that experienced age has into the vagaries of history. But for Melville's

works as one developmental totality, we find perhaps the best single meaning for "S. ye W." given in *Moby-Dick*. In the crucial chapter on "The Try-Works," the narrator says: "The truest of all men was the Man of Sorrows, and the truest of all books is Solomon's, and Ecclesiastes is the fine hammered steel of woe. 'All is vanity.' ALL. This wilful world hath not got hold of *unchristian* Solomon's wisdom yet. But he who dodges hospitals and jails, and walks fast crossing grave-yards, and would rather talk of operas than hell . . . not that man is fitted to sit down on tombstones, and break *the green damp mould* with unfathomably wondrous Solomon" [italics mine]. The paragraph which follows underscores Ishmael's growing realization that man cannot remove himself from his human heritage, that no one man can be equal to time or be impervious to the evidence of death and birth in the green mold: "But even Solomon, he says, 'the man that wandereth out of the way of understanding shall remain' (i.e. even while living) 'in the congregation of the dead.' Give not thyself up, then, to fire, lest it *invert* thee, deaden thee; as for the time it did me. There is a wisdom that is woe; but there is a woe that it madness."

Ishmael's intrusion with "(i.e., even while living)" emphasizes the ironic inversion of the Christ-to-Satan Ahab, especially when so closely followed by the word "invert." Every death is a reality for grief for the wisdom that is woe; but in turn it is only the impersonal force which allows life to continue. To rebel against the conditions—against the very principle—of life, as seen in unchristian Solomon's green-mold wisdom, is the woe that is madness. Melville always repeats his ironic technique to give dual and (only apparently) ambiguously and mutually exclusive meanings for everything, so that his images, his very language, become the symbol-mirrors that reflect alternating inversions into infinity—and are still the one and same set of mirrors. So too the dualities become a unity in the wisdom of Solomon the Wise. That devout and unchristian irreligious thinker warns that man must not remove himself from the ways of understanding, from the community of the living, as does Plinlimmon in his selfish isolation, as does the quester in his. For the Solomonic view of God is the woeful view of impersonal, amoral time, which touches earth only in the balance between life and death, the organic, naturalistic balance of the green mold. Ahab, who is completely given over to the fire and the fire-worshiping Fedallah, does kill "man's earthly household peace," by sinking the *Pequod* with his "ever encroaching appetite for God," which is only the ubiquitous, eternal blankness of the nothing that is the horror-meaning of the whale's whiteness.

And Pierre makes the Taji-mistake and the Ahab-mistake. He appeals to the Terror Stone as to a something: "if Duty's self be but a bugbear, and all things are allowable and unpunishable to man; —

then do thou, Mute Massiveness, fall on me! Ages hast thou waited; and if these things be thus, then wait no more; for whom better canst thou crush than him who now lies here invoking thee?" As far as an after life in time, based upon human morals, is concerned, all things are indeed allowable and unpunishable. But yet again, as far as time is concerned, all things are consequential as well as allowable, for time blankly visits upon man the continuum of his own history, in which man punishes and punishes and punishes himself down to the generations that vanish in the blank horizons of the future's double blue. It is no use invoking a stone (again: how can men say that they get a voice from Silence?), for man himself must answer his own prayers. The Mute Massiveness of time, like the corposants which never heard Ahab's most central and impassioned plea, cannot even know of the existence of the plea which asks if it is interested. All that Pierre foresees in his most gloomy presentiments comes to pass. Yet all that follows the plea is the "deception" of life itself. No thunder rolls. Rather, "A down-darting bird, all song, swiftly lighted on the unmoved and eternally immovable balancings of the Terror Stone, and cheerfully chirped to Pierre." For it is man who makes life and God appear to be the most malignant traitor and swindler.[16]

When we see Oro in *Mardi*, God's qualities are adumbrated: they are not reached through religion, but neither are they made to be anything as clearly definitive as *Pierre's* time. When God first appears in *Moby-Dick*, he is to Ishmael the universal joker who passes the smarting thump all round to all shoulders. He is the startlingly familiar God of Emily Dickinson's ironic poem

> I know that he exists
> Somewhere, in silence.
> He has hid his rare life
> From our gross eyes.
> 'Tis an instant's play,
> 'Tis a fond ambush,
> Just to make bliss
> Earn her own surprise!
>
> But should the play
> Prove piercing earnest,
> Should the glee glaze
> In death's stiff stare,
>
> Would not the fun
> Look too expensive?
> Would not the jest
> Have crawled too far?

---

[16] For a discussion of the deceptions of the "blue day," the light leaping from darkness and the darkness leaping from light, see the unpublished dissertation (Yale, 1952) by George R. Creeger, "Color Symbolism in the Works of Herman Melville: 1846-1852," *passim*.

By the time *Moby-Dick* is well under way, God has retreated even further from intentional connection with life and death and is, in the corposants, the personified impersonal. By the time we come to *Pierre,* God has reached his last definition for Melville, and, again, is captured in the implications that expand beyond the smart-alecky surface of Emily Dickinson's little verse,

> Faith is a fine invention
> For gentleman that see.
> But microscopes are prudent
> In an emergency.

Or, again, when Emily Dickinson tells the skeptic that, granted that the oriole's song exists as something external to the skeptic himself, yet the meaning, the definition, the importance of the song lies in him. So too, Melville does not deposit responsibility for history into the hands of any God, malignant or beneficent. The Enceladus in man must see that as one-self it is nothing—it is the mountain it assaults just as the zero-center-self of Plinlimmon is the nothing he does not communicate. As man-self, Enceladus must turn his back on nothing, and only then can he see himself as more than an agonizingly pitiful spark that flashes for less than an instant across the blank face of eternity. Only then can he see himself as the eternal something, the existence, the life principle, by which the nothing derives its identity. As Emersonian as this sounds (especially reminiscent of the poem "Brahma"), it is reminiscent of the transcendentalist only in the agreement that man's mind shapes reality. But Emerson makes man's mind the ultimate reality for all existence. Melville makes it the defining factor for humanity, which is confronted by existence which does have its own external and undefined reality. The mind exercises reality only when it copes with that which comes into man's natural experience (and this includes exaltation as well as the most crassly material). When Emerson says that his mind has created everything the universe can show him, Melville disagrees, for, he says, one cannot know what the universe may surprise him with. To say that whatever is in the mind is absolute reality is either insanity or supernaturalism. If it is insanity, then man must not listen either to this joy or this woe that is madness. If it is supernaturalism, then it merely takes the traditional concepts of God's mind, or ideality, and places them in man's mind. Emerson is constant when he says that man is God, when he both humanizes and spiritualizes nature. But, Melville argues, man's mind is not absolute because experience past is not all possible experience, is not all that is possible in the eternal and infinite physical universe. Ideality itself disappears and in place of that absolute absolute is the absolute relativity of infinite experience. And the reality of nature is the natural state. So Melville must aim away from, not toward ideal. Man's mind is reality only because it is, for man, the storehouse and courtroom for external realities. Different conditions force the mind to judge externalities differently, as Pierre discovers. The externalities themselves change as the conditions do. Translated into human history, this reality, this primacy of man's mind is always most meaningful for Melville in social rather than individual terms. Melville's theme calls not for transcendental individualism, but for enlightened and enlightening government. The problem is the social problem of natural experience, not one of absolutistic idealizations. For time, limited by its own nature, is beyond any idea of interest, and will not, cannot, look down to laugh at the heartbreaking follies of man as do even the inhabitants of *Mardi's* red star, Arcturus.

chapter 5

Billy Budd

Translated Cross, hast thou withdrawn,
Dim paling too at every dawn,
With symbols vain once counted wise,
And gods declined to heraldries?

      *   *   *

The atheist cycles—must they be?
Fomenters as forefathers we?

                       —Clarel

Morally, philosophically, emotionally, socially, Melville's search for the complete man is not the search for the knightly hero, but for the Governor. The Governor must repress man's anarchic atheism and must reorient man's frantic activities.

The quester is an atheist because he denies history and thereby rejects man's only possible God. The quietist is an atheist because he denies human commitments and thereby rejects possibility itself. The banded world is an atheist because it denies reality and thereby rejects the true nature of God and of man's potentialities. All these confidence men-atheists have one denial in common: they reject man. They deny man because they cannot recognize the importance of man-self and the subordinate position of one-self; they cannot recognize anything by means of the naturalistic perception wherein the importance of man's morality shrinks on a cosmic scale, and the importance of man's morality grows on the social and historical scale. Thus they all perpetuate a crazy history of crime and error. Sacrifice of self to ideal is not self-sacrifice at all, Melville has suggested, but rather it is that indulgence of self which is the ultimate romantic selfishness.

What is needed is a tactically wise, if often distasteful and unspectacular, sacrifice of self to the historical moment. Except for King Media, Melville so far has given us no one willing or able to practice this particularly contemporary, larger-and-smaller-than-traditional sacrifice. In *Billy Budd* he does.

The nature of the governor and the nature of the sacrifice demand an emphasis not on individualism, certainly, or self-expression per se, but on control—which is at the center of Melville's political classicism.

Melville introduces the need for planning by slyly setting the reader at ease with a promise of "that pleasure which is wickedly said to be in [literary] sinning." With such a sin Melville announces that he is "going to err into . . . a bypath" which turns out, after all, to be the direct road into the center of this "inside narrative." Enticed into the bypath, "anybody who can hold the Present at its worth without being inappreciative of the Past," finds in "the solitary old hulk at Portsmouth, Nelson's *Victory*" a symbol of the conditions of victory, of good government, and of the ruler who recognizes the need for altruistic yet impersonal self-sacrifice to the realities of history.

There are some, perhaps, who while not altogether inaccessible [to the beauty of the past] . . . may yet on behalf of the new order, be disposed to parry it; and this to the extent of iconoclasm, if need be. For example, prompted by the sight of the star inserted into the *Victory's* quarter-deck designating the spot where the Great Sailor fell, these martial utilitarians may suggest considerations implying that Nelson's ornate publication of his person in battle was not only unnecessary, but not military, nay, savored of foolhardiness and vanity. They may add, too, that at Trafalgar it was in effect nothing less than a challenge to death; and death came; and that but for his bravado the victorious admiral might possibly have survived the battle, and so, instead of having his sagacious dying injunction overruled by his immediate successor in command he himself when the contest was decided might have brought his shattered fleet to anchor, a proceeding which might have averted the deplorable loss of life by shipwreck in the elemental tempest that followed the martial one.

Well, should we set aside the more disputable point whether for various reasons it was possible to anchor the fleet, then plausibly enough the Benthamites of war may urge the above.

But the *might have been* is but boggy ground to build on. And certainly in foresight as to the larger issue of an encounter, and anxious preparation for it—buoying the deadly way and mapping it out, as at Copenhagen—few commanders have been so painstakingly circumspect as this same reckless declarer of his person in fight.

Personal prudence even when dictated by quite other than selfish considerations is surely no special virtue in a military man; while an excessive love of glory, impassioning a less burning impulse the honest sense of duty, is the first. If the name *Wellington* is not so much a trumpet to the blood as the simpler name *Nelson*, the reason for this may perhaps be inferred from the above. Alfred in his funeral ode on the victor of Waterloo ventures not to call him the greatest soldier of all time, though in the same ode he invokes Nelson as "the greatest sailor since the world began."

At Trafalgar Nelson on the brink of opening the fight sat down and wrote his last brief will and testament. If under the presentiment of the most magnificent of all victories to be crowned by his own glorious death, a sort of priestly motive led him to dress his person in the jewelled vouchers of his own shining deeds; if thus to have adorned himself for the altar and the sacrifice were indeed vainglory, then affectation and fustian is each more heroic line in the great epics and dramas, since in such lines the poet but embodies in verse those exaltations of sentiment that a nature like Nelson, the opportunity being given, vitalizes into acts [pp. 822-24].

The goal at the end of this bypath is a statement of the kind of heroism that, unlike the quester's courage, may lead to salvation, and that the reader is led to expect to find in the other Great Sailor, Captain Vere. Practical recognition of actualities is not attacked in this brief excursion—"the *might have been* is but boggy ground to build on." Both cheap hindsight and absolutist evaluations are tossed aside with the rejection of any should-have-been or might-be or must-be that does not grow out of the conditioning historical facts which inevitably become a particular historical result. Hand in hand with this rejection is the attack on "martial utilitarians," who, in this context, are the dry tactitians who can see tactics only. Strategy, empiricism, tactics, Melville says here, while of prime importance, cannot be divorced from the greatest communal aspirations—"the larger issue." The fact of the existence of aspiration, and recognition of larger issues, makes it necessary to reckon with human nobility and heroism as factors in tactical action. The nonrational gloriousness of which man is capable cannot be denied—indeed must be depended upon—in strategy which is to win the greatest human victories. In attacking the might-have-been and the Benthamites of war, Melville attacks the function of head minus heart, the power politics minus the informing vision. And because the informing vision is a social, historical vision, and because man is at once unbelievably heroic and unbelievably blind and base, the leader must combine Machiavellian circumspect foresight with the glorious and heartful act. The Machiavellian prudence channels and controls blind, base man, and the glorious act vitalizes the controlled and channeled man into the proper acts in which his inspired heroism can victoriously operate. The hero thus is a political and moral administrator. The standing in one's fullest magnificence upon the beleaguered quarter-deck of the state stems not from the personal and pathetically heroic idealism of the quester, but from the social and tactical vision of the leader who recognizes that the historical moment demands the sacrifice of self to the possible victory that the combined head and heart may achieve. Thus the shrewdly heroic Nelson, who deliberately and purposefully went out, in the shining medals of his honor, to tempt death.

Thus too, this modern Nelson-hero-Administrator is, like the quester, self-consuming. But unlike the quester, he consumes himself as an inspiration which will result in victory concerning the larger, social issue. He places himself on the altar of "the honest sense of duty," making his very using up of one-self a man-self triumph which saves rather than destroys the ship. And the difference between the Nelson-Vere-captain and the Ahab-captain exists most centrally in this matter of the empirically, communally, historically centered rather than the idealistically, self-centered predisposition. Indeed, "few commanders have been so painstakingly circumspect as this same reckless declarer of his person in fight," and "while an excessive love of glory . . . is the first . . . special virtue in a military man," Nelson's love of glory was no more motivated by Ahabian glory, or *vain*glory, than his painstaking circumspection was motivated by "personal prudence." The implication is that the gloriousness itself, which was always there, would never have been displayed had it not been the tactical move which resulted in the preservation and triumph of the human community, had it not been the socially conscious, altruistic "exaltations of sentiment . . . vitalized into *acts*." So too, Vere's captaincy is not the glory that leads the Ahab-led Ishmael to utter the Solomonic "All is vanity. ALL." Not at all vain, when Vere is ashore

in the garb of a civilian scarce any one would have taken him for a sailor, more especially that he never garnished unprofessional talk with nautical terms, and grave in his bearing, evinced little appreciation of mere humor. It was not out of keeping with those traits that on a passage when nothing demanded his paramount action, he was the most undemonstrative of men. Any landsman observing this gentleman not conspicuous by his stature and wearing no pronounced insignia, emerging from his cabin retreat to the open deck and noting the silent deference of the officers retiring to leeward, might have taken him for the King's guest, a civilian aboard the King's ship, some highly honorable discreet envoy on his way to an important post. But in fact this unobtrusiveness of demeanor may have proceeded from a certain unaffected modesty of manhood sometimes accompanying a resolute nature, a modesty evinced at all times not calling for pronounced action, and which shown in any rank of life suggests a virtue aristocratic in kind [p. 826].

The preparation for Vere made by the Nelson "divergence" exists in more than the nature of self-sacrifice. Not only must Nelson sacrifice the most gloriously beautiful self in order to insure the historically possible larger issue, but so also must Vere, in the rejection of the might-have-been, do the same. But in addition, just as there is no one left to whom Nelson can delegate the proper conduct of the ship of state ("his sagacious dying injunction overruled by his immediate successor") so there is no one left to whom Vere can delegate the proper power and insight. In the perfectly complete parallel between Nelson and Vere, Melville says that if human society can win a victory over itself, no one man can insure the perpetuity of the outcome. Perhaps the governor must be a community of rule. Perhaps, indeed, lasting victory cannot be achieved from the top down at all. Not only is there the implicit rejection of the great-man theory along with the recognition of the identity of the truly great man, but there is the frustrating irony which places destiny in the hands of the general, common man. Because of his blindness, general, common man cannot be led by his nobility (the administrator's self-sacrifice provides the leadership) and there is no avenue left open to the gregarious advancement, which is the only lasting one. Because in *Billy Budd* Melville comes most closely to grips with the problem of rule, the political alternative to his metaphysical rejections, and because the facts of his experience showed him no solution to the problem, *Billy Budd* has the angry, bitter, frustrated tone which too few readers have noticed in their agreement to call the story a testament of acceptance.

Melville orients the elements of Vere's sacrifice as historically as he does Nelson's. He sets up the conditions of Vere's choice in a specific moment which extends to the general history of order and community versus anarchic atheism, in Melville's sense, and atomistic individualism.

Billy himself, as the lure, is a familiar figure. He is the element to which Vere reacts, and it is important that Billy is dragged out of *The Rights of Man* onto *The Indomitable* "in the year of the Great Mutiny." He enters actual rather than theoretical human history at a moment when order is threatened and when the felicities of the rights of man are absent because the whole world is in another Mar-di. In the total historical picture, the man-of-war world, wrong as it is, is all that exists. Man can either, like the quester, renounce it, or can try to preserve order so that the social instruments which are the actuality may be used to attain felicity. Like tactics, order per se is not the point. Melville's political classicism cannot possibly be construed as totalitarianism. Vere, it is stated, does not maintain order for its own sake. Vere sees order as necessary for a reconciliation of opposites and a suppression of chaos-bringing disruption. The paradox is that in the predatory world, in which the gun robs man of his felicities, the wrong instrument is that very felicity itself, which in the character of Billy Budd is characterized as the nonpredatory Typee-child savage "—a Tahitian say of Captain Cook's time. . . . Out of natural courtesy he received but did not appropriate . . . like a gift placed on the palm of an outstretched hand upon which the fingers do not close."

Billy is presented in a world where the Articles of War and the Sermon on the Mount are the two opposites which compose the choice open to man in the universal history of the war. The preface to the novelette brings the choice into immediate focus. "The year 1797, the year of this narrative, belongs to a period which as every thinker now feels, involved a crisis for Christendom not exceeded in its undetermined momentousness at the time by any other era whereof there is record." It is curious that Melville sums up the universal history in the term "Christendom" (wherein one of the main actors is a pagan "Tahitian," as it were), for within this "inside narrative" one need go no further than the chaplain's interview with Billy to find Melville's Solomonic, unchristian, cultural relativism, or his view of Christendom (the official term) as a false appearance. The Tahitian is closer to the Sermon on the Mount than to "Christendom's" Articles of War. The clue to Melville's preparation for Billy lies in the assertion that it is Christendom's most momentous time. There are a few alternatives for this assertion, other than the year 1797, but they all add up to the same thing. Immediately suggested are the birth and adoration of the Christ Baby, the Passion, or the Fall. And just as Melville uses Typee or Saddle Meadows or Serenia to demonstrate universal points of development, so in *Billy Budd* Melville tells his history of humanity in a reworking of the Adam-Christ story, placing prelapsarian Adam and the Christ on a man-of-war, and demonstrating the inevitability of the Fall and the necessity of the Crucifixion.

The Preface is complete in itself as the setting in which that beautiful self, Christ, is introduced. In this setting, the Sermon is as distinct from the Articles as the French Revolution is distinct from Vere's England. The problems of rule are introduced in the implicit question, in the actuality of a world torn by chaos and ruled by the gun, what are the proper means and ends?

"Now, as elsewhere hinted, it was something caught from the Revolutionary Spirit that at Spithead emboldened the man-of-war's men to rise against real abuses, long-standing ones, and afterwards at the Nore to make inordinate and aggressive demands, successful resistance to which was confirmed only when the ringleaders were hung for an admonitory spectacle to the anchored fleet. Yet in a way analogous to the operation of the Revolution at large the Great Mutiny, though by Englishmen naturally deemed monstrous at the time, doubtless gave the first latent prompting to most important reforms in the British Navy [p. 805].

Throughout the story, the quester-like, ideal-seeking destructiveness of the Spirit of the Age broods in the background against which the major action takes place. Despite its good intentions and real justifications, the gun wielded by the spirit championing the rights of man is an emblem of the perpetuation of all the sins of history by the good-badness of tactically misdirected human aspiration. Melville insists so strongly upon the background of the narrative, that, extended as it is by its connection with a retelling of the Christ story, it becomes the actuality of all history. Simply, there is no escaping the conditions in which Vere must act:

[The Nore] was indeed a demonstration more menacing to England than the contemporary manifestoes and conquering and proselyting armies of the French Directory.

To the British Empire the Nore Mutiny was what a strike in the fire-brigade would be to London threatened by general arson. In a crisis when the Kingdom might well have anticipated the famous signal that some years later published along the naval line of battle what it was that upon occasion England expected of Englishmen; *that* was the time when at the mast-heads of the three-deckers and seventy-fours moored in her own roadstead—a fleet, the right arm of a Power then all but the sole free conservative one of the Old World, the blue-jackets, to be numbered by thousands, ran up with hurras the British colors with the union and cross wiped out; by that cancellation transmuting the flag of founded law and freedom defined, into the enemy's red meteor of unbridled and unbounded revolt. Reasonable discontent growing out of practical grievances in the fleet had been ignited into irrational combustion as by live cinders blown across the Channel from France in flames [pp. 819-20].

Again, in Chapter V, after the conditions of rule have been explored in the Nelson episode, Melville once more warns that "Discontent foreran the Two Mutinies, and more or less it lurkingly survived them. Hence it was not unreasonable to apprehend some return of trouble sporadic or general."

Into this history Christ is born. If the fall of man, for Melville, is neither a mythical nor chronological actuality, but is merely a symbol of the beginningless and symbolic facts of all human history, then again, as *Typee* suggested, Eden never was, fallen man is actual man trapped in his own history, and the prelapsarian and pure must be out of history, indeed out of time. Thus, when Melville introduces Billy as

a sort of upright barbarian, much such perhaps as Adam presumably might have been ere the urbane Serpent wriggled himself into his company.

And here be it submitted that apparently going to corroborate the doctrine of man's fall, a doctrine now popularly ignored, it is observable that where certain virtues pristine and unadulterate peculiarly characterize anybody in the external uniform of civilization, they will upon scrutiny seem not to be derived from custom or convention but rather to be out of keeping with these, as if indeed exceptionally transmitted from a period prior to Cain's city and citified man . . . [pp. 817-18].

he is implicitly advocating neither the nineteenth-century primitivism that derives from a quester-like insistence upon self, nor the eighteenth-century primitivism that derives from the sensationalism and institutionalism whose political corrolaries were based upon the social compact and the natural rights of man. Especially within the context of Billy Budd's actions it becomes evident that Melville is continuing and summing up what he had said in his other books: given the only actuality of earth and time, then the transcendent purity, the Edenic, absolute morality, is something before history and which therefore comes from nowhere—is something that is literally as impossible as Yillah or Isabel or Billy himself, as impossible as the right-wrongness of the anarchic, individualistic, rebellious insistence upon the eighteenth-century idealism which Vere must oppose. Again, recalling citified man, Melville recalls the fact that like all the other lures, Billy, despite his existence, is devoid of experience, which though it is the hideous experience of "fallen" man, is the only history there is.

The conditions of Vere's choice must be further defined within the opposition of history and ideal. Whereas anarchical revolution is the *bête noire* of the piece, neither social revolution, nor imposition of order, nor any socio-political instrument per se is defined absolutely. Both Vere and the French seek the rights of man, the lasting peace and welfare of mankind. But in the search for human felicities, uncontrolled and disorderly action ironically has and will result in the denial of those very rights. The Vere will have to suspend the rights in order to institute the communal order which makes those rights attainable. The idealist will ironically defeat those rights just as the quester defeats his own purpose. So Vere recognizes that to speak of the rights of man as an abstract ideal is meaningless. The historical duties and responsibilities of man must be recognized and practiced before the rights of man become significant or can even exist in the actuality of man's "fallen" state. Thus it is not the fact but the tactics of the French Revolution with which Vere has his quarrel, for the Revolution as a justified fact has itself, like Spithead and the Nore, in unanticipated ways, brought about a step toward betterment and the lasting peace and welfare of mankind which Vere champions. "The opening proposition made by the Spirt of the Age involved the rectification of the Old World's hereditary wrongs. In France to some extent this was bloodily effected. But what then? Straightway the Revolution itself became a wrongdoer, one more oppressive than the kings. Under Napoleon it enthroned upstart kings, and initiated that prolonged agony of continual war whose final throe was Waterloo. During those years not the wisest could have foreseen that the outcome of all would be what to some thinkers apparently it has since turned out to be, a political advance along nearly the whole line for Europeans." In short, the mutinies, the Revolution, the Rights of Man, and ideal aspirations all become merged (like the Sermon on the Mount, in opposition to the Articles of War) in the historical cycles of rightly motivated, morally justified action which is tactically mismanaged and wrongly directed against an order which, nonetheless, had to be challenged in the first place. Ordinary men, Jarl, Starbuck, Charlie Millthorpe, the majority of the ships' "people" in the French and English fleets, want what is good. But absolutely defined good, such as Billy implies, is inoperative in the actualities of history. The good can only be defined by—indeed becomes one with—the proper tactics within the historical moment. Melville is no more absolutist in his political classicism than he is in his cultural relativism; the problem becomes not one of order versus rebellion as such, or of suppression versus mass aspiration, but a problem of the proper tactics versus the improper tactics. As Vere insists in the court-martial scene, it is not the intention, but the consequences of the act that must be weighed. The problem is that of "atheism" (the well-intended but ultimately man-denying idealism) versus true "Godliness" (the communally disciplined use of the gun according to the historical view which uses the gun to destroy the gun). It is not so important that Melville may not have agreed with those thinkers who saw a political advance along the whole line for Europeans, or that he said that 1797 was or was not a year for revolution, or that he agreed or disagreed with the French Directory: the important point is the statement he reached for in using those events as symbols. That is, the moral intention, the absolute goodness by itself, is inapplicable to history and therefore a chaos bringer. The gun itself is sterile rule and power and prerogative for its own sake. Neither quester nor Machiavel, Vere is both. He recognizes that only by wedding the correct, disciplined, forced, social manipulation to a moral goal of social altruism can man achieve his Nelson-Victory over the chaos and atheism of history. Always the implication is that history is not a result of dependence upon or lack of dependence upon an absolute morality; but rather that since no absolute morality governs the cosmos, that the definition and even existence of morality arise from the historical situation which shapes its being.

Having set up the "fallen" state of man as the only context for reality, Melville now has to dramatize the impossible unrealities of man's supranatural, suprahistorical idealism. Billy Budd is first introduced in a view of the Handsome Sailor. The Handsome Sailor is not necessarily white like Billy, but, universalized by the Negro Handsome Sailor, he is the leader of apostles, the informing center whose physical and moral being sets the tone and direction of his universal followers' activity. He is

"a symmetric figure much above the average height. . . .
"It was a hot noon in July; and his face, lustrous with perspiration, beamed with barbaric good humor. In jovial sallies right and left his white teeth flashing into view, he rollicked along, the center of a company of his shipmates. These were made up of such an assortment of tribes and complexions as would well have fitted them to be marched up by Anacharsis Cloots before the bar of the first French Assembly as Representatives of the Human Race. At each spontaneous tribute rendered by the wayfarers to this black pagod of a fellow—the tribute of a pause and a stare, and less frequent an exclamation,—the motley retinue showed that they took that sort of pride in the evoker of it which the Assyrian priests doubtless showed for their grand sculptored Bull when the faithful prostrated themselves.
"Invariably a proficient in his perilous calling, he was also more or less of a mighty boxer or wrestler. It was strength and beauty. . . .
"The moral nature was seldom out of keeping with the physical make. Indeed, except as toned by the former, the comeliness and power, always attractive in masculine conjunction could hardly have drawn the sort of honest homage the Handsome Sailor in some examples received from his less gifted associates" [pp. 807-9].

When Billy himself is presented, he too is the Handsome Sailor characterized by barbaric good humor, by a tall, athletic, symmetric figure, by the ability to box well, by proficiency in his calling, by a highly moral nature. The Handsome Sailor becomes the kind of innocent that the most attractive Typee savage is, and the repeated mention of Billy's barbarian innocence and his magnificent physical appearance predetermines the genre's essential mindlessness. Once more, the prehistoric and griefless Typee mindlessness is associated with the Edenic purity of Christian innocence. Billy is constantly presented as the prelapsarian Adam, indeed, one who "in the nude might have posed for a statue of young Adam before the fall." Melville repeatedly suggests that innocence, in the need for a knowledge of the history of the only world there is, is not a saving virtue, but a fatal flaw. The very goodness of Billy's ignorance of the world, while in accord with Christian teaching, becomes the sin of nonunderstanding, noncommunicating mindlessness marked by the stutter. Melville writes:

In certain matters, some sailors even in mature life remain unsophisticated enough. But a young seafarer of the disposition of our athletic foretopman is much of a child-man. And yet a child's utter innocence is but its blank ignorance, and the innocence more or less wanes as intelligence waxes. But in Billy Budd, intelligence such as it was, had advanced, while yet his simple-mindedness remained for the most part unaffected. Experience is a teacher indeed; yet did Billy's years make his experience small. Besides he had none of that intuitive knowledge of the bad which in natures not good or incompletely so foreruns experience, and therefore may pertain, as in some instances it too clearly does pertain, even to youth [p. 854].

The problem of Billy's mindlessness is not merely one of the Christlike purity which is an absolute and predetermining absence of evil. The problem of Billy's mindlessness arises from his typically lure-like inexperience and inability to evaluate the experience he does have. Leaving no doubt at all about the nature of his rejection of ideal, Christly behavior, Melville sums up his statement about Billy by saying, "As it was, innocence was his blinder."

Billy, then, is particularized as the Adam-Christ within the general type of the Handsome Sailor: "Such a cynosure [the Handsome Sailor], at least in aspect, and something such too in nature, *though with important variations* made apparent as the story proceeds, was *welkin-eyed* Billy Budd or Baby Budd . . ." [italics mine]. Billy immediately is the beauty and childlike purity of the ideal. He is called both Beauty and Baby by his shipmates, and the detail of his "heaven-eyed" face occurs again and again. Even in the ever illuminating matter of origins (on the literal level, Billy's origins will turn out to be something quite different), Melville hints that Billy's unknown mother was one "eminently favored by Love and the Graces," and—who is his father? Well, "God knows, Sir." The Baby is not allowed to continue his straight and narrow path within the chronometrical and ideal sermon of the rights of man, but is born into the actualities of the Articles of War. "It was not very long prior to the time of the narration that follows that he had entered the King's service, having been impressed on the Narrow Seas from a homeward bound English merchantman [the *Rights of Man*] into a seventy-four outward-bound, *H.M.S. Indomitable*." In *White-Jacket* Melville used the ship image precisely in the way it was to be used repeatedly in other books: the homeward bound ship is the ship bound to heaven, to something final and absolute. The outward bound ship, whether wrongly or rightly directed, is the actual state of the world, ever seeking, ever subject to the dark waters of new and unknown experiences, ever plowing new paths in the boundless waters of infinite relativity. In the actual world, Billy continues his behavior of ideal Christliness. Chronometrically and mindlessly he turns the other cheek to all new experiences, accepting everything with animal insightlessness and the childlike faith of innocence. "As to his enforced enlistment, that he seemed to take pretty much as he was wont to take any vicissitude of weather. Like the animals, though no philosopher, he was, without knowing it, practically a fatalist."

The ordinary, hard-working, Jarl-world of common grave-lings depends upon Budd morality for the peaceful pursuits of an unarmed and productive world. When his merchant ship, the *Rights of Man*, is robbed of "man's earthly household peace" and "domestic felicity" by the arch-thief, the gun, Captain Graveling pleads with Lieutenant Ratcliffe lest the man-of-war remove the very possibility of a peaceful and moral world. "Ay, Lieutenant, you are going to take away the jewel of 'em; you are going to take away my peacemaker!" Immediately the Prince of Peace must be defined within the context of either the ideal, the Sermon and the *Rights of Man*, or hideous history, the Articles and the *Indomitable*. Immediately, first things come first, and the needs of the man-of-war world take precedence over the needs of the Ship of Peace. The bitterness of this story's irony and anger first becomes noticeable in the impressment scene. For Ratcliffe, who understands none of the things that Vere understands, and who can use the gun only in order to use the gun, makes the only possible, correct answer for all the wrong reasons. "Well," says he, "blessed are the peacemakers, especially the fighting peacemakers!" And pointing through the cabin window to the *Indomitable*, Ratcliffe adds, "And such are the seventy-four beauties some of which you see poking their noses out of the port-holes of yonder warship lying-to for me." For they, not the meek, inherit the earth.

Characteristically, Billy's transfer of worlds is accompanied by the predatory act of spoilation. Not only is the very act of impressment symbol enough, but the lieutenant bursts unbidden into Graveling's cabin, unbidden takes his ease and pleasure with Graveling's liquor, as though the act of taking were his military, world-wide right. To

him Billy's impressment has only the meaning of his own selfish amusement gained by obtaining a prize at the expense of the *Rights of
Man.* "Why, I pledge you in advance the royal approbation," he says
sarcastically to Graveling. Ratcliffe will not allow Billy to transfer
his possessions from one ship to the other. The characteristics of the
ideal cannot be applied to the characteristics of the real. What Billy
can take with him is what Billy—"Apollo with his portmanteau"—can
carry in a man-of-war's sea-bag in order to live a man-of-war life. But
as for the rest of Billy's possessions, why, "you can't take that big box
aboard a warship. The boxes there are mostly shot-boxes."

And what the thief, Ratcliffe, says about his brother-slave-master
thief, the gun, is history's hideous but inescapable truth. In a bit of
preparation for Billy's felling Claggart, Melville indicates that when
the Christ is a peacemaker, he must be a fighting peacemaker, and
must suspend innocent peacefulness for the actuality of the moment.
In a mindless parallel to Vere's position, Billy uses his fists as the only
means for removing the necessity for using his fists. Talking about the
chaotic living conditions aboard ship, Graveling says,

But Billy came; and it was like a Catholic priest striking peace in an Irish
shindy. Not that he preached to them or said or did anything in particular;
but a virtue went out of him, sugaring the sour ones. They took to him like
hornets to treacle; all but the bluffer of the gang, the big shaggy chap with
the fire-red whiskers. He indeed out of envy, perhaps, of the newcomer, and
thinking such a "sweet and pleasant fellow," as he mockingly designated
him to the others, could hardly have the spirit of a game-cock, must needs
bestir himself in trying to get up an ugly row with him. Billy forebore with
him and reasoned with him in a pleasant way . . . but nothing served. So,
in the second dog-watch one day the Red Whiskers in presence of the
others, under pretense of showing Billy just whence a sirloin steak was cut
—for the fellow had once been a butcher—insultingly gave him a dig under
the ribs. Quick as lightning Billy let fly his arm. I dare say he never meant
to do quite as much as he did, but anyhow he gave the burly fool a terrible
drubbing. It took about half a minute, I should think. And, Lord bless you,
the lubber was astonished at the celerity. And will you believe it, Lieutenant, the Red Whiskers now really loves Billy—loves him, or is the biggest
hypocrite that ever I heard of [pp. 811-12].

There is therefore, before the story opens, a history of experience
to which Billy has been exposed. But his actions, even though dictated by the unchristly actualities of experience, were unplanned, un-
intended, mindless, and spontaneous as lightning. For Billy, precisely
as for Isabel and Yillah, experience might just as well never have
been. Billy is incapable of subtleties, "for Billy, though happily en-
dowed with the gaiety of high health, youth and a free heart, was yet
by no means of a satirical turn. The will to it and the sinister dex-
terity were alike wanting. To deal in double meaning and insinuations
of any sort was quite foreign to his nature." Like Isabel, Yillah, and the
white whale, Billy is alone in the world, and without connections in

his human family. Beneath the exposure to experience—the orange-tawny dye of the tar-bucket and the glow of the seaman's tan—there is the lily and the rose. He is Lily-Yillah's rose-flower in the bud. He is "all but feminine in purity [and] in natural complexion . . . where, thanks to his seagoing, the lily was quite suppressed and the rose had some ado *visibly* to flush through the tan." And despite the life of experience (the seagoing), like the young Pierre, Billy has not had a view of woe.

No merrier man in his mess: in marked contrast to certain other individuals included like himself among the impressed portions of the ship's company; for these when not actively employed were sometimes, and more particularly in the last dog-watch when the drawing near of twilight induced revery, apt to fall into a saddish mood which in some partook of sullenness. But they were not so young as our foretopman, and no few of them must have known a hearth of some sort, others may have had wives and children left, too probably, in uncertain circumstances, and hardly any but must have acknowledged kith and kin, while for Billy, as will shortly be seen, his entire family was practically invested in himself [p. 814].

Not until it is too late does he recognize the inescapable trap laid for innocence, which initiates him into the wisdom and woe that brings "to [his] face an expression which was as a crucifixion to behold." Not until touched by the hatred reminiscent of the sons of Aleema does the innocence fade and does "the rose-tan of [Billy's] cheek look struck as by white leprosy." And it is the innocence which attracts the Satanism of the Ahabian man whose experience has demonized his heart in the fires of the madness that comes from woe. The imagery completes the picture of Billy as the tempted Adam-Christ pursued by the Spoiler, Claggart, for Billy is "as Adam presumably might have been ere the urbane Serpent wriggled himself into his company."

Billy's famous stutter introduces the idea that the inevitable relationship with evil, or history, is precisely what makes the Baby Buddlike Beauty a murderous and murdered thing. For as a man, Billy too is subject to external history, and must learn to evaluate experience. When Melville says that innocence was Billy's blinder, he says that as a behavior pattern for man to "square his life by," Billy can only offer what is really the original sin of unknowledge. Again Melville uses the Christian mythos and symbology in order to make the empirical reversion of what to the unchristian Solomonic wisdom had been the inversion to begin with. The irony which makes the innocence-stutter a sin is enriched by its inevitable relationship, as a sin, to Satan, suggesting that because of his mindless purity, heartful Billy had always been subject to and would inevitably attract the attention of Claggart. Billy had no

visible blemish . . . but an occasional liability to a vocal defect. Though in the hour of elemental uproar or peril, he was everything that a sailor should be, yet under sudden provocation of strong heart-feeling his voice otherwise

singularly musical, as if expressive of the harmony within, was apt to develop an organic hesitancy, in fact more or less of a stutter or even worse.
In this particular Billy was a striking instance that the arch interferer, the
envious marplot of Eden still has more or less to do with every human
consignment to this planet of earth. In every case, one way or another he is
sure to slip in his little card as much as to remind us—I too have a hand
here [pp. 818-19].

And Satan sent his subtlest card when he signed his name with innocence.

The man of experience can not believe the reality of the appearance
that Billy makes. The Dansker, for instance, at first is merely amused
by the incongruity of a being, like Billy, aboard the *Indomitable*. At
first it is merely the amusement of wondering how, when, and where
the pretense will be destroyed by the inevitable initiation. But as the
Dansker becomes aware that Billy is what he seems to be, the Dansker's amusement disappears in thoughtful consideration of the symbolic situation which innocence and the inevitable initiation imply.

Now the first time that [the Dansker's] small weazel-eyes happened to
light on Billy Budd, a certain grim internal merriment set all his ancient
wrinkles into antic play. Was it that his eccentric unsentimental old sapience
primitive in its kind saw or thought it saw something which in contrast
with the warship's environment looked oddly incongruous in the handsome
sailor? But after slyly studying him at intervals, the old Merlin's equivocal
merriment was modified; for now when the twain would meet, it would
start in his face a quizzing sort of look, but it would be momentary and
sometimes replaced by an expression of speculative query as to what might
eventually befall a nature like that, dropped into a world not without some
man-traps and against whose subtleties simple courage lacking experience
and address and without any touch of defensive ugliness, is of little avail;
and where such innocence as man is capable of does yet in a moral emer-
gency not always sharpen the faculties or enlighten the will [p. 836].

Thus irony compounds irony; the irony of the man-trap, Claggart's,
accusation of Budd, is given the further twist of a truth uttered by
the liar, of the sin of innocence attacked by the evil and experienced
man: "You have but noted [Budd's] fair cheek," says Claggart to
Vere, "A man-trap may be under his ruddy-tipped daisies." The
Dansker's elemental sapience makes him the man who can see what is
going on in the swirling fogs that surround the necessities of action.
(Later in the story Melville images the actual, historical present as
"obscuring smoke.") The Dansker is called old Board-her-in-the-smoke
because he was wounded in a boarding action upon an enemy vessel.
When the Dansker enlightens Billy about Claggart's enmity, Melville
directs attention to the old sailor's scar, the emblem of the insights
gained through the experience which has earned him his nickname:
"The old man, shoving up the front of his tarpaulin and deliberately
rubbing the long slant scar at the point where it entered the thin
hair, laconically said, 'Baby Budd, *Jemmy Legs*' (meaning the master-
at-arms) 'is down on you.'"

However, the Dansker has not learned the one thing that Nelson and Vere know: sapient empiricism is not enough. Once in a lifetime a man impractically may have to expose himself to the dangers which he had always guarded against with practical strategy. Sometimes a man must chance his own destruction and play the hero. What for the quester is characteristic behavior must sometimes be performed by the true administrator, not as the self-indulgence it may so insidiously appear to be, but as a calculated risk. The Dansker cannot do this. For him the true behavior is the direction of wisdom toward that personal prudence which both Vere and Nelson reject. He is the typical G.I. who knows "the score": "Years, and those experiences which befall certain shrewder men subordinated life-long to the will of superiors, all this had developed in the Dansker the pithy guarded cynicism that was his leading characteristic." So he can see the truth, but his resigned and misdirected action is a development of noncommunicative cynicism by means of which he protects himself. " '*Jemmy Legs!*' ejaculated Billy, his welkin eyes expanding; 'what for?' . . .

"Something less unpleasingly oracular [Billy] tried to extract; but the old Chiron thinking perhaps that for the nonce he had sufficiently instructed his young Achilles, pursed his lips, gathered his wrinkles together and would commit himself to nothing further." He can only hint at murder, but must, in the last analysis, allow the murder to take place nonetheless. Thus he cannot prevent the rising of the issue which may threaten social solidarity and communal order. Because he cannot make the kind of self-sacrifice of which Vere is capable, he can reform nothing.

But Captain the Honorable Edward Fairfax Vere is a man whose experience had not been lost in innocence nor yet sterilized in that cynicism which makes the inactive and practical and circumspect Dansker only a more humane and understandable Plinlimmon. Vere is totally active. He will not delay in making decisions, even when the decision is totally painful and when just a three-day wait would allow him to dump the entire problem in the lap of a superior officer. Yet, like Nelson, he is not the enthusiast or the gloryhog. Totally aware of the fact of consequences, he does not subordinate reflection to physical courage, which, Melville said, is the one characteristic that man shares with the beasts of the field. Vere's is the communal prudence; he is "thoroughly versed in the science of his profession, and intrepid to the verge of temerity, though never injudiciously so."

As clear as Vere's position may seem to be, however, he, like Claggart, provides a problem. Vere's social philosophy is apparent within the story. His cosmic philosophy is not. Because the reader must supply Vere's and Claggart's cosmic motivations, *Billy Budd* is incomplete. Yet, although Melville could not justifiably devote space to either Vere's or Claggart's education (*Billy Budd* is the most impossible thing Melville attempted), Vere's cosmic view can be extrapolated from his social view and from the other books. In brief, the man's moral pragmatism and empiricism and emphasis on social order make it apparent that he has learned from the blank sea, at which he always stares, the same lesson that Pip learned from the blank sea in which he almost drowned. Presumably he has learned history's lesson of a naturalistic universe. In any case, unspecified as it is, his experience has resulted in the wisdom that is woe, and that demands of man a closer scrutiny and control of his own morality and actions than ever before. Vere is neither innocently mirthful like Billy, nor cynical like the Dansker. He is prominently and predominantly serious. His seriousness comes from history, and not from idealism. Hardheadedly realistic, Vere rejects the pretentious Titanism of the quester. Whether he realizes that there is nothing in the blankness to strike, like whether he realizes the fact of a naturalistic universe, is not anchored in direct evidence within the story. One can assume the affirmative in both cases, for in his nonidealistic actions, Vere subordinates self to community and desire to history; thus his wisdom that is woe does not slip over into the woe that is madness. He becomes the one man who sees and who is not the confidence man or the zero or the quester. Unlike Ahab, who is the one man to drive and run the ship, even to the point, Melville realizes, where it can be he alone who first spies the whale, Vere is the administrator who can allow subordinates to help direct affairs no matter how poignant any particular case may be for him. For Ahab the ship and the whale are self. For Vere the ship and naval order are society. Ahab replaces the world with his self and can only disregard the forms and needs and uses of society. Vere also captains society, but he does not misuse it. Ahab would dictatorially sentence or reprieve. Vere, however, feels that he must not only preserve social form by making the proper judgments seen to issue from the social machinery set up to decide upon tactics, but that he must also educate that machinery in the process. The one time Vere is permitted quester-like secrecy is in the closet scene with Billy, where he discloses personal feelings. Because he can force his decisions to surmount personal feelings, and because the consequences of personal and heedless reactions have been demonstrated in Billy's career, the specifics of Vere's personal reactions are not needed in the story. Painfully, Vere the man cannot exist in this story. Vere the administrator is the need. In drawing the curtain of secrecy, Melville evidenced thematic as well as aesthetic taste. Vere and Billy could not have spoken or acted in any way but that which Melville supposes, and the actualization of those actions and words would have broken the story's fine, constant edge of anger with a serrated space of lugubriousness. It would be lugubriousness because one's emotional associations with Vere arise from seeing that Vere does not weep. The entire motifs of appearances and self-consumption demand that Vere not be either in view or in life when he does give in to the heart beneath the tunic of the King's service, for then he would be one of us, not the ruler; his tears would make him but one more of the "people," who are controlled by, but who do not control, the moment. It is of fundamental importance to know that Vere can weep and wants to weep. It should be (as Melville makes it) impossible to see him weeping. Melville must show only that Vere has earned a right to the ownership of his personal feelings, that he is aware of the demands of the heart and that the relationship those feelings allow Vere to have with the external world is "noble" rather than mad. For "there is no telling the sacrament, seldom if in any case revealed to the gadding world wherever under circumstances at all akin to those here attempted to be set forth, two of great Nature's nobler order embrace. There is privacy at the time, inviolable to the survivor, and holy oblivion the sequel to each diviner magnanimity, providentially covers all at last."

Indeed the depth and sincerity of Vere's feelings make him the man of necessary heart as well as mind and power. "The first to encounter Captain Vere in act of leaving the compartment was the senior Lieutenant. The face he beheld, for the moment expressive of the agony of the strong, was to that officer, though a man of fifty, a startling revelation. That the condemned one suffered less than he who had mainly effected the condemnation was apparently indicated. . . ."

Because then, he is not the heartless Machiavel merely, Vere is the man who can understand the beauty of absolute morality, who can stare out at the amoral message of the blank sea, and who can, therefore, weep over Billy. For, as "with some others engaged in various departments of the world's more heroic activities, Captain Vere, though practical enough upon occasion would at times betray a certain dreaminess of mood. Standing alone on the weather-side of the quarter-deck, one hand holding by the rigging he would absently gaze off at the blank sea. At the presentation to him then of some minor matter interrupting the current of his thoughts he would show more or less irascibility; but instantly he would control it." Personal, nostalgic, romantic, as well as philosophical thought may occupy Vere, but this man is not the Taji or Ahab or Pierre. This man sees himself as the captain of the small bit of man-of-war mortality, the only life there is, caught in the blank, eternal immensity of time. He does not go insane as does poor, weak Pip. He rechannels his thoughts, making earth's needs paramount, and returns to even the minor matter which pertains to the conduct of society. Unlike the quester, Vere does not indulge himself. Only in personal matters, when he is the father rather than the administrator, does he reveal his agony. The quester can never control himself as, Vere knows, the leader must. When faced with an opposition between his personal desires and the demands of his position, he too is dreamily tormented by private yearning, "but instantly he would control it." As he asks the members of the court-martial, "But something in your aspect seems to urge that it is not solely that heart that moves in you, but also the conscience, the private conscience. But tell me whether or not, occupying the position we do, private conscience should not yield to that imperial one formulated in the code under which alone we officially proceed?" Thus the public man's conscious consuming of his private self. Thus the individualism, the ideal morality, and the primitive heartfulness—the Sermon on the Mount—placed squarely in opposition to public order—the Articles of War. And in one of Vere's speeches, Melville combines privatism, intention, individualistic and personal response (heartful as they may be), with the mindless chaos over which the "forms, measured forms" must triumph by giving effective shape to the idealism and absolute morality which the private self craves:

"Ay, Sir," emotionally broke in the officer of marines, "in one sense [Billy's blow] was [a capital crime]. But surely Budd purposed neither mutiny nor homicide."

"Surely not, my good man. And before a court less arbitrary and more merciful than a martial one that plea would largely extenuate. At the last Assizes it shall acquit. But how here? We proceed under the law of the Mutiny Act. In feature no child can resemble his father more than that Act resembles in spirit the thing from which it derives—War. In His Majesty's service—in this ship indeed—there are Englishmen forced to fight for the King against their will. Against their conscience for aught we know. Though as their fellow-creatures some of us may appreciate their position, yet as Navy Officers, what reck we of it? Still less recks the enemy. Our impressed men he would fain cut down in the same swath with our volunteers. As regards the enemy's naval conscripts, some of whom may even share our own abhorrence of the regicidal French Directory, it is the same on our side. War looks but to the frontage, the appearance. And the Mutiny Act, War's child, takes after the father. Budd's intent or non intent is nothing to the purpose" [p. 881].

In Vere, Melville has the unopportunistic character through whom he can morally pronounce the necessity for pragmatic judgment. Moreover, unlike the bureaucrats who wrote the official version of Budd's deed, Vere sees through official, conventional appearances and does not save the officer caste for its own sake at all— indeed he condemns that caste to the necessities and responsibilities for the public judgments which slay the private judge. He realizes that one must defend the forms and appearances in order to use them in the struggle to reform the actualities which makes the "frontage" necessary. For Vere the historical must always take precedence over the ideal: first things first. "Speculatively regarded," Vere says, "[Billy's

case] might be referred to a jury of casuists. But for us here acting
not as casuists or moralists, it is a case practical and under martial
law practically to be dealt with. . . ."

"But . . . while thus strangely we prolong proceedings that should
be summary—the enemy may be sighted and an engagement result.
We must do; and one of two things must we do—condemn or let go."

Placed in the necessity for action, man cannot appeal to anything
beyond the wooden walls of his world. He must take his moral basis
for acts that would otherwise be meaninglessly cruel from a recognition
of the fact that his morality is dictated by history, as well as vice versa,
and that he must be obedient—in order to attain anything other than
a mere repetition of immorality—to his own relative and immediate
actualities in time. "But in natural justice," asks Vere, "is nothing but
the prisoner's overt act to be considered? How can we adjudge to
summary and shameful death a fellow-creature innocent before God,
and whom we feel to be so?—Does that state it aright? You sign sad
assent. Well, I too feel that, the full force of that. It is Nature. But
do these buttons that we wear attest that our allegiance is to Nature?
No, to the King. Though the ocean, which is inviolate Nature primeval,
though this be the element where we move and have our being as
sailors, yet as the King's officers lies our duty in a sphere correspond-
ingly natural? So little is that true, that in receiving our commissions
we in the most important regards ceased to be natural free agents."
One cannot emulate the universe. First of all, nature in man may not
be nature in the universe. Secondly, though nature in man may be
the spontaneous heartfulness of primitive, childlike, barbaric Typee,
two-thirds of nature is dark and Typee cannot cope with it. Time has
brought man beyond the point where the simplicities of Typee-rela-
tionships are effective any longer. The leader's self-sacrificing allegiance is to a recognition of the historical reality (the King) with
which the out-of-time primeval-beneath-the-brass-buttons cannot cope.
Thus Vere brings the reader full circle back to the historical reality
set up in the Preface, and reveals the lonely, self-denying, self-sterilizing role that must be played by the man that the Good Officer, the
Good Administrator, should be.

"Lieutenant," [Vere replies to that officer's request that Billy's penalty be
mitigated] "were that clearly lawful for us under the circumstances consider the consequences of such clemency. The people" (meaning the
ship's company) "have native sense; most of them are familiar with our
naval usage and tradition; and how would they take it? Even could you
explain to them—which our official position forbids—they, long moulded by
arbitrary discipline have not that kind of intelligent responsiveness that
might qualify them to comprehend and discriminate. No, to the people the
foretopman's deed, however it be worded in the announcement will be plain
homicide committed in a flagrant act of mutiny. What penalty for that
should follow, they know. But it does not follow. Why? They will ruminate.
You know what sailors are. Will they not revert to the recent outbreak at

the Nore? Ay, they know the well-founded alarm—the panic it struck throughout England. Your clement sentence they would find pusillanimous. They would think that we flinch, that we are afraid of them—afraid of practicing a lawful rigor singularly demanded at this juncture lest it should provoke new troubles. What shame to us such a conjecture on their part, and how deadly to discipline. You see then, whither prompted by duty and the law I steadfastly drive. But I beseech you, my friends, do not take me amiss. I feel as you do for this unfortunate boy. But did he know our hearts, I take him to be of that generous nature that he would feel even for us on whom in this military necessity so heavy a compulsion is laid" [p. 882].

Just as true individual identity paradoxically results from subordination of one-self to man-self, so Vere's kind of self-sterilizing, unlike the quester's, leads to potent effectiveness.

Vere is Melville's complete man of action, mind, and heart. His experience demands that his acts proceed from an understanding of history, and, empirically, "his bias was toward those books to which every serious mind of superior order occupying any active post of authority in the world, naturally inclines; books treating of actual men and events no matter of what era—history, biography and unconventional writers, who, free from cant and convention, like Montaigne, honestly, and *in the spirit of common sense* philosophize upon *realities*" [italics mine]. And coupled with heartful and mindful empiricism is an eclectic time sense which sees all history as the unfolding of a pattern, all aspects of man's life equatable in different eras in the blank and inevitable passage of time. "In illustrating of any point touching the stirring personages and events of the time he would be as apt to cite some historic character or incident of antiquity as that he would cite from the moderns." Thus, though set off from the rest of mankind as a man of superior insight and power, Vere never passes from the way of understanding. He can effect the kind of border-crossing eclecticism which the quester, who tried to cross borders, needed so desperately. Nonidealistic eclecticism gives men like Vere direct insight into the heart of the matter, and their "honesty prescribes to them directness, sometimes far-reaching like that of a migratory fowl that in its flight never heeds when it crosses a frontier." His entire rationale for being is based upon the final characteristic necessary for the complete man: his goal is the betterment of the race and the communal attainment of the earthly felicities. Of course, almost every Melvillean character desires this goal, but it is not until Vere that goal and tactics are merged at last. Indeed, others may be political classicists simply because they are conservative or reactionary; but as for Vere, "while other members of that aristocracy to which by birth he belonged were incensed at the innovators mainly because their theories were inimical to the privileged classes, not alone Captain Vere disinterestedly opposed them because they seemed to him incapable of embodiment in lasting institutions, but at war with the peace of the world and the true welfare of mankind." Vere's own political classicism is based upon a knowledge of tactics which can attain the revolutionary goals of the revolutionaries he opposes.

Because Vere is not primarily concerned with self, he knows when and how to delegate authority. Because he knows that few men can read the sea and human history, he knows the limitations of delegation. He must bear within himself all the tortures of choice and yet present to the ship's people a demeanor of calm decision. His focal realization is that as he goes, so goes the world—always, though, within the moment of history which shapes him.[1] The cost, to the leader, of proper leadership is a frightful one, for the administrator must be all work and no play. It is germane to this consideration of sterility that Vere is a bachelor. With one exception, he leaves behind no lasting seed, and cannot delegate self in time. He must feed upon himself. He cannot regenerate; he can only reinform. History makes the man; the man can only choose the size of his own identity in history. Unmarried except to his "honest sense of duty," Vere can only lead to the statement that Robert Penn Warren concluded from a study of Melville's poetry: Nature is time and cycle. All continues again, and history, as time, is redemption as well as fate. The lessons are lost and only dim myths of the physical struggle remain. In short, meliorism is trapped in determinism just as determinism is trapped in meliorism.[2]

As the major figure in such a thematic statement, Vere, in the closet interview with the Handsome Sailor, emerges as the story's real central character. Because he understands the beauty of the primitive simplicity and heartful innocence that he must deny, Vere has Billy Budd within his own inner being—there is the primeval beneath the brass buttons just as there is the altruistic motivation beneath the rigorous tactics. There is more to be said of Budd's origins and his relationship to Vere in any consideration of Vere as the central figure, but John Claggart must be scrutinized before that centrality is seen in its clearest light.

The satanic imagery that incessantly characterizes Claggart identifies him as the demonized man, who has always appeared as the quester. Claggart is not engaged in active search, yet, but for his Plinlimmonism, he is the quester reincarnate. His dark pallor, his isolation and "seclusion from the sunlight," the lurid light that comes to his eyes, the fact that he is an alien about whose origins no truth is known, all indicate the man who has been removed from humanity by a stone heart which has been hardened in the man's own internal hell-fires. The pale, high, forehead to which attention is called as

---

[1] Wendell Glick notes the problem of prudence. See "Expediency and Absolute Morality in *Billy Budd*," *PMLA*, LXVII (1953), 103-10. The article offers a suggestive presentation of the choices open to Vere.

[2] "Melville the Poet," *KR*, VIII (1946), 208-23.

one of Claggart's identifying features, indicates mind and will as leading characteristics. Here is a man whose misty history hints at the quester-like experience which drives one to the woe that is madness. Indeed, if Billy is associated with the pre Cain-city of innocence, Claggart is associated with all the experience of citified man. "Civilization, especially if of the austerer sort, is auspicious" to Claggart's depravity. "It folds itself in the mantle of respectability." Chapter XI is devoted to the removal of any doubt about the double fact of Claggart's experience and insanity. And this man of woeful experience is driven to longing and to fury by the implications of the looks of Baby Beauty Budd.

Claggart's was no vulgar form of [envy]. Nor, as directed toward Billy Budd did it partake of that streak of apprehensive jealousy which marred Saul's visage perturbedly brooding on the comely young David. Claggart's envy struck deeper. If askance he eyed the good looks, cherry health and frank enjoyment of young life in Billy Budd, it was because these went along with a nature that as Claggart magnetically felt, had in its simplicity never willed malice or experienced the reactionary bite of that serpent. To him, the spirit lodged within Billy, and looking out from his welkin eyes as from windows, that ineffability it was which made the dimple in his dyed cheek, suppled his joints, and dancing in his yellow curls made him preeminently the Handsome Sailor. One person excepted [Vere], the master-at-arms was perhaps the only man in the ship intellectually capable of adequately appreciating the moral phenomenon presented in Billy Budd. And the insight but intensified his passion, which assuming various secret forms within him, at times assumed that of cynic disdain—disdain of innocence—to be nothing more than innocent! Yet in an aesthetic way he saw the charm of it, the courageous free-and-easy temper of it, and fain would have shared it, but he despaired of it [p. 845].

Again, like the problem of Vere's experience and motivations, the same problem applied to Claggart indicates the incompleteness of this "inside narrative." The story is the capstone of Melville's thematic structure, and the meaning of the story can only exist "inside" the totality of Melville's works. Taji, Ahab, and Pierre leave no more that need be said to explain Claggart, but in *Billy Budd* Melville does not and cannot incorporate those characters, which it had taken three novels to develop, into a novelette which does not place Claggart as the central character. Perhaps unconsciously Melville depended upon what he took for granted, by this time, about the demonized man— perhaps consciously. At any rate, he depended—he did not create. Thus in *Billy Budd*, Claggart can only be another inexplicable heartless creature of the deep, one of the surprises that the universe always sends out from her frozen, teeming north to add to the store of external realities potential in man's experience. Consequently Melville does the only thing he can do. He evades the problem of Claggart by assigning—rightly, but incompletely—to that man a "mystery of iniquity," a "Natural Depravity." It is significant, however, that limited as he is by the focus of his story, Melville yet takes time to make it clear that the mystery of Claggart's hatred lies in, and is projected from, the realm of human nature, human experience, human perception, and human idealization. The mystery lies not in the absolute or the supernatural; it lies in the various perceptions of external reality.

Long ago an honest scholar my senior, said to me in reference to one who like himself is now no more, a man so unimpeachably respectable that against him nothing was ever openly said though among the few something was whispered, "Yes, X— is a nut not to be cracked by the tap of a lady's fan. You are aware that I am the adherent of no organized religion much less any philosophy built into a system. Well, for all that, I think that to try and get into X—, enter his labyrinth and get out again, without a clue derived from some source other than what is known as *knowledge of the world*—that were hardly possible, at least for me."

"Why," said I, "X— however singular a study to some, is yet human, and knowledge of the world assuredly implies the knowledge of human nature, and in most of its varieties."

"Yes, but a superficial knowledge of it, serving ordinary purposes. But for anything deeper, I am not certain whether to know the world and to know human nature may not be two distinct branches of knowledge, which while they may coexist in the same heart, yet either may exist with little or nothing of the other" [pp. 840-41].

In the chapter ("Lawyers, Experts, Clergy") immediately following the discussion of X—, Melville makes it clear that neither assumed absolutes, legalities, nor theological idealizations will explain the mystery. Claggart's nature does not depend from any God that Religion assumes; nor does it depend upon the sociologist's "environment." The demonism of Claggart depends upon the Ahabian perception of what experience teaches about man's cosmic status. This perception is not the sophistication of a Worldly Wise-Man, who would not be able to explain Claggart. It is a philosophical reading of history, not a legalistic recognition of history. The worldly wisdom which knows the artificialities of codes without reading the underlying meanings of human experience, such is not the woeful wisdom of the philosophizing Solomon. "Coke and Blackstone hardly shed so much light into obscure spiritual places as the Hebrew prophets. And who were they? Mostly recluses." [3] Since Melville cannot create Ahab in *Billy Budd*,

---

[3] Here, because the context of the quester's story is missing, the reintroduction of the isolated Solomonic insight is a jarring error. In the other novels there was needed the honest, nonconformist perception that could stand apart from the banded world and see nature and experience truly. But the story of the false Prometheus, who has the nobility of an honest, if erroneous, perception, as well as the story of the true education (Ishmael, Media) have long since been finished. Melville has already taken these stories for granted in *Billy Budd*. He had to, for now that the past lessons had been reached and passed, he was writing the corollary of *application* of that knowledge. Thus, all his "correct" people must now be involved in society, and the Hebrew prophet saw truth, that recluse is an echo from Melville's literary past, whose motivation, but not whose isolation, belongs no longer in the exploration of the political administration of the truths the recluse saw. There is nothing within *Billy Budd* to provide the proper context for the Hebrew recluse, for the only recluse *Billy Budd* provides, properly, is the bad man, Claggart.

he combines the incomplete presentation of the wisdom that is woe (Vere, truth) and the woe that is madness (Claggart) by evaluating Claggart in contrast to Vere. The contrast is an over-all thing, but perhaps is most noticeable in the matter of appearances, whose necessity both Vere and Claggart recognize. Unlike the kind of and use of appearance attributed to Nelson and Vere, Claggart's appearance and his use of appearances suggest anything but the hero. His "chin, beardless as Tecumseh's, had something of the strange protuberant heaviness in its make that recalled the prints of the Rev. Dr. Titus Oates, the historic deponent with the clerical drawl in the times of Charles II and the fraud of the alleged Popish Plot." The man's studied obsequiousness constantly suggests that he is a prince of lies. He is "Ananias." Handling his corpse is like handling a dead snake. He is a subtle serpent. "The superior capacity he immediately evinced, his constitutional sobriety, ingratiating deference to superiors, together with a peculiar ferreting genius manifested on a singular occasion, all this capped by a certain austere patriotism abruptly advanced him to the position of master-at-arms." His iniquity and depravity have "no vulgar alloy of the brute . . . but invariably are dominated by intellectuality. . . . There is a phenomenal pride in [them]." Claggart's motivations are set off from Vere's with this: "toward the accomplishment of an aim which in wantonness of malignity would seem to partake of the insane, he will direct a cool judgment sagacious and sound." And even the tactics are contrasted, for concerning Claggart, an "uncommon prudence is habitual with the subtler depravity." The personal circumspection and the monomania mark Claggart as a creature of self. Like the Dansker, he knows the ways of the world, for the mythlike rumors about his past are filled with hints of an experienced, unsavory, woeful murderousness. Urbane, totally disguised, false and unctuous, he uses his knowledge of the world to satisfy his monomania. Vere, however, will not settle for dissemblance in others, for his own dissembling position demands a constant, never relenting, wearing hold of realities. When Claggart tries to play to appearances, softening, he thinks, Vere's disposition by refusing to refer directly to the practice of the pressgangs, then "at this point Captain Vere with some impatience interrupted him:

" 'Be direct, man; say impressed men.' "

In sum, the contrast offers the central reason that neither the existentialist nor the transcendentalist may enlist Melville's aid. Both Vere and Claggart have had and comprehended full experience. But Claggart has made self the instrument of reality, and his woe is madness. Vere has made society the instrument of reality, and his woe is wisdom. For Vere externalities may have a more fundamental reality than the realities of self. Not so for Claggart. Claggart rules his world for his own aims, and Vere rules his world for selfless aims.

Claggart feeds himself to his own monomania, and uses appearances to further the reachings of his demonized hatred. Vere feeds himself to an altruistic sense of duty and uses appearances in the staggering attempt to control externalities for the lasting peace and welfare of mankind.

The Claggart-Prince of Liars lies about the appearances of experience—which he knows are lies. Everyone accepts those lies as truths, and Claggart lies when patriotically he seems to accord with what everyone accepts. His relationship to appearances and his relationship to Billy Budd are the same. Budd becomes the surface of an existence whose true facts are anything but handsome, and Claggart would avenge himself upon what drove him to demonism by exposing the lie of the handsome appearances. His feeling for Baby is Ahab's feeling for the whale, with the fury compounded of the added hatred Ahab would have felt had the whale further mocked him by being a smiling mirage of beauty, promising goodness and purity, so that not even other sailors would recognize it for the dangerous thing it was. It would be inexpressibly wonderful to believe in absolute goodness, to know that such chronometrical appearances but mirrored horological facts. But, in "view of the marked contrast between the persons of the twain, it is more than probable that when the master-at-arms . . . applied to the sailor the proverb *Handsome is as handsome does;* he there let escape an ironic inkling, not caught by the young sailors who heard it, as to what it was that had first moved him against Billy, namely, his significant personal beauty." And if Claggart hates the comely visage of the Handsome Sailor, still does he envy the lie which is accepted by all because of its beauty, so that the woeful man's hatred is strengthened. It is all much like the hating, despairing, wistful reaction of the "old" Pierre looking back at the younger Pierre in Saddle Meadows. Thus Claggart looks at Billy Budd yearningly as well as hatefully, wistfully as well as scornfully, lovingly as well as balefully. Claggart knows the mess occasioned by acceptance of an apparently benevolent chronometrical thing. For the apparently inviolable being is himself but a product of mortal origins, (He is not better than I!: the hatred and envy), and he misdirects men's sight of reality (Don't believe him!: the hatred and despair). This is the ironic significance Claggart finds in the scene wherein Billy messes the "mess" by spilling his greasy soup, and which prompts Claggart to say, "Handsomely done, my lad! And handsome is as handsome did it too!" For all men are subject to the same actualities, and no man's appearances make him invulnerable to the pitching and rolling of the ship of life. Had another sailor spilled the soup, Claggart would have proceeded "on his way without comment, since the matter was nothing to take notice of under the circumstances." He cannot tolerate the sight of the man whose appearances seem to

associate him, in men's eyes, with an indulgent reprieve from consequences, an immunity to what experience has proved to be the actuality of existence. Claggart has been driven to madness by whatever
his experience has embraced of the two-thirds of the world that is
dark. The woe which is his constant bitterness resulting from his own
vulnerability to, and consequent insight into, existence, cannot tolerate
the Beautybudd appearance which would seem to indicate that three-
thirds of the world is light, and to promise an eternally beautiful
flower.

The actualities of experience are the inescapable circumstances
symbolized in the preface's treatment of the mutiny and the French
Revolution. Because Billy's appearance denies the facts of life, Claggart would destroy the appearance by visiting those facts upon the
Budd's experience. Precisely like the quester, Claggart, although ini-
tially he is right, thus becomes the champion and advocate of the
horrors that murder the community. The very circumstances of mutiny
and the French Revolution, for instance, are allied to Claggart in the
rumors about his foreign birth and in the reintroduction of those circumstances in Chapter VIII, which is devoted to an introduction of
Claggart. Thus subtly Claggart, like the Directory, is associated with
"an aspect like that of Camoens' Spirit of the Cape, an eclipsing
menace mysterious and prodigious . . ." and with "this French portentous upstart from the revolutionary chaos who seemed in act of
fulfilling judgment prefigured in the Apocalypse." Always the mysteries of iniquity are returned to the human sphere, for like Ahab,
Claggart himself becomes agent and principle of the very horrors
which drove him to woeful madness in the first place. So every sight
of Billy re-intensifies Claggart's envious hatred, and "there can exist
no irritating juxtaposition of dissimilar personalities comparable to
that which is possible aboard a great warship fully manned and at
sea. There, every day among all ranks almost every man comes into
more or less of contact with every other man. Wholly there to avoid
even the sight of an aggravating object one must needs give it Jonah's
toss or jump overboard himself. Imagine how all this might eventually
operate on some peculiar human creature the direct reverse of a
saint?" Claggart can neither jump nor give the Jonah's toss. Yet he must
destroy Billy's innocent appearance and immunity, for they are the
lie his madness cannot tolerate. This is the motivation for his actions.
And to all the "Pale ire, envy, and despair," Billy must be blind because he is innocent.

The madness of Claggart is evident in his confusion of what Billy
is with what Billy represents to him. Billy is but a husky, primitive
child, after all. He is subject to consequences: he fears the whipping
he witnesses at a disciplinary exhibition. He is not immune: the Ar-
morer and the Captain of the Hold do distrust him because of Clag-

gart's machinations. The "*thews* of Billy were hardly compatible with that sort of sensitive spiritual organization which in some cases instinctively conveys to ignorant innocence an admonition of the proximity of the malign." In short, Claggart commits the same unforgivable sin that the quester does. He identifies the lure only by means of a projection of his own insanity, and would pursue this self-vision to the detriment of all the world. In striking at an idea, Claggart throws open the door to historical chaos by pursuing the idea at the risk of unsettling the necessary order of the ship. And once more the murderous confusion of tactics arises from idealism even if the idealist is not hotly crazy like Ahab, but is capable of a "cool judgment sagacious and sound." He can not see man-self because one-self is always in the way. He can no longer see history because the ideal—ironically, born of historical man—entirely fills his eye.

Vere, like Claggart, must confront Baby Budd with an ultimate rejection. With pained love rather than with envious hatred Vere must reject what Budd represents to him. As administrator of the society whose order Claggart's machinations have threatened, Vere must condemn the actual as well as the representative Budd. To Claggart, Billy represents the false appearances of the world and is a hateful idea. To the Dansker, Billy represents an anomaly and is a curiosity. To Vere, Billy represents the human heart, and is a beautiful but inoperative idea. Like all Melvillean lures and doubloons, Billy, to the reader, is the totality of all the perceptions of the individual characters. Pragmatically, because he too rejects (albeit reluctantly) the idea and condemns the man, Vere is Claggart. But this is only a surface similarity. The sorrowful man whose wisdom was tutored by experience is also within Vere, so that Claggart, in his *initial* being, is Vere. It is history that has formed Vere's being. It is Claggart who represents the history which Vere recognizes in order to destroy it. Claggart is the reason just as Billy is the reason, that the brass buttons must take precedence over the primal heart. Claggart is the reason presented by the evils of history which he finally comes to represent, the gun which Vere uses because he hates the gun; Billy is the reason presented by the very definition of the primal heart, the innocence which must always be at the mercy of the gun and is unable to recognize the evils of history in order to use the evils of history in order to destroy the evils of history. Thus Budd and Claggart are at once the idealistic side of the polarities presented in the "Preface." They are externalizations of Vere, and it is this that makes him the central character. Billy is associated with Vere's beautifully motivated self; Claggart is associated with Vere's harshly necessary tactical self. The difference between Claggart as a being and Claggart as part of Vere is the difference between self-absorption on the one hand and self-dissection, self-control, self-subordination on the other. That is, Vere controls and uses—unlike Claggart he does not become—the hideous truth that both he and Claggart see. Vere controls and uses—unlike Billy he does not become—the ideal love and innocence and goodness that both he and Billy know. The war between Claggart and Billy is the internal war between heart and mind which constantly tears Vere apart in his merger of the two. He needs both; he loves one and hates the activities of the other. He takes his identity from the recognition of what he and Claggart share in common; yet the motivation for his identity is but the desire for the goodness that is the Billy Budd within him. That is, if there is a continuum, a common denominator in humanity, it is the human heart, which desires goodness. But the goodness is redefined by different conditions, so that understanding of conditions, or tactics, is the only method man has with which to identify himself with his underlying self, his heart. Tactics, historical lessons, identity, must all be relearned in each historical moment by each generation. That is the historical identity that dies, like the individual being. But each generation gives birth to new generations, passing on the mystery of the heart-yearning, the aspiration (which is the idealism that makes Melville partly Ahab), along with the historical conditions which the dead identities have created and from which the new men must gain their identities by learning to cope with them (which is the empiricism and materialism that makes Melville Vere). His heart, along with the consequences of history, Vere inevitably leaves as his human heritage to the future. The human heart and the future are heirs of the history he leaves. His own historical identity he cannot leave: the others are inescapable heirlooms, but this must be earned. And the heart of Vere, the inevitable child that each generation leaves to each next generation as part of being human, the heart is the area of Billy's relationship to Vere.

Vere, "the austere devotee of military duty letting himself melt back into what remains primeval in our formalized humanity may in the end have caught Billy to his heart even as Abraham may have caught young Isaac on the brink of resolutely offering him up in obedience to the exacting behest." Biblical reference of course reemphasizes the fact and nature of Vere's sacrifice. But it also suggests the nature of Billy's relationship to Vere. And Billy, as part of Vere, is suggested in more than the Abraham-Isaac analogy. "Billy Budd was a foundling, a presumable bye-blow, and, evidently, no ignoble one. Noble descent was as evident in him as in a blood horse." And without really introducing anyone else but Claggart, the Dansker, and Vere, Melville hints, "for Billy, as will shortly be seen, his entire family was *practically* invested in himself" [italics mine]. The Dansker is old enough to be Billy's father, but he is not noble. Claggart has a certain nobility, but not the right kind, certainly, and he is only "five-and-thirty" besides. But Vere is truly noble, Melville points out more than once, and as for age, "he was old enough to have been Billy's father." The possibility that Baby is Vere's own natural off-spring, the goodness of Vere's own heart, not only sharpens the significance of Vere's sacrifice, but strengthens the thematic consideration of the administrator as the hero, or the only interested God available to man. And even in the extremity of the only choice open to him, when he is robbed of all that his son symbolizes by all that the Satan-gun-thief symbolizes, Vere forces himself to behave according to the need for preservation of the humanity he commands and for which he alone is responsible. For as Father of the Adam who falls and the Christ who is sacrificed, Vere is the only anthropocentric God. He knows that he must control destinies and decide fates in order to gain the goal of the indestructible human heart, and immediately he reverts to the only means for gaining the proper destiny, and he becomes the tactician. He exercises the proper prudence. He forearms against the possible mutinous effect of the court-martial decision. Realizing that intentions make no difference, Vere succeeds in preventing an undesirable consequence of his act. Claggart met the unanticipated consequence of Billy's fist, for all his misdirected personal prudence. His monomania prevented his seeing the wider symbolism, the social vision, that characterizes Vere's every act, and while Claggart's prudence can only result in chaos, Vere's might result in reformation. In this is the note of affirmation that Melville strikes, finally, in his last book: though intentions make no difference in the consequences of an act, the direction of thought which forms the intentions create a different kind of act which, in its administration, brings different consequences.

Vere necessarily kills the chronometrical Christ for man's own good, so that the death of the false Messiah may bring a redemptive horological paradise on earth. For if Billy, in the chronometrical act of killing Claggart, were allowed to set the example for the world, the effect would be tacit permission for the mutiny and the spontaneous, individualistic, idealistic, atheistic anarchy which brings chaos again. Baby Christ learned the lesson Father Vere had to teach him. As Billy's beautifully good and heartbreakingly innocent relationship with that paradox, a man-of-war's chaplain, makes clear, he is too much the primitive child to comprehend anything intellectually. His "sailor way of taking clerical discourse is not wholly unlike the way in which the pioneer of Christianity full of transcendent miracles was received long ago on tropic isles by any superior *savage* so called." Robbed of complete innocence by evil, by the fact of the gun (when he lies in the darbies, his glimmering whiteness is now "more or less soiled"), he can only understand what is good and right with the goodness and rightness of his helpless heart. And his "God bless Captain Vere!" is the "I forgive you Father, for you know what you must do," which not only emphasizes Budd's goodness but which also emphasizes Vere's stature. Billy does not stutter now, but makes the one clear and final statement of the chronometrical innocence by which he lived. He is the Christ who still turns the other cheek to the man-of-war world, and, except for his new knowledge, takes his crucifixion as he took his impressment. And Vere, while recognizing that Billy leads to hopelessly inoperative behavior, also recognizes in Billy the heartful goodness of the primal human heritage. And when Billy blesses Vere, at "the pronounced words and the spontaneous echo that voluminously rebounded them, Captain Vere, either through stoic self-control or a sort of momentary paralysis induced by emotional shock, stood rigidly erect as a musket in the ship-armorer's rack." Even the simile works. At the moment that he kills the elemental goodness in man, Vere's reaction is both emotional shock and self-control. On the one hand he has his clearest perception of just what it is he kills, and at the same time realizes that if he had to, he would do it all over again. Necessarily he becomes the appearance not of the primal thing inside him, which he sacrifices, but of the gun, the thief-emblem of the world he must preserve, use, and change in order to preclude the conditions of sacrifice. Indeed, when Billy lies in the chains, he lies on the gun deck, which is given the religious imagery of a cathedral—with the gun-bays as the confessionals. Lest the ironic bitterness be lost even here, Melville hints that it is even as Christ hanging between the two thieves that the Baby is "now lying between the two guns, as nipped in the vice of fate."

When Vere dies, he calls his primal identity, his son-self of the indestructible human heart. Removed finally from the rigors of the gun-bearing world and from the pressures of control and from the self-devouring and self-killing sterility of command, he would relax into the something primeval within him and rejoin the perfection of man's heartfelt aspirations. His historical identity cannot continue. But the human heart does. So Vere goes home. He calls "Billy Budd, Billy Budd." And his call is an exhortation and a welcome. "That these were not the accents of remorse, would seem clear from what the attendant said to the *Indomitable's* senior officer of marines who as the most reluctant to condemn of the members of the drumhead court, too well knew though here he kept the knowledge to himself, who Billy Budd was." Yet, this quotation reintroduces the bitterness which is the closing note of *Billy Budd's* irony. On the one hand the officer of marines is a good and heartful man, but a man without Vere's historical identity. There is the possibility that this officer does not know Billy's identity any more than Millthorpe knew Plinlimmon or Pierre. Or there is the possibility that in his very heartfulness, the officer of marines, like some of the other crew members, idolized Billy. In this case too, the cycle would be repeated if the man Vere leaves behind him is an embryonic quester. In any case, probably both ironies are intended, for the net result is the final irony that it is the military officer who bears the memory of the chaos-bringing yet primally good Christ. Thus Melville reintroduces the motif of delegated authority. Man, like the Polynesian, is primarily good and primarily blind. The obscuring smoke of the chaos in which man has seasoned himself and his history must be pierced. But even the true hero, who correctly boards in the smoke, cannot as one man redeem the world, for his own historical identity, with all that is involved within it, is the one thing that can not be delegated in time. And, Melville adds, the effective identity must be ready in advance, for "Forty years after a battle it is easy for a non-combatant to reason about how it ought to have been fought. It is another thing personally under fire to direct the fighting while involved in the obscuring smoke of it. Much so with respect to other emergencies involving considerations both practical and moral, and when it is imperative promptly to act. . . . Little ween the snug card-players in the cabin of the responsibilities of the sleepless man on the bridge."

That the lessons are lost and that the cycle continues all over again is evident in three "digressions" tacked on to the end of the "inside" narrative.[4] The first is the section wherein Vere is killed by the ship named—the *Atheiste*. The *Atheiste* continues the wrongs of history, for it takes over from a name which is reminiscent of Isabel's mother and her other-worldly associations: this French ship had formerly been the *St. Louis*. The wrongs of the prerevolutionary nation are translated into the wrongs of the postrevolutionary nation—one kind of atheist becomes another kind of atheist under new name and management. And those who deny the peace of the world and the true welfare of mankind are those who kill Vere. The paradox is that the seamen of France kill the man whose goals are identical with those for which the tactically misdirected French Revolution had been fought. Vere had always known that men on both sides, wanting but the same goodness for which the human heart hungers, after all, cut each other down in the actualities of all the warfare attendant upon the wrong directions to the common peace and welfare. No final resolution has been effected, for Vere can re-inform so that reformation may be possible; but he himself, limited by time, cannot regenerate.

The second "digression" is the *News from the Mediterranean* which appears in an authorized "naval chronicle of the time." The account reports the official version, wherein Claggart is the good but wronged man, and wherein Billy is the villain. Thus appearances for their

---

[4] My "digressions" are not arranged as Melville lists his. After the "digressions" of the conversation between the Purser and the Surgeon, and the sea burial of Billy, the narrator goes on to say that the further "digressions" of the sequel to the story can be told in three additional short chapters.

own sake are preserved. There is even an inversion of origins in the account. Claggart, the alien, is pictured as the true patriot, and Billy, the trueborn Englishman, is made suspect of association with all the dimly French origins that actually characterized Claggart. The very basis of proper behavior is inverted. The official account could never admit that the strong arm of order enforcement itself could allow the officer to be the villain and the impressed man the saint. This is order for its own sake, command for the sake of prerogative, appearances for the protection of privilege. This kind of preservation of official appearances is a mindless thing. It is cast and bureaucracy, but it is not the good administration that carries with it the true motives for Vere's siding with official law. The administrator is no God merely by virtue of his position. If he is heartless or mindless, he can offer only official preference, not truth, and he becomes as much a perpetuator of the wrongs of history as was the dictatorial Mrs. Glendinning or the early king Media.

The third "digression" is most basic to the story, and it comprises the conversation of the Purser and the Surgeon together with the ballad of "Billy in the Darbies."

Neither the Purser nor the Surgeon are the men to explain what happened at Billy's execution. The Purser is a ruddy and rotund little accountant of a man who in a few words is presented as a man of no mind, insight, or imagination. The Surgeon is the worst kind of pontificator upon dry facts, being able to cope with experience only in the measurable quantities of what is already known, and avoiding all the very real problems which he cannot explain. Neither of these men are capable of aspiration or of evaluating new experience or of re-evaluating the old. Theirs is the meaningless empiricism of the circumscribed prudential. These two men tell the reader that Billy did not die as hanged men always die. There was no spasmodic movement of the corpse. For neither of these men can Billy be a symbol, be anything but a corpse. It is in the irony of presenting the picture of Billy's death through the eyes of men who cannot evaluate what they see that the suggestion is established that Billy is not a corpse. The meaning of this suggestion is intensified in the Ballad. Members of the *Indomitable's* crew revere Billy's memory and follow the progress of the yard on which Billy was hung, for "to them a chip of it was as a piece of the Cross." Billy's memory is perpetuated in a kind of Passion-hymn which is narrated in the first person, as if from Billy's point of view. The narrative action of the Ballad seems to be taking place in Billy's mind while he lies in the darbies, just before the execution. But the last two sentences bring the shock of recognition of a type, the realization that this is the voice of the "dead" man in the deep . . . dormant . . . waiting.

> . . . Sentry, are you there?
> Just ease these darbies at the wrist,
> and roll me over fair.
> I am sleepy, and the oozy weeds about me twist.

Billy never died. The aspiring yearning and goodness of man's heart is indestructible. So too, as Vere's defeat indicates, is history. Either heartfulness will continue in a new history made by men like Vere, or history will remain unchanged and heartfulness will continue as the chaos of the French Revolution or as the predisposition which will prompt another quester. The furious hopefulness of the work is in the indestructibility of human aspiration. The furious hopelessness of the work is that nothing but the wrong channels for that aspiration remain. So the human heart will continue to be the trap of the lure, the primitive perfection, the chronometrical Adam-Christ, who still exists in the deeps of human history and experience, mired by the oozy weeds and events of the man-of-war world. As lure, it can do nothing to pave the mire and raze the weeds, can be nothing but that which the quester will follow, at which the Satan will spring, by which the ship-world's common "people" will be deceived, and the cycle will continue . . . and continue . . . and continue.

This last book is not an "acceptance" either of God or of expediency for its own sake. *Billy Budd* accepts only what all the books before it accepted: that if history is the determinant of society, so too society is the determinant of history; that if man is not the cosmic creator and killer, he is at least his own social and individual creator and killer. *Billy Budd* accepts not an absolute fate to which man must bow, but rather it offers the bitterness of the proposition that man may never create the kind of fate that he can place at his own disposal. But for the method for attaining the yearnings of the heart, even in defeat, Melville could easily be entirely characterized by the bitter fatalism which characterized his civil war poem, "The Conflict of Convictions," in which he wrote,

> Power unanointed may come—
> Dominion (unsought by the free)
>   And the Iron Dome,
> Stronger for stress and strain,
> Fling her huge shadow athwart the main;
> But the Founder's dream shall flee.
> Age after age shall be
> As age after age has been,
> (From man's changeless heart their way they win);
> And death be busy with all who strive—
> Death with silent negative.
>   YEA AND NAY—
>   EACH HATH HIS SAY;
>   BUT GOD HE KEEPS THE MIDDLE WAY.
>   NONE WAS BY
>   WHEN HE SPREAD THE SKY:
>   WISDOM IS VAIN, AND PROPHESY.

Melville was not able to deduce a changed history from the facts of his times, and therefore could not create a Captain Vere who was in charge of not one ship but all of society—for having then created the proper leader, he would have had to create the picture of the Utopian good society, a task for which in his history and his realism Melville could find no justification. It is the mass of men, the society, that holds the choice of fates; so Vere, as hero, could not be allowed to triumph, and he had to die. As an artist Melville was too honest a symbolist—too honest a liar—too realistically immersed in the destructive element of reflection upon truth to create a shallow happy ending of the universally reformed society, which would be a deception to the facts of his world and time. Like Joyce, Melville was trying to create the uncreated conscience of his human race. And he could find that conscience properly directed only in a man like Vere, for the conscience, the morality, and the act could not be divorced one from the other. It is only the Vere who can lead the Jarl and Samoa and Lucy and Starbuck and Bulkington through the correct courses of conscious and heartfelt action, no matter how official and heart-denying those actions might appear to be. It is this implicit prescription for behavior, together with the God-time-zero which facelessly puts forth the face of all the infinite possibilities of phenomena, that accounts for the dualities and "ambiguities," in all their modifications, in the enormous world of Herman Melville.

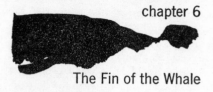

chapter 6

The Fin of the Whale

(The poor old Past,
The Future's slave,
She drudged through pain and crime
To bring about the blissful Prime,
Then—perished. There's a grave!)
    —"The Conflict of Convictions,"

In *Billy Budd,* Melville arrived at the traditional knot in the center of instrumental definition. In the very fact that he could not undo the intricacies of Vere's failure, the essentially naturalistic Melville exposed the particular kind of idealism that is as much his characteristic as is common-sense empiricism. An operational attempt at truth creates definitions according to function rather than according to absolute. In simple examples, the system works perfectly well. For instance, if one uses a butter knife to turn a screw, then the butter knife is defined as a screw driver. The definition is one-directional. It works from the end, the turn of the screw, to the means, the instrument, so that the end and the means become inseparable. The backwards, single direction of definition holds, but only when the end is a "visible truth" so that it exists complete in itself in a point present which can shed a defining light back to the actions which led up to it and became one with it.

However, the problem changes when it is applied to an end which is not actualized, to something like "the good human society," for instance. For with the end still unborn in future time, there is no specific entity from which the actions aiming forward to the creation of that entity can be defined. In that case the specific acts, the hanging of a man or the reprieve, the gun or the particular piece of legislation, require a definition according to something that is going to be. In the recognition of an informing vision which gives validity to different intentions inherent in different acts, lies Melville's own idealism. Thus

Melville seems to present four possible alternatives: ideal action motivated by social ideal (one must act according to the behavior which would exist in the ideal to be achieved); ideal action motivated empirically (history or the cosmos presents the actualized ideal according to which one can act); empirical action motivated empirically (the "practical" pursuit of power for its own sake in the actuality of a power-seeking world); and empirical action motivated by social ideal (the recognition of power motives adapted to a reformation of history). The first is ruled out as visionary purism, something that is totally ineffective. The second, closer to the idealism of a man like Thoreau, is ruled out as a too self-full misreading of history or of the cosmos. The third is ruled out as Plinlimmonism, the selfishness of the Machiavel who would use history for self. The fourth is what Melville accepts in his creation of Vere, and it is the particular Melvillean recognition of the need for an ideal. In this way, perhaps without any such consciously held philosophical purpose, Melville began an integration of America's idealistic past and materialistic present. Yet, because so few people merged social ideal with practical history, Melville could not project his integration into the future as the good society. And in this way Melville became the historically and socially oriented, rather than cosmically and socially oriented, empirical idealist. It is this, finally, which is the split between a perception like Melville's and a perception like, say, Thoreau's, which also aimed at a new man and a new society in its idealistic acceptance of much empiricism.

Interested as he was in both history and in books, perhaps Melville's naturalism can fruitfully be approached by a comparison of his own orientation with representative productions of either cosmic or aesthetic idealism. And if a concluding argument about Melville's philosophical position is to be taken from any one book, then, of course, *Moby-Dick* should be that book. And if any one section of *Moby-Dick* offers a thematic center, "The Try-Works" is that section.

"The Try-Works" does indeed offer Melville's opposition to both cosmic and aesthetic idealism. Ishmael is guiding that Anacharsis Clootz expedition, the *Pequod*, the ship of man, the ship of history, the ship of state. The crew is toiling redly at the fiery task of boiling out whales on the midnight ship, and "then the rushing Pequod, freighted with savages and laden with fire, and burning a corpse, and plunging into that blackness of darkness, seemed the material counterpart of her monomaniac commander's soul." The fires, like the Parsee's fire-worship of an evil God, are equated with the hell-fire of Ahab's idealism; the direction taken by the plunging ship is equated with the supranatural direction of Ahab's quest.

"So seemed it to me, as I stood at her helm, and for long hours silently guided the way of the fire-ship on the sea. Wrapped, for that interval, in darkness myself, I but the better saw the redness, the madness, the ghastliness of others. The continual sight of the fiend shapes before me, capering half in smoke and half in fire, these at last begat kindred visions in my soul, so soon as I began to yield to that unaccountable drowsiness which ever would come over me at a midnight helm." This is the education of the quester. He boldly and directly faces all the fiend shapes of experience, yet wrapped in darkness himself, he gives bare phenomena a philosophical quality that derives from his own perception until, finally, his own redness and madness and ghastliness are intensified by the horrors of existence from which he does not flinch, and which in turn are intensified by his own redness, madness, and ghastliness. Finally, the hell-blinded vision of his own sight becomes to him the fact of all creation, and he must strike against the kind of creator that is measured in his vision of the creation. But Ishmael is to realize that the only way to strike through that mask is to strike inward.

But that night, in particular, a strange (and ever since inexplicable) thing occurred to me. Starting from a brief standing sleep, I was horribly conscious of something fatally wrong. The jaw-bone tiller smote my side, which leaned against it; in my ears was the low hum of sails, just beginning to shake in the wind; I thought my eyes were open; I was half conscious of putting my fingers to the lids and mechanically stretching them still further apart. But, spite of all this, I could see no compass before me to steer by; though it seemed but a minute since I had been watching the card, by the steady binnacle lamp illuminating it. Nothing seemed before me but a jet gloom, now and then made ghastly by flashes of redness. Uppermost was the impression, that whatever swift, rushing thing I stood on was not so much bound to any haven ahead as rushing from all havens astern. A stark, bewildered feeling, as of death, came over me. Convulsively my hands grasped the tiller, but with the crazy conceit that the tiller was, somehow, in some enchanted way, inverted. My God! what is the matter with me? thought I. Lo! in my brief sleep I had turned myself about, and was fronting the ship's stern, with my back to her prow and the compass. In an instant I faced back, just in time to prevent the vessel from flying up into the wind, and very probably capsizing her. How glad and how grateful the relief from this unnatural hallucination of the night, and the fatal contingency of being brought by the lee!

If one stares at the fires of idealism, one stares but at the projections of self. Blinded by ideal, even with the eyes open, one loses sight of the real, physical, material, social, historical world. Then, like Ahab, one leaves the one area of reality that there is; one leaves the only hope of the very reformation he would seek; one rushes to the blankness of zero. The world-ship, already pointed in Ahab's monomaniacal direction, is government and morality idealistically steered, and thus "whatever swift, rushing thing I stood on was not so much bound to any haven ahead as rushing from all havens astern." At that moment, the warning of "The Mast-Head" chapter comes back to Ishmael— you may believe that you glidingly merge with the ultimate reality when you merge with what you think is ideality; but slip your hand or foot one inch, and then in horror you recognize—too late—that you have jeopardized the only reality, your social, physical, historical existence. So Ishmael almost duplicates Ahab's unforgivable sin. By leaving reality, he becomes inverted. His hierarchy of values is turned upside down, and all the last things come first, all the first things come last. In effect, he loses the control of government, he inverts his contact with reality, and almost kills mankind. His surrender to self is almost his sacrifice of the human community. Thus Ishmael prepares for Ahab, and prepares for his own eventual salvation by rejecting a cosmically idealistic vision in favor of empirical, historical vision and social brotherhood. Thus, too, inversely, Ahab prepares for the necessity of Vere. Ishmael leaves no doubt about what he has learned: the light of idealism is false and inverting and will kill one by removing him from contact with, and therefore from any possible control over, the reality and light of the natural world:

"Look not too long in the face of the fire, O man! Never dream with thy hand on the helm! Turn not thy back to the compass; accept the first hint of the hitching tiller; believe not the artificial fire, when its redness makes all things look ghastly. To-morrow, in the natural sun, the skies will be bright; those who glared like devils in the forking flames, the morn will show in far other, at least gentler, relief; the glorious, golden, glad sun, the only true lamp—all others but liars!" Thus if there is an absolute reality, it is natural existence. And what Ishamel emphasizes here is the external reality of phenomena seen in the light of the natural world. He is not emphasizing the transcendental belief that if seen in the proper light all creation is good and but a projection of one's own soul; no, for he goes on to state the existence of that which began the vicious circle of perception which drove the quester mad in the first place. He goes on to affirm the independent externality, reality, and positive horror of much of life:

"Nevertheless the sun hides not Virginia's Dismal Swamp, nor Rome's accursed Campagna, nor wide Sahara, nor all the millions of miles of desert and of griefs beneath the moon. The sun hides not the ocean which is the dark side of this earth, and which is two thirds of this earth. So, therefore, that mortal man who hath more of joy than sorrow in him, that mortal man cannot be true—not true, or undeveloped. With books the same." There follows the memorable passage, already discussed, about unchristian Solomon, and sorrow, and the green damp mold, and the vanity which is the cosmic idealist's replacing of reality with self. The untrueness, or lack of development, in men as well as in books, is precisely what Melville repeatedly said about transcendental—particularly Emersonian—morality and perception, in the man and in the man's writings. Moreover—and this is the quester's nobility—man must not avoid the uglinesses of the natural world. The smell of mortality, the sights and mysteries of existence which, like the sharks and whales and squids, are dark things to man's sight, are all part of the reality with which man must cope, within which man must fashion his destiny. The incomprehensible wonders of nature and the "scurvy, empirical" nature of one's own self cannot and must not be looked at by means of a cosmic or aesthetic idealism, for such looking is blinding, is an evasion, and dooms man to an inability to cope with those very wonders which stimulate the mistakenly idealistic direction of the real aspiration which lies in the human heart. Do not deny the primacy of your mind, but channel that primacy into recognition of its place in the externalities of natural, the only, reality. For,

even Solomon, he says, "the man that wandereth out of the way of understanding shall remain" (*i.e.* even while living [like Ishmael, blind even with eyes open]) "in the congregation of the dead." Give not thyself up, then, to fire, lest it invert thee, deaden thee; as *for the time* it did me. There is a wisdom that is woe [the recognition of all the darknesses in a naturalistic universe]; but there is a woe that is madness [the quester's cosmically idealistic response to the darknesses which experience has made him recognize].[1] And there is a Catskill eagle in some souls that can alike dive down into the blackest gorges, and soar out of them again and become invisible in the sunny spaces. And even if he for ever flies within the gorge, that gorge is in the mountains; so that even in his lowest swoop the mountain eagle is still higher than any other birds upon the plain, even though they soar.

So again, with books as with men, the highest, completest truth is the truth of the naturalistic perception. There is the aspiring perception within some men that will not avoid, but will dive down into, the dark side of life and know its reality; there are men who will yet try to find the highest, finest, moral space of life within the truth of existence. And because they deal with truth rather than self, they remain, even in their plunges, higher than the deluded birds of the plains.

Few examples are required to indicate the dimensions of opposition between Melville's perception and the cosmic idealism of his age.

---

[1] R. W. B. Lewis has an excellent section on the demonized man. See his treatment of Nathan Slaughter, of Bird's *Nick of the Woods*, in *The American Adam* (Chicago, 1955), pp. 105-9. Lewis also judges "The Try-Works" to be a "guide" for a reading of Melville. See *American Adam*, pp. 127-52, especially pp. 130-34. Lewis lights "The Try-Works" with a "transvaluation of values." "Here, then, in 'The Try-Works,' we have a series of displacements. Artificial light gives way to natural light, darkness to morning, and the imperative to the indicative. Then dawn and sunlight yield to darkness, to the moon and 'the dark side of the earth'—to hell, to sickness, and to death. But hell and death are the source at least of a new and loftier life, new 'sunny spaces' and new imperatives. Those sunny spaces are not the same bright skies of . . . ['the morn']. The moral imagination which contemplates the sunny spaces . . . has been radically affected by the vision of hell and death. . . . The sunny spaces (tragic optimism) relate to the earlier morning skies (empty-headed cheerfulness) as does the Catskill eagle to 'the other birds upon the plain'; it is the sky, as the eagle is a bird—but bird and sky have been raised to a higher power" (pp. 133-34). I believe that the change from idealistic to naturalistic perception is the basis for the symphonic development of what Lewis calls "the different degrees of moral alertness."

Perhaps two of the most dramatic instances are furnished by Walt Whitman. In "Darest Thou Now O Soul" (from *Whispers of Heavenly Death*), the transcendental perception sees eternity and infinity (Whitman's use of Space and Time in this poem is an equation with ideality) as the obtainable realm of ultimate reality beyond the natural world:

Darest thou now O soul,
Walk out with me toward the unknown region,
Where neither ground is for the feet nor any path to follow?
No map there, nor guide,
Nor voice sounding, nor touch of human hand,
Nor face with blooming flesh, nor lips, nor eyes, are in that land.
I know it not O soul,
Nor dost thou, all is a blank before us,
All waits undream'd of in that region, that inaccessible land.
Till when the ties loosen,
All but the ties eternal, Time and Space,
Nor darkness, gravitation, sense, nor any bounds bounding us.
Then we burst forth, we float,
In Time and Space O soul, prepared for them,
Equal equipt at last, (O joy! O fruit of all!) them to
        fulfill O soul.

From the point of view of Ishmael's nightmarish lesson, this is the inversion of the tiller, the loosening of the hold upon the time and space and flesh and voice and path that are the only existence this side of zero. For Ahab the motivation is vengeful fury. For Whitman it is love and joy. But regardless of the specific emotion, morality itself depends from an assumed absolute state of being which, to the naturalist, can only be a state of non-being mistakenly created by the misdirected aspiration of the perceiver's self. The very assumption of joy and absolute goodness in that bright, final reality which has no dark side to it is even more explicit in "Passage to India" (from *Autumn Rivulets*), which, in using the image of the ship, highlights Melville's opposition:

Passage indeed O soul to primal thought . . .
O soul, repressless, I with thee and thou with me,
Thy circumnavigation of the world begin,
Of man, the voyage of his mind's return.
To reason's early paradise,
Back, back to wisdom's birth, to innocent intuitions,
Again with fair creation.
O we can wait no longer,
We too take ship O soul,
Joyous we too launch out on trackless seas,
Fearless for unknown shores on waves of ectasy to sail,
Amid the wafting winds, (thou pressing me to thee, I thee to me,
        O soul,)

Caroling free, singing our song of God,
Chanting our chant of pleasant exploration.

°   °   °   °

Passage, immediate passage! the blood burns in my veins!
Away O soul! hoist instantly the anchor!
Cut the hawsers—haul out—shake out every sail!
Have we not stood here like trees in the ground long enough?
Have we not grovel'd here long enough, eating and drinking like
        mere brutes?
Have we not darken'd and dazed ourselves with books long enough?
Sail forth—steer for the deep waters only,
Reckless O soul, exploring, I with thee, and thou with me,
For we are bound where mariner has not yet dared to go,
And we will risk the ship, ourselves and all.
O my brave soul!
O farther farther sail!
O daring joy, but safe! are they not all the seas of God?
O farther, farther, farther sail!

Typee and *Billy Budd* have said enough about return to the ideal
beginnings, the Eden, the paradise, whatever place or time that
represents the child fresh from the hands of God and trailing clouds
of glory. Not so much bound to any haven ahead as rushing from all
havens astern, were this a "chant of vengeful exploration" this would
be the song of Ahab. Both of these poems are about death. It might
seem unfair to deprive Whitman of naturalistic exuberance, for the
poems may be interpreted simply as a statement of joy in the thing,
in the continuum which is the nitrogen-cycle structure of nature. Nor
can one deny Whitman's joy of natural life. However, Whitman's joy-
of-life, especially as he later concentrated it in his concept of death,
is not joy-giving for its physical reality, but for the cosmic ideality symbolized by death's transmutation of life. Death is joy-giving because
it becomes the supranatural realization of cosmic ideality: it becomes
the "payment" on what Kenneth Burke has demonstrated as the
"promissory principle" of Whitman's view of material existence.[2]
Again, the difference between Whitman's "naturalism" (especially the
later Whitman and particularly after the third edition of *Leaves of
Grass*) and Melville's is not the fact of symbolism but the nature of it.
For Whitman, all nature can be embraced, for all his poems are the
yawp which present phenomena's symbolic meaning as a result of the
budding, barbaric, joyful, transcendental experience. The symbolic

---

[2] "Policy Made Personal," *Leaves of Grass One Hundred Years After,* ed. Milton
Hindus (Stanford, 1955), p. 76. Burke adds that "Somewhere between the
grounding of his position in time, and its grounding in eternity . . ." Whitman
takes for "an 'over-arching' term . . . 'nature' in ways that, while clearly referring
to the materialistic on one side, also have pontificating aspects leading into a
Beyond, along Emersonian lines. . . . Democracy was Nature's 'younger brother,'
and Science was 'twin, in its field, of Democracy in its.' But such equations were
idealistically weighted to one side . . ." (p. 76).

meaning thus assigned to nature, and to death, which is the continuator of the symbolism, becomes, from the perspective of Melville's
naturalism, an argument (*primarily*) for cosmic rather than social
idealism. In this sense Whitman's use of death is a fine presentation of
what Melville rejects, for it is a presentation of a journey away from
the historical and conditional to the suprahistorical and to the cosmic
absolute. It is the "joy" and "fruit of all" which is not physical continuation per se, but which is the payment and oneness with spiritual
absoluteness—of which physical continuity was the promise. In short,
for Melville, it is an impossibility because it is oneness with God as a
cosmic, moral, spiritual good and goodness [3]—which isn't there. In
the ultimate rejection of the historical and conditional, Whitman's re-
nowned celebration of the body and the common man and physical
existence, while seeming to offer the most democratic embrace of love,
paradoxically is really not as democratic as the embrace of the apparently misanthropic political classicist, Melville. Whitman embraces all
because he thinks he embraces God, the spirit for which the thing
is but the symbol in its political, expansionist, and physical manifestations. But as for the body and the common man and physical existence as such, those are but "trees in the ground . . . mere brutes." If
the thing itself, the conditional, were all there is, Whitman could
not accept it. Despite appearances, Whitman's "acceptances" are ultimately the same idealism as that of the "colder" Thoreau and the
more "intellectual" Emerson. From the naturalistic point of view,
Whitman accepts natural life for what he thinks it symbolizes, not for
what it is. Indeed, regardless of modifications, the idealist finally must
make ideal superior to the physical and the historical, and—as Whitman does here—reject them as such. So too, finally, the naturalist eventually must hold to the opposite extremity. Melville accepts man for
what he is, wherein is his hatred and woe, and also for what he might
be within the physical and historical reality, wherein is his joy of
aspiration. And Whitman too makes what in the Melvillean view is
the Ahabian unforgivable sin. He turns his back on the physical and
historical in his outward passage to the deepest waters of ideal,
"where mariner [except for Taji and Ahab and landlocked Pierre]
has not dared to go." And he "will risk the ship, ourselves, and all."
Finally there is no difference between this paean of joy and the
paean of grief of Taji and Ahab who scream that there should be total
wreck if wreck there be. For Melville, when Whitman says he will
risk "the ship . . . and all," the ALL is more significant than the idealist
suspects. For Melville, cosmic idealism grasps neither reality nor the
human condition truly.

---

[3] For God as either the Ideal of The Good or as the Ideal of Goodness, see
A. O. Lovejoy, *The Great Chain of Being* (Cambridge, Mass., 1936), Chapters
I, II, III, *et passim.* Transcendental thought combines both in the self.

The "mere brutishness" of existence that the naturalist, in his materialism, accepts and that the idealist, in his cosmic moralities, rejects,
is also the core of the difference between Melvillean "Rabelaisianism"
and moral idealism's twin brother, aesthetic idealism.[4] Even though
Melville may have his joke about flatulence and sex, certainly he
is not the kind of writer who composes paeans to the animal aspects
of existence. However, he accepts those levels; people are people, and
Melville's repugnance for people exists on political or philosophical,
but not on physical, levels. It is, indeed, the inescapable conditions and
fate of physical existence that account for most of Melville's wide and
democratic embracing of a joint-stock world in all meridians, for his
cultural democracy and his insistence on brotherhood. We all smell
the same, and, says Melville, despite aesthetic, ascetic, and religious
precepts, if champagne and oysters be the food of the body, then pay
good attention to the enjoyment of champagne and oysters. Compare
Melville's naturalistic attitude with that of the aesthetic idealist,
Baudelaire, from whose *Mon Coeur Mis a Nu* W. H. Auden has
selected a section pertinent to this contrast: Talking about his "ideal
man, the Dandy" Baudelaire says, "Woman is the opposite of the
Dandy. Therefore she should inspire horror. Woman is hungry and
she wants to eat, thirsty and she wants to drink. She is in rut and she
wants to be possessed. Woman is *natural*, that is to say, abominable.
    "The Dandy should aspire to be uninterruptedly sublime. He should
live and sleep in front of a mirror.
    "The more a man cultivates the arts, the less he fornicates. A more
and more apparent cleavage occurs between the spirit and the brute."[5]
    The healthiness of Melville, in contrast to the delicacies and minc-
ing self-centeredness of narcissism implicit in the Dandy, is itself
enough to exorcise the ghost of the more extreme conjectures of early
psychobiographic Melville criticism. But more important here than a
vindication of Melville the man is the contrast in ideas of self, order,
and life. In comparison to the selfless circumspection of Nelson and
Vere, the idealistic aesthete can find no beauty but in admiration of a
hermetically sealed, uncontaminated self. Melville, with his questers,
and Hawthorne, with his Goodman Browns and Birthmarks, both
recoiled in horror from the last, last crime of soul suicide, which is
always the removal of self from common humanity. The imposition of
order that this bowelless man who "should live and sleep in front of a

---

[4] Perry Miller, in *The Raven and the Whale* (New York, 1956: see index, p.
368), defines the specific meanings of Rabelaisianism as created by Melville's
literary environment. Although I take for granted some of the same meanings, I
use the general term here in its less specific and more popular sense, that of
earthy zest in natural existence.
[5] *The Enchafed Flood* (New York, 1950), pp. 87-88. Despite what I consider
to be some twisted uses of Melville, Auden's book is a magnificent and fertile
study to which every student of romanticism must owe a debt.

mirror" recognizes is not only selfish, but antinatural. Ultimately it can either have no meaning for the community and for life, or else it must have the meaning of sterility and murder. Finally, therefore, the one-self and antinatural aspects of aesthetic idealism are immoral because they deny the principle of life itself. Like the homosexuality they imply, they can only be a perversion, an artificiality, a "self-expression" in the narrowest sense with which our age of psychiatric romanticism narcissistically concerns itself under the aegis of either "Art" or "Therapy." They cannot pierce through the mask to the conditions of actuality with which every position—even the aesthetic—must cope, not only because the very assumption of a position is itself a hierarchy of moral choices, but because they too reject the truths about reality and the human condition.

Along with Fitzgerald's Nick Carraway, Melville always seemed to be saying, "Conduct may be founded on the hard rock or the wet marshes, but after a certain point I don't care what it's founded on." Whatever its foundation, whatever its excuse, human conduct finally must be historically responsible and communal. There must be not "cleavage" but juncture of "spirit," mind, and "brute," for any one alone is the murderousness of one-self rather than the generation of man-self. Thus many years before literary naturalism became ill-defined in the narrow channels of literary Naturalism, Melville the classical democrat, the ethical relativist, the devout empiricist, demonstrated that naturalistic perception in the years of the modern could and must take from woe not only materialism, but also the humanism and the deep morality of social idealism, which are the true beginnings of wisdom.

"You may think, in your own mind [wrote Melville] that a man is unwise,—indiscreet, to write a [profound and unpopular] work . . . when he might have written one perhaps, calculated merely to please the general reader, & not provoke attack, however masqued in an affectation of indifference or contempt. But some of us scribblers, My Dear Sir, always have a certain something unmanageable in us, that bids us do this or that, and be done it must—hit or miss." [6] Often he missed. But when he hit, he hit hard and struck through to the center of unquenchable, undrownable, human hope and greatness. And the "six-inch chapter" that "is the stoneless grave of" *Moby-Dick's* Bulkington is a monument to the human heart, to man himself, as well as to the one-man Melville, who met the white wave beyond the dimly looming shores. Talking not about the Ahabian or Whitmanesque outward voyage, but about the "intrepid effort of the soul to keep the open independence of her sea" in the face of all the heartbreaking restrictions and debasements that Hautia's banded world tries

---

[6] Eleanor Melville Metcalf, *Herman Melville, Cycle and Epicycle*, p. 63.

to force upon man's mind, Melville wrote, "But as in landlessness alone resides the highest truth, shoreless, indefinite as God—so, better is it to perish in that howling infinite than be ingloriously dashed upon the lee, even if that were safety! For worm-like, then, oh! who would craven crawl to land. Terrors of the terrible! is all this agony so vain? Take heart, take heart, O Bulkington! Bear thee grimly, demigod! Up from the spray of thy ocean-perishing—straight up, leaps thy apotheosis!"

And that, too, is the human heritage.

Index

ILLINI BOOKS

IB-1	Grierson's Raid: A Cavalry Adventure of the Civil War	D. Alexander Brown	$1.75
IB-2	The Mars Project	Wernher von Braun	$ .95
IB-3	The New Exploration: A Philosophy of Regional Planning	Benton MacKaye, with an Introduction by Lewis Mumford	$1.75
IB-4	Tragicomedy: Its Origin and Development in Italy, France, and England	Marvin T. Herrick	$1.95
IB-5	Themes in Greek and Latin Epitaphs	Richmond Lattimore	$1.95
IB-6	The Doctrine of Responsible Party Government: Its Origins and Present State	Austin Ranney	$1.25
IB-7	An Alternative to War or Surrender	Charles E. Osgood	$1.45
IB-8	Reference Books in the Mass Media	Eleanor Blum	$1.50
IB-9	Life in a Mexican Village: Tepoztlán Restudied	Oscar Lewis	$2.95
IB-10	*Three Presidents and Their Books: The Reading of Jefferson, Lincoln, and Franklin D. Roosevelt	Arthur E. Bestor, David C. Mearns, and Jonathan Daniels	$ .95
IB-11	Cultural Sciences: Their Origin and Development	Florian Znaniecki	$2.25
IB-12	The Legend of Noah: Renaissance Rationalism in Art, Science, and Letters	Don Cameron Allen	$1.45
IB-13	*The Mathematical Theory of Communication	Claude E. Shannon and Warren Weaver	$ .95
IB-14	Philosophy and Ordinary Language	Charles E. Caton, ed.	$1.95
IB-15	Four Theories of the Press	Fred S. Siebert, Theodore Peterson, and Wilbur Schramm	$1.25
IB-16	Constitutional Problems Under Lincoln	James G. Randall	$2.95
IB-17	Viva Mexico!	Charles Macomb Flandrau, edited and with an introduction by C. Harvey Gardiner	$1.95
IB-18	Comic Theory in the Sixteenth Century	Marvin T. Herrick	$1.75

* Also available in clothbound editions.

IB-19	Black Hawk: An Autobiography	Donald Jackson, ed.	$1.75
IB-20	Mexican Government in Transition	Robert E. Scott	$2.25
IB-21	John Locke and the Doctrine of Majority-Rule	Willmoore Kendall	$1.25
IB-22	The Framing of the Fourteenth Amendment	Joseph B. James	$1.45
IB-23	The Mind and Spirit of John Peter Altgeld: Selected Writings and Addresses	Henry M. Christman, ed.	$1.25
IB-24	A History of the United States Weather Bureau	Donald R. Whitnah	$1.75
IB-25	Freedom of the Press in England, 1476-1776: The Rise and Decline of Government Controls	Fredrick Seaton Siebert	$2.25
IB-26	Freedom and Communications	Dan Lacy	$ .95
IB-27	The Early Development of Henry James	Cornelia Pulsifer Kelley, with an introduction by Lyon N. Richardson	$1.95
IB-28	*Law in the Soviet Society	Wayne R. LaFave, ed.	$1.95
IB-29	Beyond the Mountains of the Moon: The Lives of Four Africans	Edward H. Winter	$1.75
IB-30	*The History of Doctor Johann Faustus	H. G. Haile	$1.45
IB-31	One World	Wendell L. Willkie, with an introduction by Donald Bruce Johnson	$1.75
IB-32	William Makepeace Thackeray: Contributions to the Morning Chronicle	Gordon N. Ray, ed.	$1.45
IB-33	Italian Comedy in the Renaissance	Marvin T. Herrick	$1.75
IB-34	Death in the Literature of Unamuno	Mario J. Valdés	$1.25
IB-35	*Port of New York: Essays on Fourteen American Moderns	Paul Rosenfeld, with an introductory essay by Sherman Paul	$2.25
IB-36	*How to Do Library Research	Robert B. Downs	$1.45
IB-37	Henry James: Representative Selections, with Introduction, Bibliography, and Notes	Lyon N. Richardson	$3.50

* Also available in clothbound editions.

IB-38	*Symbolic Crusade: Status Politics and the American Temperance Movement	Joseph R. Gusfield	$1.75
IB-39	*Genesis and Structure of Society	Giovanni Gentile, translated by H. S. Harris	$1.95
IB-40	The Social Philosophy of Giovanni Gentile	H. S. Harris	$2.45
IB-41	*As We Saw the Thirties: Essays on Social and Political Movements of a Decade	Rita James Simon, ed.	$2.45
IB-42	The Symbolic Uses of Politics	Murray Edelman	$2.45
IB-43	White-Collar Trade Unions: Contemporary Developments in Industrialized Societies	Adolf Sturmthal, ed.	$3.50
IB-44	*The Labor Arbitration Process	R. W. Fleming	$2.45
IB-45	*Edmund Wilson: A Study of Literary Vocation in Our Time	Sherman Paul	$2.45
IB-46	*George Santayana's America: Essays on Literature and Culture	James Ballowe, ed.	$2.25
IB-47	*The Measurement of Meaning	Charles E. Osgood, George J. Suci, and Percy H. Tannenbaum	$3.45
IB-48	*The Miracle of Growth	Foreword by Arnold Gesell	$1.75
IB-49	*Information Theory and Esthetic Perception	Abraham Moles	$2.45
IB-50	Outlawing the Spoils: A History of the Civil Service Reform Movement, 1865-1883	Ari Hoogenboom	$2.95
IB-51	*Community Colleges: A President's View	Thomas E. O'Connell	$1.95
IB-52	*The Joys and Sorrows of Recent American Art	Allen S. Weller	$3.95
IB-53	*Dimensions of Academic Freedom	Walter P. Metzger, Sanford H. Kadish, Arthur DeBardeleben, and Edward J. Bloustein	$ .95
IB-54	*Essays on Frege	E. D. Klemke, ed.	$3.95
IB-55	The Fine Hammered Steel of Herman Melville	Milton R. Stern	$2.95

* Also available in clothbound editions.

University of Illinois Press   Urbana, Chicago, and London